Muskegon, Michigan
welcomes

TALL SHIPS CHALLENGE™

August 7-11, 2003
Heritage Landing
Tall Ship Site

ASTA
American Sail Training Association

For more information on events and attractions in Muskegon County, call
1-800-250-WAVE
231-724-3100 or 231-893-4585

www.visitmuskegon.org • www.sailmuskegon.com

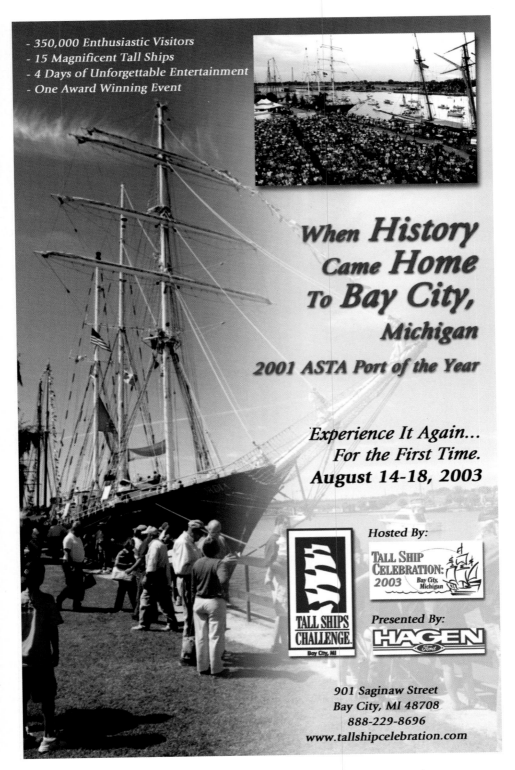

- 350,000 Enthusiastic Visitors
- 15 Magnificent Tall Ships
- 4 Days of Unforgettable Entertainment
- One Award Winning Event

When *History* Came *Home* To *Bay City,* Michigan

2001 ASTA Port of the Year

'Experience It Again...
For the First Time.
August 14-18, 2003

Hosted By:

TALL SHIP
CELEBRATION:
2003 Bay City, Michigan

TALL SHIPS
CHALLENGE.
Bay City, MI

Presented By:

HAGEN
Ford

901 Saginaw Street
Bay City, MI 48708
888-229-8696
www.tallshipcelebration.com

Port of San Francisco
Welcomes the
Tall Ships Challenge®

✑ GREENPORT HARBOR ✎
LONG ISLAND, NEW YORK

Photo: Gil Amiaga

An authentic, working deep water port
surrounded by seaside farms & vineyards...

Tall Ships 2000® Cruise Port
Americas' Sail Host–1995 & 1998

Visit Mitchell Park & Marina.
Deep water dockage, vintage carousel, amphitheater
and boardwalk—all in the heart of the village!
Easy walk to stores, galleries, beach,
hospital & Historic District.

Special arrangements made for visiting tall ships.

Services available include hauling, shipbuilding,
welding, engine repair & hardware.

For more information contact:
Mayor David E. Kapell, Village of Greenport
236 Third Street, Greenport, New York 11944
631-477-3000 • FAX 631-477-1877
or hail the harbormaster on VHF channel 9

Tall Ships® Chicago 2003

July 31 to August 4, 2003

Produced by the Mayor's Office of Special Events
For more information call 312-744-3315,
TTY 312-744-2964
www.cityofchicago.org/specialevents

Navy Pier 312-595-PIER, Outside the Chicagoland area
call 1-800-595-PIER or click on
www.navypier.com

**MAYOR'S OFFICE OF
SPECIAL EVENTS
CHICAGO**
RICHARD M. DALEY, MAYOR

City of Chicago Richard M. Daley, Mayor

Bark Europa

2002/2003

Cross Pacific
Tall Ships Challenge
Cape Horn
South Georgia
Antarctica
Cross Atlantic

Europe

In search of adventure

For more information:

Rederij Bark Europa B.V.
Vissershavenweg 65-I
NL-2583 DL Den Haag
The Netherlands

Phone   : +31 (0)70 331 7475
Fax   : +31 (0)70 354 2865
E-mail   : info@barkeuropa.com
Web-site : www.barkeuropa.com

The cruise line
that loves sailing
as much as you do.

THE MEGA-YACHT SAILING EXPERIENCE:

~ *Choose to help sail and navigate.*

~ *No crowds, only 170 or 227 guests.*

~ *7 and 14- night sailings.*

~ *Exotic ports of call few ships visit.*

~ *The romance of a true sailing ship.*

~ *International cuisine.*

~ *Full range of water sports*

~ *Rich nautical heritage*

Star Clippers offers intimate, 7 and 14-night mega-yacht sailing adventures in the Caribbean, French & Italian Rivieras, Spain & Balearic Islands, Greek Isles & Turkey, and the Far East. Star Clipper and Star Flyer each carry only 170 guests, the new Royal Clipper, the largest true sailing ship in the world, carries 227 guests.

 STAR CLIPPERS

www.starclippers.com   *Ship's Registry: Luxembourg*

Free Brochure: 800-442-0556

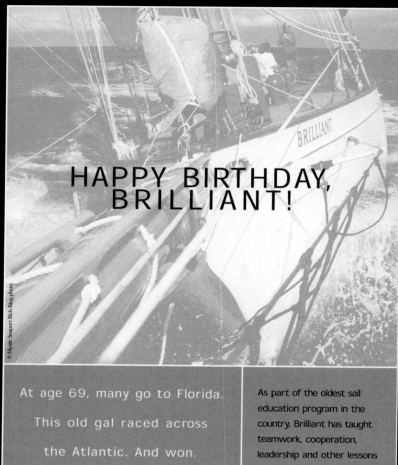

HAPPY BIRTHDAY, BRILLIANT!

At age 69, many go to Florida.

This old gal raced across

the Atlantic. And won.

She turns 70 this year.

Think she's slowing down?

Think again.

As part of the oldest sail education program in the country, Brilliant has taught teamwork, cooperation, leadership and other lessons of the sea to more than 8,000 people. That's a lot of cake.

How can you celebrate? Give Brilliant (and yourself) the gift of membership.

MYSTIC SEAPORT®
THE MUSEUM OF AMERICA AND THE SEA™

Exit 90 off I-95 in Mystic, Connecticut
www.mysticseaport.org · 888.9SEAPORT

TALL SHIPS CHALLENGE®
RACE SERIES

An annual series of sail training races, rallies, cruises and port festivals organized by the American Sail Training Association in conjunction with host ports:

2002 - The Pacific
2002 TALL SHIPS CHALLENGE® Race Series:

August 8-12, 2002	Richmond (Vancouver-area), British Columbia
August 15-19, 2002	Seattle, WA
Aug. 28-Sept. 2, 2002	San Francisco, CA
September 6-10, 2002	Los Angeles, CA
RACE 1: August 20-27	Seattle (Cape Flattery) to San Francisco
RACE 2: September 2-5	San Francisco to Los Angeles

Additional Pacific events:

May and June, 2002 Sail Korea 2002 in Korea and Japan
July 30-Aug. 2, 2002 Transpacific race: Yokohama to Richmond, BC

2003 - The Great Lakes
2003 TALL SHIPS CHALLENGE® Race Series: *

June 28-July 1, 2003	Toronto, Ontario (tentative)
July 10-13, 2003	Cleveland, (Ohio Bicentennial)
July 17-20, 2003	Toledo, (Ohio Bicentennial)
July 30-Aug. 3, 2003	Chicago, IL (Tall Ships® Chicago)
Aug. 7-10, 2003	Muskegon, MI
Aug. 14-17, 2003	Bay City, MI
Aug. 21-24, 2003	Sarnia, Ontario

2004 - The Atlantic
2004 TALL SHIPS CHALLENGE® Race Series: *

June 17-21, 2004	Charleston, SC
June 25-29, 2004	Philadelphia, PA or Norfolk, VA
July 1-5, 2004	Baltimore, MD
July 9-15, 2004	Boston, MA
July 17-21, 2004	Rhode Island
July 24-28, 2004	Portland, ME
July 31-Aug.4, 2004	Halifax, Nova Scotia

* Dates subject to change; check with ASTA or the host ports before making travel arrangements.

Sail Tall Ships!
2002

Mapping out the 2002 TALL SHIPS CHALLENGE®
Race Series:

TALL SHIPS
CHALLENGE.

Richmond, BC

Seattle, WA

San Francisco, CA

Los Angeles, CA

Photo credit: Chris Bowser

Sail Tall Ships!

This book is dedicated to the families of all of those who lost their lives on September 11, 2001 in New York City, Washington, DC and Somerset County, Pennsylvania.

A Directory of Sail Training and Adventure at Sea

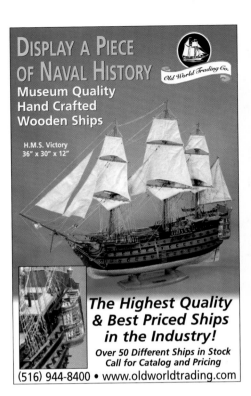

Table of Contents

The mission of the American Sail Training Association is to encourage character building through sail training, promote sail training to the North American public, and support education under sail.

Published by:
American Sail Training Association (ASTA)
PO Box 1459, 559 Thames Street
Newport, RI 02840 USA
Phone: (401) 846-1775; Fax: (401) 849-5400
E-mail: asta@sailtraining.org
Web site: http://www.tallships.sailtraining.org

Acknowledgments
Many of the photographs in this edition of Sail Tall Ships! were supplied by:

Thad Koza
Tall Ships Photography
24 Mary Street
Newport, RI 02840 USA
Phone: (401) 846-5274

MAX
Bywater Lodge-Pierside
Lymington, Hants SO41 5SB
United Kingdom
Phone: + 44 (0) 1590 672047

Wojtek Wacowski
102 E. Lorain Street
Oberlin, OH 44074
Phone: (440) 775-3158

Michael Kahn
PO Box 335
Unionville, PA 19375
Phone: 610-383-9250

We would like to thank Ms Cindy Hammel, Ms Rebecca Priddy, Captain Randall Peffer and Sheridan House, Captain James Gladson, Mr. Richard King, Mr. Michael J. Meighan, Ms. Alix Thorne, Mr. Rafe Parker and Mr. Drew McMullen for submitting material or granting permission to reprint their remarks. We would also like to thank Ms Sally Anne Santos for her assistance in selling advertisements, and the advertisers who made the production of this Directory possible.

Registered Trademarks
The following registered trademarks and service marks are owned by the American Sail Training Association:

Tall Ships®
Tall Ships are Coming!®
Tall Ships 2000®
Tall Ships Challenge®

ASTA

TALL SHIPS 2000®

TALL SHIPS CHALLENGE

Sail Tall Ships! A Directory of Sail Training and Adventure at Sea 14th edition

Compiled and edited by Lori A. Aguiar, ASTA Program Coordinator
Design by Artinium Design, 3 Davol Square, Box 148, Providence, RI 02903
Consulting by Pucino Print Consultants, 631 Fletcher Road, North Kingstown, RI 02852
Printed in Canada by Dollco Printing

ISBN 0-9636483-7-3

Cover photo: *Hawaiian Chieftain* (left) and *Lady Washington* in San Francisco Bay.
Photo by Benson Lee

Welcome Aboard!

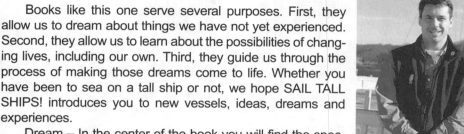

Books like this one serve several purposes. First, they allow us to dream about things we have not yet experienced. Second, they allow us to learn about the possibilities of changing lives, including our own. Third, they guide us through the process of making those dreams come to life. Whether you have been to sea on a tall ship or not, we hope SAIL TALL SHIPS! introduces you to new vessels, ideas, dreams and experiences.

Dream – In the center of the book you will find the spectacular work of world famous maritime photographers Thad Koza and Michael Kahn. We also take pleasure in introducing you to the exciting perspectives of Wojtek Wacowski. While we often think of tall ships as being from the past, all of these wonderful images are of sail training vessels today!

In his essay "Sailing for Whales" (adapted with permission from Logs of the Dead Pirates Society - Sheridan House 2000), Captain Randy Peffer tells a magical story about a sail training voyage off the coast of Massachusetts where the objective may have been to spot a whale but the result was the rite of passage for the young crew aboard the schooner *Sarah Abbot*.

Learn - In 2003, the American Sail Training Association will celebrate our 30th anniversary and in SAIL TALL SHIPS! you can learn all about the history of our organization which started out as just a handful of vessels gunkholing in the Northeast Atlantic to now more than 250 vessels that perform sail training around the globe.

In 2001, we successfully launched the TALL SHIPS CHALLENGE® Series of sail training races, rallies and port visits in the Great Lakes. You can read about this exciting event from an intern's perspective in Cindy Hammel's essay entitled "An Intern's Challenge." There is also a lot of other additional information on the TALL SHIPS CHALLENGE® Series for 2001, 2002 (Pacific Coast), 2003 (Great Lakes) and 2004 (Atlantic Coast).

If you are thinking of embarking on a sail training voyage and you feel you need to "learn the ropes" first, read 2001 Henry H. Anderson, Jr. Sail Training Scholarship Recipient Rebecca Priddy's humorous essay "*Concordia* for Dummies."

On the more serious side, we have reprinted recent speeches by three leaders in the sail training industry: Alix T. Thorne, Rafe Parker and Captain James Gladson.

Sail - Finally, SAIL TALL SHIPS! will help you chart a course to your adventure at sea. Sail training experiences are valuable for "youth of all ages" and voyages of any duration and distance. Whether you are a K-12 teacher scouting field trips for the day, a college junior away for a semester at sea, a couple celebrating an anniversary on an adventure-travel sailing expedition, a family on a weekend excursion on a Maine windjammer or an older adult on an Elderhostel Adventures Afloat program, this book contains the information to make your experience successful and to create memories that will last for a lifetime.

So we hope you dream, learn but most importantly SAIL TALL SHIPS!

Peter A. Mello, Executive Director

A Brief History of the American Sail Training Association

In the summer of 1972 Barclay Warburton III, of Newport, Rhode Island, his two sons, and several friends, sailed his brigantine *Black Pearl* across the Atlantic to participate in a tall ships race from Cowes on the south coast of England to Malmo in Sweden, organized by what was then known as The Sail Training Association. He was so inspired by the enthusiasm and spirit he saw in that international gathering of tall ships and young people that he set out to create a similar organization in order to bring the same kind of spirit to the United States, and through his efforts the American Sail Training Association was founded the following year. ASTA soon became the first national association to formally affiliate with what eventually became known as the International Sail Training Association-a family that has since grown to more than 16 members around the globe.

The Tall Ships Races in which the *Black Pearl* took part had first been held in 1956, when a London solicitor, Bernard Morgan, had the idea of bringing what he imagined to be the last of the world's great square-riggers together for a race as a sort of last hurrah-a farewell salute-for the Great Age of Sail. A committee was formed, and with the support and assistance of the Portuguese Ambassador in London, a race was organized from Torbay, on England's Cornish coast, to Lisbon. Five square-rigged schoolships entered the race: Denmark's *Danmark*, Norway's *Christian Radich* and *Sorlandet*, Belgium's *Mercator*, and Portugal's first *Sagres*.

St. Lawrence II (back) and *True North of Toronto.* TALL SHIPS CHALLENGE® Great Lakes 2001, Parade of Sail, Kingston, Ontario.

The event proved to be anything but a funeral procession, however, and it has since grown into an annual series that would astonish its original organizers. Today, hundreds of tall ships from around the world come together annually for friendly competition in international and regional Tall Ships Races organized by ISTA and national affiliates such as ASTA. These races, along with waterfront festivals in designated start and finish ports, bring together the ships and young people of most European countries, Russia and the former Soviet states, the Americas, and the Pacific Rim. The key elements uniting these events are an emphasis on youth—from the beginning, ISTA's racing rules have required that no less than half those onboard participating vessels be between 15 and 25 years of age—and a formula for rating participating vessels which allows vessels ranging in size from the largest square-riggers down to yachts of 30 or more

feet in length.

ASTA's efforts in its first decade were primarily focused on organizing tall ships races on the ISTA model, but from the mid-1980's to the mid-1990's (when it began intensive planning, in conjunction with ISTA, for Tall Ships 2000®) it worked on a multitude of activities broadly aimed at promoting sail training and supporting education under sail in North America. Thus at the beginning of the 21st century, the American Sail Training Association has evolved into both an organizer of tall ships races and a strong industry association for the growing numbers of vessels involved in providing opportunities for people of all ages to take part in a seagoing experience aboard a sailing vessel. With an organizational membership of over 250 vessels, ASTA serves as a forum for information exchange, professional development, and program standards. Through such initiatives as the Council of Educational

Ship Owners, which worked successfully for the passage of the Sailing School Vessels Act of 1982 and the Sailing School Vessels Council, founded the following year, ASTA has continued to work with the US Coast Guard and other agencies to create and maintain a friendly regulatory climate for the development of sail training.

Safety at sea has been an enduring emphasis, and in conjunction with the Australian bicentennial gathering of tall ships in Sydney in 1988, a group of ASTA members organized the first international discussion on safety standards, practices, and equipment for sail training programs. Since 1992, ASTA and ISTA have jointly sponsored the annual International Sail Training Safety Forum, which in 1999 drew more than 160 professional sail trainers from 16 nations. Also in the 1980's, ASTA developed the concept of the Sail Training Rally; a competition among crews both at sea and ashore, which provides trainees with an opportunity to demonstrate their seamanship skills in a friendly but competitive format. During shoreside events, the general public can observe the sort of teamwork and maritime skills that are learned on board sail training vessels at sea.

Over the years, the American Sail Training Association has undertaken many other projects to meet the needs of a rapidly growing sail training community. These include a variety of publications including this Directory, forums, an Annual Conference on Sail Training which attracts substantial international attention and participation; a Marine Insurance Program; a Billet Bank to assist vessels in finding qualified crewmembers, and vice versa; a growing program of scholarships and grants to support trainees, vessels, and professional crew; and a constantly expanding Web site. In 2001, building on the spectacular success of Tall Ships 2000®, ASTA launched its most ambitious project to date—an annual series of tall ships races known as TALL SHIPS CHALLENGE®. Starting with the highly successful series in the Great Lakes in 2001, the series will move to the Pacific Coast in 2002, back to the Great Lakes in 2003, and to the Atlantic Coast in 2004.

TALL SHIPS CHALLENGE® Great Lakes 2001. Port Colborne, Ontario.

2002 Board of Directors

Chairman - Captain Christoper Rowsom - Baltimore, Maryland
Vice Chairman - Mr. Thomas Gochberg - New York, New York
Vice Chairman - Mr. Jeffrey Parker - McLean, Virginia
Secretary - Mr. Per Lofving - New York, New York
Treasurer - Mr. B. Devereux Barker III - Danvers, Massachusetts
Fund Development Committee Chair - Mr. George Lewis, Jr. - Boston,Massachusetts
Sail Training & Education Committee Chair - Ms Nancy H. Richardson - Maplewood, NJ
Technical Committee Chair - Captain Ken Neal-Boyd - Woods Hole, Massachusetts
Executive Director - Mr. Peter A. Mello - Mattapoisett, Massachusetts

Class of 2004
Mr. Alexander M. Agnew - Portland, Maine
Mr. Dexter Donham - Dover, Massachusetts
Mr. James Kerr, Esq. - New York, New York
Mr. John McCollough - Portsmouth, Rhode Island
Mr. Thomas M. McKenna - Philadelphia, Pennsylvania
Mr. Joseph Ribaudo - Hingham, Massachusetts
Captain Jeffrey Troletzsch - Oriental, North Carolina
Mr. F. C. "Bunky" Wichmann - Charleston, South Carolina
Captain Ken Neal-Boyd - Woods Hole, Massachusetts

Class of 2003
Captain Richard Bailey - Bridgeport, Connecticut
Captain Martyn J. Clark - Victoria, British Columbia
Mr. Chuck Fowler - Olympia, Washington
Captain James Gladson - San Pedro, California
Captain Joseph A. Maggio - Coconut Grove, Florida
Captain William D. Pinkney - Mystic, Connecticut
Captain Doug Prothero - Halifax, Nova Scotia
Captain John C. Wigglesworth - Ipswich, Massachusetts

Class of 2002
Ms Alice Cochran - Sausalito, California
Mr. George Lewis, Jr. - Boston, Massachusetts
Mr. Clarke Murphy - New York, New York
Captain Michael J. Rauworth, Esq. - Boston, Massachusetts
Captain Walter Rybka - Erie, Pennsylvania
Ms Alix T. Thorne - Georges Mills, New Hampshire
Mr. Barclay H. Warburton IV - Newport, Rhode Island

Commodores Council
Mr. Henry H. Anderson, Jr. - Newport, Rhode Island
Mr. Bart Dunbar - Newport, Rhode Island
Ms Nancy H. Richardson - Maplewood, New Jersey
Ms Gail Shawe - Baltimore, Maryland
Ms Pamela Dewell Smith - Newport, Rhode Island
VADM Thomas R. Weschler, USN (Ret.) - Newport, Rhode Island
CAPT David V. V. Wood, USCG (Ret.) - Newport, Rhode Island

ASTA Staff
Mr. Peter A. Mello - Executive Director
Mr. Steven H. Baker - Race Director
Ms Lori A. Aguiar - Program Coordinator
Mr. Nicholas M. Baker - Program Assistant

Tall Ships Challenge®

Tall ships and sail training vessels from Europe, Oceania, North America and the Caribbean are bound for the West Coast of Canada and the U.S. this summer to participate in the 2002 TALL SHIPS CHALLENGE® Race Series.

Featuring five weeks of sail training races, cruises, nautical rallies and port festivals, the series is organized by ASTA to celebrate and promote sail training for youth as well as education and adventure travel opportunities for participants of all ages. Several million visitors are expected to come to city waterfronts to view or board the vessels and to learn about life on board ship from the crew and trainees during this annual series which rotates from the Pacific to the Great Lakes to the Atlantic and possibly the Gulf Coast.

The 2002 TALL SHIPS CHALLENGE® Series warms up with a 4250-mile feeder race across the North Pacific from Yokohama, Japan to Richmond, British Columbia, Canada to connect the series with Sail Korea 2002 which will take place in Korea and Japan in May and June at the same time as the FIFA World Cup Soccer Championship.

Race 2 runs more than 800 nautical miles from Seattle, Washington to the northern California port of San Francisco from August 19 - 28 and race 3 will bring the fleet 360 miles to Los Angeles in southern California September 2 - 6.

The 2002 host ports have planned many social and cultural activities for trainees and crews while the vessels are in port. Richmond and perhaps San Francisco are also hosting ASTA Sail Training Rallies, a series of nautical competitions among crew and trainees. Rally events typically include pulling boat races, bucket brigades, knot-tying relays, heaving line toss/hawser pull, tug of war and a captains' sailing dinghy race.

2002 port festival schedule:

Richmond, British Columbia, Canada – August 8-12
Seattle, Washington, USA – August 15-19
San Francisco, California – August 28 – September 2
Los Angeles, California – September 6-10

The 2003 TALL SHIPS CHALLENGE® Race Series will return to the Great Lakes with visits to Canadian and US ports. One of the highlights of the 2003 series will be the chance to help commemorate the State of Ohio's 200th anniversary.

The tentative 2003 port schedule is:

June 28 - July 1, 2003 – Toronto, Ontario (tentative)
July 10-13, 2003 – Cleveland, Ohio (Ohio Bicentennial)
July 17-20, 2003 – Toledo, Ohio (Ohio Bicentennial)
July 30 - August 3, 2003 – Chicago, Illinois (Tall Ships® Chicago)
August 7-10, 2003 – Muskegon, Michigan
August 14-17, 2003 – Bay City, Michigan
August 21-24, 2003 – Sarnia, Ontario

In 2004, the TALL SHIPS CHALLENGE® Series will make its Atlantic Coast debut. Interested ports include Jacksonville, FL, Charleston, SC, Norfolk, VA, Baltimore, MD, Philadelphia, PA, New London, CT, Boston, MA, Rhode Island, Portland, ME and Halifax, Nova Scotia. Firm dates so far include Baltimore's U.S.S. Constellation Sesquicentennial July 1-5, 2004 and Sail Boston 2004 July 9-15.

Visit the ASTA website for updates and racing schedules.

Tall Ships Challenge® 2001-Great Lakes
An ASTA After-Action Report

The 2001 series was divided into four ASTA-organized races:

1. Across Lake Ontario from Kingston, Ontario to the Welland Canal en route to Port Colborne, Ontario;

2. Across Lake Erie from Port Colborne to Cleveland, Ohio;

3. Detroit/Windsor to Bay City, Michigan in Lake Huron; and

4. Bay City to the Straits of Mackinac in Lake Huron en route to Green Bay, Wisconsin and Muskegon, Michigan.

ASTA, along with eight American and Canadian Great Lakes port cities, 30 sail training vessels from six countries, and nearly 1000 crewmembers and sail trainees representing 14 nationalities joined together for a very successful inaugural TALL SHIPS CHALLENGE® Race Series during the summer of 2001.

The series was designed to celebrate and promote sail training for youth but also opportunities for education under sail and adventure travel for participants of all ages. Several million visitors came to city waterfronts throughout the Great Lakes to view or board the vessels and talk with crewmembers and trainees about their experiences.

For the port cities and their local sponsors, it was a chance to showcase their historic and often recently-renovated waterfronts and to bring crowds to their city centers – in most cases, the TALL SHIPS CHALLENGE® fleet and related port festivals drew larger crowds than any previous city events. The TALL SHIPS CHALLENGE® port visit and Grand Parade of Sail were the highlights of Detroit and Windsor's 300th anniversary celebrations.

With two first places and two second places, the 75-foot schooner *Grand Nellie* from the US Virgin Islands (with all-female trainees) was the overall winner on corrected time and also the winner of the Youth Sail Training Division in which *St. Lawrence II* from Kingston, Ontario placed second and *Highlander Sea* from Dartmouth, Nova Scotia was third. *Pride of Baltimore II* from Maryland was second overall on corrected time and first in the Cruising Division ahead of *True North of Toronto* and the sailing school ship *Concordia* based in the Bahamas.

In addition to our appreciation of the efforts put forth by the host port cities and the thousands of volunteers, and participating sail training vessels and their crews, we at ASTA would like to recognize the US Coast Guard in District 9 (Great Lakes) for supplying escort vessels/ communications/ safety vessels throughout the series, for their assistance in planning and logistics, and to the Cleveland Marine Safety Office for dedicating a "Sail Training Room" at the Coast Guard Club.

Tall Ships Challenge®
Great Lakes 2001 Race Results

Race 1 – Youth Sail Training Division
1. *Highlander Sea*
2. *Grand Nellie*
3. *St. Lawrence II*
4. *Norfolk Rebel*
5. *Fair Jeanne*

Race 1 – Cruising Division
1. *Pride of Baltimore II*
2. *True North*
3. *Road to the Isles*

Race 2 – Youth Sail Training Division
1. *Grand Nellie*
2. *St. Lawrence II*
3. *Pathfinder*
4. *Playfair*
5. *Fair Jeanne*
6. *Norfolk Rebel*
7. *True North*

Race 2 – Cruising Division
1. *Pride of Baltimore II*

Race 3 – Youth Sail Training Division
1. *Grand Nellie*
2. *Highlander Sea*
3. *St. Lawrence II*
4. *Appledore IV*
5. *Norfolk Rebel*
6. *True North*
7. *Fair Jeanne*

Race 3 – Cruising Division
1. *Pride of Baltimore II*
2. *Concordia*

Race 4 – Youth Sail Training Division
1. *St. Lawrence II*
2. *Grand Nellie*
3. *Highlander Sea*
4. *Norfolk Rebel*
5. *True North*

Race 4 – Cruising Division
1. *Pride of Baltimore II*

Overall Results – Youth Sail Training Division
1. *Grand Nellie*
2. *St. Lawrence II*
3. *Highlander Sea*
4. *Norfolk Rebel*
5 *Fair Jeanne*
6. *True North*
7. *Pathfinder*
8. *Playfair and Appledore IV* (tied)

Overall Results– Cruising Division
1. *Pride of Baltimore II*
2. *True North*
3. *Concordia*

Overall Series Winner
1. *Grand Nellie*
2. *Pride of Baltimore II*

Cook Longest at Sea
True North

Long Distance Award (furthest distance traveled to participate in the TALL SHIPS CHALLENGE®)
Concordia

SAIL TALL SHIPS!

Tall Ships Challenge® Race Series
ASTA Sail Training Rally
Port Colborne, Ontario - July 2001

Heaving Line Toss & Hawser Pull

Events:

Bucket Brigade
1. *St. Lawrence II* – "Blue Watch"
2. *Fair Jeanne* and *Pathfinder* (tied)
4. *Grand Nellie*
5. *St. Lawrence II* – "Red Watch"

Heaving Line Toss & Hawser Pull
1. "5 Shoes & 1 Sandal" with trainees from *Fair Jeanne*, *HMS Tecumseth* & *St. Lawrence II*
2. *Grand Nellie*
3. *St. Lawrence II* – "Blue Watch"
4. *St. Lawrence II* – "Red Watch"
5. *Fair Jeanne*
6. *Pathfinder*

Knot-tying Relay
1. *St. Lawrence II* – "Blue Watch"
2. *St. Lawrence II* – "Red Watch"

Sailing Dinghy Race
1. *Pathfinder*
2. *Concordia*
3. *Norfolk Rebel*
4. *St. Lawrence II*
5. *Fair Jeanne*

Overall Rally Winner:
St. Lawrence II

Bucket Brigade

SAIL TALL SHIPS!

Tall Ships Challenge® 2001
An Intern's Challenge

By: Cindy Hammel

The BLUENOSE II "She does not race, but she sure is fast!"

The wind can either toss a scrap of paper across the dock, or push 18 tons of a tailored forest across a never ending body of water. On deck, a rigorous work ethic, teamwork, and camaraderie harness that wind to carry the tall ships to a finish line and the next port in the TALL SHIPS CHALLENGE® race series. Whatever the crew and trainees learn at sea-be it navigation, the principles of lift and drag, how to channel their own fear to carry them aloft-they also discover life skills and meet personal challenges that will remain with them years after their first CHALLENGE.

I was initially looking for any internship that would put me in an interesting part of the country, where I could find experiences I would not otherwise encounter. When I found an internship that offered a taste of media, event coordination, web-design, writing opportunities, development, and education, not to mention travel, and a summer surrounded by tall ships, the search ended, and the Executive Director of the American Sail Training Association, Peter Mello, welcomed me on board.

Picture this: You have been in Newport, Rhode Island working for ASTA for approximately two weeks, then suddenly find yourself in Kingston, Ontario, to kick off the TALL SHIPS CHALLENGE® 2001. Here is your hotel room, here is the ASTA Race Office. Here are the people you will need to know and recognize for the next week. This is Lake Ontario, this is Kingston, this is the event site map. Memorize as much as possible to make your life easier later on. When you go to dinner you are recognized for the blue polo shirt and race team name badge. This is what it is like to hear your event on the tip of every tongue in the city. A visitor yourself in every port, you have just a few hours to locate yourself before the ships and the onlookers start pouring in.

Waiting in line for a latte in a Port Colborne coffee shop, a man in front of me buys a paper and asks the woman behind the counter if the special section on the Tall Ships is inside.

"It should be." "Do you know when the parade starts tomorrow?" "I don't. I'm sorry," she answers him, then turns to me. "What can I get you?"

The gentleman before me had been examining my name badge. Now he eagerly asks me about the Parade of Sail that will soon swamp the town with both tall ships and tourists coming to see them. "The parade should start around four. Of course the precise time will depend on your location along the waterfront. They will also be sailing at about three knots, so it should be slow enough for a good viewing." He thanks me, relieved. Oh, yes, I had answers.

I drift through that first reception already amazed by my position, which has so many different perspectives on an event of this magnitude. From sponsors, contracts, event coordination, ticket sales, customs, merchandise and logo arrangements, programs, media communication and miscommunication, from the captains and crew, to the ASTA office, not to mention plans for 2002 and 2003, I have a privileged insight in all directions. When someone referred to me as the "right hand of god," as Steve Baker's race assistant-they were probably closer than they could have known. The interns have a unique perspective and the liberty to drift between the different worlds involved with the event.

While the tall ships' nostalgic grandeur dazzles the public, the people on board give each ship her own personality, and passion for sail training. This spirit lies at the heart of the race series. On the event site, we run the ASTA booth, this year headed by Kazu, my fellow intern, Massachusetts Maritime Academy Cadet and seasoned tall ship sailor. Here we spread the ASTA mission, bringing education under sail to the public, as well as ASTA merchandise. I can't even count the number of times I am asked, "How can I sail on a tall ship?" Some people wander off before I can even tell them that ASTA is responsible for the entire race series, but others pick up a directory and leave with their jaws hanging open, shocked to discover that they too can sign onto a ship that they previously thought sailed only through Disney films.

Working the booth in Detroit, a man approaches me with a dazed look on his face. He wants to sail. I explain ASTA, education under sail and how "sail training is for youth of all ages." "I have nautical stuff all over my house," he says. "I'm obsessed with sailing ships, but I've never sailed. I've had the TALL SHIP CHALLENGE® on my calendar since last October, and now you're telling me that I can sail?" "Yes." He thinks a moment, then says, "...I might have to do that."

This man returns to the booth at least four times throughout the day, amazed at how easily he could get on board, "What kind of gear will I need? How long can I sail for? What if I don't have any experience?" He leaves late that afternoon, a directory tucked under one arm, and three different pages turned down, asking himself, "Why not? There's no reason not to do this. I've been working behind a desk my whole life and dreaming about this." When I'm not on the waterfront, I find myself back in the office compiling racing handouts with Steve Baker, to entertain and bedazzle the sleepy captains at the race briefing the next morning. Otherwise, I find myself wedging my way between the crowds to collect racing forms and crew lists. As silly as it sounds, I get a rush from cutting in line on "official business" with my VIP tags flapping in the wind to ask, "is the Captain on board?" The person I cut off gives my name badge a closer look, thinking, "This woman must be terribly important" especially when the captain hands the paperwork through the rigging and kindly invites me for "a spot of tea later on."

Jeff on the *Grand Nellie* dubs Nicole, another intern, and myself, the "ASTA-roids," or the "ASTA chicks that orbit the tall ships." Nicole has been a part of this for years, sailing on the *St. Lawrence II*, *True North*, and *Royaliste*. She told me, "I no longer belong to any one ship. We are like the tall ship groupies. We just follow them around all summer."

I find my peer social group among the crew community. Although I am part of the ASTA official race team, I am removed enough for the crew and captains to speak candidly with me, giving me their friendship as well as a more professional perspective on the Challenge.

They are here for sail training, for the irreplaceable character building challenges, experiences, and friendships the trainees and crew find on the water and in port. Between Cleveland and Detroit some of the ships anchor off of Pelle Island, where they can celebrate the sail training community without the pressure of the crowds, and refresh themselves for the excitement awaiting them at Detroit's 300th birthday celebration.

A parade of sail brings the ships into port, and the trainees see hundreds of thousands of little specks packing the waterfront staring right back at them. The organizers may not understand what it means to make a parade course where the largest main sail will have to jibe; this was one area where I had a privileged view at the very different perspectives at work in the event. However, as long as the captains get their septic tanks pumped when they arrive, they will joke about frustrations at the open bar reception that evening. My advice to ports: provide an open bar reception, so they can joke that evening. I never would have thought septic pumping could make so many people so happy. Or maybe it's just the open bar.

The Captains' Receptions, the on-deck sponsor parties, and the crew parties illustrate yet another dimension of the summer. The crowds go home; the captains don their dashing blue blazers and may or may not bother with socks. I get to clamor out of my sticky polo and remind myself how to put on a dress. "What's your draft?" could be a pick-up line here. This was my chance to kick back and get to know the organizers, the ship officers, and other people involved in the event a little better. This can turn into a networking haven if you talk to the right people, which also compensates for an intern's minimal wages.

To the crew and trainees, port is a promise of showers, laundry, and the small pleasures only a person who has been at sea can truly appreciate. I remember running into a crewmember in Windsor, happily chattering about his exciting day, "I got to use my bank card, and I got a Slurpee at Seven-Eleven, and saw a Circle K, and now I'm going to the library to check email, and tonight some of us are meeting at the Irish pub up the street…" When you ask for the "head" people look at you strangely, until you remember that on land the head is more commonly called the restroom, or washroom, or le toilette, depending on which part of the world or even where in a city you find yourself. Granted, as an intern, I found myself in port more than at sea, but every once in a while the opportunity to sail arises, and you jump on it. My opportunity happily arose on the historic *Bluenose II*, Canada's ambassador schooner from Nova Scotia.

"Here, put your hands here. Pull out, then down, like this. Ready?" said Andrew, a member of the *Bluenose II* crew. Reaching over my shoulders he placed his hands above mine on a rope the thickness of a large cucumber. We leaned, then sank all our weight to our knees, hand over hand. Lean, sink, lean, sink. The main sail slowly rose into the clear blue sky over Lake Erie. Taylor's hands whipped the rope around the cleat—three figure eights, flip, and pulled the

ASTA interns and volunteers join executive director, Peter Mello in the ASTA booth in Detroit, MI, during the TALL SHIPS CHALLENGE® Great Lakes 2001.

ASTA Interns Cindy and Nicole mingle with crew members.

sheet taught. I tumbled back into Andrew's chest as the wind caught the sail and the ship heeled. He grinned and propped me upright. The *Larinda* passed across our port bow, close hauled on a port tack. The *Mist of Avalon* soon had her sails up and was jockeying for position off our port stern. Lake Erie tossed around the swarms of small motorboats, out to watch the start of the race just off of the Welland Canal entrance at Port Colborne, Ontario. Next stop: Cleveland, Ohio. The *Bluenose II*, however, "does not race. But she sure is fast," according to her home office.

That evening we dropped anchor in the middle of Long Point Bay. Later that night I padded across the deck in my bare feet, and paused to admire the stars' reflection resting on the water. Lake Erie was calm, and a gentle breeze caught my hair and blew it across my face. I pushed it aside, but the wind had caught my heart as well, before I could duck down through the hatch and into the galley. Below, the crew was watching a movie and drinking coffee. I couldn't think of any-where I would rather be, of any floor that would feel better than the soft mahogany rocking beneath my feet. Sarah smiled when I walked in, and Simon moved over to make room for me on the bench. This could be home. Somewhere behind my back my imagination had created a sailor in me. I loved the crew. I loved the ship. I was even starting to love the crowds that would greet us in Cleveland; hundreds and hundreds of faces with the same awestruck looks, kinked necks gazing aloft, and all because of us and our ships. Some of them would find themselves sailing to the next port; others would hopefully leave with a better understanding of the maritime world, its history, and the opportunities it offers.

Driving back to Newport after the series I felt that at some point down the eastbound freeway sneaking between Lake Ontario and Lake Erie, I would have to cry. It might not happen until I got back to Rhode Island, or until I ran across an old friend in Boston, but with every small wheat field that rolled past my win-dow, the distance between the tall ships and myself grew both in geography and time. A summer of excited crowds, of hot blue skies sliced open by one ton tim-bers waving hundreds of feet above my head through a steady embrace of main-stay sheets, softened by baggy wrinkles creates a skyline all of its own in my mind's eye.

The Tall Ships are Coming!® Yes, we are. A fleet of floating history, of mar-itime knowledge, of educational opportunities, personal challenges and character-building experiences, and especially a community of wonderful people who keep the sail training spirit alive year after year, and here's to that "spot of tea" next summer.

Additional Events with Invitations to ASTA Member Vessels

August 16-18, 2002: 2nd Annual Thunder Bay Tall Ships® Festival, Alpena, MI
Sponsored by the National Marine Sanctuary Foundation
Contact: NMSF Executive Director Lori Arguelles at (703) 714-2371.

Sept. 6-8, 2002: Boats Books and Brushes, New London, CT.
Sail New London's Maritime Arts Festival
Contact: Nancy Tyler at 800-634-1919 ext. 707 or email: sailnl@aol.com

Sept. 14-15, 2002: Sail for America, New York Harbor
One year after the tragic events of Sept. 11, 2001 – the plan is to have the greatest gathering of sailboats ever in the history of the harbor. This will be a symbolic rebirth for the City of New York and a tribute to the soaring spirit of America.
Contact: New York Harbor Sailing Foundation, Inc.,
393 South End Avenue,
New York, NY 10280: Tel: (212) 786-1743
Contact the ASTA office for additional information.
You may also contact Michael Fortenbaugh, Commodore of the Manhattan Yacht Club at 212-786-3323. or email: mike@myc.org

May 15-18, 2003: Sail Jacksonville 2003, Jacksonville, FL
Contact: Capt. Bob Russo, Bluewater Maritime School
Tel & fax: 904-247-3366 or email: tugco@aol.com

July 9-13, 2003: International Children's Conference on the Environment and Tall Ships® Festival, New London, CT
Created by the United Nations Environmental Programme (UNEP) following the 1992 Earth Summit, the ICCE hosts children and their chaperones from more than 100 countries, encouraging them to learn about global best-practices, initiate innovative environmental change and make lasting international friendships.
Contact the ASTA office for additional information.
You may also contact: Nancy Tyler at 800-634-1919 ext. 707 or
email: nptyler@aol.com

August 15-17, 2003: Sail Lunenburg 2003, Lunenburg, Nova Scotia
250th Birthday of Lunenburg, Canada's Favorite Tall Ship Port
Contact: Sail Lunenburg 2003, P.O. Box 195, Lunenburg, N.S. B0J 2C0 Canada
Tel: 902-634-9958   Fax: 902-634-1907 Email: acreaser@tallships.ca

The Henry H. Anderson, Jr. Sail Training Scholarship Fund has been established to assist youth ages 14 - 19 in achieving a sail training experience. Year 2001 Recipients - total of $6500:

Individual

Rebecca Priddy — *Concordia*/Class Afloat
Raven Bier — *Robert C. Seamans*/SEA
Ryan M. Tharp — *Corwith Cramer*/SEA
Travis M. Killian — *St. Lawrence II* - TALL SHIPS CHALLENGE® Great Lakes 2001
Sarah B. Hansen - *Corwith Cramer*/SEA
Claire F. Connors - *Corwith Cramer*/SEA
Callie Garrett Van Koughnett - *Corwith Cramer*/SEA
James Taylor — *Lady Maryland*/Living Classroom Foundation
Christoper Michael Nemes — *Spirit of Massachusetts* /Ocean Classroom Foundation
Katelyn Baker Miller — *Spirit of Massachusetts* /Ocean Classroom Foundation

The ASTA Sailing Vessel Assistance Grant has been established to support vessels that are not necessarily operating as USCG-inspected Sailing School or Passenger Vessels. Priority will be given to requests that further the mission and goals of the American Sail Training Association or are consistent with ASTA's stated mission. Year 2001 Recipients - total of $3000:

Providence - Providence Maritime Heritage Foundation - Providence, RI
Quinnipiak - Schooner Sound Learning-New Haven, CT
Roald Amundsen - Lebenlernen auf Segelschiffen e.V. (Learning to Live on Sailing Ships),-Eckernförde, Germany

The ASTA Crew Development Grant has been established to provide financial assistance to professional crewmembers of ASTA vessels in order to meet new and existing requirements for maintaining as well as advancing their USCG licenses, and to encourage the highest possible standards of safety training for individuals or groups of ASTA members. Year 2001 Recipients - total of $5000:

Austin Becker
Christine M. Cleary
Michael Dawson
Elizabeth Doxsee
Donald Keel
Richard King
Norseman
Erica Sachs
Ronald Smith

For specific guidelines and criteria or for an application, please visit the Scholarship/Grant page of the ASTA Web site at www.tallships.sailtraining.org

Class Afloat/Great Lakes Adventure
Aboard Concordia

Dear ASTA,

I would like to thank everyone from ASTA for a wonderful experience this summer in the 2001 TALL SHIPS CHALLENGE®, and for giving me the opportunity to receive the Henry H. Anderson, Jr. Sail Training Scholarship. I had an awesome time on the *Concordia*, met many people I'll be sure to keep in touch with, and I learned an incredible amount about tall ships in general.

When I first got on the ship, I was a bit intimidated because I was the youngest one aboard. Most of the students that were on the ship were freshmen and sophomores in college, and I was just a little junior in high school. After a few days on the ship when we actually started doing watches and cleaning the boat, it got very tiring. Since I had gone sailing last year also, I adjusted to the sleeplessness of all the work and study. All of the pro-crew welcomed me, and made me feel at home. When I would be walking around in port with my friends I met on the ship, we would even call the ship "home." All of the work was worth the experience. It was so much fun, it's almost indescribable. Someone has to actually experience it to understand what anything is, or how anything is done. I would definitely love to do this again in the near future. I think that anyone who likes adventure and new experiences would have liked this trip. The fact that there is no escaping from anything on the ship, from little misunderstandings, to doing work, is just so neat, because at home you can just put it all behind you. On the ship everyone has to work together, whether or not they want to. This trip gave me lots of self-confidence and I learned how to work together. The living arrangements are so closed in, you get to know everyone on the ship really well, and it's almost as if you are forced to know everyone, just because you are going to be living with them for that month. The *Concordia* was a huge ship compared to *Corwith Cramer*, the last ship I was on. Even though our cabins were small, I was surprised that we even had cabins, instead of little "bunks" like the last trip.

While we were in port, we could visit other ships, and meet the crew on those ships. I met lots of people from all different ships. I was surprised when I took ["special crew"] tours below decks of the different ships. The "Bat Boat" was so tiny! I can't imagine what it must be like down there when it's really hot outside. The *Larinda* was extremely decorative and different than any other ship, and their sails were pretty neat too. My favorite ship I saw this summer was the *Amara Zee*, the "tall ship theater." I am really interested in theater and live acting, and this ship amazed me because I had joked around with my mom about a tall ship with actors on it before I left on this trip. I couldn't believe that there is actually a ship that people perform plays on. The ship was my two biggest interests combined, and something that I had only imagined. I learned all about all of the ships I saw, and could point out which ship is which in a picture.

I had an awesome time this summer, and I'd like to thank ASTA again for the scholarship I received. I would especially like to thank Peter, Nancy, Kazu, Steve, and Nicole for everything they helped me with while I was in port.

Sincerely,

Becca Priddy

Concordia for Dummies

Being aboard two different tall ships in the past two summers I have learned a lot about the ships and sailing. When my mom first told me that I was going to be sailing from New York to Boston for five days on what she called a "tall ship," I really wasn't too excited. First of all, I live in Arizona. There's no ocean, sea or big body of water that I could possibly sail on. I had never been sailing on any boat (or "ship" for that matter) and I didn't even know what a tall ship was. But now that I've sailed twice the past two summers, I can tell you what a tall ship is. Basically, a tall ship is a pirate ship that real people sail all over the world on.

Before I go on, in order for someone who has no clue about, well, anything, I have created a vocabulary list to help that person better understand what I would like to call "Ship Gibberish."

Helpful Places

Bridge – Where the helm is, Galley – Kitchen, Mess – Where you eat, Helm – The wheel you steer the ship with, Below Deck – Downstairs, Above Deck – Upstairs, Bow – The front of the ship, Stern – The back of the ship, Starboard – The right side of the ship when facing the bow, Port – The left side of the ship when facing the bow, Midships – The middle of the ship, Classroom – Classroom, Head – Toilet, Cabin – Room, Mess Deck – Above the mess, Mizzen Deck – Behind the bridge above the classroom, Yards – The horizontal mast-like things off of the fore mast with sails rolled up on them, Fore Mast – most forward mast, Main Mast – middle mast, Mizzen Mast – last mast.

Lines and Commands

Line – rope, Haul – with all your might, Ease – slowly let go. LET GO, or else! Faster – faster. Sweat down – a process of making the line extremely tight. Dobry – good. Make fast – wrap the line around the pin in a figure-8 clockwise. Spanks - thanks. Set – put up a sail. Douse – take down a sail. Halyard – line used to set the sail (haul to set, let go to douse). Downhaul – line used to douse a sail (haul to douse, let go to set). Sheet – line used to change the positioning of a sail. Buntlines – lines used to pull down the square sails. Clue lines – similar to buntlines. Gaff Preventer – line helps move the main and mizzen sails.

Other Useful Words

Scuppers – those nasty black things on the sides of the ship that serve as gutters and must be cleaned by the 8 – 12 watch every morning. Schmutca – old, dirty rag used to clean the scuppers. Ratlines – the horizontal ropes on the "ladder" to climb up. Shrouds – vertical cables on the "ladder" to climb up. Work line – empty line. Superstructure – those "buildings" on the ship (there are two of them). Harness – keeps you from falling if you slip. Berth – bed/bunk. Mast – those three things sticking up out of the ship. Crosstree – the little platforms every 1/3 of the way up the mast. Bowsprint – the net at the bow. Aloft – up. Watch – time for you to be on deck. Gordon – the ship's plastic pink flamingo.

This summer, I sailed on a tall ship called the *Concordia* for a month during the Great Lakes Challenge. We started in Cleveland, sailed for Detroit, Sarnia, Bay City, Mackinaw City, Green Bay, Muskegon, and Chicago. *Concordia* is a 188-foot barquentine with 120-foot masts, and can sail in water as shallow as 13 feet. Below deck, she is full of cabins. My cabin was like a tiny hotel room. It had 4 berths, its own head, and shower, and it even had small cubbies to put my clothes in. Everyone thought that this small room was unlivable. To me the cabin was a mansion. The fact that there were actual cabins, with a head and a shower to each, with a real door was almost unbelievable considering the last ship I sailed on. I lived in a cubby, and there were 4 heads and 3 showers on the whole ship.

So far, the ship is huge, right? Well, big ships mean lots of sails to memorize. *Concordia* has 15 sails on three different masts, the fore mast, main mast and mizzenmast. Just to brag about all I've learned on this trip, I've decided to list all of the sails, from bow to stern, bottom to top. Ready? Outer jib, inner jib, fore staysail, course sail, lower topsail, upper topsail, t'galant topsail, royal topsail, main staysail, t'galant staysail, royal staysail, main sail, main sail gaff, mizzen sail, mizzen sail gaff. There you go, all 15 of *Concordia's* sails.

Well, lots of sails mean lots of lines to memorize. (Oh joy!) So, when Piot, one of the ship's bosuns, starts screaming out commands for different lines, it is pretty helpful to know what he is talking about. When you're on a ship like *Concordia*, words like sheets, buntlines, clue lines, halyard, downhaul, gaff preventer, ratlines, shrouds, crosstree, and work lines all become a part of your daily vocabulary. As well as the usual commands, haul, ease, let go, make fast, and the occasional hurry up, or get your harness, being screamed during sail maneuvers.

So I think I have covered all the basics, now on to the daily life. First, there are three watches. What a watch is, is when we are on the water, there are 2 people on both sides of the bridge watching for buoys, ships, boats, or anything at all and report any sightings to the captain, or whoever might be on the bridge. Someone on watch might also be steering at the helm. A watch usually has about 6 – 8 people on it and everyone on that watch must be on deck during their watch. They must be ready at all times for sail maneuvers, too. You can sleep on watch, as long as you are not on the lookout, but you still must be on deck. There are three watches, 8 – 12, 12 – 4, and 4 – 8. The 8 – 12 watch always has to scrub the deck and clean scuppers every morning. (Personally I like the 12 – 4 watch the best).

Besides normal watch there is also galley duty for breakfast, lunch, and dinner. Breakfast galley starts at 7:00 am, lunch at 11:30 am, and dinner at 5:30 pm. If you are on galley you must wash dishes before the meal, set the tables, serve, wash all the dishes after the meal including pots and pans used to make the meal, clean the mess, and for dinner, sweep and mop the mess and galley. And when you're done with all of that, Rob (a.k.a. our executive chef) always has something else for you to do!

As if that took up enough of your 24 hours? Of course not! Don't forget about class. Since, while on this trip, I am also taking a college class, I also had a class from 9 – 11 am for human ecology and 1 – 2 pm for sail training. It wasn't a pain at all to have class along with galley duty and watch, but I do have to admit it takes up a lot of your day. Sleep is hard to find, but work isn't.

Fun, however, is NEVER hard to come by on the *Concordia*. During the day most people play card games, and if you're lucky someone might even bring UNO. In your spare time you might study, read, or just sit around talking to the pro-crew about the ship. Another thing to do during spare time is study and memorize the sails and lines. Everyone on the ship gets to know each other really well. The people you bunk with become your close friends because of the small living space between everyone. Everyone must work together for the ship to sail. Teamwork skills are extremely helpful on *Concordia* so be prepared for that.

With this information, you are now ready to sail on the *Concordia*! (Even if you live in Timbuktu). So, good luck, and have fun!

SAIL TALL SHIPS!

The American Sail Training Association Announces the 2001 Sail Training Awards

<u>ASTA Sail Training Program of the Year 2001:</u>
St. Lawrence II

- Awarded to current ASTA member.
- Awarded to program which significantly contributes to the development of seamanship, navigation skills, teamwork, and leadership skills.
- Must be offered by a USCG (or national equivalent) inspected vessel.
- Must be offered by certified/qualified personnel.
- Must have clear training goals and curriculum which is compatible to the ASTA syllabus and logbook.
- Students must have the opportunity to demonstrate knowledge at sea. (They can't be given a program and remain as passive passengers.)

Captain Bob Hodgson of the *St. Lawrence II*

<u>ASTA Sea Education Program of the Year 2001:</u>
Great Lakes Schoolship Program of the Inland Seas Education Association

- Awarded to a program offered by a current ASTA member which
- Significantly contributes to the educational credibility of program under sail.
- Must be offered in conjunction with school, school system, school group or other recognized educational institution.
- Must have a clear curriculum of educational goals which are compatible with curriculum goals of traditional schools.
- Must have qualified instructors on a certified vessel.

Kim Biocchi accepts the Sea Education Program of the Year award from Captain David Wood on behalf of the Inland Seas Education Association.

SAIL TALL SHIPS!

ASTA Sail Trainer of the Year 2001:
Captain Bob Hodgson
St. Lawrence II

• Must be an ASTA member.
• May be either a Captain, crew member,
  volunteer, board member, etc.
• Contribution: The demonstration of
  leadership by means of empowerment
  and inspiration.

Captain Doug Prothero, ASTA board
member, presents Captain Bob Hodgson
of the St. Lawrence II with the Sail Trainer
of the Year Award.

ASTA Port City of the Year 2001:
Bay City, Michigan

• Awarded to a city/municipality which
  demonstrates significant support of ASTA,
  an ASTA Member Organization, or
  furthers public recognition of sail training.

Chairman Chris Rowsom presents the
Port of the Year Award to Shirley Roberts
of Bay City, Michigan

ASTA Volunteer of the Year 2001:
Hisakazu Nakayama

• Awarded to current ASTA member.
• Awarded to an individual who significantly
  advances ASTA's overall mission.

Hisakazu "Kazu" Nakayama receives his
award from Peter Mello, ASTA
Executive Director

For a Lifetime of Dedication to Sail Training:
Captain Lane Briggs
Presented November 2, 2001

• Awarded to an individual who has dedicated his/her life's work to getting people to sea under sail and
• Who has worked to preserve the traditions and skills of sail training.

Captain Lane Briggs accepts the ASTA Lifetime Achievement Award from his son, Captain Jesse Briggs)

The Perry Bowl
Grand Nellie

• Awarded to the Top Finishing ASTA Member Vessel in the TALL SHIPS CHALLENGE® Great Lakes 2001 Races.

Captains Jeff and Ellen Troeltzsch of the Grand Nellie are presented with The Perry Bowl by Race Director, Steve Baker

Special Recognition Award

• In Grateful Appreciation for Years of Service and Dedication in Support of the ASTA's Mission.

CAPT David V. V. Wood, USCG(Ret.) Chairman 1998 - 2001

Retiring Chairman, Captain David Wood, receives thanks and recognition for his years of dedicated service, from the ASTA board, staff, and membership.

Ryan Tharpe, ASTA Henry H. Anderson, Jr. Scholarship recipient, "aloft" for the first time (SSV *Corwith Cramer*)

Sailing for Whales

Adapted from Logs of the Dead Pirates Society (Sheridan House). Reprinted with permission.
by: Captain Randall Peffer

Ship's Log: July 8, 1600 hrs, 10 miles due west of Stellwagen Bank, wind southwest 18 knots, barometer falling.

As Ahab said in *Moby Dick*, "The deed is done." Here we are: a small boat on a gray sea sailing west toward the coast of Massachusetts--homeward bound from a blue water adventure. The wind comes in blustery puffs out of the southwest, but the eight-foot swells rolled in from the southeast. There is a storm brewing somewhere near Bermuda. Phillips Academy's 55' research schooner SARAH ABBOT climbs and slides between waves like small houses. Eight souls aboard: six high school marine science students, scientist, mate, and captain.

In his novel *Youth*, Joseph Conrad spoke of the "bond of the sea" and the "fellowship of the craft" that develops aboard a traditional vessel. For Conrad, some of his most powerful memories of going to sea rooted in a voyage aboard a queer, old wooden windship like SARAH ABBOT "when we were young and at sea; young and had nothing on the sea that gives nothing, except hard knocks?" Aboard the traditional vessels of the American Sail Training Association (ASTA), that experience is not lost for 21st century mariners. And yesterday, like a thousand "green" crews before us, we took our leave from familiar shores and struck off into the cold Atlantic on what Herman Melville had called "the high and mighty business of whaling."

Why are we out here? First, as a group of biology students in Phillips Academy/Andover's Oceans program, the crew is currently studying a unit on whales, and now they wanted to see whales in the wild. Second, as explorers of history we have this idea that we really cannot not understand the essence of the Massachusetts coast without sailing in the wake of its whalers.

In the golden age of whaling, Massachusetts ships, like Melville's crew on the PEQUOD sailed across the Atlantic and around Africa to the Pacific whaling grounds. Such voyages took three years; ours trip to and from the Stellwagen Bank Marine Sanctuary off Cape Cod will last three days. Instead of harpoons we pack cameras. In lieu of filling barrels, we have tried to capture whales on roles of film.

Yesterday, the new crew of teenagers joined the schooner SARAH ABBOT in Marion. In spite of a dank, smothering fog, the crew bagged aboard with laughter and energy. So in late afternoon we set out on what promises to be 125 miles of sailing before we return to Marion again. We left under jib, mainsail, and motor with no better than a quarter mile visibility in the fog. Each of the crew stood a trick at the helm. They steered carefully and kept sharp lookout, practicing for their responsibilities that would come. As night settled over our voyage, the crew swaddled themselves in sweaters or slickers, gathered shoulder to shoulder in the cockpit, and sang old camp songs. They seemed particularly fond of the theme song from the TV comedy Gilligan's Island.

At seven o'clock in the next morning I roused the entire crew. We needed everyone to help steer and keep watch. We still had thick fog, but experience told me that we would be in the whales' territory within the hour. As the crew ate their cereal and took their turns at the helm, an eerie quiet settled over the vessel. All you could hear was the hum of the wind in the sails. But at some point a new sound broke the desolation: the vessel's dog, a Rotweiler mix named Yankee, roused herself from sleep under the table in the main saloon, came on deck, and began to sniff at the air, snort, and pace--her claws clicking against the deck. She smelled whales.

With the visibility improving to two hundred yards, we began to search, sailing a zigzag pattern as SARAH ABBOT worked her way to the northeast along the western edge of Stellwagen. Everyone was on deck--clinging to the halyards, looking for a cloud of vapor from a whale's blow, a dark back, a dorsal fin breaking the surface, or the Wilson's storm petrels, small black and white birds that follow the whales and feed on the leftovers.

"Whale up, two o'clock, a half mile," called a girl from the bow. A few seconds later I saw a small minke--maybe twenty feet long--break the surface for a breath of air. The whale was the color of the gray ocean, and it was racing away from us to the east.

I had to make a drastic change of course to keep the minke in sight, and the commands went forward to the crew: "All hands, heads up. Stand by your sail handling stations; prepare to jibe; jibe ho." Amid the clatter and commotion of the jibe, we lost the minke in the fog. Up on the foredeck someone swore. He spoke for us all.

An hour or more passed. The crew sagged in their sweaters and slickers at their lookout stations. Then Yankee began to sniff the air and pace the deck again. Suddenly, a whale surfaced with a burst of air that sounded like steam rushing from a boiler. As the whale's V-shaped head started to submerge, its dark back arched slowly, and foot-by-foot a body that seemed as big as a submarine showed itself above the waves. Finally, the dorsal fin broke the surface and made a perfect triangle against the sky before sliding back beneath the waves. About eight feet beneath the surface, we could see a massive tail fanning the water into a boiling eddy as it slid out of sight.

I gave the helm to the scientist and told her to hold her course as I climbed into the lower rigging of the mainmast to get a better view of the whale. From 15 feet up, I could see the dark form of the whale patrolling about 10 feet below the surface. With the magnification of the water the whale looked substantially longer and wider than SARAH ABBOT. At least 60 feet long. Focusing my eyes, I could see the white scythe marking on the whale's lower right jaw clearly identifying this animal as the so-called "greyhound of the sea," Balaenoptera physalus --a fin whale. The close cousin of the largest animal on the planet the blue whale.

The presence of this fin whale gave us a clue as to what bait fish were in the area. The most likely answer was herring--shoals of herring. Fin whales love the critters, and we would probably find the remains of herring in the samples of orangish whale feces we scooped up to analyze.

Now, here we were with the second largest specie of animal in the world swimming in formation with us--barely ten feet off our port rail. At 30-second intervals its head broke the surface to breath. The crew steadied themselves with their hands on the rigging and clicked away with their cameras.

Then, without warning, I saw the whale make a sharp lunge as its body turned toward SARAH ABBOT and picked up speed. "It's going to hit us," shouted one of the crew. I saw one girl grasp the foremast. A boy looked like he was saying his prayers. "Hold your course," I called to the scientist at the helm.

From my perch in the rigging, I saw the animal's dark body begin to slide under the schooner. Three seconds later the whale rose within ten feet of the boat on the starboard side. Water poured off its back like rushing streams. The animal rolled on its right side, and for two or three seconds its left eye broke the surface of the water and held SARAH ABBOT, the crew, and me in its stare, lock-

ing pictures of us in its memory. Then the whale dropped its head, arched its back a bit, and exhaled. A cloud of fishy vapor settle over SARAH ABBOT. But this moment was not the climax of some kind of Native American vision quest. No curtain of surface reality peeled away to offer me a glimpse into the very soul of life or God or even New England maritime history. No such luck. I saw no vision. Just a schooner drenched with about 20 gallons of whale snot. Still, it took my breath away. I felt my whole face curling into a silly grin like a kid caught with his hand in the cookie jar. And as I looked around the deck, I saw that my crew was smiling too.

One of the crew wrote in his journal:

"Now, after seeing my first whale, I can relate to the reasons young boys have always gone to sea. I understood how they had a desire to seek their dreams and find themselves in the face of these waves and mighty monsters. I can make the connection to my forefathers because I felt nervous, a little afraid, and small when I confronted a whale and the wide green ocean for the first time." So it goes.

Crew Development to the Ice

by Richard King

I received an ASTA Crew Development Grant to help me travel to the Antarctic Peninsula. I sailed aboard the MV *Professor Multanovskiy* a 236-foot, ice-strengthened Russian research vessel that was converted to hold about 54 ecotourists. The voyage was short, only ten days. We sailed from Ushuaia, Argentina, through the Beagle Channel, then down to the South Shetland Islands. After we peeked into the Weddell Sea, the ship doubled back to trace the western edge of the Peninsula before returning to Ushuaia via Cape Horn. I went on the voyage as part of my graduate study, specifically to see the Antarctic cormorant, otherwise known as the Imperial Blue-eyed Shag. This seabird sticks within fifteen miles from land, so both Cook and Shackleton were elated to see them. Captain James Cook wrote in his journals that "the shags and the soundings were our best pilots." Ernest Shackleton wrote that when they approached South Georgia at the end of their open boat journey, cormorants told them land was near: "These birds are as sure an indication of the proximity of land as a lighthouse is, for they never venture far out to sea." The early sealers probably used cormorants for navigational aids, too, and they definitely used these birds and their eggs for fresh food. In the beginning of the 20th century, the Blue-Eyed Shag was a delicacy among whalers. Journal accounts describe cormorants flying so near to the crosstrees that whalers whacked them out of the air. I didn't manage to catch or eat an Antarctic cormorant, but I saw plenty, often mixed among the penguins.

I also went on the trip to see what I had read so much about. Cape Horn, man. I saw it up close. And it was just as the books describe: high cliffs, soaring albatross, and a honking wind from the west. Crepuscular rays lit the cliffs to add to the majesty of it all. We saw several species of icebergs, and big seas and wind in the Drake Passage. We had enough snow on deck one morning for a snowball fight. We saw orca whales with a pup, circling a crabeater seal on an ice flow. The orcas seemed to be teaching the young whale, "Go on, just nose up the flow, and he'll come rolling off. Then you bite him. Go on." We saw wandering albatross gliding in 40 knots. Penguins leapt off into the bow wake, "porpoising." but they are small, it looks less like dolphins and more like Neptune is hucking a few dozen black and white Nerf footballs out of the water. One afternoon, the ship hove to beside some pack ice, just cut right alongside, bow into the ice, and turned the engines off. We had Zodiac tours among the ice flows, the growlers. (A half dozen spare outboard propellers hang in the ship's bosun's locker). The sun set around eleven at night and rose near to three in the morning. The air and hills and breath were Colorado crisp. I kept a journal daily. Here is one entry:

23 December 2001
2052
Bransfield Straight
sw of Deception Island
approx. 63 ° 10' S, 61 ° 00' W

The Brave Research Team assumes command on deck five, aft. It has been dusk for hours. Not too cold, but wet flakes of snow. My gloves are wet. There were reports of 30-foot seas last night. I find it hard to believe, but that's the rumor flying around. Sorry I missed it...

We visited Half Moon Island this morning, as an alternative to another spot because of the high winds. Half Moon is an aptly-named curl of land. We anchored in the bay and Zodiacked to the beach, then walked over to the other side. The water, white-capped, but Caribbean turquoise, then snowy peaks in the background. I looked for crabs under rocks but found none— thousands of limpet shells, the only rocky intertidal invertebrate I have seen. Did see some lamanaria-like algae on the beach, some half-buried under rocks. Here I found a Weddell Seal's full skeleton (identified by Chris, our guide). The Weddell is the south-

When was quite cool. Here ... a reliable(?) green hue from ... of orcas swimming around a ... closer the seal as we saw it yesterday — ship turned around to watch the orca, one with a baby swimming beside. They were "playing" with this seal — I wish they could have knocked the seal to get him — the seal was pulled ... and we ship him —

ernmost mammal in the world. Too cool for school. Could see the whole thing, the vestigial hip bones, the big thick skull. The teeth worn down like I saw in a National Geographic video. The Weddell Seal uses its teeth to keep a hole in the ice over the winter. Our ship, bright white in the water, snowy peaks, streaks of brown-rarely reds and greens-Antarctica is all blue shades, white, grey, occasional browns of rock, greens of algae, mosses. Saw snowy sheathbills up close.. .

Saw a couple cormorants flying high-like the whalers' journals at Mystic Seaport described-this is the third time I have seen cormorants flying high near the ship beside the top deck, hovering a bit. I have started marking cormorant sightings on the chart. Saw no cormorants on the island with a spotting scope survey, though they were flying in the harbor. Perhaps they were nesting in a spot I couldn't see. ..

In the afternoon we went to Deception Island and Whaler's Cove, site of a 20th century whaling station, the southernmost one in the world, but now it is partially buried in volcanic mud. Saw some brontosaurus-sized whale bones, abandoned science stations. Barrel staves half-buried in brown mud, as were faded wood water boats-the huge rusted tanks, stories high, had been shot with bullets from WW II the guide said. Interesting how recent the history is here—the 1940's and 50's.

Noticed that though Antarctic cormorants and penguins are colored nearly exactly the same, that the underwings of cormorants, unlike penguins, are black. Perhaps this if for camouflage, hunting fish under water--the white against the water when looking up at the sky from a fish's point of view is not so important for a cormorant who swims with his feet, his wings against his body, while a penguin "flies" underwater, showing his underwings...will need to learn more about this when I get back...

Took a few sights today—most of them drastically off, 17 + miles and yet the horizon looked so clear and I thought my angles, height of eye, were good based on a real close Local Apparent Noon the other day—I can't identify what error I am making. At least I'm consistently wrong. My last one off by 8 or less, but hmmm...

Each day getting to know the passengers and crew a bit. The crew, all Russian, and I think they enjoyed the *Kruzenshtern* cadet cap that I wore on day three or four, the one I traded for during OpSail 2000. Occasionally a Russian crew member will appear that I have not seen before—out of the ship's depths. I am a tired man but so much I want to do and only two more days on the Antarctic Peninsula then bound homish for Tierra del Fuego. Fingers crossed for seeing Cape Horn. A fine, fine day. Out.

I got to know the Russian crew a bit because I have some tall ship sailing experience. No other passengers were nerdy enough to bring their own chart or work on shooting the sun. I think the bridge liked that. The radio man showed me the weather fax he doctored to look like a woman's rear end. But having some sailing experience hurt me sometimes. When we were doing our "Prepare to Abandon Ship" drill on the first day, the instructors told us to meet "by the bar on deck 4." When the alarm sounded, I went aft and stood under the steel bar between the two lifeboats. The rest of the group were inside by the bar crunching beer nuts and wearing lifejackets inside. It was humbling being a passenger again, piled into the Zodiacs and herded ashore without any one to wink at.

Along the trip, I picked up a brochure called "Students on Ice," a high school educational trip which heads to the Arctic and the Antarctic Peninsula. I saw that a shipmate I had sailed with eight years ago—hadn't seen her since--is one of the founders. Fortunately, when our voyage ended in Ushuaia I was able to track her down. She is starting up a fantastic program, getting students to The Ice. I hope we can get more students down there. I am not sure how. It is expensive. The sights are profound, and it might not remain so pristine. More tourists travel to Antarctica each year, but the ships that take them to Antarctica, however, seem genuinely concerned about maintaining environmental standards and minimizing human impact. Tourist eyes have worked in some parts of the Antarctic by pushing to clean abandoned research station dumping areas.

I like to think that my trip has already paid off with the students with whom I work. I teach with the Williams College at Mystic Seaport Maritime Studies Program and occasionally with Ocean Classroom Foundation, and as we read Poe's *The Narrative of Arthur Gordon Pym of Nantucket*, which ends in Antarctica, or as we read Coleridge's "Rime of the Ancient Mariner" or any maritime work that mentions Cape Horn, I am now able to contribute a new perspective, however small. I can add a bell clear mind's eye image of some of these settings. I am tremendously grateful for the generosity of the American Sail Training Association's Crew Development Grant.

Launching the Twin Brigantines
Irving Johnson and Exy Johnson

Saturday, April 27, 2002

Captain Jim Gladson, Founder and President, Los Angeles Maritime Institute

We are here today to celebrate the launching of these "Twin Brigantines". These magnificent pieces of sculpture would stand alone in any public place as elegant works of art. In fact vessels of this sort are often described as the largest mobile objects of art.   But as you can see our ships are just begging for floatation.

Simply to build these vessels as monuments to honor Irving and Exy Johnson and their contributions to the betterment of life on this planet would be reason enough for the effort. But during the time we have been crafting these vessels another significant project has been just as busy. There is a factory or an assembly line somewhere in the region that is producing "at risk" kids at a prodigious rate.

Now I am a "tree hugger" from way back; I'm all in favor of saving spotted owls and blue butterflies and dolphins and whales and old growth sequoias. But there is one endangered species we cannot possibly afford turn our backs on and that's our next generation.

In years past, vessels like these were constructed for commerce to transport cargo, or passengers, or for exploration, or research, or for recreation; and sometimes even for warfare. In fact these vessels are designed and being built as warships for the 21st Century. Our enemies are ignorance, fear and ineptitude; and above all lack of confidence.

I thank you for your support. But we still need your help to complete these ships and fit them out so that they can go forth and do battle with the conditions that produce so many kids whose personal visions do not yet include the expectation of a future with personal success.

Captain Jim Gladson of the Los Angeles
Maritime Institute

Asta Executive Director Peter A. Mello and Robert Johnson.

Exy and Matthew Johnson

The guest of honor – Exy Johnson

All those who made it possible!

Exy Johnson (in the water) and *Irving Johnson* just
prior to launch

Exy Johnson and *Irving Johnson*
just prior to launch

Ocean Star – Sea-mester programs
An Adventure in Education

By Michael J. Meighan, Program Director, Sea-mester

Photo Collection by Mauricio Handler

Learning is, at its best, an active process. Studies show that interest and assimilation of knowledge are far greater when the process is multi-faceted and calls upon us to use our intelligence in ways the traditional learning environment cannot. Sea-mester programs are designed to do just that; learn by doing, seeing and experiencing those things that most students only read about in books. Based upon principles of experiential and adventure education, Sea-mester takes 14 high school graduates and college students aboard the traditionally-rigged schooner, *Ocean Star*, for 80- and 40-day semesters. During their time aboard, students complete college-accredited academics alongside sailing and scuba diving certification training, research and service projects. Rather than being passengers, students (shipmates) are the crew responsible for piloting *Ocean Star* from the British Virgin Islands throughout the Eastern Caribbean basin to Grenada and back.

The voyage begins in the BVIs, providing an ideal training ground to initiate the sailing and diving certification work and introduce the academics, with students taking all of the courses offered. The courses of Introduction to Oceanography, Basic Seamanship, Introduction to Speech Communication and Student Leadership Development have been specifically chosen as they mesh the experiential and academic aspects of the program. The academic modules combine more traditional class presentations with interactive and practical activities. The more hands-on approach to learning brings subjects from the text book into real-life application.

By the time *Ocean Star* departs the BVIs, every student is scuba-certified, and those certified prior to the voyage have progressed to a more advanced level.

The crew are challenged early on in the voyage with an overnight sail, as the vessel makes passage eastward to Saba, Statia and Nevis before reaching Grenada. The next seven weeks are spent routing north via the Grenadines, Tobago Cays, St. Vincent, St. Lucia, Martinique, Dominica, Guadeloupe and the Saints, Antigua, St. Barts and St. Martin. As the semester progresses, shipmates are given increasing responsibility for the planning and executing of island-to-island passages and land excursions. Each crew member is given the opportunity to lead, as instructors and tutors shift to an afterguard role. The cultural, geological and aquatic diversity seen over such a small geographic area lends itself to all of the experiential and academic studies. The expeditions, projects and shore excursions undertaken facilitate the adventure learning and group service ventures. Diving becomes instinctive as training continues and scuba skills are used in cooperation with marine science theory to collect scientific data for organizations such as Seascape Research and Education Foundation in Bequia, the Reef Ball Coalition in Dominica and the SMMA in St. Lucia.

Academics Brought to Life

Deborah Moroney, M.S., has been teaching the oceanography course aboard Sea-mester since 1998. For her, Sea-mester is able to accommodate many types of learning styles, unique to each individual. However, the true value of this type of education lies in the mastery of concepts through repetition. "Many of the tasks onboard, be they interpersonal relations, seamanship skills or oceanographic research, must be done on a regular basis. Because the students practice these skills routinely, they become second nature and the students have learned for a lifetime, not just for the test." In her mind, the advantage of this experience over the traditional classroom approach is the teachable moment. "... A moment when something unexpected happens in nature that is interesting to teach. For example, a teachable moment is sailing by Montserrat at 2 am while it is erupting and lava is pouring down the

mountainside. Can there be a better way to explain the volcanic nature of many of the Caribbean islands?" A bonus for the students living aboard with their instructors is that there are no office hours to follow. Students can ask questions of the instructor at the dinner table or while hiking the highest peak in the Lesser Antilles. For Moroney, the highlight of this living experience is to be there when students gain a true understanding of the subject for themselves. "Teachers are facilitators of learning. They do not make the learning happen; instead they make it easier for learning to occur. The real learning goes on outside the classroom when the students are studying and I see when the material begins to click. This is what motivates me to teach in this capacity." Moroney admits that although a great setting, college life aboard ship in the Caribbean requires students to be self-motivated and disciplined, but the rewards can be both academic and personal. On a personal level, students benefit when they take a step towards independence. Every shipmate is the "skipper of the day" several times throughout the voyage. They are responsible for ensuring activities occur on schedule, making sure everyone knows what they are doing, moving the vessel, etc. This gives each student the chance to develop their own leadership style in a safe environment and allows

them to gain confidence in themselves." These opportunities for learning and camaraderie are most appreciated by the shipmates themselves. Ellis Pepper, a high school graduate from Maine, says of her Sea-mester experience, "high school was never like this, and I'm sure college won't quite match up either. To learn concepts and then be forced to practice these concepts in order to live and get from one place to another is a fulfilling way to learn. To work in classes with and be taught by people who also know everything about you, from your sleeping habits to your dreams and ambitions, makes me want to work hard."

The introduction to speech communication and student leadership development courses this spring, were taught by Marguerite West, M.S., Ph.D. Cand., who joined Sea-mester for the first time. With eight years of teaching experience behind her, West believes the Sea-mester program takes experiential learning to

a deeper and more sustainable level. "Rather than contrived activities that emulate real life, the experiences at sea are real from the start. Students are entrusted with significant responsibility in every aspect of life aboard and see the impact of their contributions on a daily basis, oftentimes immediately. Each task on the boat is rich with opportunities for learning and personal development, from making important leadership decisions as skipper of the day, to planning and preparing meals for 18 people as chef of the day, to the ongoing process of relating and working with other shipmates... Because of the duration of the program, students not only learn about who they are now, but have the opportunity to develop new strengths." On the advantages of shipboard education over a conven-

tional environment, West says, "it's difficult to facilitate the development of interpersonal communication and leadership skills in a traditional classroom format. Although the concepts may seem easy to grasp on a cognitive level, they're hard to apply to real life. In the traditional classroom, students may walk away with new

vocabulary and some understanding of the ideas involved, but it's unlikely that the quality of their relationships will see a significant change as a result of the experience. In contrast, life onboard constantly demands listening, contributing your ideas, making decisions as a group, resolving interpersonal conflicts and collaboration, among other things." She also sees value in the experience as a rite of passage. "We tend to associate the arrival into adulthood with the legal right to drink alcohol. I believe the Sea-mester voyage can provide students with more satisfying markers of maturity; the opportunity to experience themselves as responsible, competent, accomplished and capable of succeeding in

the face of challenges." Stephanie Baccarella, a senior at Rutgers University, agrees that knowledge could be extracted from every experience aboard. "I have taken 90 credits at university, but not a single $150 textbook nor 400 person lecture has been able to teach me a sliver of the life knowledge I obtained on *Ocean Star*. Challenging more than just my knowledge in one subject, I challenged myself to accomplish tasks that I had no idea I could do. The feeling of exhilaration after sailing through a storm off Martinique is more rewarding than the superficial satisfaction from an A in organic chemistry. While a traditional classroom fulfills the need to feel successful in society by filling your brain with transient knowledge, living on a school ship develops one's character, soul and mind."

Shipboard education is by no means a new concept. Program director, Captain James Stoll, has been working with youth education at sea since the 1970's: "Truly great teachers can make the classroom come alive even when surrounded by four walls. We enhance the setting by placing these great teachers in an ever-changing, living classroom where the horizons become limitless. For this reason, it's no wonder that over the past 30 years, I've seen our students learn more per moment during a live-aboard voyage. The sea has long provided access to adventure. Those who look for challenges grow from their experience and often find new facets of themselves inside." Changing trends demonstrate that there is a place for experiential education within the formal academic arena. More and more colleges and universities are encouraging students to participate in such experiences, not just as an adjunct part, but as an integral component of their education.

Spirit of Elissa Award

On March 22, 2002, Daniel K. and Alix T. Thorne were honored at the Spirit of Elissa Award Dinner hosted by the Galveston Historical Foundation, Galveston, TX. Alix is president of Ocean Classroom Foundation, trustee of Mystic Seaport, ASTA board member and long standing supporter of sail training and education under sail. An excerpt of her speech follows:

You have heard what Dan and I have done for ELISSA over the years, but I want to turn that around to tell you what ELISSA has done for me....

What has ELISSA done for me? To answer that, I have only to look at the people around me in this room and see how many elements of my current life grew out of that magic time in the mid 80's when I came to ELISSA. Indeed, the 4-month voyage from Galveston to New York in 1986 has taken on an aura of awe and wonder to all volunteers since then, and to professional crew who long to sail her more than a few miles from the jetties. But what was that 1986 trip really like?

It was a time of long hot days of hard work trying to make ELISSA look her best, and even longer days in ports from Miami to New York giving tours to the hundreds of visitors who crossed her decks. Thirty or so crew slept on canvas cots made fast to the railings in the exhibition area of the cargo hold, with the lights and noise at the change of watch a constant factor. Meals were eaten on paper plates, standing or sitting on the deck and shoveling it in before the wind tore the plate from your hand or the rain washed away the food. Daily swim calls with the communal bottle of Liquid Joy were our only showers. And we tacked, over and over we tacked, until our hands were calloused and we could hear each command in our dreams. But it was magic and not a one of us would have given up our place on board.

It was a time when all those mysterious bits and pieces of dockside training came together in a system and a lifestyle with a long and honorable tradition which is called seamanship. It was no longer about who could climb farther or faster, or who could tie the most knots or name the most lines. It was about reacting the proper way to each new situation with awareness and understanding of the big picture as well as knowing your job within it. We didn't have uniforms that matched, and we came in all shapes, sizes and ages from all walks of life, but we became shipmates together. And when we sailed ELISSA past the Statue of Liberty in New York Harbor, bursting with pride and emotion it was – well, indescribable.

(from left to right) Captain Lane Briggs, Alix Thorne, and Dan Thorne aboard the *Elissa*.

Lots of us have our sea stories, moments in time that will always be recalled in vivid detail. Here is mine: Well into the ELISSA voyage, just off the shores of Bermuda, we ran into a fast hard-hitting squall line. It was just after breakfast, with chores and work parties getting underway. A couple of us were sent aloft on the foremast to sea stow the upper topsail. I threw on my foul weather jacket and safety belt and started up. When the squall hit, I was on the yard, and I remember my jacket blowing over my head and the sail whipping and cracking in my face, throwing arms and legs in all directions to get the sail under control, reaching and wrapping the gasket round and round – no points for neatness here. When the rain hit, it was like a description in a passage by Richard Henry Dana …"It came in one body like a falling ocean".

I watched in horror as the outer jib filled violently with too much wind, and the jib boom curved off to leeward and with a huge explosion broke in half. All the Conrad, Dana and Hornblower sagas and legions of sailing adventure books flashed in my head as I tried to anticipate what would happen next – would the mast itself collapse in a heap of tangled rigging and jagged wood – was my fantasy of life as a foretopman going to end so melodramatically ?

But below me, it was all hands to their stations and everyone moved into place smoothly. I don't even remember coming down to the deck and moving to my assigned spot on the mizzen mast. But I was there working on the spanker, all focus on my responsibilities as I had learned them. Meanwhile the damage forward was assessed, the broken spar and torn sail hauled back on deck, and the winds were once more calm and gentle. As sea stories go, a relatively mild one.

Joseph Conrad has written that "….he who loves the sea also loves the ship's routines." And I had just had my first lesson in the importance of that statement. Here we were, the self-confessed rag-tag crew made up partly of housewives and retired businessmen, a few teenagers and other amateurs but with the all-important core of professionals who had drilled us over and over in those very routines until we were able to follow orders in whatever new situation came our way. We had become seamen.

When I say that I am a supporter of the American Sail Training Association, or that I worked on the HMS ROSE engaged in sail training, or that I run programs of sail training and sea education on board my Ocean Classroom schooners, it is usually received a bit blankly-how nice-teaching sailing, must be fun. Sometimes I hear my family refer to my times at sea as being on "a cruise". But if I could ever find the right words to describe the transformation that can happen to those who are lucky enough to have a working sea voyage under sail – then perhaps we could have a fleet of ELISSAs.

What other situation can you think of where you can take kids, or even "youth of all ages", put them in strange moving environment, make them learn a new language, tell them that there is an absolute right way and wrong way for every job on board – or as Captain Bailey used to say to us on ROSE, " It's not your way, it's not my way, it is THE WAY". Have them suffer through cold and wet or scorching sun and sea sicknesses, sleep deprivation, blistered hands, and even perhaps sheer terror – and then watch them leave with a new swagger in their step, a confidence and pride in their accomplishments and a promise that "it has changed my life." One former student of ours on the SPIRIT of MASSACHUSETTS wrote that "in the beginning he was desperately homesick, longing for life at home, but when he went home after 6 weeks, he had a new meaning for "seasick" – a longing for life at sea."

Sailing on ELISSA, I entered a wonderful world of maritime professionals. Lots of people sail their boats or cruise far and wide in their yachts, but there is a very special group of people who have devoted their careers to making sure that the very highest standards and traditions of seamanship are passed on to the next generation. They make sure not only that the vessels meet all the standards of safety laid out by the US Coast Guard, but that the crew understand the working of the ship – helm, lookout, sail handling, boat check – all of the elements of proper watchstanding traditions.

I keep referring to Joseph Conrad, but if it is about ships and sailors, he usually says it best. In writing about shipboard work, he said it is ".....made up of accumulated tradition, kept alive by individual pride, rendered exact by professional opinion, and like the higher arts, it is spurred on and sustained by discriminating praise."

Depending on the vessel and its officers, that praise might be pretty hard to come by – but indeed, it is that praise and approval which forms the sense of accomplishment that volunteers on ELISSA or students on sail training vessels take home with them. And here I would like to recognize and thank some of those professionals who I have been privileged to sail with and learn from –

Captain Lane Briggs of the tugantine NORFOLK REBEL, who this year was awarded the Lifetime Achievement Award by the American Sail Training Association. He is a friend to ships and sailors wherever he goes.

Captain Richard Bailey of the full-rigged ship HMS ROSE who encouraged me to make the commitment to take the USCG exams and move up from deckhand to AB to a mate position. Hundreds of "youth of all ages" have sampled a slice of life on a squarerigger thanks to him.

And most especially, I want to thank our own ELISSA officers – Captain Steve Cobb, Captain Kip Files, Captain Jesse Briggs, Captain Jon Finger – all of whom have been or are currently involved with preserving and sailing historic vessels. A continuation of a long tradition of making a living on and from the sea, but where today's cargo is students and vacationers instead of cotton and bananas.

If we are going to make the stupendous effort to preserve a wonderful slice of maritime history such as ELISSA, it is just as important to preserve the skills and traditions of seamanship that are needed to ensure that when the mooring lines are cast off, that ELISSA is sailed with all the respect, pride and professionalism that she deserves – and to recognize that over her lifetime, it is ELISSA who has absorbed the accumulated spirit of all who have walked her decks and climbed her rigging, and that is why when all sails are set and she comes up to full and by she seems to take an extra exhilarating leap forward. There can't be another vessel in the world who has had so many tears cried over her and songs sung to her.

And without the volunteers, those exhilarating moments at sea could not happen. Over 20,000 hours a year of maintenance work has kept ELISSA ready to sail whenever permission is granted. On Sunday afternoon, she was an attraction vessel with tourists roaming the decks. On Monday morning, the Coast Guard inspector okayed her to leave the dock. It was a smooth and seamless transition and the highest compliment to the volunteers is that the Captain and his mates know that they can arrive that last day and have total confidence that ELISSA will be fit and ready to sail.

And if Dan and I have given enough back to be deserving of this recognition, then I just want to say thank you back to the Galveston Historical Foundation and the Texas Seaport Museum and all the staff and volunteers whose pride and determination have kept ELISSA and her traditions alive.

SAIL TALL SHIPS!

Key-note address given by Rafe Parker

President of Sea Education Association,
Woods Hole, Massachusetts, U.S.A.
ISTA Conference, Alicante, Spain,
Friday, 16th November, 2001

Ladies and Gentlemen, Fellow mariners and educators, and all those who work to send young people to sea:

It is a delight and a privilege to have the opportunity to make this address. I stand here before you with nearly forty years of active involvement in outdoor education, thirty years of which has been involved in designing, funding and conducting educational programmes that operate on the ocean in offshore deep water sailing ships. I am nevertheless in awe of what this audience represents in terms of the depth of experience and level of professionalism in providing powerful educational experiences for those who wish to go to sea aboard your ships. It is with much humility and respect, therefore, that I deliver this address.

No one escapes the magic and challenge of going to sea. Inevitably, the sea experience has a subtle, but profound, influence on every aspect of the lives of those who sail our ships. It is a powerful catalyst that raises the qualities within each individual to a conscious level, providing him or her with the raw material with which to influence one's society and environment.

I submit and firmly believe that the traditional tall ship is the finest vehicle for learning ever devised by man.

Through this extraordinary vehicle of learning we have the gift of providing an educational opportunity that is second to none. And that is the essence of what we do – we teach. We provide a dimension to education that is as vital as the science and mathematics that is taught in our schools and our universities.

But why is it important for today's generation to experience a ship of the past when it has trouble enough keeping pace with the present and anticipating its future? Because we ask so little of our youth. Because our wonderful sophisticated society is enormously rich in technology – yet desperately poor in experience, that precious resource with which values are molded and leaders are made.

Whether we like it or not we are firmly and unquestionably in the business of education and as educators we have the opportunity to make a difference in the lives of those who dare to participate in our programs. As educators, we have a commitment to enhance and enrich the quality of education within our home school system, and ultimately our homeland, at a time when it is desperately needed the most. Our school children are bored and disgruntled. Their schooling holds little relevance or immediacy to them. Their teachers struggle to hold their students' attention and respect.

High schools urgently need to find ways to create a challenging and meaningful curriculum while maintaining the academic standards that will allow their students to compete in the work place. A tall ship can offer both. It is very clear that traditional education can no longer be satisfied with incremental improvement in a world of exponential change. We can play a role in affecting that change. And the world of education is ready to embrace what you have to offer.

In the United States, in Europe, Scandinavia and Japan, and in many other parts of the world more and more schools and universities are coming to acknowledge the need to provide a transforming experience. An experience that not only challenges the student academically, but also physically and emotionally while creating an environment that rekindles within them the excitement of discovery, and a greater sense of themselves.

The National Science Foundation, the premier source of funding for all research and education in the U.S., recently put out a report entitled, "Shaping the Future". Throughout the 150 page document the central theme is the belief "that every student can learn within a supportive climate, which builds inquiry, a sense of wonder and excitement of discovery, plus communication and teamwork, critical thinking, and life-long learning skills." Does this have anything to do with sail training?

The U. of N.Y. at Stony Brook has published a report that puts forth the concept "that the education of our youth should be research driven". Education must put greater emphasis on active, collaborative learning; focus on the processes of inquiry and discovery; and rekindle the unique curiosity with which every child is born.

Outward Bound in the U. S. has developed a model for middle and high schools that is quietly changing the landscape of how teachers teach through the idea of "expeditionary learning". Over 100 schools in the U.S. now teach their students to learn through the need to prepare themselves for an expedition outside of the classroom. They must work with their teachers to gain the knowledge they will need to successfully complete their expedition which usually lasts from three weeks to a month.

We can no longer alter our students to fit the abilities of educational institutions; we must alter the institutions to fit the needs of our students. We must seek ways to provide our youth with an education that rekindles their need to learn in an environment that is physically, emotionally, and intellectually challenging.

So, how can we continue to integrate the two dimensions – sail training and mainstream education? How can we create a rich and powerful learning experience that extends the student intellectually and physically in a rigorous, interactive, interdisciplinary curriculum? How can we reach out to new horizons?

I would like to share with you some insights into how Sea Education Association attempts to answer that question.

Sea Education Association's mission is to provide an opportunity for people from all walks of life to better understand the oceans in all its forms and to develop a greater respect for themselves, for others and for their ocean planet.

Based in Woods Hole, USA, one of the world's great centers of oceanography, SEA conducts its flagship course SEA Semester, an undergraduate programme that is run six times a year. Since its inception, thirty years ago, over five thousand students, usually in their second or third year have traveled to SEA's campus to start this three month long capstone experience.

Ashore, at SEA's campus in Woods Hole, the first half of the semester (six weeks) is spent studying three courses: Oceanography, which includes the development of a research project; Nautical Sciences which involves ship design, ship operations, piloting and celestial navigation; and Maritime Studies which includes maritime history, law and literature, as well as current maritime affairs. Each course is taught by a Chief Scientist, a Captain (who is a Master Mariner), and a maritime history professor.

During these six weeks the students take three sets of exams for each of the three courses. If they successfully complete their exams they will then join their Chief Scientist and Captain aboard one of our three ships to begin the second six weeks of the semester. There they will be joined with three mates and three assistant scientists, an engineer and a steward.

Once aboard their vessel which operates in the North Atlantic from Newfoundland to Venezuela and the Caribbean, as well as the Eastern Pacific, the students (now separated into three crews of twenty five) begin the process of learning what it takes to operate the ship and to gather the data, information and samples with which to complete their research project.

By the end of the first four weeks of their six week cruise, which will ultimately cover an average of three thousand miles, the students take over the full operation of their vessel. Reporting directly to their captain and chief scientist, each student in turn will take on the responsibility for the smooth running of the vessel and the scientific mission of the cruise. They literally bring their ship back to her final port. Every graduate receives a full semester's academic credit and is awarded over half the sea time needed to qualify for a U.S. Coast Guard A.B. license. Sixty five percent of all graduating students are women.

SEA's first ship, *Westward*, a 125' stays'l schooner, was built by Abeking and Rasmussen in Germany in 1961. Our second ship, *Corwith Cramer*, a 134' brigantine, was built in Bilbao, Spain in 1987. Our most recent vessel, *Robert C. Seamans*, also a brigantine, was designed by Laurent Giles, of Lymington, England, and built in Tacoma (near Seattle) in 2001, four months ago. All three ships are fully equipped to conduct oceanography in every part of the world, sampling the ocean to a depth of 5,000 meters.

Finally, I would like to end my talk with a vision of where we might all be ten years from now if we have been able to successfully develop a presence in mainstream education. It is described in the form of a press release.

"This morning, at a ceremony held at the United Nations in New York, the Secretary General, Anne Marie Soulierre, presented its prestigious education award to the International Society of Ocean Educators for outstanding contributions made through its extraordinary programs to the quality of education within the school systems of twenty five Member Nations.

"Formerly known as the International Sail Training Association, the I.S.O.E, first conceived these programs just over ten years ago during its extraordinarily successful conference in Alicante, Spain. Today, over eight thousand high school students representing over 700 high schools from 25 Member Nations have successfully graduated from I.S.O.E.'s flagship accredited program, Sea Change.

"Sea Change is a three month high school program which serves as an alternate school term for second and third year high school students. The first six weeks are spent ashore at the students' home school studying a variety of subjects relating to the sea, such as maritime history and literature, marine policy, ship design, celestial navigation and piloting and finally, coastal and off-shore marine science. They will also develop a research project which, if they pass all their exams, they will take to sea with them. They will then join one of 32 traditional tall ships for the remaining six weeks. During this cruise they will apply their knowledge gained in the class room to the unforgiving realities of life aboard a blue water vessel. While assisting in the operation of their ship, the students will undertake their research projects that they began ashore. If successful, they will graduate with full academic credit.

"120 of the top graduating students from Sea Change have received the coveted I.S.O.E. Fellowship in Expeditionary Learning. Funded by the Ford Foundation, the World Bank and the Bic Corporation, each Fellowship provides support for the recipient's university tuition for one year. Over 200 universities throughout the Member Nations recognize and support Sea Change by awarding its graduates with advanced placement credits to their institutions".

The release goes on to say, "With its Headquarters based in Cadiz, I.S.O.E. is recognized internationally as a leader in promoting the concept that an educational program that extends the student physically, emotionally, and intellectually, as well as academically, is a richer and more powerful learning experience, raising the quality of education and the lives of those who participate in its programs."

This is a vision that brings back into the lives of our youth a meaningful and transforming educational experience at a time when it is needed the most. More than at any other time in our history, young people need the kind of value-forming experience that we can offer.

e.e. cummings wrote, "We do not believe in ourselves until someone reveals that deep inside us something is valuable, worth listening to, worthy of our trust, sacred to our touch. Once we believe in ourselves we can risk curiosity, wonder spontaneous delight or any experience that reveals the human spirit."

Through our ships and a well conceived curriculum, we have the extraordinary capability of bringing to our childrens' education the process of expeditionary learning that will, perhaps for the first time, reveal that deep within them they do have something of value, worth listening to, worthy of our trust, sacred to their touch.

With a strong leadership and steadfast commitment, this vision can become a reality. It can happen.

But it will take a leap of faith and the willingness to believe in ourselves and in our mission.

After all, how can we ask our youth to reach out and explore distant horizons if we, as educators, do not have the courage to lose sight of the shore.

Remember Goethe's wonderful couplet:

Whatever you do, or dream you can, begin it. Boldness has genius, power and magic in it.

Sultana Under-Sail

by Drew McMullen

For anyone who happened to be in Chestertown, Maryland on the weekend of March 24, 2001, the events of those few days were something that they likely will not soon forget. How often do you get the opportunity to see a 50 Ton, 18th century schooner backed down the main street of a 300 year old colonial town and then hoisted several stories through the air before touching down in the calm waters of the Chester River?

This was the scene in Chestertown for the launch of the schooner *Sultana*. After almost four years of hard work on the part of the shipwrights of Swain Boatbuilders, hundreds of volunteer laborers and the unwavering support of the entire State of Maryland, this reproduction of a 1768 century Royal Navy revenue cutter was successfully christened and launched.

The original *Sultana's* was built in 1767 in the Boston shipyard of notable American shipwright Benjamin Hallowell. Conceived as a combination cargo schooner/yacht, *Sultana* was sold to the British Royal Navy in 1768, only months after her roughed-out hull slid off the ways at the Hallowell yard and into Boston Harbor. At only 52 tons burthen, *Sultana* was an unlikely candidate for Royal Navy service. Her diminutive size prevented her from carrying even a single carriage gun. Upon her purchase *Sultana* instantly became the smallest schooner ever to serve in the Royal Navy, a distinction she retains to the present day.

Sultana's small size did give her certain advantages, principal among them speed, maneuverability and the ability to venture into shallow waters. This made her ideal for service as a Royal Navy "revenue cruiser," employed enforcing British customs duties such as the infamous Townsend Acts or "Tea Taxes". Sultana spent the years from 1768-1772 patrolling the waters of colonial North America, spending great amounts of time on the Narragansett, Delaware and Chesapeake Bays. For the entirety of this period the schooner was under the command of Lieutenant John Inglis and Master David Bruce who together managed a crew of 23 sailors.

The new *Sultana* was and is the brainchild of John Swain, an accomplished sailor and builder of traditional wooden watercraft for over thirty years. From her inception *Sultana* was conceived as a hands-on venue for education in history and environmental science. Even during the construction of the schooner, students played an integral role, with over 3000 of them coming to the *Sultana* Shipyard in Chestertown to learn about shipbuilding and to help with construction.

After completing her rigging, outfitting and sea-trials in the spring of 2001,

Sultana was appropriately commissioned on the Fourth of July and promptly set forth on a 10-week tour of the Chesapeake Bay. Over 10,000 people boarded and or sailed on the schooner during port visits to Baltimore, Annapolis, Harve de Grace, St. Michaels, Oxford, Cambridge, Solomon's Island, and St. Mary's City.

In the fall of 2001 *Sultana* began fulfilling her true mission as the "Schoolship of the Chesapeake." The schooner works with students of all ages, offering three and five-hour under-sail programs as well as multi-day live aboard experiences. Several curriculum options are offered to school groups sailing on *Sultana*. These include programs that focus on environmental science/ estuarine ecology, colonial history and traditional sail training.

The schooner's unique curricula were developed with the assistance of a regional advisory board composed of teachers and administrators from both public and private schools in Maryland, Virginia and Pennsylvania – the three principal states that compose the Chesapeake Bay Watershed. All of *Sultana's* educational programs are designed to complement the public school educational goals and outcomes for these three states in marine/ estuary science and colonial history for students from 4th through 8th grade. The curricula are also easily adapted for the needs of specific schools and groups, including learning disabled students, at risk and adjudicated youth, college and senior groups. Both *Sultana's*

SAIL TALL SHIPS!

ecology and history curricula are complemented by an extensive "in class" curriculum unit, two weeks in length, that is utilized by teachers in the classroom prior to a *Sultana* trip.

Sultana's small size (52 feet on deck, 43 gross tons) and traditional 18th century hull and rig provide a learning atmosphere for students that is simultaneously challenging and accessible. The largest running rigging on the vessel is only 7/8" in diameter and each of her six working sails (main, fore, staysail, jib, fore topsail and main topsail) can be handled easily in most weather conditions by even a small group of fourth graders. One aspect of *Sultana* that has proven to be especially popular with students is her meticulously re-created crew quarters and main-hold, which were painstakingly reproduced directly from the original 1768 Royal Navy survey of the vessel. Below decks includes an authentic brick galley stove, six men's cabins, the surgeon's cabin (complete with 18th century surgical gear – ouch!), the lieutenant's cabin, the magazine and even a "bread room." Students are encouraged to don 18th century sailor's clothing, taste authentic hard tack, and navigate with an octant, log-line and sandglass.

When the focus of a *Sultana* educational program shifts from history to ecology so too does the layout of the schooner, both above and below decks. Thanks to a significant gift from Lamotte Chemical Company in Chestertown, and the Shared Earth Foundation *Sultana* is equipped with a full array of modern scientific equipment including a variety of trawl nets, dredges, water chemistry equipment, optical and video microscopes and even an extensive reference library. In most respects the vessel can be quickly converted to a fully equipped research trawler in a matter of minutes.

While the growth of students' academic knowledge and understanding is a

central component of *Sultana's* mission, so too is the goal of having fun. The *Sultana* experience is designed to develop a life long love for the ecosystem of the Chesapeake Bay and its human history. The theory is that if students have a great time on *Sultana* learning about and experiencing the Chesapeake and its history that they will be more likely to pursue their classroom studies in these areas and pay attention to environmental and historic issues when they become adults.

54

As every ASTA member vessel knows, the expense of operating and maintaining a traditional sailing vessel while offering complex and diverse educational programs can be extremely daunting. Quality education under sail is not an inexpensive proposition. While many private schools have the ability to pay the full tuition for a *Sultana* educational program ($700 for three hours for 32 students) many public schools would find it difficult to squeeze their already tight budgets to accommodate a *Sultana* trip. In order to make *Sultana* educational programs available to a diverse a student population Sultana Projects, Inc, the organization that owns and operates *Sultana*, has established a School Support Fund which raises money in order to reduce the cost

of a program by 50% for the average public school. In 2002 the Sultana School Support Fund will provide over $60,000 of tuition assistance, making a *Sultana* trip a reality for over 3,000 public school students who might not otherwise be able to enjoy this opportunity.

Sultana's operating budget is also supported by a substantial endowment established while the vessel was under construction. Work on building the endowment will continue through 2005, by which time it is expected to grow to over 3-million dollars.

Sultana's 2002 calendar is already nearly full and over 7,000 students are expected to sail on the schooner. *Sultana* will once again be making port visits to Baltimore, Annapolis, St. Michael's and Washington, D.C. To learn more about *Sultana* and to see details of her sailing schedule and curricula visit the schooner's website at www.schoonersultana.com.

INTERNATIONAL CHILDREN'S CONFERENCE
ON THE ENVIRONMENT

TALL SHIPS® FESTIVAL

The Wind Brings the World to New London for ICCE 03

The International Children's Conference on the Environment

A Tall Ships® Festival

A friendly New England port city

Join us in New London, CT for an environmental tall ships festival commemorating the United Nations Environment Programme's global conference challenging children from around the world.

Please contact Richard Brown, City Manager for more information

860.447.5201 (tel)
860.447.7971 (fax)
181 State Street
New London, CT 06320

photos by: Don Couture

New London, CT USA
July 9-13, 2003

Information to help you plan your sail training experience.

Sail training in San Francisco Bay on board the S/V *Nehemiah*

Take Responsibility for Your Adventure

One of the most important products of sail training is the development of a sense of judgment about what and whom you can rely on, and to what degree. This applies to: the compass, the weather forecast, your shipmates, the depths on the chart, the strength of the anchor cable, the vigilance of the lookout on the other ship, and many other things. Sail training also builds a reasoned sense of self-reliance. All of this starts from the moment you begin to think about a voyage. Use the information in this Directory to begin to evaluate and decide what might be the best sail training experience for you.

Recognize who you are dealing with and what is included. When you book a sail training trip, you are dealing with the vessel owner or its representatives-ASTA is not involved. You must evaluate whether the financial and business arrangements make sense for you. If there is connecting travel involved, for example, find out if you must make the arrangements, or if it is somehow tied into those you make with the vessel. What happens if you miss your ship because your plane is delayed, or vice versa? Do you need trip insurance? Have you confirmed with the vessel owner any possible customs or immigration issues? Will you need a passport or a pre-purchased air ticket? You must seek out the answers to these questions.

Make informed, responsible decisions about risk and safety, level of challenge, physical suitability and other important issues. One of the important reasons to embark on a sail training trip is to engage the world in a different, stimulating, and challenging way-if you want to stay warm and dry, you should stay at home by the fireplace. Much of the point is to come face-to-face with the elements. At the very least, this probably means that you will find yourself wet, chilled, or tired at some point in a challenging voyage. But everyone's threshold for this is different, and you need to find out what you are likely to be experiencing in order to find out if it is well matched for you.

Since the beginning of time, going to sea has been recognized as carrying an element of risk. These days, we more commonly think about risk in connection with highway travel or aviation, but the idea is the same: you get a pre-flight safety brief on an airliner, you get a lifeboat drill on a cruise ship. Part of the value of sail training is addressing these issues head on. You need to decide whether you are comfortable with the combination of risks and safety measures connected with your proposed sail training trip.

For example, will you be able to go aloft? Will trips in smaller craft be involved? Will you be expected to stand watch at night? Do the demands of the ship match your physical and health capabilities? Are you on medication that will (or may) become necessary during the voyage, or do you have a condition (for example, hemophilia or epilepsy) that may require special access to medical attention; if so, is the vessel operator aware of this? Will you be able to get up and down the ladders, in and out of your berth, and along a heeled-over deck? If there is an emergency, will you be needed to handle safety equipment or to help operate the vessel?

Remember that sail training is often not intended to be like a vacation. Some vessels, on the other hand, may offer leisurely voyages, where very little will be asked of you. You should arrive at a clear understanding of these issues prior to setting sail.

In short, you must satisfy yourself that the trip you are looking into is the right thing for you to do, considering safety, risk, suitability, challenge, comfort, convenience, educational value, cost, and any other factors you consider important.

Does the American Sail Training Association have a hand in any of this? In a word—no! ASTA is your "bulletin board" to introduce you to opportunities. However, the American Sail Training Association does not operate any vessels, and has no ability or authority to inspect, approve, or even recommend vessels or programs because programs are constantly evolving and changing.

The American Sail Training Association is a nonprofit organization with a limited staff. It serves as a forum for the sail training community, but it has no authority over what programs are offered, or how vessels are operated. The information in this Directory is supplied by the vessel operators, and ASTA can not possibly verify all the information, nor visit all the ships in order to evaluate programs. For these reasons, you must take the information in this Directory as a starting point only, subject to change and correction, and proceed directly with the vessel operator. The American Sail Training Association is not an agent or business partner for the vessel operators, and is not a travel agent.

ASTA believes in the value of sail training as a concept, but remember, from the moment you step beyond looking at this book, the decision and the resulting experiences rest with you.

Choosing a Sail Training Program

The four essential components of any sail training program are a seaworthy vessel, a competent captain and crew, qualified instructors, and a sound educational program appropriate and suited to the needs of the trainees on board.

There are as many sail training programs as there are ships, and choosing the right one depends a great deal on your personal needs and desires. Sail training differs from going on a cruise ship, in that you are expected to take part in the running of the ship by handling sail and line and standing watch, as well as working in the galley (the ship's kitchen) or performing routine cleaning or maintenance duties. To what degree depends on the sail training program you select.

Do you want a program that specializes in marine biology or adventure travel? Would you like to ship out for a day, a week, a school semester—or, for as long as it takes to circumnavigate the world? Are you interested in maritime history? In celestial navigation? Whales? Do you want the unique challenge of climbing aloft in a square-rigger? A race across the Atlantic? Maine lobster dinners aboard classic windjammers? Exotic ports of call? Will you be bringing your wheelchair? Would you like to receive academic credit?

The answers to the above questions provide a profile for just some of the options available to you. As to what sail training programs require of you—beyond an eager willingness to get the most out of your voyage—the requirements are few:

Safety First!:

Take a close look at the vessel's credentials. In the US, check to see if the vessel operates under United States Coast Guard regulations. Does the vessel currently hold a USCG-issued Certificate of Inspection (see page 62, "Regulations for US Sailing Vessels") or comparable certification from the authorities of the country in which it is registered? If it is a non-US vessel you should ensure that the vessel operates in accordance with the maritime safety rules of that country. In most cases this is supervised by a government agency similar to the US Coast Guard. The resources section of the ASTA Web site lists the latest known Web sites of some of these agencies.

Talk to the program provider! Ask questions! Read the organization or company's literature; check out their Web site. Most important: visit the ship if you can. Get a sense of the professionalism of the operation and the quality of its program. Find out about the experience level of the captain and officers. How long have they served the ship you are looking into? If you will be joining the vessel in a distant port, or if it does not hold a current USCG Certificate of Inspection, be especially diligent in your research. Ask the program operator for the names of past trainees or clients and give them a call and ask about their experience. The amazingly diverse range of opportunities featured in this book provides each of us with a variety of options.

Many ships venture no more than 20 miles from a harbor and are rarely underway overnight; others offer offshore voyaging and the challenge of distant passages where severe weather and water conditions may be unavoidable. Being underway around the clock requires watch duties night and day, demanding both physical and mental stamina and perseverance.

Experience:
With very few exceptions, no prior sailing experience is required of trainees. Some programs do accept non-paying volunteers as crewmembers, but typically require experience in similar vessels or a long-term commitment-or both. Paying positions typically require a license-"Able-bodied Seaman" papers document a minimum of 180 days spent underway and successfully passing an exam administered by the US Coast Guard. Licenses are awarded to crew based on additional time underway, the tonnage of vessels served in, waters sailed, technical training, and additional testing.

Swimming Ability:
Trainees are encouraged to have the ability to feel comfortable in and around the water; however, many programs have no formal swimming requirements.

Age:
Most voyages are planned with a specific age group in mind. This varies from program to program, but many sail training programs start accepting unaccompanied trainees from the age of 14 (ninth grade). Ask what the composition of the ship's complement will be and, if you plan to send a young person on an extended voyage, what the in-port supervisory arrangements will be. Day sails and dockside education programs are readily available for elementary school students and overnight trips can be arranged for older school groups as well. There are a tremendous variety of adventure programs for adults of all ages, including "Elderhostel" voyages for seniors.

Academic credit:
Some vessels are tied directly to academic institutions that grant academic credit to trainees who successfully complete sail training programs as part of a course of study or project in a wide range of subjects. Some educational institutions will also grant credit for on-board independent study.

Co-education:
Just about every sail training vessel in the US sails with both male and female professional crew and programs are typically co-ed. Others are designed specifically for groups such as the Girl Scouts or in conjunction with a single-gender school or affiliated program.

Cost:
Prices vary considerably, ranging from $25 to $150 per person per day, depending on the nature and the duration of the program and the type of vessel.

Financial aid:
A few vessels have limited financial assistance available, and some trainees, Scouting, and school groups have successfully sought private, business, and/or community support to help defray the cost of sail training. In addition, there are a small number of independent organizations that provide financial aid to trainees, usually through matching grants. Check with the sail training program you are interested in to see what opportunities may be available.

Regulation of US Sail Training Vessels

Virtually all vessels are subject to some form of regulation by the national maritime authority of their "flag state"-the country in which they are registered. In the United States, these regulations are written and enforced by the US Coast Guard, pursuant to laws enacted by Congress. Under the Safety of Life at Sea (SOLAS) Convention, administered by the International Maritime Organization (IMO), vessels of any nation signatory to the convention and over a certain size or carrying more than 12 passengers and operating internationally must comply with the requirements of the Convention with regard to construction, safety equipment, manning, crew training, etc. Compliance is documented in a "SOLAS Certificate" issued by the ship's national maritime authority.

US-registered vessels listed in this directory will generally fall into one of the following categories: Small Passenger Vessel, Sailing School Vessel, Oceanographic Research Vessel, and Uninspected Vessel. For each category there is a comprehensive set of regulatory requirements governing construction and arrangement, watertight integrity and stability, lifesaving and firefighting equipment, machinery and electrical systems, vessel control and equipment, and operations.

With the exception of Uninspected Vessels, all categories of US-registered vessel are subject to Coast Guard inspection on an annual basis. Upon satisfactory completion of the inspection, a Certificate of Inspection (COI) is issued, and must be permanently displayed on board the vessel. The COI spells out what waters the vessel may operate in (its authorized route), how many passengers or sailing school students may be carried, how many crew must be carried and what qualifications the master and crew must have, the requirement for and location of lifesaving and firefighting equipment, and so forth. Although not inspected annually, Uninspected Vessels (which are generally vessels less than 65 feet in length and carrying 6 or fewer passengers for hire) must still comply with requirements for safety equipment and a licensed skipper. The type of COI to be issued to inspected vessels is determined by both the size and construction of the vessel and the operating intentions of the owner. Some vessels carry dual certification.

The Coast Guard also prescribes the qualifications for the officers and crew of inspected vessels, and requires both that they have certain minimum levels of experience and training and that they be examined and issued licenses or documents before they can lawfully serve on board.

Following is a brief description of the various types of certifications governing the operation of US-flagged vessels:

Sailing School Vessels (SSV) are inspected under Title 46, Subchapter R of the Code of Federal Regulations (CFR). An SSV is a vessel of less than 500 gross tons carrying six or more sailing school students or instructors, principally propelled by sail, and operated by a nonprofit educational organization exclusively for the purpose of sailing education. Sailing School Vessels are required to pass regular inspection by the USCG in order to maintain their certification.

Passenger Vessels are certified according to size and number of passengers (not engaged in educational activities or in the operation of the vessel) carried under Title 46 of the CFR:

Subchapter C - Uninspected vessels which operate with no more than six passengers.

Subchapter T - Small passenger vessels of under 100 gross tons that carry more than six passengers and are required to pass regular USCG inspection of the ship and all onboard equipment.

Subchapter K - Small passenger vessels of under 100 gross tons that carry more than 150 passengers and are required to pass regular USCG inspection of the ship and all onboard equipment.

Subchapter H - Passenger vessels more than 100 gross tons that carry passengers for hire and are required to pass regular USCG inspection of the ship and all onboard equipment.

Attraction Vessel certification is required whenever a vessel is open to public boarding or conducts dockside programs. The vessel may be permanently moored to a pier, or it may also be certified under one or more of the above subchapters, but the Attraction Vessel COI (ATCOI) certifies its safety for dockside programs and visitation only.

Oceanographic Research Vessels (ORV) are certified under Subchapter U of Title 46 of the CFR. An ORV is a vessel employed exclusively in either oceanographic (saltwater) or limnologic (freshwater) instruction and/or research, and is not necessarily equipped for passengers or other non-professionals.

For more information, access the United States Coast Guard through the link on ASTA's Web site or contact the Government Printing Office for the above listed sections of the Code of Federal Regulations.

Shipping Out

Photo by Jim Taylor

Each year, ASTA asks one of its Member Organizations for the equipment list they provide to potential trainees, for use in this Directory. This list is a general guide only. Requirements may vary from vessel to vessel. Check for specific requirements of the program you are condisering. The following "gear list" was provided by S.A.L.T.S. (Sail and Life Training Society) owner and operator of the *Pacific Grace* (pg. 236) and *Pacific Swift* (pg. 237).

S.A.L.T.S. SUMMER PROGRAM

GEAR LIST

Every trainee should bring the following items:

-1 sleeping bag (pillow optional)
-2 or 3 pairs of jeans or slacks
-1 old pair runners (or deck shoes)
-2 - 4 warm sweaters or sweat shirts
-1 swim suit
-1 toque, hat or cap
-4 or 5 shirts or tops
-sleepwear
-1 pair sandals
-1 pen, 1 pencil and eraser
-Water bottle for shore excursions

-necessary towels, soap, toothbrush, etc
-rain gear (pants and jacket)
-1 pair rubber boots (or deck boots)
-1 warm jacket
-2 - 4 pairs shorts
-1 pair gloves (for cool nights and/or hauling lines)
-1 change socks and underwear (for each day at sea)
-flashlight (for nightwatch)
-plastic bag for wet gear
-writing pad and binder for Sailor's Handbook
-Log Book if returning from last year

SAIL TALL SHIPS!

Supplementary List: (recommended but not mandatory)
1 pair dividers, and 1 set parallel rules for trainees taking the Intermediate Certificate, reading material, Bible, musical instrument* and "long john underwear".

Avoid large suitcases (duffel bags and soft luggage recommended) - bring only what you can stow on your own bunk.

* Please check with office before bringing large instrument (e.g. guitar)

ANY UNCLAIMED/UNMARKED "LOST AND FOUND" ITEMS WILL BE HELD AT THE S.A.L.T.S. OFFICE ONLY UNTIL THE END OF THE SEASON (APPROXIMATELY SEPTEMBER 30) AND WILL THEN BE DONATED TO A WORTHY CAUSE.

Photo by Mark Kaarremaa

What is a Tall Ship?

"... how tall is a tall ship? The answer to this is rather similar to that of 'How long is a piece of string?' Perhaps John Masefield stated it best in his famous poem Sea Fever:

'And all I ask is a tall ship and a star to steer her by.' "

from *Sail Training, The Message of the Tall Ships* by John Hamilton

A "tall ship" is not a strictly defined type of sailing vessel. Most of us use the term to mean a large, traditionally rigged sailing vessel, whether or not it is technically a "ship." The United States Coast Guard's training ship *Eagle*, for example, is technically a barque. A tall ship can also be a schooner, brigantine, barquentine, brig, ketch, sloop, or a full-rigged ship depending on the number of masts and the cut of the sails.

For the purpose of classification and race rating, the International Sail Training Association divides tall ships into three classes and several sub-classes:

Class A: All vessels over 160 feet in overall length, regardless of rig, and all square-rigged vessels over 120 feet (Square-rigged vessels include ships, barques, barquentines, brigs, and brigantines, but not square-topsail schooners)

Class A Division II: All square-rigged vessels less than 120 feet in length

Class B: Fore-and-aft rigged vessels between 100 feet and 160 feet in length

Class C: All other fore-and-aft rigged vessels at least 30 feet long at the waterline

The American Sail Training Association owns the registered trademark Tall Ships® as it relates to the organization of sailing events and races and related commercial activity.

Ships' Shapes

Sail training vessels are as varied as the programs operated on board them. Below are examples of the different rig configurations used by ASTA's Member Vessels. On the following page you will find a diagram of the different sails carried by a full-rigged ship as well as a glossary of terms commonly used in this book.

wo-Masted Schooner

Brigantine

Topsail Schooner

Full-Rigged Ship

Barquentine

Three-Masted Schooner

Brig

Sail Names: Glossary of Terms

SAIL NAMES

1. Fore mast
2. Main mast
3. Mizzen mast
4. Flying jib
5. Outer jib
6. Inner jib
7. Fore topmast staysail
8. Fore sail, fore course
9. Fore lower topsail
10. Fore upper topsail
11. Fore lower topgallant sail
12. Fore upper topgallant sail
13. Fore royal
14. Main royal staysail
15. Main topgallant staysail
16. Main topmast staysail
17. Main sail, main course
18. Main lower topsail
19. Main upper topsail
20. Main lower topgallant sail
21. Main upper topgallant sail
22. Main royal
23. Mizzen royal staysail
24. Mizzen topgallant staysail
25. Mizzen topmast staysail
26. Main spencer
27. Crossjack, mizzen course
28. Mizzen lower topsail
29. Mizzen upper topsail
30. Mizzen lower topgallant sail
31. Mizzen upper topgallant sail
32. Mizzen royal
33. Spanker

TERMS

Sparred length - The length between the extremities of any spars that overhang the bow or the stern of a vessel, such as a bowsprit or a boomkin.

LOA - Length overall. The length between the forwardmost and the aftermost points on the hull of a vessel.

LOD - Length on deck. The length between the forwardmost and the aftermost points on a specified deck measured along the deck, excluding sheer.

Sheer - The fore-and-aft curvature of a vessel's main deck from bow to stern.

LWL - Length on the waterline. The length between the forwardmost and the after most points on a vessel's waterline.

Draft - The depth of water required to float a vessel.

Beam - Width of a vessel at its widest part.

Rig height - Maximum height of rig above waterline.

Freeboard - The vertical distance from the waterline to the freeboard deck, usually measured amidships.

Freeboard deck - The uppermost deck that is designed to be watertight.

GRT - Gross registered tonnage. The volume, expressed in units of 100 cubic feet to the ton, of a vessel's total enclosed spaces below the weather deck and enclosed spaces above the deck including the bridge and accommodations.

USCG Barque *Eagle*

**252 OPPORTUNITIES TO LEARN
FROM THE SEA, UNDER SAIL**

777 (Triple Seven)

Association. Yacht *777's* owner served as one of the first cadets aboard the *Black Pearl*. This excellent experience of transatlantic passage, tall ships races, and the character-building values embodied in sail training brings together the vessel and her crew to continue the tradition.

Yacht *777* was built in 1963 for the Fastnet Race of that year. Built under Lloyd's supervision and to the highest standards of UK racing rules, she has crossed the Atlantic many times, traveling the traditional cruising circuit from New England down to the lower Caribbean.

Established in 1993, Proper Yacht, Inc. follows the tradition begun by Barclay Warburton III with the formation of the American Sail Training

Flag:	USA
Rig:	Sloop
Homeport/waters:	Charleston, South Carolina: Coastal US to Caribbean
Who sails?	Individuals, students, and families of all ages.
Season:	Year-round
Cost:	$100 per person per day. $500 per person per week.
Program type:	Sail training for volunteer and paying crew and trainees. Sea education programs in marine science, maritime history, historic reenactments, and ecology in cooperation with accredited institutions and organized groups, and as informal, in-house programming.

Specifications:			
	Sparred length: 41' 3"	Draft: 6' 6"	Sail area: 1,400 sq. ft.
	LOD: 39'	Beam: 11' 8"	Tons: 10 GRT
	LOA: 41'	Freeboard: 4'	Power: diesel
	LWL: 37'	Hull: wood	

Built:	1963; R J. Prior and Sons, UK
Coast Guard certification:	Sailing School Vessel (Subchapter R)
Crew:	2. Trainees: 4
Contact:	Charles Hatchell
	Proper Yacht, Inc.
	PO Box 7
	Little River, SC 29566
	Tel: 843-830-3506; Fax: 843-767-1405
	E-mail: yacht777@gte.net
	Web site: http://www.properyacht.com

The Delaware Bay Schooner Project operates the schooner *A.J. Meerwald,* New Jersey's official tall ship, as an experiential classroom. This authentically restored 1928 Delaware Bay oyster schooner sails from her homeport, Bivalve, New Jersey, as well as annual visits to cities and coastal towns throughout New Jersey, Pennsylvania, and Delaware (occasional special trips into the Chesapeake and the Northeast Atlantic seaboard).

Students range from fourth-graders to senior citizens; subject matter ranges from the history of Delaware Bay oystering to present water quality issues. Stewardship of the environment and preservation of our maritime heritage are the primary goals of all activities on the *A.J. Meerwald,* regardless of their target audience, length of program, and/or port of origin.

The Delaware Bay Schooner Project also conducts shore-based programs, lecture series, hosts Delaware Bay Day (the first Saturday in June), and provides leadership on watershed issues throughout the Delaware Estuary. Members and volunteers are the lifeblood of the organization and are always welcome.

Flag:	USA
Rig:	Gaff-schooner
Homeport/waters:	Bivalve, New Jersey: Delaware Bay and coastal New Jersey
Who sails?	School groups, 4th grade through college, families, scouts, teachers, businesses, associations, and anyone interested in a Meerwald experience.
Cost:	$25 per person per sail, $2,500 group rate per day (charter)
Program type:	Sail training for professional crew and volunteer and paying trainees. Three-hour educational sails, summer camp, family sails, teacher workshops, overnight programs, team building, and special "theme" sails (i.e. birding, oystering, etc.). Sea education in marine science, maritime history, ecology, team building, and watershed awareness in cooperation with accredited institutions and other groups, and as informal, in-house programming.

Specifications:			
	Sparred length: 115'	Draft: 6'	Sail area: 3,560 sq. ft.
	LOA: 85'	Beam: 22' 1"	Tons: 57 GRT
	LOD: 81' 7"	Rig height: 67' 8"	Power: diesel
	LWL: 78' 3"	Freeboard: 3' 6"	Hull: wood

Designer:	Charles H. Stowman and Sons, Dorchester, New Jersey
Built:	1928; Dorchester, New Jersey, Charles H. Stowman and Sons Shipyard
Coast Guard certification:	Passenger Vessel (Subchapter T)
Crew:	11, augmented by volunteers
Contact:	Meghan Wren, Executive Director
	Delaware Bay Schooner Project
	2800 High Street, Bivalve
	Port Norris, NJ 08349
	Tel: 856-785-2060; Fax: 856-785-2893
	E-mail: ajmeerwald@snip.net
	Web site: http://www.ajmeerwald.org

Abaco

Abaco was designed by John Alden in 1921 and built by W.B. Calderwood at Manchester Marine, Manchester, Massachusetts for Mr. Robert Saltonstall. She is owned and operated by Captain Peter L. Warburton, son of the late Barclay H. Warburton III, founder of ASTA.

Abaco operates half-day, day, weekend and week-long sail training, adventure cruising, chartering and team building experiences, as well as seamanship classes. Individuals, families, and groups, of all ages and types, are encouraged to plan their next voyage, vacation, adventure, outing or educational experience aboard this classic beauty!

Abaco carries up to six passengers or trainees. She operates in South Carolina, Florida, and/or the Bahamas during the winter months, and sails in Chesapeake Bay and New England waters during the summer months. When participating on the passage north or south, or for any portion of any voyage, passengers are the crew and are able to experience all aspects of ship life. Duties on board *Abaco* include steering, sail handling, cooking, watch standing, navigating, and much more. All duties are performed under the direction of *Abaco's* captain and crew. Experience is not necessary. Whether you are a novice or a seasoned sailor, you are sure to further your sailing knowledge, challenge your own abilities, develop a sense of "team,"experience personal growth, and have fun!

Flag:	USA
Rig:	Main staysail schooner
Homeport/waters:	Newport, Rhode Island: New England, Maryland, Coastal Northeast (summer), South Carolina, Florida Bahamas (winter)
Who sails?	School groups from middle school through college, individuals, families, corporate groups, charter groups
Season:	Year-round
Cost:	Call for details
Program type:	Sail training for paying trainees. Informal programming in maritime history and ecology. Passenger day sails, overnight voyages and adventure vacations.

Specifications:	Sparred length: 53'	Draft: 7'	Sail area: 2,000 sq. ft.
	LOD: 45' 6"	Beam: 11' 8"	Tons: 20 GRT
	LOA: 45' 6"	Rig height: 62'	Power: 85 HP diesel
	LWL: 33'	Freeboard: 5'	Hull: wood, Color: whilte

Designer:	John G. Alden
Built:	1921; W.B. Calderwood, Manchester, Massachusetts
Coast Guard certification:	Uninspected Vessel
Crew:	2. Trainees: 6
Contact:	Captain and Mrs. Peter L. Warburton
	East Passage Packet Co., LLC
	Fazio, 57 Palmetto Dunes
	Hilton Head Island, SC 29928
	Tel: 843-842-2432, E-mail: schoonerabaco@cs.com

Adastra was built by Irwin Yachts in 1986. Originally named the *Tasa Grande*, she operated in the charter trade throughout the Caribbean and East Coast. Today she makes her home in Key West, Florida and is available for day sails, sunset cruises, and private charters.

Flag :	USA
Homeport/waters:	Key West, Florida: Florida Keys, East Coast US
Who sails?	Groups and Individuals of all ages.
Season:	Year-round
Program type:	Private charters, day sails and sunset cruises
Specifications:	Sparred length: 78' LOA: 65'
	Draft: 6' Beam: 17'
	Rig height: 83'
Designer:	Irwin Yachts
Built:	1986; St. Petersburg, Florida, Irwin Yachts
Crew:	2. Trainees/Passengers: 6 (day sails), 6 (overnight)
Contact:	Captain Kevin Foley
	National Boat Owner Association
	4404 N. Tamiam Trail
	Sarasota, FL 34234
	Tel: 800-248-6572
	E-mail: info@nboat.com
	Web site: www.nboat.com

Adirondack

The schooner *Adirondack* is the third of five schooners to come out of the Scarano Boat Building yard, beginning with the 59-foot schooner *Madeline* and the 61-foot *Woodwind* in 1991, and followed by the 105-foot schooner *America* in 1995 and a sister ship, *Adirondack II*, launched in August 1999. *Adirondack* combines the virtues of turn-of-the-century American schooner yachts with the latest in laminated wood technology. Offering an enviable combination of stability and speed, the *Adirondack* fulfills the builder and owner's ambition of providing a quality sail for people of all ages and experience.

Flag:	USA
Rig:	Gaff schooner
Homeport/waters:	New York, New York: New York Harbor
Who sails?	School groups from elementary school through college, individuals and families.
Program type:	Sail training with paying trainees. Passenger day sails.

Specifications:			
	Sparred length: 80'	Draft: 8'	Sail area: 1,850 sq. ft.
	LOD: 64' 6"	Beam: 16'	Tons: 41 GRT
	LOA: 65'	Rig height: 62'	Power: twin 50 HP diesels
	LWL: 58'	Freeboard: 3' 4"	Hull: wood

Built:	1996; Albany, New York, Scarano Boat
Coast Guard certification:	Passenger Vessel (Subchapter T)
Crew:	3. Trainees/passengers: 49
Contact:	Rick Scarano, Manager
	Sailing Excursions, Inc.
	c/o Scarano Boat, Port of Albany
	Albany, NY 12202
	Tel: 800-701-SAIL; 518-463-3401; Fax: 518-463-3403
	E-mail: mail@scaranoboat.com
	Web site: http://www.scaranoboat.com

The schooner *Adirondack II* is the latest sailing vessel to be launched from the Scarano yard in Albany, New York. Launched in August of 1999, the near-sister ship of the *Adirondack* joins the fleet of schooners known for their performance-oriented design/construction combined with classic traditional aesthetics (see *Coronet*).

"This year's model" expands on the idea that safety, comfort, and style are paramount considerations. Passengers can experience the exhilaration of being aboard the huge new day sailer, with its wide-open cockpit that can comfortably accommodate larger groups of trainees and passengers (up to 65). While dockside, spacious cockpit doghouses double as serving space for food and beverages or classroom navigation paperwork.

Adirondack II affirms that modern wood composite construction and 19th-century elegance blend seamlessly to the benefit of all.

Flag:	USA		
Rig:	Gaff schooner		
Homeport/waters:	Newport, Rhode Island: Narragansett Bay.		
Specifications:	Sparred length: 80'	Beam: 16'	Sail area: 1,800 sq. ft.
	LOD: 64' 6"	Draft: 8'	Tons: 41 GRT
	LOA: 65'	Rig height: 62'	Hull: wood
	LWL: 58'	Freeboard: 3' 4"	Power: twin 50 HP diesels
Built:	1999; Albany, New York, Scarano Boat		
Coast Guard certification:	Passenger Vessel (Subchapter T)		
Crew:	3. Trainees/passengers: 65		
Contact:	Rick Scarano, Manager		
	Sailing Excursions, Inc.		
	c/o Scarano Boat, Port of Albany		
	Albany, NY 12202		
	Tel: 800-701-SAIL, 518-463-3401; Fax: 518-463-3403		
	E-mail: mail@scaranoboat.com		
	Web site: http://www.scaranoboat.com		

The Schooner *Adventure* is one of the last of the Gloucester fishing schooners, an icon of our nation's fishing industry and Gloucester's heritage. *Adventure* was built in 1926, near the end of the commercial Age of Sail, in Essex, Massachusetts. Designed by McManus as a "knockabout", without a bowsprit for the safety of the crew, the 122' *Adventure* represents the pinnacle of schooner design, embodying grace, speed, and functionality.

Immortalized by Rudyard Kipling's novel *Captains Courageous*, Gloucester's fishing schooners, known as "*Gloucestermen*", were famous throughout the world. Fast and able under sail and carrying 14 dories, *Adventure* was the "highliner" of the North Atlantic fleet, earning more money than any other fishing vessel of her era. At the time of her retirement from fishing in 1953, *Adventure* was the last American dory-fishing schooner working in the North Atlantic.

Refitted as a windjammer, *Adventure* carried passengers along the coast of Maine until 1987. Her grace, beauty, and prowess as a sailing vessel earned her the nickname "Queen of the Windjammers." In 1988, *Adventure* was given to the people of Gloucester to be preserved as Gloucester's historic tall ship. A rare survivor, *Adventure* is a unique vessel from an extraordinary era in American history. A National Historic Landmark, *Adventure* serves as a living memorial to the more than 5,000 Gloucester fishermen lost at sea, and was selected as an Official Project of "Save America's Treasures" by the National Trust for Historic Preservation.

Adventure is being restored as a 1926 Gloucester fishing schooner and will resume sailing once work is completed. The schooner will be used as a community resource for educational programming, focusing on maritime, cultural, and environmental issues, and will sail as a living symbol of Gloucester's maritime heritage. The vessel is available for dockside tours, educational programs, and maritime events.

Flag:	USA
Rig:	Gaff topsail schooner
Home port/waters:	Gloucester, Massachusetts
Program type:	Dockside interpretation. Educational programs for schools.

Specifications:	LOA: 122'	Draft: 13' 6"	Sail area: 6,500 sq. ft.
	LOD: 122'	Beam: 24' 6"	Tons: 130 GRT
	LWL: 109'	Rig height: 110'	Hull: wood

Designer:	Tom McManus
Built:	1926; Essex, Massachusetts, John F. James & Son Yard
Coast Guard certification:	Moored Attraction Vessel (dockside)
Contact:	Sally Curry
	Gloucester Adventure, Inc.
	PO Box 1306, Gloucester, MA 01931-1306
	Tel: 978-281-8079; Fax: 978-281-2393
	E-mail: scurry@schooner-adventure.org
	Web site: http://www.schooner-adventure.org

In 1913 the schooner *Adventuress* sailed from Maine to the Bering Sea via the straits of Magellan and served the Bar Pilots of San Francisco Bay until 1952. Although originally commissioned to gather Arctic specimens, *Adventuress* now sails to increase awareness of the majesty and vulnerability of Puget Sound. Since 1989, Sound Experience, a nonprofit environmental education organization, has provided hands-on education aboard *Adventuress* in response to the area's urgent environmental issues. Today, *Adventuress* is a National Historic Landmark and a Puget Sound treasure - the crowning jewel of the Pacific Northwest's collection of wooden ships.

Volunteer and paid crew receive environmental and sail training. The ship's apprentice program for youth 14-18 and month-long internships for adult sailor/educators also feature extensive sail training. Sound Experience is proud to own and operate *Adventuress* and to keep her a "working" vessel - Protecting Puget Sound Through Education. The non-competitive environment fosters cooperation, teamwork, leadership, and sailing skills for Elderhostelors, Boy and Girl Scout Troops, youth groups, schools, and individuals of all ages who enjoy raising her massive sails and standing watch to hand, reef, and steer this classic tall ship. Truly a boat for the people, *Adventuress* provides empowering, life-changing experiences to more than 3,500 youth and adults each year.

Flag:	USA
Rig:	Gaff topsail schooner
Homeport/waters:	Port Townsend, Washington: Puget Sound/Salish Sea
Who sails?	School and other groups from elementary school through college, individuals and families.
Season:	March to November
Cost:	$30 per person ($20 for youth) for 3-5 hour sail, $1,260 per day for adult groups ($800 youth groups). Overnights: $2,500 per day adult groups ($1,725 youth groups). Scholarships available.
Program type:	Sail training for paying trainees. Sea education in marine science, maritime history, and ecology. Passenger day and overnight sails. Dockside interpretation during port visits.

Specifications:			
	Sparred length: 135'	Draft: 12'	Sail area: 5,478 sq. ft.
	LWL: 71'	Beam: 21'	Sail number: TS 15
	Rig height: 110'	Tons: 82 GRT	Power: 250 HP diesel

Designer:	B.B. Crowninshield
Built:	1913; East Boothbay, Maine, Rice Brothers
Coast Guard certification:	Passenger Vessel (Subchapter T)
Crew:	4-5, 8-10 instructors. Trainees: 45 day, 25 overnight. Age: 8-adult
Contact:	Jenell DeMatteo
	Sound Experience
	2310 Washington Street
	Port Townsend, WA 98368
	Tel: 360-379-0438; Fax: 360-379-0439
	E-mail: soundexp@olypen.com Web site: http://www.soundexp.org

schooners, Thomas F. McManus.

After a major three-year reconstruction, the summer of 1998 marked her first season sailing the waters of southern New England. She is a product of Vineyard Haven craftsmanship as the lion's share of her rebuild took place in Vineyard Haven Harbor. *Alabama* now joins *Shenandoah* in the Coastwise Packet Company fleet.

The ex-pilot schooner *Alabama* is an authentic example of a typical Gloucester fishing schooner of the early 1900s. She was built for the Mobile Bar Pilot Association in Pensacola, Florida in 1926 and designed by the greatest New England designer of Gloucester

The *Alabama* runs 6-day sailing trips for kids ages 9 to 14 from late June through late August. She also runs day sails and is available for private charter each year from June 1 through June 23 and August 25 through mid-October.

Flag:	USA
Rig:	Gaff schooner
Homeport/waters:	Vineyard Haven, Massachusetts: Southern New England
Who sails?	School groups from elementary through college and individuals of all ages.
Cost:	$650 per child per week, $750 per adult per week (Sunday night through Saturday noon)
Program type:	Sail training for paying trainees ages 9 – 14. Private charters and public day sails. Two-week college credit courses offered for students and adults through Boston University

Specifications:			
	Sparred length: 120'	Draft: 12' 6"	Sail area: 5,000 sq. ft.
	LOD: 85'	Beam: 21'	Tons: 85 GRT
	LOA: 90'	Rig height: 94'	Power: twin diesels
	LWL: 78'	Freeboard: 5'	Hull: wood

Designer:	Thomas F. McManus
Built:	1926; Pensacola, Florida, Pensacola Shipbuilding Company
Coast Guard certification:	Passenger Vessel (Subchapter T)
Crew:	6. Trainees: 49 (day sails), 27 (overnight)
Contact:	Captain Robert Douglas
	Coastwise Packet Company
	PO Box 429
	Vineyard Haven, MA 02568
	Tel: 508-693-1699; Fax: 508-693-1881
	Web site: http://www.coastwisepacket.com

The scow schooner *Alma* was built at Hunters Point in San Francisco Bay in 1891 and is the last of approximately 400 scow schooners that carried cargo in the San Francisco Bay area at the turn of the century. She is owned and operated by the San Francisco Maritime National Historical Park and docked at Hyde Street Pier near Fisherman's Wharf. The San Francisco Maritime National Park Association supports operations of the *Alma* at the many maritime festivals and parades in the Bay area.

Alma sails from March until November and is crewed by volunteers, representing and interpreting a time when commerce moved by boat around the Bay. The *Alma* volunteer program enables trainees and apprentices to learn about traditional sailing and wooden boat maintenance. No fees are required as all crew volunteer to sail and maintain the *Alma* and other park vessels at Hyde Street Pier.

Flag:	USA
Rig:	Schooner, two-masted
Homeport/waters:	San Francisco, California: San Francisco Bay
Who sails?	Adult education groups, individual students and adults, families.
Program type:	Sail training for crew and apprentices. Sea education based on informal, in-house programming focused on maritime history. Dockside interpretation. Affiliated groups include the National Maritime Museum Association, San Francisco National Maritime Historical Park, and National Park Service.

Specifications:			
	Sparred length: 88'	Draft: 3' 6"	Sail area: 2,684 sq. ft.
	LOD: 61' 4"	Beam: 23' 6"	Tons: 47 GRT
	LOA: 62'	Rig height: 76"	Power: twin diesels
	LWL: 59' 5"	Freeboard: 4'	Hull: wood

Designer:	Fred Siemers
Built:	1891; San Francisco, California, Fred Siemers
Crew:	6. Trainees: 28 (overnight), 40 (day). Age: 14+
Contact:	Captain Al Lutz
	San Francisco Maritime National Historical Park
	Building E, Fort Mason Center
	San Francisco, CA 94123
	Tel: 415-561-7000; Fax: 415-556-1624
	E-mail: al_lutz@nps.gov
	Web site: http://www.nps.gov/safr/local/alma.html

Alvei

After an extensive 8-year refit, *Alvei's* accommodations, deck, and rigging have been completely renewed. Underway since October 1995, *Alvei* has completed half a circumnavigation, sailing from Portugal to Australia. She now sails long trade wind passages using the old sailing ship routes.

Alvei's rig, the main topsail schooner, was the preference of privateers during the early 19th century. *Alvei* has 137 lines of running rigging to handle 16 sails, providing experience in both fore-and-aft and square-rigged sail handling.

A sailor from a hundred years ago would be at home on *Alvei*. It takes a team of people using block and tackle, to "sweat & tail" as they set and handle sails. Raising the anchor, rowing the shore boat, and laundry are all done by hand.

The crew, both regular and trainees, stand watch at sea, four on and eight off; in port it's one day on and two days off. Duties include steering, lookout, sail handling, painting, tarring, sewing, cooking, and rigging. *Alvei* has a full-participation crew.

Flag:	Vanuatu
Rig:	Main Topsail Schooner
Homeport/waters:	Port Vila, Republic of Vanuatu; tropical waters worldwide
Who sails?	Adults 18 and over
Season:	Year-round
Cost:	$25 per person per day
Program type:	Sail training for volunteer and paying trainees. Sea education based on informal in-house participation. Coastal and offshore passages.

Specifications:			
Sparred length: 126'	LOD: 92'	LOA: 126'
LWL: 87'	Draft: 10'	Beam: 19'
Rig Height: 85'3"	Freeboard: 2'6"	Sail area: 5,700 sq. ft.
Power 160 HP Diesel	Hull: steel	

Designer:	Unknown; rig, Evan Logan
Built:	1920; Montrose, Scotland
Contact:	Margy Gassel, Shore Crew
	604 Masonic Avenue
	Albany, CA 94706
	Tel: 510-526-7157
	E-mail: alvei@yahoo.com
	Web site: http://www.alvei.com

The Caravan Stage Barge *Amara Zee* is the new touring vessel of the Caravan Stage Society, Inc. Built in 1997, the *Amara Zee* is based on a Thames River Sailing Barge blended with the best of contemporary marine and theater technology. With its shallow draft and lowering masts, the Stage Barge can access almost any waterfront community in North America. The spars are utilized for scenery, lights, sound equipment, and special effects. All performances are staged on deck, with the audience sitting on the shore.

The *Amara Zee* was built by the theater company with the assistance of a number of marine professional volunteers and financed by over 600 manufacturing companies with in-kind donations of equipment, materials, and services. The Caravan's original productions express contemporary concerns and issues in an engaging and compelling format that is both entertaining and inspirational.

Flag:	Canada		
Rig:	Ketch (sailing barge)		
Homeport/waters:	East Coast of US		
Program type:	Theatrical performances.		
Specifications:	LOA: 90'	Draft: 3' 6"	Sail area: 5,100 sq. ft.
	Rig height: 90'	Beam: 22'	Power: twin 120 HP diesels
	Hull: steel		
Contact:	National Caravan Stage Company, Inc.		
	140 Seventh Avenue South		
	St. Petersburg, FL 33701		
	Tel: 917-208-6976, 727-515-8163		
	E-mail: office@caravanstage.org		
	Web site: http://www.caravanstage.org		

American Eagle

The 12-meter yacht *American Eagle* was launched in Stamford, Connecticut, in 1964, and won 20 out of 21 races in the June and July America's Cup defender trials. In 1968, she was bought by Ted Turner, a 31-year-old sailor from Atlanta, Georgia. During his years racing *American Eagle*, Turner became one of the finest 12-meter helmsmen in the world and was selected by the New York Yacht Club to defend and win the America's Cup with *Courageous* in 1977.

American Eagle offers a memorable experience for you and your guests. Take the wheel and sense the sheer power and exhilaration that only the big twelves provide. An experienced three-man crew will make your pleasure a priority while ensuring safety aboard. Rediscover Narragansett Bay or the historic America's Cup course on Rhode Island Sound on one of the greatest 12-meter yachts ever built. *American Eagle* is based in Newport but upon request can be available at the port of your choice from New York to Maine by the day or the week. Call or write for more information.

Flag:	USA
Rig:	Sloop
Homeport/waters:	Newport, Rhode Island: New England and Chesapeake Bay
Who sails?	Individuals and groups of all ages
Cost:	$2100 group rate per day, $75 per person for evening sails
Program type:	Sail training for paying trainees. Passenger day sails, corporate team building, corporate racing, individual and group charters.

Specifications:			
	Sparred length: 69'	Draft: 9'	Sail area: 1,850 sq. ft.
	LOA: 68'	Beam: 12' 8"	Tons: 28 GRT
	LOD: 68'	Rig height: 90'	Power: diesel
	LWL: 46'	Hull: wood	

Designer:	A.E. Luders
Built:	1964; Stamford, Connecticut, Luders
Coast Guard certification:	Passenger Vessel (Subchapter T)
Crew:	3. Trainees/passengers: 12 (day sails)
Contact:	Herb Marshall/George Hill
	America's Cup Charters
	PO Box 51
	Newport, RI 02840
	Tel: 401-849-5868; Fax: 401-849-3098
	Web site: http://www.americascupcharters.com

The graceful three-masted schooner *American Pride* was built in 1941 as a two-masted "schooner-dragger." She spent over 40 years commercially fishing the Grand Banks and George's Banks. In 1986, completely restored and with a third mast added, she operated as a charter boat out of Bar Harbor, Maine. In October 1996, she was purchased by the American Heritage Marine Institute (AHMI) and sailed to her new home in Long Beach, California.

The AMHI offers hands-on educational programs which stress science, marine biology, history, and sail training. Programs encourage teamwork, good communication, problem solving, and leadership. Sail training programs, team building, and private group charters are available for teens and adults, with destinations and length of voyage varying.

AHMI is actively engaged in sharing the thrill of sailing with sick or abused children, and regularly donates sails to child welfare groups and fundraising guilds. A professional crew and strong volunteer group generously gives time, talents, and resources in support of the programs.

The once-successful fishing schooner now majestically sails the southern California waters, her huge red sails highly visible as she gracefully shares the adventures and romance of the tall ship with all that come aboard.

Flag:	USA
Rig:	Schooner, three-masted
Homeport/waters:	Long Beach, California: Southern California.
Who sails?	Elementary/college students, corporate team building, individual/private, Summer youth camps.
Season:	Year-round
Cost:	Rates vary depending on program, please contact Institute for more information.
Program type:	Scientific or living history educational programs, sail training, team building, sailing adventures for individuals and groups

Specifications:	Sparred length: 129'	Draft: 10'	Sail area: 4,900 sq. ft.
	LOD: 101'	Beam: 22'	Tons: 203 GRT
	LOA: 105'	Rig height: 98'	Power: diesel
	LWL: 92'	Freeboard: 6'	Hull: wood

Built:	1941; Muller Boatworks, Brooklyn, New York
Coast Guard certification:	Passenger Vessel (Subchapter T)
Crew:	6 (paid and volunteer). Trainees/passengers: 100 (day sails), 48 (overnight)
Contact:	Helen H. Clinton, Director
	American Heritage Marine Institute
	21520 "G" Yorba Linda Blvd., # 444
	Yorba Linda, CA 92887
	Tel: 714-970-8800; Fax: 714-970-8474
	E-mail: americprd@aol.com
	Web site: http://www.americanpride.org

Amistad

PHOTO COURTESY MYSTIC SEAPORT MUSEUM

Freedom Schooner *Amistad*, currently completing the *Amistad East Coast Friendship Tour,* will tour the Gulf Coast, Great Lakes, West Coast, Europe and Africa through 2005. The focus of these tours is to provide an enriching experience for hundreds of thousands of schoolchildren and adults through an interdisciplinary curriculum, dockside exhibits, in-school presentations and educational sailing programs. *Amistad* is owned, operated, and protected by AMISTAD America, Inc. The mission of AMISTAD America is to teach the historic lessons of perseverance, cooperation, leadership, justice and freedom inherent in "The *Amistad* Incident of 1839" to individuals, families and school children through a variety of experiences from onboard and dockside exhibits to half-day excursions. Themes are interdisciplinary, blending communication skills, geography, math, and social studies while making history relevant among people of diverse backgrounds. While sailing and maintaining *Amistad* is the primary task for crew members, crew are also expected to greet the public and tell the story of "The *Amistad* Incident" during dockside tours and private sails. To crew or volunteer aboard *Amistad* and for general information, visit our website www.amistadamerica.org or call us at (203) 498-9000 or (866) AMISTAD. The homeport for Freedom Schooner *Amistad* is New Haven, Connecticut.

Flag:	USA
Rig:	Topsail schooner
Homeport/waters:	New Haven, Connecticut: East Coast of the United States.
Who sails?	School groups from elementary schools through college.
Program type:	Sail training for crew and apprentices and with paying trainees. Maritime history and a full range of programming are expected. Sea education in cooperation with accredited institutions and other groups. Passenger day sailing and dockside interpretation during home and port visits.

Specifications:

Sparred length: 129'	Draft: 10' 2"	Sail area: 5,000 sq. ft.
LOA: 85'	Beam: 22' 4"	Power: twin diesels
LOD: 81'	Rig height: 90'	Hull: wood
LWL: 79'		

Designer:	Tri-Coastal Marine
Built:	1998-2000, Mystic Seaport, Mystic, Connecticut
Coast Guard certifications:	Sailing School Vessel (Subchapter R), Passenger Vessel (Subchapter T)
Crew:	8, combination paid and volunteer. Trainees/passengers: 49
Contact:	Amistad America, Inc.
	199 Crown Street
	New Haven, CT 06510
	Tel: 203-495-1839; Fax: 203-495-9647
	E-mail: info@amistadamerica.org
	Web site: http://www.amistadamerica.org

Named for the Greek goddess of the sea, Aphrodite, this trim 100' brig arose from the "sea-foam" dreams of her captain, Aent Kingma. Scion of a family of cargo and charter canal boat captains, Captain Kingma designed this unique 16-passenger vessel when the opportune time presented itself in 1995.

Crewed by Captain Kingma, a cook, first mate, and one or two of his own children, the *Aphrodite* is a popular addition to the tall ship fleet of northern Europe. Offering deluxe, informal cruises along the coasts of the North and Baltic seas, and also visiting the English and French coasts, the *Aphrodite* has participated in the major maritime festivals at Douarnenez, France; Rostock, Germany; Ebsjerg, Denmark; and of course, Amsterdam, The Netherlands.

With eight double cabins, the brig affords opportunities for "adventure sailing" in an intimate and collegial setting. Each cabin is equipped with bathroom facilities and showers. Guests on board can help with the sail lines or retire to cozy nooks on deck or below with a favorite book. Cruises are generally 5 to 7 days in duration, but often seem far too short for a true appreciation of this neat, comfortable sailing brig.

Flag:	The Netherlands
Rig:	Brig
Homeport/waters:	Stavoren, The Netherlands: European coastal waters.
Who sails?	Individuals of all ages, families, corporate groups.
Season:	March to November
Cost:	$200 per person per day, $2500 group rate (or charter) per day.
Program type:	Sail training and sea education for individuals, groups, families, and companies as informal programming. Sail training for adults as paying trainees. Passenger day sails and overnight passages.

Specifications:			
	Sparred length: 100'	Draft: 6' 4"	Sail area: 4,162 sq. ft.
	LOD: 77'	Beam: 21' 3"	Tons: 94 GRT
	LOA: 81'	Rig height: 74'	Power: Iveco 360 HP
	LWL: 70'	Freeboard: 7'	Hull: steel
	Hull color: white	Spar: steel/wood	

Designer:	J. M. de Vries/M. Bekebrede/A. Kingma
Built:	1994; Lemmer, The Netherlands
Certification:	Passenger vessel, Holland and Dutch shipping inspection.
Crew:	3-6. Trainees/passengers: 50 (day sails), 16 (overnight)
Contact:	Captain Aent Kingma, Owner
	Koeweg 3
	NL-8715 JW Stavoren, The Netherlands
	Tel: +31-514-68-1989; Fax: +31-514-68-1302
	E-mail: aentkingma@tref.nl
	Web site: http://www.maritime.org.nz/aphrodite

Appledore II

The *Appledore II* is a traditional gaff-rigged schooner designed for ocean sailing. Launched in 1978 at the Gamage Ship Yard in South Bristol, Maine, Bud McIntosh circumnavigated the world on her maiden voyage, an adventure documented in Herbert Smith's *Dreams of Natural Places and Sailing Three Oceans*. *Appledore II* makes day sails from her homeport of Camden, Maine from late June until mid-October. During the winter months, she undertakes snorkel trips on North America's only living coral reef, as well as sunset cruises from Key West, Florida. She carries up to 49 passengers on day sails and can accommodate up to 26 overnight.

The crew of the *Appledore II* is committed to sail training, and they are trained in sailing, celestial navigation, and marlinespike seamanship through operation of the vessel on day sails as well as two 2,000-mile offshore voyages yearly. Interested persons are encouraged to contact us for possible payroll or volunteer positions. We have opportunities for not only crew, but business positions on an entry level.

Flag:	USA
Rig:	Gaff topsail schooner.
Homeport/waters:	Camden, Maine: Maine to the Florida Keys
Season:	June to October (Maine); December to May (Florida)
Cost:	$20 per person per trip
Who sails?	School groups from elementary school through college, individuals and families.
Program type:	Sail training for crew and apprentices. Sea education based on informal, in-house programming. Passenger day sails. Dockside interpretation.

Specifications:	Sparred length: 86'	Draft: 10' 6"	Sail area: 2,815 sq. ft.
	LOA: 82'	Beam: 18' 9"	Tons: 63 GRT
	LOD: 65'	Rig height: 75'	Power: 210 HP diesel
	LWL: 53'	Freeboard: 8'	Hull: wood

Designer:	Bud McIntosh
Built:	1978; Gamage Shipyard, South Bristol, Maine, Herb Smith
Coast Guard certification:	Passenger Vessel (Subchapter T)
Crew:	7. Trainees/passengers: 49 (day), 26 (overnight)
Contact:	John P. McKean, President
	Schooner Exploration Associates, Ltd.
	"0" Lily Pond Drive
	Camden, ME 04843
	Tel: 207-236-8353, 800-233-PIER (summer)
	PO Box 4114, Key West, FL 33041-4114
	Tel: 305-296-9992 (winter)

The schooner *Appledore IV* is owned and operated by BaySail, a private, non-profit organization. Tall ship adventures aboard the *Appledore IV* help to support BaySail's mission: "To foster environmental stewardship of the Saginaw Bay watershed and the Great Lakes ecosystem and to provide personal development opportunities for learners of all ages through shipboard and land based educational experiences."

BaySail's environmental education program begins and ends in the classroom with materials designed to prepare students for their sailing experience and reinforce the lessons learned while on board the *Appledore IV*. During the three-and-a-half-hour excursion, trained volunteer teachers lead small groups of students through activities including collecting and analyzing water, sediment, and plankton samples. Land use, maritime history, navigation, and weather observation are also discussed.

BaySail is developing a sail training program, which is envisioned to be an intensive training experience on board the *Appledore IV*. It will be designed to teach at-risk youth about the importance of self-reliance, teamwork and respect for authority in an environment few have ever experienced. Communication skills and self-esteem will be enhanced as trainees work independently and as a team on every aspect of *Appledore IV* operations.

Appledore IV is available for private charter to companies, organizations, and other groups of up to 48 people and for public sails on weekends from May through September.

Flag:	USA
Rig:	Topsail schooner
Homeport/waters:	Bay City, Michigan: Saginaw Bay and Lake Huron
Who sails?	Elementary students through adults.
Season:	April to October
Cost:	$30 per adult, $15 per student (3-hour sail); $1000 group rate/private charter (3-hour sail)
Program type:	Marine science and ecology education in cooperation with accredited institutions. Sail training for volunteer and paying trainees. Affiliated with K-12 public schools, Saginaw Valley State University, Boys & Girls Clubs of Michigan.

Specifications:			
	Sparred length: 85'	Draft: 8' 6"	Sail area: 3,500 sq. ft.
	LOD: 65'	Beam: 18' 5"	Tons: 70 GRT
	LOA: 65'	Rig height: 76'	Power: 135 HP diesel
	LWL: 53'	Freeboard: 6'	Hull: steel

Designer:	Bud McIntosh
Built:	1989; Palm Coast, Florida, Treworgy Yachts
Coast Guard certification:	Passenger Vessel (Subchapter T)
Crew:	4. Trainees/passengers: 48 (day sails)
Contact:	Cynthia L. Smith, Executive Director, BaySail
	901 Saginaw Street, Bay City, MI 48708
	Tel: 989-893-1222; Fax: 989-893-7016
	E-Mail: clsmith@chartermi.net
	Web site: http:// www.tourbaycitymi.org

a replica of a 19th Century schooner and was designed and built by Captain Frank Fulchiero for the day passenger trade. She carries 49 passengers on the waters of Block Island and Long Island Sounds for 2 to 3 hour day sails, charters, and marine science/ coastal ecology programs. The Coastal Ecology Program utilizes various sampling and testing techniques to provide students with a better understanding of marine and coastal ecosystems. Volunteer and intern positions are available for this program which runs in Spring and Fall. Paid crew positions include: deckhand, 1st and 2nd mate, and licensed captain.

Voyager Cruises operates the *Argia* out of Mystic, Connecticut during the months of May through October. She is

Flag:	USA
Rig:	Gaff tops'l schooner
Homeport/waters:	Mystic, CT: Block Island and Long Island Sounds
Who sails?	Individuals and groups of all ages
Season:	May through October
Cost:	$36 per person per day, $2500 group rate (charter) per day
Program type:	Sail training for paying trainees. Sea education in marine science, maritime history, and ecology in cooperation with accredited institutions and other organized groups. Passenger day sails.

Specifications:			
	Sparred length: 81'	LOD: 56'	LOA: 56'
	LWL: 48'	Draft: 7' 6"	Beam: 20'
	Rig height: 75'	Freeboard: 5'	Sail area: 1,800 sq. ft.
	Tons: 20 GRT	Power: 100 HP diesel	

Designer:	Frank Fulchiero
Built:	1986; Reedville, Virginia, Jennings Boat Yard and Frank Fulchiero
Coast Guard certification:	Passenger Vessel (Subchapter T)
Crew:	5. Trainees/passengers: 49 (day sails), N/A (overnight)
Contact:	Amy Blumberg, owner/captain
	Voyager Cruises
	15 Holmes Street
	Mystic, CT 06355
	Tel: 860-536-0416; Fax: 860-536-0416
	E-mail: alblumberg@yahoo.com

Aries was built in 1962 to the highest possible standards by C.A. Crosby Co. in Osterville, Massachusetts. Materials include mahogany carvel planking from Honduras on Connecticut white oak frames with Sitka spruce masts and spars. Virtually everything else on board is teak, from the hand-carved ram figurehead tucked beneath the bowsprit to the raised eagle on the transom. Solid and comfortable with a large cockpit and berths for four, the classic cabin is a testimony to the fine yacht-builder's art. In addition to the schooner's four working sails, she hoists a flying jib, two jib-cut topsails and a powerful fisherman. With deadeyes and ratlines on both masts, fifty belaying pins on board, and a dozen gun ports (alas, no cannon), the *Aries* has the look and feel of a two-hundred year old privateer. Having seen only light day sailing duty in her early years, the *Aries* languished in a shed for more than fifteen years before being discovered by her present owner, re-powered,

and put back to sea. In addition to private excursions up and down the New England coast, the *Aries* is available for charter out of Plymouth and Duxbury harbors in Massachusetts, and is used for traditional sail training at the Duxbury Bay Maritime School.

Flag:	USA
Rig:	Schooner
Homeport/waters:	Duxbury, Massachusetts: New England
Who sails?	Groups and individuals of all ages.
Program type:	Sail training and sea education in cooperation with the Duxbury Bay Maritime School and other organized groups. Private charters. Dockside interpretation during port visits.

Specifications:	Sparred length: 45'	Draft: 4' 5"	Sail area: 900 sq. ft.
	LOD: 36'	Beam: 12'	Tons: 10 GRT
	LOA: 37'	Rig height: 45'	Power: 51 HP diesel
	LWL: 30'	Freeboard: 2'6"	Hull: wood
	Hull color: black w/white stripe	Spar material: wood	

Designer:	W. D. Knott, Barnstable, Massachusetts
Built:	1962; Osterville, Massachusetts, C. A. Crosby Co.
Crew:	3. Trainees/passengers: 6
Contact:	Andrew Olendzki, Owner
	C. Barnes Davis, Charter Captain
	152 James Street
	PO Box 192
	Barre, MA 01005
	Snug Harbor Station, Duxbury, MA 02331
	Tel: 978-355-2985 or 781-789-SAIL

Aurora

Aurora, formerly known as the *Francis Todd*, is a two-masted schooner built in 1947 by Newbert & Wallace of Thomaston, Maine, for work in the fishing industry. *Aurora* retired from fishery work in 1991. The vessel has been rebuilt to offer ample seating, a spacious deck plan, and amenability to charter arrangements. *Aurora* is the perfect venue for entertaining and special occasions. The vessel is inspected and certified by the US Coast Guard as a Passenger Vessel. She is stable, seaworthy, and professionally maintained for comfort and safety. *Aurora* is based in Newport, Rhode Island and sails New England waters, principally Narragansett Bay.

PHOTO BY ONNE VAN DER WAL

Flag:	USA
Rig:	Gaff topsail schooner
Homeport/waters:	Newport, Rhode Island: Narragansett Bay
Who sails?	School groups from elementary through college, as well as individuals, families, corporate, and social groups.
Program type:	Passenger day sails and informal sail training.

Specifications:			
	Sparred length: 101'	Draft: 8'	Sail area: 2,800 sq. ft.
	LOD: 80'	Beam: 17'6"	Tons: 53 GRT
	Rig height: 82'	Hull: wood	Hull color: black/green w/gold stripe

Designer:	Newbert & Wallace
Built:	1947; Newbert & Wallace, Thomaston, Maine
Crew:	3. Trainees/passengers: 75
Contact:	IDC Charters, Inc.
	Goat Island Marina
	Newport, RI 02840
	Tel: 401-849-6683
	Web Site: http://www.newportexperience.com

Built in 1924 for Newport, Rhode Island millionaire Marion Eppley, *Bagheera* represents a time when unlimited wealth and classical tastes combined to produce some of the finest vessels in the history of yachting and yacht racing. For many years, *Bagheera* was the boat to beat in campaigns from the Great Lakes to the Bahamas, and as far as Morocco and the Mediterranean. She twice won the prestigious Chicago-Mackinac Race, and was used for the training of naval cadets during the Second World War.

After the war *Bagheera* cruised extensively all over the world, eventually making her way to the West Coast.

Throughout the 1980's, *Bagheera* was a familiar sight along the San Diego waterfront, sailing for hire, and competing in many classic yacht races.

Now, after an extensive six-month restoration, *Bagheera* is in San Francisco Bay, certified by the US Coast Guard, and operated by an experienced, well trained crew. She can comfortably carry 30 passengers for day sails.

Flexible programs and schedules are available for group charters. *Bagheera* sails primarily from Richmond, in the East Bay.

Flag:	USA
Rig:	Staysail schooner
Homeport/waters:	San Francisco, California: San Francisco Bay, California
Who sails?	School groups from elementary school through college, individuals and families.
Program type:	Sail training for volunteer and paying trainees. Sea education based on informal, in-house programming. Passenger day sails.

Specifications:			
	Sparred length: 72'	Draft: 7' 6"	Tons: 21 GRT
	LOD: 54'	Beam: 14' 6"	Power: 72 HP diesel
	LOA: 55' 6"	Rig height: 65'	Hull: wood
	LWL: 44'	Freeboard: 4'	

Designer:	John G. Alden
Built:	1924; East Boothbay, Maine, Rice Brothers
Coast Guard certification:	Passenger Vessel (Subchapter T)
Crew:	2. Trainees/passengers: 25-30
Contact:	Captain Jonathan Friedberg and Becky Waegell
	Bagheera Charters, LLC
	7700 Eagle's Nest Road
	Sacramento, CA 95830
	Tel: 916-683-4915, 1-87-SCHOONER (toll-free)
	E-mail: bagheera@theship.com
	Web site: http://www.bagheera.theship.com

As a deepwaterman, *Balclutha* and a 26-man crew rounded Cape Horn with grain for Great Britain, and later ran Pacific Coast lumber to Australia. Each year as a salmon packet, the vessel carried hundreds of men (with boats and supplies) to the salmon-fishing grounds of Alaska. *Balclutha* even had a brief Hollywood career. The vessel was rescued from decay by the San Francisco Bay Area community in 1954, and has been restored as a memorial to the men and times of the grand days of sail.

Today, *Balclutha* (now designated a National Historic Landmark) is open to the public daily as part of the San Francisco Maritime National Historical Park. Park Service rangers conduct regular tours and present a variety of history programs aboard, and the vessel hosts special events such as the Park's annual Sea Music Concert Series, and maritime-related theater productions.

In 1886, Charles Connell & Company built a three-masted, riveted steel ship "to the highest class in Lloyd's registry" near Glasgow, Scotland. Her owner, Robert McMillan, named that 256-foot vessel *Balclutha*—the Gaelic name for Dumbarton, Scotland.

Flag:	USA
Rig:	Full-rigged ship
Homeport/waters:	San Francisco, California
Program type:	Dockside sea education in maritime history.

Specifications:	Sparred length: 301'	Draft: 22' 7"	Tons: 1,689 GRT
	LOD: 256' 6"	Beam: 38' 6"	Hull: steel
	Rig height: 145'		

Designer:	Charles Connell
Built:	1886; Scotland, Charles Connell
Contact:	William G. Thomas, Superintendent
	San Francisco Maritime National Historical Park
	Building E, Fort Mason Center
	San Francisco, CA 94123
	Tel: 415-561-7000; Fax: 415-556-1624
	Web site: http://www.nps.gov/safr/local/balc.html

The *Bat'kivshchyna* is a converted steel-hull Russian fishing supply boat which has been reinforced with ferro-cement. The design and conversion was accomplished by Dmytro Biryukovich, a civil engineer in Kyiv, Ukraine and an expert in ferro-cement applications.

Captain Biryukovich intends to circumnavigate the world promoting tourism and foreign business investments in his beloved Ukraine. During the TALL SHIPS CHALLENGE® in the summer of 2001, the *Bat'kivshchyna* partnered with the Children of Chernobyl Relief Fund in raising funds for, and awareness of, the medical and health needs of Ukrainian children affected by the radioactive fallout caused by the Chernobyl nuclear

power plant explosion in 1986. (This power plant was permanently closed on 15 December 2000.)

The *Bat'kivshchyna* has become an icon for a free Ukraine, which celebrated its 10th year of independence in 2001.

Flag:	Ukraine
Rig:	Gaff rigged schooner
Homeport/waters:	Kyiv, Ukraine: Dnipro River, Black Sea (summer)
Season:	April through October
Who sails?	Trainees of all ages.
Program type:	Sail training for volunteer and paying trainees. Sea education as informal in-house programming. Dockside interpretation at every opportunity.
Cost:	$100 per person per day, $1500 (day sails) group rate per day (20 max.)

Specifications:			
	Sparred length: 97'	Draft: 10'	LOD: 80'
	LOA: 87'	LWL: 68'	Beam: 17'
	Tons: 80 GRT	Rig height: 68'	Freeboard: 3'6"
	Hull: steel reinforced with ferrous cement		
	Power: 150 HP diesel	Hull color: black	

Designer:	Dmytro Biryukovich
Built:	1991; Kyiv, Ukraine, Dmytro Biryukovich
Crew:	3. Trainees: 20 (day sails), 10 (overnight)
Contact:	Roy Kellogg
	Discover Ukraine Expedition
	16D Heroes of Stalingrad
	Flat 57
	Kyiv 04210
	Ukraine
	Tel: +38 044-461-3194; Fax: +38 044-461-3194
	Web site: http://www.batkivshchyna.net

HMS Bee

Although incorporating modern technology, *HMS Bee* is a faithful reproduction of an early 19th century naval vessel. Her exterior and interior reflect the realities of a sailor's life of that time. The schooner *Bee* proudly sails from the Discovery Harbour Provincial Historic Site in Penetanguishene, Ontario, under an "Honorary Warrant" of the Royal Navy.

The *HMS Bee* is a replica of a Royal Navy transport schooner which operated on the Upper Great Lakes in the years immediately following the War of 1812. Commissioned by the Province of Ontario, the vessel was constructed in 1984 by provincial staff and volunteers on the naval site where the original schooner sailed.

The volunteers and staff of the Marine Heritage Association operate the vessel on beautiful Georgian Bay, June through September. Our rig is in the 19th century tradition, as is the dress and manor of the crew. During your visit to Ontario, join the officers and crew in the naval fashion of 1812.

Flag:	Canada
Rig:	Gaff schooner
Homeport/waters:	Penetanguishene, Ontario, Canada: Georgian Bay and upper Great Lakes
Season:	June to September
Program type:	Living history and seamanship. Sail training for paying trainees. Dockside interpretation during port visits.

Specifications:	Sparred length: 78'	Draft: 5' 6"	Sail area: 1,672 sq. ft.
	LOA: 48' 6"	Beam: 14' 6"	Tons: 25 GRT
	LWL: 42'	Hull: GRP and wood	Power: 90 HP diesel

Certification:	Operates under the Canadian Sail Training Association guidelines
Designer:	Steve Killing
Built:	1985; Penetanguishene, Ontario, Canada, Charlie Allen
Crew:	12 officers and leading hands.
Contact:	The Marine Heritage Association
	PO Box 353
	Midland, Ontario L4R 4L1 Canada
	Tel: 705-549-5575/800-MHA-5577; Fax: 705-549-5576
	E-mail: marineheritage@on.aibn.com
	Web site: http://www.marineheritage.ca

PHOTO BY BIL LINGARD

The Los Angeles Maritime Institute is the educational affiliate of the Los Angeles Maritime Museum. Through the Topsail Youth Program, the Institute provides character-building sail training adventures for youth. The schooners *Swift of Ipswich* and *Bill of Rights* are learning environments that nurture the development of knowledge, skills, and attitudes that are necessary for the education of today's youth, but difficult to teach in a traditional classroom.

The schooners sail with crews of mariner-educators who encourage the growth of awareness, understanding, communication, and teamwork, along with maturing of the traits of persistence, patience, endurance, courage, and caution.

Topsail can be adjusted to fit the age, interests, and abilities of any participants. Single-day events are for exploration, fun, and an introduction to the sea and sailing. Multi-day programs typically provide a life-changing experience for participants.

The Los Angeles Maritime Museum and all of its affiliates take pleasure in offering hospitality, on an as-available basis, to visiting tall ships and other "educationally significant" vessels.

Flag:	USA
Rig:	Gaff-rigged topsail schooner, two-masted
Homeport/waters:	Los Angeles, California: coastal California and offshore islands.
Who sails?	Referred youth-at-risk and groups catering to students and adults.
Season:	Year-round
Program type:	Educational

Specifications:			
	Sparred length: 136'	Draft: 10'	Sail area: 6,300 sq. ft.
	LOD: 94'	Beam: 23'	Tons: 95 GRT
	LOA: 129'	Rig height: 100'	Power: 210 HP diesel
	LWL: 85'	Freeboard: 5' 8"	Hull: wood

Designer:	McCurdy, Rhodes & Bates
Built:	1971; South Bristol, Maine, Harvey F. Gamage
Coast Guard certification:	Passenger Vessel (Subchapter T)
Crew:	5 (day); 8 (overnight); 5 instructors. Trainees: 52 (day sails); 39 (overnight)
Contact:	Captain Jim Gladson
	Los Angeles Maritime Institute
	Berth 84, Foot of Sixth Street
	San Pedro, CA 90731
	Tel: 310-833-6055; Fax: 310-548-2055

Black Jack

toric Ottawa River. Up to 30 youth, aged 12 to 16, participate in 11-day sail training programs which depart from Canada's capital city for the river and voyage to an 18-acre wilderness island camp. At the island, trainees live aboard traditional logging barges from where they set out to explore the river. In addition to sailing aboard *Black Jack*, trainees also sail 27-foot traditional Drascome luggers and share a variety of other camp activities.

Thomas G. Fuller was one of Canada's most decorated WW II naval war heroes, earning the name "Pirate of the Adriatic" and holding the distinction of the longest time served in offensive war action. His wartime experience taught him the value of installing confidence and resourcefulness in our youth, through adventure at sea. Bytown Brigantine Inc. was established in 1983 by the Fuller family as a charitable foundation to provide opportunities for young people to experience adventure in the time-honoured traditions inherent in square rigged sailing, aboard the family's donated brigantines *Black Jack* and *Fair Jeanne*.

Rebuilt in 1952 from the hull of a 1904 tugboat by the late Captain Thomas G. Fuller, *Black Jack* is an 87-foot brigantine, operated by Bytown Brigantine, Inc. Carrying 3,000 sq. ft. of sail, the ship is now used as a centrepiece for a sail training program operated on Canada's his-

Flag:	Canada			
Rig:	Brigantine			
Homeport/waters:	Ottawa, Ontario, Canada: Upper Ottawa River			
Who sails?	Middle school, high school and college students as well as individuals of student age			
Cost:	$65 Canadian per person per day			
Program type:	Sail training for paying trainees, overnight voyages, Tall Ship Adventure Camp			
Season:	May to October			
Specifications:	Sparred length: 90'	Draft: 6'	Sail area: 3,000 sq. ft.	
	LOD: 68'	Beam: 15'	Tons: 42.25 GRT	
	LOA: 87'	Rig height: 72'	Power: 235 HP diesel	
	LWL: 57'	Freeboard: 3'	Hull: steel	
Built:	1904; Scotland			
Coast Guard certification:	Passenger Vessel (Subchapter T)			
Crew:	6.			
Contact:	Simon A. F. Fuller, President			
	or Robbin Zrudlo, Foundation Manager			
	Bytown Brigantine, Inc.			
	2700 Queensview Drive			
	Ottawa, Ontario K2B 8H6, Canada			
	Tel: 613-596-6258; Fax: 613-596-5947			
	E-mail: tallshipinfo@tallshipsadventure.org			
	Web site: http://tallshipsadventure.org			

SAIL TALL SHIPS!

Built in 1938 by Lincoln Vaughan for his own use, *Black Pearl* was purchased by Barclay H. Warburton III in 1958. Long a believer in the sea as a teacher, Warburton selected the rig as a good one for sail training. In 1972 Warburton sailed the *Black Pearl* to England to participate in that summer's European tall ships race, becoming the first American to do so. On his return to Newport, Warburton founded the American Sail Training Association.

Black Pearl is currently owned and operated by the Aquaculture Foundation, a nonprofit trust formed to promote quality education in marine studies. Her programs take her throughout Long Island Sound, as well as into the North Atlantic, Gulf of Mexico, and Caribbean. At present, the Foundation is engaged in a capital campaign to raise $1.25 million for *Black Pearl's* complete renovation.

Flag:	USA
Rig:	Brigantine
Homeport/waters:	Bridgeport, Connecticut: Atlantic Ocean and Caribbean Sea
Who sails?	School and other groups and individuals aged 16 to 65. Affiliated groups include University of Bridgeport, Housatonic Community College, and seven Connecticut school districts.
Season:	May to October
Program type:	Sail training for crew and paying trainees. Sea education in marine science, maritime history, and ecology in cooperation with accredited schools and colleges. Passenger day sails and overnight voyages.

Specifications:	Sparred length: 79'	Draft: 9'	Sail area: 2,000 sq. ft.
	LOD: 52'	Beam: 14'	Tons: 28 GRT
	LWL: 43'	Rig height: 63'	Sail number: TS US-33
	Freeboard: 6'	Power: diesel	

Designer:	Edson Schock
Built:	1938; Wickford, Rhode Island, C. Lincoln Vaughan
Crew:	3-4 (day), 4-8 (overnight). Trainees: 6
Contact:	Edwin T. Merritt, Executive Director
	The Aquaculture Foundation
	525 Antelope Trail
	Shelton, CT 06484
	Tel: 203-372-4406; Fax: 203-372-4407
	E-mail: tmerritt@pcnet.com
	Web site: http://www.tallshipblackpearl.org

Bluenose II

for the International Fishermen's Trophy series of races between Canada and the US, *Bluenose* was undefeated under her legendary Master, Captain Angus J. Walters of Lunenburg. Her likeness became a national emblem and it is depicted on stamps and the ten-cent coin of Canada. Launched on July 24, 1963, *Bluenose II* was built from the same plans at the same yard and by some of the same men. The only difference lies in the accommodations for the co-ed crew of 18 and the modern navigation and communication instruments. She serves as a goodwill ambassador for the Province of Nova Scotia, participating in tall ship events throughout the Western Hemisphere.

The original *Bluenose*, launched on March 26, 1921, was a typical Nova Scotian Grand Banks fishing schooner. Built at Lunenburg both for fishing and

Bluenose II's 12 deckhands receive instructions from the officers in all manners of seamanship. Today she sails in the best *Bluenose* tradition, and all officers and deckhands are encouraged to enhance their skills and certifications.

Flag:	Canada
Rig:	Gaff topsail schooner
Homeport/waters:	Lunenburg, Nova Scotia, Canada: East Coast of Canada and the US.
Who sails?	Individuals and groups. Affiliated institutions include the Fisheries Museum of the Atlantic, Lunenburg; the Maritime Museum of the Atlantic, Halifax; Nova Scotia Nautical Institute, Port Hawkesbury; and the Canadian Navy, Halifax.
Season:	April to November
Cost:	Adults, $20, children under 12, $10 (per two-hour sail).
Program type:	Sail training for crew. Passenger day sails. Dockside interpretation.

Specifications:

Sparred length: 181'	Draft: 16'	Sail area: 11,139 sq. ft.
LOD: 143'	Beam: 27'	Tons: 285 GRT
LWL: 112'	Rig height: 132'	Power: twin 250
Hull: wood		HP diesels

Designer:	William J. Roué, Halifax, Nova Scotia, Canada
Built:	1963; Lunenburg, Nova Scotia, Canada, Smith & Rhuland Shipyards
Certification:	Canadian Coast Guard certified
Crew:	18
Contact:	Senator Wilfred P. Moore, Chairman
	Bluenose II Preservation Trust
	PO Box 1963, 121 Bluenose Drive
	Lunenburg, Nova Scotia B0J 2C0, Canada
	Tel: 902-634-1963; Fax: 902-634-1995
	E-mail: ship@bluenose2.ns.ca
	Web site: http://www.bluenose2.ns.ca

Bonnie Lynn is one of the most unique of the Maine Windjammer fleet. She is a modified version of designer Merrit Walter's Trade Rover, the hull being built by Treworgy Yachts and then the interior and rigging completed in Maine. Being a serious offshore cruising vessel, she is built to very high standards. The steel hull is 57' on deck, with an overall length of 72'. She was completed in July of 1998 and has been actively chartering since then.

Bonnie Lynn charters from the Virgin Islands through the Grenadines in the winters, and returns to her homeport of Islesboro, Maine in the summers, where she charters from New England to Nova Scotia. She is Coast Guard certified for 38 passengers for day sail and 10 for ocean. Extraordinary means have been taken to make this a most comfortable and seaworthy vessel. Although she has a very traditional look, passengers rest in the serenity and luxury of modern day technology and amenities. Her charters range from day sails and term charters to offshore cruising. Future plans include a circumnavigation with guests.

Flag:	US
Rig:	Schooner
Homeport/waters:	Islesboro, Maine: New England (summer), Caribbean (winter).
Who sails?	Families and groups.
Program type:	Sail training for volunteer crew and for volunteer and paying trainees. Dockside interpretation during port visits.

Specifications:			
	Sparred length: 72'	Draft: 7'	Sail area: 2,500 sq. ft.
	LOD: 57'	Beam: 15'3"	Tons: 32 GRT
	LWL: 49'	LOA: 57'	Rig height: 63'
	Power: 220 HP diesel	Hull: steel	Hull color: black

Designer:	Merrit Walter
Built:	1997; Palm Coast, Florida, Islesboro, Maine; Treworgy
Certification:	Passenger Vessel (Subchapter T)
Crew:	3. Passengers, trainees: 38 (day sails); 10 (ocean)
Contact:	Captains Bonnie and Earl MacKenzie
	PO Box 41
	Islesboro, ME 04848
	Tel: 401-862-1115 (summer)
	E-mail: mack@midcoast.com
	Web site: http://www.bonnielynn.com

Bounty

Built in 1960 in Lunenburg, Nova Scotia for the movie "Mutiny on the Bounty," by MGM Studios, this ship has starred in many other film productions such as "Treasure Island," and "Yellowbeard," along with numerous documentaries. *Bounty* has successfully operated as a sail training vessel for many years. Due to her commitment to sail training and preserving the art of square rigged sailing, the US Navy selected the *Bounty* to help prepare and teach the officers and crew to sail the USS CONSTITUTION for the first time in more than 100 years.

Now owned and operated by the HMS Bounty Organization, LLC, the ship will make its homeport in Greenport, Long Island and will continue the tradition of teaching 18th century seamanship skills through sail training voyages, sailing the East Coast of the US and Canada. Since acquiring the *Bounty* in February of 2001, the organization has spent 10 months restoring the ship so that she may sail once again. The restoration involved replacing 2500 linear feet of frames and over 5000 linear feet of planking from the keel up, along with new plumbing, electricity, and galley. This ship will be a work in progress for the next few years. The HMS Bounty Organization, LLC is very grateful to have the opportunity to preserve such an historic vessel for future generations.

The *Bounty* will be available for sail training, festival appearances, corporate entertaining, film appearances, and private charters.

Flag:	USA
Rig:	Full-rigged ship, three-masted
Homeport/waters:	Greenport, Long Island, New York; North East US and Canada (summer), Caribbean (winter)
Who sails?	Students, individuals, and groups of all ages. Daily, 3-day, 4-day, and weekly passages available.
Season:	Year-round
Program type:	Sail training for paying trainees. Sea education in maritime history and ecology in cooperation with organized groups and as informal, in-house programming. Dockside interpretaion during port visits.

Specifications:			
Sparred length: 169'	Draft: 13'	Sail area: 10,000 sq. ft.
LOD: 120'	Beam: 30'	Tons: 412 GRT
LOA: 130'	Rig height: 115'	Hull: wood
Power: 535 HP diesel, electric drives		

Designer:	The British Admiralty
Built:	1960; Lunenburg, Nova Scotia, Smith & Rhuland
Coast Guard certification:	Attraction Vessel; working towards Passenger Vessel certification (Subchapter T)
Crew:	18. Trainees/passengers: 12, (149 with Subchapter T certification)
Contact:	Margaret Ramsey, Director of Seaside Operations
	HMS Bounty Organization, LLC
	PO Box 141, Oakdale, NY 11769
	Tel: 631-588-7900 or 866-HMS-BOUNTY (866-467-2686) ; Fax: 631-471-4609
	E-mail: mramsey@tallshipbounty.org
	Web site: http://www.tallshipbounty.org

The schooner *Bowdoin* is the flag-ship of Maine Maritime Academy's sail training fleet, and the official sailing vessel of the state of Maine. Built in 1921 specifically for cruising in Arctic waters, she is one of the strongest wooden vessels ever constructed. Between 1921 and 1954 she made 26 voyages to the far north under the command of her first master, explorer Donald B. MacMillan.

Today, with the characteristic ice barrel on her foremast, *Bowdoin* serves the students of the Maine Maritime Academy and the educational community of New England with a broad range of programs in seamanship, ocean studies, and curriculum development. Offerings begin at the high school level, and range from cruises on Penobscot Bay to extended passages to

Greenland and Labrador. These semi-annual cruises represent a unique opportunity in the world of sail training.

Bowdoin

Flag:	USA
Rig:	Schooner
Homeport/waters:	Castine, Maine: Gulf of Maine, Canadian Maritimes
Who sails?	School groups from high school through college as well as individuals of all ages. Affiliated institutions include the Maine Maritime Academy.
Season:	May to October
Cost:	$1,500 group rate per day (charter)
Program type:	Sail training for professional crew and paying trainees. Fully accredited sea education in marine science, maritime history, and ecology as well as informal, in-house programming. Passenger overnight passages. Limited dockside interpretation during port visits.

Specifications:			
	Sparred length: 100'	Draft: 10'	Sail area: 2,900 sq. ft.
	LOD: 83'	Beam: 20'	Tons: 66 GRT
	LOA: 88'	Rig height: 70'	Power: 190 HP diesel
	LWL: 72'	Freeboard: 4'	Hull: wood

Designer:	William Hand
Built:	1921; East Boothbay, Maine, Hodgdon Brothers Shipyard
Coast Guard certification:	Sailing School Vessel (Subchapter R), Passenger Vessel (Subchapter T)
Crew:	6. Trainees: 40 (day sails), 11 (overnight)
Contact:	Linda Strathdee, Continuing Education Coordinator Maine Maritime Academy Castine, ME 04420 Tel: 207-326-2211; Fax: 207-326-2218 E-mail: continuinged@mma.edu Web site: http://www.mainemaritime.edu

Brandaris

Brandaris, the 63-foot Dutch-design sailing vessel was launched in 1938 as the private yacht of William De Vries Lentsch, Jr., shipyard owner and famous Dutch designer. After a colorful escape from German occupation in WW II, *Brandaris* participated in the evacuation of Dunkirk. Now berthed in Wickford, RI, she is available for public excursions, sailing charters, and special occasion functions from weddings to funerals.

Brandaris also offers a Classroom Afloat program featuring educational field trips and curriculum based experiential learning programs. Many of these programs have received sponsorship from corporate and grant-based underwriters at no charge to schools.

Flag:	USA
Rig:	Cutter/Sloop
Homeport/waters:	Wickford, Rhode Island: Narragansett Bay, Rhode Island
Who sails?	School groups from elementary school through college, individuals, families, charter groups.
Season:	Year-round
Program type:	Sail training for volunteer and paying trainees. Sea education in marine science, maritime history and ecology in cooperation with organized groups. Passenger day sails and overnight voyages, dockside interpretation during port visits.

Specifications:			
	Sparred length: 63'	Draft: 2'6"	Sail area: 1,317 sq. ft.
	LOD: 55'	Beam: 18'	Tons: 60 GRT
	LOA: 58'	Rig height: 59'	Power: 135 HP Ford
	LWL: 53'	Freeboard: 4'6"	Hull: riveted iron
	Spar: spruce	Hull color: white	

Designer:	William De Vries Lentsch, Jr.
Built:	1938; Amsterdam Shipyard, Amsterdam, The Netherlands
Coast Guard certification:	Passenger vessel (Subchapter T), Inland, Near Coastal
Crew:	2. Trainees: 32 (day sails)
Contact:	Captain Douglas Somers, Owner
	Brandaris Sailing Charters/Friends of Brandaris
	7 Main Street
	Wickford, RI 02852
	Tel: 401-294-1481; Fax: 401-294-1938
	E-mail: brandaris@earthlink.net

Winner of the Tall Ships 2000® transatlantic race from Halifax to Amsterdam and captained by ASTA's 2000 "Sail Trainer of the Year," George Moffett, *Brilliant* is the traveling ambassador of Mystic Seaport, our nation's leading maritime museum. In service for more than 45 years - the oldest sail-education program in the nation - *Brilliant* has introduced more than 8,000 people to the lessons a sailing ship naturally teaches. Board this classic schooner and become the crew; steer, handle sails, cook and clean as you learn the venerable maritime tradition of "for the good of the ship." *Brilliant* has two other ASTA awards to her credit: "First in Class" in the 2000 Boston to Halifax race and "Sail Training Vessel of the Year" in 1996. She also won the 1997 Nantucket Lighthouse Opera Cup.

Her typical season includes spring, summer and fall sailing in southern New England waters (between Long Island and Nantucket) with overnight stops that may include Shelter Island, Newport, Block Island and Martha's Vineyard. Trainees (ages 15-19) sail six to ten day programs, July - August. Adults (20+) sail May, September and October with four-day weekends (Friday morning - Monday afternoon).

Flag:	USA
Rig:	Gaff schooner, two-masted
Homeport/waters:	Mystic, Connecticut: New England, Nova Scotia, Chesapeake Bay.
Who sails?	Teens ages 15-19 and Adults 20+. Participants must be physically fit, agile, and competent swimmers. Affiliated institution is Mystic Seaport.
Season:	May to October.
Cost:	Teens $790, Sunday - Friday. Adults $650-750 Friday - Monday. Financial assistance is available
Program type:	Sail training with paying trainees. Sea education in cooperation with organized groups such as Scouts, based on informal, in-house programming.

Specifications:	Sparred length: 74'	Draft: 9'	Tons: 30 GRT
	LOD: 61' 6"	Beam: 14' 8'	Power: 97 HP diesel
	LOA: 61' 6"	Rig height: 81'	Hull: wood
	LWL: 49'		

Designer:	Sparkman & Stephens
Built:	1932; City Island, New York, Henry B. Nevins
Coast Guard certification:	Sailing School Vessel (Subchapter R), Passenger Vessel (Subchapter T)
Crew:	3 (day sails), 4 (overnight). Trainees/passengers: 9-10 (day sails), 6 (overnight)
Contact:	Brilliant Program, Museum Education Division
	Mystic Seaport
	PO Box 6000
	Mystic, CT 06355-0990
	Tel: 860-572-5323; Fax: 860-572-5355
	Web site: http://www.mysticseaport.org/brilliant

C.A. Thayer

wood mill in Grays Harbor, Washington, to San Francisco, but she also carried lumber as far south as Mexico, and even ventured offshore to Hawaii and Fiji. Later, the vessel supplied the Alaskan salt-salmon canneries, anchoring out during the summer, then returning in September with the season's catch packed in her hold. From 1925-1950, *C.A. Thayer* carried men north to the Bering Sea cod-fishing grounds. In fact, *C.A. Thayer's* last voyage in that trade marked the end of commercial sail on the West Coast. Purchased by the State of California in 1957, and transferred to the National Park Service in 1977, this National Historic Landmark is a rare survivor from the days when strong canvas sails billowed over tall deckloads of freshly-milled fir and redwood.

Once, hundreds of sailing schooners carried lumber to San Francisco from Washington, Oregon, and the California Redwood Coast. Built in 1895, *C.A. Thayer* was part of that mighty Pacific Coast fleet. *C.A. Thayer* usually sailed from the E.K.

Today, the vessel hosts a slate of unique school education programs presented by the San Francisco Maritime National Park Association, and is open to the public as part of the San Francisco Maritime National Historical Park.

Flag:	USA
Rig:	Schooner, three-masted
Homeport/waters:	San Francisco, California
Program type:	Dockside sea education programs in maritime history.
Specifications:	Sparred length: 219' Draft: 11' 3" Tons: 453 GRT
	LOD: 156' Beam: 36' Hull: wood
	Rig height: 105'
Designer:	Hans Bendixsen
Built:	1895; Fairhaven, California, Hans Bendixsen
Contact:	William G. Thomas, Superintendent
	San Francisco Maritime National Historical Park
	Building E, Fort Mason Center
	San Francisco, CA 94123
	Tel: 415-561-7000; Fax: 415-556-1624
	Web site: http://www.nps.gov/safr/local/thayer.html

Captain Lance Holmquist is the owner/operator of Calypso Watersports and Charters. He grew up in California, owned a dive business in Australia before he moved to the Florida Keys and sailed the Caribbean Sea for over a decade. Let him introduce you to the magic of sailing and tropical reefs, watch him prepare the catch of the day and join in at "tribal art" jam sessions. His great personality together with his knowledge and passion for boats, the sea and life in the tropics will guarantee your cruise to become a great experience!

S/V *Calypso Explorer* is a 105-foot gaff rigged schooner. Built in Bath, Maine, she is designed following the lines and layout of a traditional 18th century coastal trader. With accommodations for a total of 28 people in 8 staterooms in a spacious interior your group will step back in time as you hoist the sails for another adventure. Like aboard

all our vessels you will become part of the crew as you pilot this classic through the tropical waters of the Florida Keys. Her experienced crew will introduce you the secrets of sailing and navigating as well as to life on the islands and under the ocean surface.

Flag:	USA
Rig:	Gaff topsail schooner, two masted
Homeport/waters:	Key Largo, Florida: Florida Keys
Who sails?	Groups and individuals of all ages
Program type:	Sail training for paying trainees, sea education in cooperation with organized groups. Passenger day sails and overnight passages.

Specifications:			
	Sparred length:105'	LOD:65'	LWL:60'
	Draft:7'6"	Beam:21'	Rig height:75'
	Freeboard:6'	Sail area:3,000 sq. ft.	Tons:73 GRT
	Power:136 HP diesel	Hull:ferro/steel	

Designer:	M. D. Lee
Built:	1975; Bath, Maine, Long Beach Shipyard
Coast Guard certification:	Passenger Vessel (Subchapter T)
Crew:	3. Trainees/passengers: 49 (day sails), 28 (overnight)
Contact:	Lance Holmquist
	Calypso Watersports and Charters
	PO Box 2037
	Key Largo, Fl 33037
	Tel: 305-451-1988; Mobile: 305-451-1988
	E-mail: altmeier@terranova.net
	Web site: http://www.calypsosailing.com

Calypso Gypsy

S/V *Calypso Gypsy* is an 80-foot sailing yacht designed and built for charter, the combination of classic lines and reliable technology makes her a remarkable vessel. Four spacious staterooms forward and separate crew quarters aft can carry private parties or large groups up to 20 guests in equal comfort. The professional crew will enable you enjoy a relaxing cruise or you may try a real hands on sailing experience. As the flagship of the Boy Scouts of America High Seas Adventure Program in the Florida Keys she sails the warm clear waters of the Caribbean and the Gulf of Mexico.

Flag:	USA
Rig:	Staysail ketch
Homeport/waters:	Key Largo, Florida: Florida Keys, Caribbean, Gulf of Mexico
Who sails?	Groups and individuals of all ages. Sea Scouts.
Program type:	Sail training for paying trainees, sea education in cooperation with organized groups. Passenger day sails and overnight passages.

Specifications:

Sparred length: 78'	LOD: 65'	LOA: 60'
LWL: 58'	Draft: 7'2"	Beam: 18'
Rig height: 70'	Freeboard: 8'	Sail area: 2,400 sq. ft.
Tons: 60 GRT	Power: 6 cyl GM diesel	Hull: composit fiberglass

Built:	1968
Coast Guard certification:	Passenger Vessel (Subchapter T)
Crew:	3. Trainees/passengers: 45 (day sails), 20 (overnight)
Contact:	Lance Holmquist

Calypso Watersports and Charters
PO Box 2037
Key Largo, Fl 33037
Tel: 305-451-1988; Mobile: 305-451-1988
E-mail: altmeier@terranova.net
Web site: http://www.calypsosailing.com

S/V *Calypso Poet* is a 44-foot center cockpit cutter yacht built by CSY. Rebuild in 1994, she is a yacht you can take "to the end of the world" or just to lovely beach in the islands. She is on charter for Calypso Watersports in the Bahamas, Caribbean Islands and South Florida. The *Calypso Poet* is able to accommodate up to six guests plus crew. Due to her easy handling under sail & power, she will make your sailing vacation an unforgettable experience. Relax under white sails and watch her cut gently through the ocean to a distant shore.

Flag:	USA
Rig:	Cutter
Homeport/waters:	Key Largo, Florida: Bahamas, Caribbean Islands, South Florida
Who sails?	Groups and individuals of all ages.
Program type:	Private charters

Specifications:	Sparred length: 46'	LOD: 42'	LOA: 44'
	LWL: 40'	Draft: 5'2"	Beam: 13'
	Rig height: 52'	Freeboard: 5'	Sail area: 1,250 sq. ft.
	Tons: 15 GRT	Power: 85 HP diesel	

Built:	1994
Coast Guard certification:	six pack (Uninspected Vessel)
Crew:	3. Trainees/passengers: 6
Contact:	Lance Holmquist
	Calypso Watersports and Charters
	PO Box 2037
	Key Largo, Fl 33037
	Tel: 305-451-1988; Mobile: 305-451-1988
	E-mail: altmeier@terranova.net
	Web site: http://www.calypsosailing.com

Canadian Expedition Project-Hawk

Canadian Sailing Expedition's newest vessel, *Hawk*, was originally named the Lord St. Vincent and launched from the Cooks and Welton Shipyard in Beverly, United Kingdom. She was an Icelandic Beam Trawler and fished until the late 1970's. In the early 1990's, she was refitted to a Stand-by vessel, as part of the Saint-class fleet, and used in the North Sea petroleum industry as the re-named St.

Anne. She was in service until November 2000. Purchased by Canadian Sailing Expeditions in May 2001, she was delivered from Scotland to Nova Scotia via the Azores.

Hawk will be refitted to a Barquentine. She will have 28 ensuite cabins, capable of carrying 56 passengers on extended coastal expeditions. The ship will be re-named upon the completion of her refit.

During the summer months, the ship will cruise throughout the Atlantic Canadian region on multi-day expeditions. Passengers will be introduced to communities along the coast via the traditional sea route. At all times possible, the vessel will be under sail. During the winter, the ship will sail throughout the Caribbean.

Canadian Sailing Expeditions is dedicated to providing opportunities for people of all ages to explore our sea-coast in the traditional way.

Flag:	Canada
Rig:	Barquentine
Homeport/waters:	Halifax, Nova Scotia, Canada: North American waters and the Caribbean
Who sails:	Groups and individuals of all ages
Season:	Year-round
Program type:	Sail training for paying trainees, private charters, day sails and overnight passages
Specifications:	Sparred length: 220' LOD: 165' LOA: 175'
	LWL: 150' Draft: 13' Beam: 30'
	Freeboard: 7' Tons: 622 GRT Power: Cat 3508
Built:	1962; Beverly, United Kingdom, Cooks and Welton Shipyard
Certification:	Transport Canada
Trainees/ passengers:	56 (day sails), 56 (overnight)
Contact:	Captain Doug Prothero, Owner/operator
	Canadian Sailing Expeditions
	PO Box 2613
	Halifax, NS B3J 3N5 Canada
	Tel: 902-429-1474; Fax: 902-429-1475
	E-mail: doug@canadiansailingexpeditions.com
	Web site:http://www.canadiansailingexpeditions.com

Cape Rose, the ex-*Danielle Louise*, was restored to her original launch name in the spring of 2001. She sailed the entire eastern seaboard in the year 2000, from historic Key West to the scenic ports of Downeast Maine, participating in maritime festivals and nautical events along the way. She is seaworthy, comfortable, and a good boat on all points of sail.

Hull construction is of multi-chine steel with the topside radiused in sections, giving the appearance of a round bilge boat when on the water. Below the waterline, she was given a modern underbody, for good performance and maneuverability. The combination of traditional gaff rig, her modern underbody; and her spacious deck area give her performance, helm response and comfort, which surprises most who sail on her.

This rugged schooner is a perfect platform for sail training programs. Wellness and personal growth are the focus of professionally-facilitated workshops. The training fosters team-building, cooperation, self-sufficiency, and leadership. Awareness and appreciation for the shipboard and marine environments are emphasized. Programs are customized to meet the specific needs of the participants.

Flag:	USA
Rig:	Main topsail gaff rigged schooner
Homeport/waters:	Wickford, Rhode Island: East Coast US
Who sails:	Individuals and groups of all ages
Program type:	Sail training for volunteer and paying trainees. Sea education in cooperation with accredited institutions and other organized groups. Dockside tours, receptions, and interpretation during port visits. Participation in festivals and special events.
Season:	Year-round

Specifications:

Sparred length: 72'	LOD: 50' 2"	LWL: 39' 3"
LOA: 52'	Draft: 6' 5"	Beam: 15' 9"
Tons: 32 GRT	Rig height: 56' 1"	Sail area: 1,733 sq. ft.
Freeboard: 4'	Power: 212 HP diesel	Hull: steel
Hull color: green	Spar material: aluminum	

Designer:	Dudley Dix
Built:	1987; South Africa, Brian Alcock
Crew:	3. Trainees/passengers: 6
Contact:	Diane Luchild, President
	Sail into Wellness
	36 Kennedy Blvd.
	Lincoln, RI 02865-3602
	Tel: 401-419-6155; Fax: 760-588-3160
	E-mail: Diane@SailintoWellness.com
	Web site: http://www.SailintoWellness.com

Carlyn

Yawls, schooners, ketches, and sloops have been a big part of our tradition since Camp Four Winds* Westward Ho was founded in 1927. In 1996 the Camp commissioned the yawl *Carlyn*. During summer months *Carlyn* takes campers, aged 9-16, for daysails and overnights, teaching basic shipboard skills such as line handling, navigation, sailing, cooking, and cleaning. We sail in Washington's San Juan Islands and the Canadian Gulf Islands. In the Spring and Fall, Salish Sea Expeditions charters *Carlyn*, offering 1-5 day marine science programs for 5th-12th grade classes in Puget Sound. Crew opportunities are available in all three seasons. See the ASTA Billet Bank for details.

Flag:	USA
Rig:	Yawl
Homeport/waters:	Orcas Island, Washington; Inland waters, Washington and British Columbia
Who sails?	5th-12th graders, spring and fall; 9-16 year olds in the summer.
Program type:	Marine Science spring and fall; sail training in summer.

Specifications:

Sparred length: 65'	LOD: 61'	LWL: 57'
Draft: 8'	Beam: 14'	Rig Height: 64'
Sail Area: 1,490 sq.ft	Tons: 28 GRT	Power: 71 HP diesel
Hull: Strip Planked and Fiberglass.		

Designer:	Scarano Brothers, Albany, NY. 1996
Built:	Scarano Brothers, Albany, NY. 1996
Coast Guard certification:	Passenger Vessel (Subchapter T)
Crew:	4. Trainees/passengers: 34 (day sails); 13 (overnight)
Contact:	Adam Kaplan, Director
	Camp Four Winds*Westward Ho
	PO Box 140
	Deer Harbor, WA 98243
	E-mail: info@fourwindscamp.org
	Web site: http://www.fourwindscamp.org
	Tel: 360-376-2277; Fax: 360-376-5741

Challenge is a 96-foot three-masted staysail schooner. She has a strong modern rig making her a swift sailer and good windward performer. In the spring, summer, and fall *Challenge* carries out a busy schedule of port visitation, private charters, corporate team building, and day-sail educational programs for elementary through high school students. Great Lakes port visits include waterfront sail-pasts and interactive dockside activities. Private charters are fully catered parties under sail, with music, dancing and a licensed bar. Teambuilding events are custom designed intensive management training programs, often offered in cooperation with one of our management-consulting partners. The educational program, "A Sail Through Time", has a hands-on, interactive curriculum

emphasizing regional history, social science, and ecology. Since its inception in 1991 the 1-1/2 hour "A Sail Through Time" program has hosted over 55,000 students from both Canada and the United States. *Challenge* begins her season in May and can be seen sailing the waters of Toronto Bay and Lake Ontario through early fall.

Flag:	Canada
Rig:	Staysail schooner, three-masted
Homeport/waters:	Toronto, Ontario, Canada: Lake Ontario
Who sails?	Individuals and groups of all ages. Challenge operates a day sail training program in conjunction with The Pier – Toronto's Waterfront Museum.
Season:	April to October.
Program type:	Day sail training program. Vessel also conducts corporate charter and public day sails.

Specifications:	Sparred length: 96'	Draft: 8'	Sail area: 3,500 sq. ft.
	LOD: 86'	Beam: 16' 6"	Tons: 76 GRT
	Rig height: 96'	Hull: steel	Power: Volvo 160
	Freeboard: 5'		

Designer:	Bob Johnston
Built:	1984; Port Stanley, Ontario, Kanter Yachts
Certification:	Transport Canada Certified Passenger Vessel
Crew:	6 professional paid crew. Trainees: 70 (day sails)
Contact:	Roger Nugent, President
	Great Lakes Schooner Company
	249 Queen's Quay West, Suite 111
	Toronto, Ontario M5J 2N5, Canada
	Tel: 416-260-6355; Fax: 416-260-6377
	E-mail: roger@greatlakesschooner.com
	Web site: http://www.greatlakesschooner.com

Christeen

years, *Christeen* served not only as an oyster dredge but also as a cargo carrier and live aboard between Connecticut, New York and New Jersey. After surviving 16 major hurricanes, numerous nor'easters, two sinkings and severe neglect, *Christeen* was returned home to Oyster Bay in 1992 and completely restored in 1999.

The *Christeen* is the oldest remaining oyster sloop in North America and a National Historic Landmark. She was originally built in 1883 for Captain William Smith in Glenwood Landing, New York to harvest oysters in nearby Oyster Bay and Cold Spring Harbors. Over her 118

Christeen's new mission is to serve as a floating classroom. Her Coast Guard Certified Captains and experienced crew will instruct passengers about maritime history, marine science, coastal ecology and aquaculture. The *Christeen* is available for education, member and public sails, special events, and corporate charters.

Flag:	USA
Rig:	Gaff Rig Sloop
Homeport/waters:	Oyster Bay, NY: Long Island Sound
Who sails?	Students of all ages, individuals, families, groups
Season:	April – October
Cost:	Shipboard Marine Science 2 1/2-hour program - $550 Private Charters - $600 for 3-hour sail, call for group rates
Program Type:	Marine science, maritime history, marine trades (i.e. commercial fishing, oystering)

Specifications:			
	Sparred length: 60'	LOD: 40'	LOA: 52'
	LWL: 35 '6"	Draft: 3'	Beam: 15'2"
	Rig Height: 50'	Freeboard: 18"	Sail Area: 960 sq. ft.
	Tons: 11 GRT	Power: 63 HP diesel	Hull: wood

Designer:	Traditional
Built:	1883; Glenwood Landing, NY
Restored:	January 1998 - October 1999; Jakobson Shipyard, Oyster Bay, NY
Coast Guard certification:	Passenger Vessel (Subchapter T)
Crew:	3. Trainees/passengers: 20 adults, 25 adults/children
Contact:	Clint Smith, President
	Christeen Oyster Sloop Preservation Corporation, Inc.
	P.O. Box 146, West End Avenue
	Oyster Bay, NY 11771
	Tel: 516-922-1098; Fax: 516-922-3970
	E-mail: christeen@thewaterfrontcenter.org
	Web site: http://www.thewaterfrontcenter.org

Clearwater

The *Clearwater* is the only full-sized replica of the 18th and 19th-century merchant vessels known as Hudson River sloops. Since 1969, *Clearwater* has served both as a platform for hands-on environmental education and as a symbol for grassroots action. The sloop is owned and operated by Hudson River Sloop Clearwater, Inc., a nonprofit membership organization dedicated to defending and restoring the Hudson River and related waterways.

The sloop sails seven days a week, carrying as many as 50 passengers for three to five-hour education programs. Adults and children take part in a wide range of activities involving water life, water chemistry, sail raising, steering, piloting, and more. A US Coast Guard-licensed captain is in charge, and an education specialist directs the program. The permanent crew are complemented by apprentices

aged 16 and older, an education assistant, and volunteers. During a month on board, apprentices are given in-depth training in many aspects of sailing and maintaining a wooden ship and in the education program.

Flag:	USA
Rig:	Gaff topsail sloop
Homeport/waters:	Poughkeepsie, NY: Hudson River, New York Harbor and Long Island Sound
Who sails?	Individuals, families, and groups.
Season:	April 15 to November 15 (daily education program); winter maintenance program.
Cost:	$6-$30 per person per day, $40 per week for crew/trainee bunk, $850-$2500 group rate. Membership is $30 per year for individuals, $10 for low-income.
Program type:	Sail training for crew and apprentices. Sea education in marine science, maritime history, and ecology. Passenger day sails. Dockside interpretation during port visits. Clientele includes school groups from elementary school through college and individuals of all ages.

Specifications:	Sparred length: 106'	Draft: 6' 6"	Sail area: 4,350 sq. ft.
	LOD: 76' 6"	Beam: 24'	Tons: 69 GRT
	LOA: 76' 6"	Rig height: 108'	Power: 190 HP diesel
	LWL: 67'	Hull: wood	

Designer:	Cy Hamlin
Built:	1969; South Bristol, Maine, Harvey Gamage Shipyard
Coast Guard certification:	Passenger Vessel (Subchapter T)
Crew:	6 (4-month), 3 (1-month), 6 (1-week).Trainees: 50 (day sails)
Contact:	Captain, Hudson River Sloop Clearwater, Inc.
	112 Little Market Street
	Poughkeepsie, NY 12601
	Tel: 845-454-7673; Fax: 845-454-7953
	E-mail: captain@mail.clearwater.org
	Web site: http://www.clearwater.org

Clipper City

Clipper City is a replica of a Great Lakes lumber schooner of the same name, which sailed from 1854 until 1892. The plans for the Clipper City of 1985 were obtained from the Smithsonian Institution and adapted for modern use. Clipper City sails Baltimore's Inner Harbor and the waters of the Chesapeake Bay from April through October each year. providing two and three-hour public excursions for tourists in the Baltimore area and private charters for corporate groups and families. She sails up to 21 times each week and has carried over 30,000 passengers in a single season. Clipper City is also available for winter charter.

Flag:	USA
Rig:	Gaff topsail schooner
Homeport/waters:	Baltimore, Maryland: Chesapeake Bay (summer), Caribbean Sea (winter)
Who sails?	Individuals and groups
Season:	Year-round

Specifications:	LOD: 120'	Draft: 14'	Sail area: 10,200 sq. ft.
	LOA: 158'	Beam: 27' 6"	Tons: 210 GRT
	Hull: steel	Rig height: 135'	Power: CAT 3208 SS

Built:	1985; Jacksonville, Florida
Contact:	William L. Blocher, General Manager
	Clipper City, Inc.
	5022 Campbell Blvd., Suite F
	Baltimore, MD 21236
	Tel: 410-931-6777; Fax: 410-931-6705
	E-mail: info@sailingship.com
	Web site: http://www.sailingship.com

The beautiful Sparkman and Stephens-designed *Columbia* was the first 12-meter to defend the America's Cup. Skippered by legendary sailor and auto racing champion Briggs Cunningham, she was a refinement of the successful 1939 Vim. Close competition in the defender's trials of 1958 prepared her for an easy win over British challenger *Spectre*. Now, after many years in Europe, where she received a well-appointed interior and teak decks, *Columbia* has joined the America's Cup Charters 12-meter fleet in Newport, Rhode Island. She is perfect for leisure sails, racing, and team building from any port between Maine and the Chesapeake. Sail aboard a winner – no sailing experience necessary!

Flag:	USA
Rig:	Sloop
Homeport/waters:	Newport, Rhode Island: New England and Chesapeake Bay
Who sails?	Individuals and groups of all ages
Cost:	$2100 group rate per day, $75 per person for evening sails
Program type:	Sail training for paying trainees. Passenger day sails, corporate team building, corporate racing, individual and group charters.

Specifications:	LOD: 67'	Draft: 9'	Sail area: 1,800 sq. ft.
	LOA: 67'	Beam: 11' 6"	Tons: 28 GRT
	LWL: 46'	Rig height: 92'	Power: diesel
	Hull: wood		

Designer:	Sparkman and Stephens
Built:	1958; City Island, New York, Nevens
Coast Guard certification:	Passenger Vessel (Subchapter T)
Crew:	3. Trainees/passengers: 14
Contact:	George Hill/Herb Marshall
	America's Cup Charters
	PO Box 51
	Newport, RI 02840
	Tel: 401-849-5868; Fax: 401-849-3098
	Web site: http://www.americascupcharters.com

Concordia

basis of strong academic profiles, demonstrated strength of character and social suitability, health and fitness, and on their degree of commitment and dedication.

Class Afloat is a nonprofit educational program affiliated with high schools across the United States and Canada. Its mission is to broaden student's understanding of international issues while preparing them for responsible global citizenship in the 21st century.

The concept of "taking the classroom to the world" is intended to encourage self-sufficiency, cooperation, and a clear awareness of other cultures. Each semester, 48 qualifying students work as crew and study aboard the *Concordia*, a modern tall ship.

Over 700 international students have joined Class Afloat and sailed the world for an entire academic year. Applications from 11th and 12th-grade coeds are encouraged, and applicants who are seeking a unique and challenging "year out" program are also accepted. Crewmembers are selected on the

A fully-certified faculty instructs students in a full curriculum including social studies and global issues, anthropology, marine biology, and physical education. Optional, non-credit enrichment courses are also offered in seamanship, celestial navigation, and the history and traditions of the sea.

Flag:	Bahamas
Rig:	Barquentine, three-masted
Homeport/waters:	Nassau, Bahamas: worldwide, unrestricted
Who sails?	11th and 12th-grade high school and college students. Affiliated institutions include West Island College (high school), College Marie-Victorian, Hingham High School, I.S.A.M, and A.I.E.S.
Season:	Academic year. Summer programs offered for students and adults
Cost:	$15,900 per student per semester, $25,900 per student per year.
Program type:	Full-curriculum academics and marine biology for high school students.

Specifications:		
Sparred length: 188'	Draft: 13' 6"	Sail area: 10,000 sq. ft.
LOA: 154'	Beam: 31'	Tons: 495 GRT
LOD: 152' 6"	Rig height: 115'	Power: 570 HP diesel
Freeboard: 8'	Hull: steel	

Certification:	Lloyds 100A1 and LMC
Built:	1992; Poland
Crew:	8. Instructors: 8. Trainees: 48. Age: 16-19, Coed
Contact:	Eric Prud'Homme, Director of Development
	Class Afloat – West Island College International
	851 Tecumseh
	Montreal, Quebec H9B 2L2 Canada
	Tel: 514-683-9052, 1-800-301-SAIL; Fax: 514-683-1702
	E-mail: eprudhomme@classafloat.com
	Web site: http://www.classafloat.com

SAIL TALL SHIPS!

The *Contessa* offers elegance and comfort under sail. Exterior features that distinguish *Contessa* from many other charter yachts include wide spacious decks, a very large enclosed and shaded cockpit and a large fantail deck for sunbathing, fishing or hammock-napping while under sail and for cocktails in the evening at anchor. The deck layout extends "al fresco" living to the world of the beautiful Caribbean.

Below you will find luxurious living accommodations. The main saloon is traditional teak, with colorful fabrics and décor with a Caribbean flair and a beautiful dining table comfortably seating eight. This feeling of elegance is carried throughout *Contessa* from the beautiful queen sized aft stateroom to the two forward cabins each with a double and single berth, all having private bathrooms.

Contessa offers romance to some and a wonderful family experience to others. Whether seeking the thrill of a sailing adventure or a peaceful, pampered sail through the beautiful turquoise waters of the Caribbean, *Contessa* will take you on the vacation of your dreams.

Flag:	USA
Rig:	Ketch
Homeport/waters:	Dallas, Texas: British Virgin Islands to the Bahamas
Who sails?	Individuals and groups of all ages
Season:	Year-round
Cost:	Varies according to program.
Program type:	Sail training for paying trainees in cooperation with organized groups such as Sea Scouts. Private charters.

Specifications:	LOA: 55' 9"	LWL: 45' 4"	Draft: 5' 6
	Beam: 15' 7"	Rig height: 60'	
	Sail area: 1,205 sq. ft.	Hull: Fiberglass	

Coast Guard certification:	Passenger Vessel (Subchapter T)
Crew:	2. Trainees/passengers: 18 -20 (day sails), 6 (overnight)
Contact:	David W. Majors, President/owner
	Caribbean, Inc.
	601 Woodland
	El Paso, TX 79922
	Tel: 915-298-6600; Fax: 915-877-5247
	E-mail: dmajors@prologis.com
	Web site: http://www.yachtcontessa.com

Copper Sky

Specializing in marine wilderness and wildlife adventures, 88-foot Canadian staysail schooner *Copper Sky* has always been a 'hands on' vessel for anyone aboard interested in gaining seafaring skills. We provide sail training opportunities on our Vancouver to Mexico voyage in the fall, and Mexico to Vancouver in the spring. Since completion in 1987, *Copper Sky* has operated as an inspected passenger, charter, and sail training vessel. With twelve berths in six cabins for guests or trainees, and separate quarters for up to six crew, she operates in British Columbia in summer, and Mexico in winter.

Steel hulled for strength and safety, *Copper Sky* is beautifully finished with a teak and mahogany interior, & equipped with three heads and hot showers. She is available for charter to organizations, groups, families and friends, film production & for corporate events & incentives. Tour operators are invited to inquire regarding our Queen Charlotte Islands and Sea of Cortez natural history voyages.

Youth of all ages from 15 years are invited to join us during the TALL SHIPS CHALLENGE® 2002 events sailing between Vancouver and Los Angeles.

Flag:	Canada
Rig:	Staysail schooner, two masted, third mast planned
Homeport/waters:	Vancouver, Inside Passage, Queen Charlotte Islands, summer; Sea of Cortez and Socorro Island, Mexico, winter.
Who sails?	Youth trainees, individuals and groups
Season:	May to September: British Columbia. October to April: Mexico
Cost:	$100 per day for trainees, others $125/day for 3-week legs to $225/day for one-week legs

Specifications:	Sparred length: 88'	LOD: 74'	LOA: 88'
	LWL: 66'	Draft: 8'	Beam: 16' 6"
	Rig height: 66'	Sail area: 2,400 sq. ft.	Tons: 58.5 GRT
	Power: 145 HP diesel	Hull: steel	

Designer:	J. Simpson Ltd.
Built:	1985: Hull by Nels Lindholm, Britannia Beach, British Columbia, Canada
	1987: Rig, interior, & machinery, Octagon Boatworks, Delta, BC, Canada
	1993: New 17' midsection added, Fashion Blacksmiths Ship Yard, Crescent City, CA
Coast Guard certification:	Transport Canada: Ship's Safety Branch, Home Trade 3, for 12 passengers overnight berthed, total including crew 20. 30 for day sailing
Mexico:	certified passenger vessel for hire for up to 20 persons berthed.
Contact:	Russell Weisner
	Copper Sky Sailing Adventures - Canadian Nature Cruises
	6781 Westview Drive.
	Delta, BC V4E-2L7 Canada
	Tel: 604-596-7077; Fax: 604-596-7703
	E-mail: coppersky@dccnet.com
	Web site: http://www.naturecruises.com/

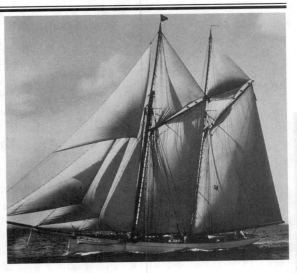

Coronet is America's most historic yacht, and the last remaining grand yacht from the gilded age. Built in 1885, she has voyaged far and wide during her career, twice circumnavigating the globe. She won the 1887 transatlantic race against the schooner *Dauntless*. She also transported a scientific expedition to Japan in 1896 to view a total eclipse of the sun.

In 1995 *Coronet* was acquired by the International Yacht Restoration School (IYRS) in Newport, RI. Founded in 1993, IYRS teaches the skills, history and related sciences needed to restore classic yachts. Over the next several years, IYRS will carry out a comprehensive and well-documented restoration to return *Coronet* to her late 19th century condition. She will have no engines, electricity or modern equipment. When completed, she will sail as the school's flagship and a living museum of yachting history.

Coronet is open to visitors dockside at IYRS from May to October each year. The public will also be able to view the ship once restoration begins. For history, photographs, documentation drawings, updates on the restoration project and information about IYRS's programs, visit www.iyrs.org.

Flag:	USA
Rig:	Gaff topsail schooner
Homeport/waters:	Newport, Rhode Island
Season:	May to October
Program type:	Walk-on visitation and dockside interpretation for individuals and groups of all ages.

Specifications:		
Sparred length: 190'	Draft: 12'	Sail area: 8,300 sq. ft.
LOD: 133'	LOA: 133'	LWL: 125'
Beam: 27'	Tons: 174 GRT	Freeboard: 6'
Hull: wood	Hull color: white	

Designer:	Smith & Terry, Christopher Crosby, William Townsend
Built:	1885; Brooklyn, New York, C & R Poillon
Contact:	International Yacht Restoration School
	449 Thames Street
	Newport, RI 02840
	Tel: 401-848-5777; Fax: 401-842-0669
	E-mail: info@iyrs.org
	Web site: http://www.iyrs.org

Corsair is a sailing whaleboat, an open boat designed to be launched from a larger ship while at sea. She was built at Puget Sound Naval Shipyard in 1939 for use in the Navy's fleet sailing program. As the US prepared for war, the Navy stripped its ships and our whaleboats were sent ashore. The sailing program was never reinstated, and surplus Navy whaleboats found their way to Sea Scout units around the country, offering thousands of youth the opportunity to learn sailing, seamanship, and teamwork on the water. Of those boats, only a handful remain.

The Sea Scout Ship Corsair has been serving the youth of the Bay Area for over 60 years, offering programs that teach sailing, seamanship, and leadership to young men aged 14-21. Her sister ship, Viking, offers similar programs for young women. The two ships sponsor many joint activities. In addition to the annual two-week summer cruise in the Sacramento Delta, the Bay Area Sea Scouts organize day sails, races, weekend outings, dances, and regattas. New members are always welcome, both young and adult.

Flag:	USA
Rig:	Ketch
Homeport/waters:	San Francisco, California: San Francisco Bay and tributaries
Who sails?	High school students and individuals. Affiliated institutions include Sea Scouting, Boy Scouts of America, San Francisco Bay Area Council.
Program type:	Sail training for male trainees, aged 14-21. Sea education in marine science and maritime history in cooperation with other groups.

Specifications:	Sparred length: 30'	Draft: 4' 6"	Sail area: 600 sq. ft.
	LOD: 30'	Beam: 8'	Freeboard: 2'
	LOA: 30'	Rig height: 35'	Hull: wood
	LWL: 28'		

Designer:	US Navy
Built:	1939; US Navy, Puget Sound Naval Shipyard
Crew:	Up to 18
Contact:	Nick Tarlson, Skipper
	Sea Scout Ship Viking
	220 Sansome Street, Ste. 900
	San Francisco, CA 94104
	Tel: 415-956-5700; Fax: 415-982-2528
	E-mail: seascouts@dictyon.com
	Web site: http://www.tbw.net/~chriss/scouts/

Corwith Cramer

Education Association (SEA), working through ASTA, was instrumental in helping the Coast Guard shape these regulations. The *Cramer* was built in Bilbao, Spain, and it took the largest floating crane in northern Spain to launch her. She is a safe, stable vessel and an excellent platform for SEA's educational and oceanographic research missions. The *Corwith Cramer* is owned and operated by the SEA, Woods Hole, Massachusetts.

See also the *Robert C. Seamans.*

The *Corwith Cramer* was the first ship built to the USCG's regulations for Sailing School Vessels. The Sea

Corwith Cramer

Flag:	USA
Rig:	Brigantine
Homeport/waters:	Woods Hole, Massachusetts: worldwide
Who sails?	Educators and students who are admitted by competitive selection. Over 150 colleges and universities award credit for SEA programs.
Season:	Year-round
Program types:	Marine and maritime studies including oceanography, nautical science, history, literature, and contemporary maritime affairs. SEA programs include SEA Semester (college level, 12 weeks long, 17 credits), SEA Summer Session (college level, 8 weeks long, 12-credits), and SEA Seminars for high school students and K-12 teachers. All programs include a seagoing component on board the sailing school vessels *Robert C. Seamans* and/or *Corwith Cramer.*

Specifications:	LOA: 134'	Draft: 13'	Sail area: 7,380 sq. ft.
	LWL: 87' 6"	Beam: 26'	Power: 500 HP diesel
	Hull: steel	Tons: 158 GRT	

Designer:	Woodin & Marean
Built:	1987; Bilbao, Spain, ASTACE
Coast Guard certification:	Sailing School Vessel (Subchapter R)
Crew:	6 professional mariners and 4 scientists. Trainees: Up to 25 in all programs
Contact:	Sea Education Association, Inc.
	PO Box 6
	Woods Hole, MA 02543
	Tel: 508-540-3954, 800-552-3633; Fax: : 508-546-0558
	E-mail: admission@sea.edu
	Web site: http://www.sea.edu

Courageous, the famous two-time America's Cup champion, was the first 12 Metre built from aluminum to successfully defend the America's Cup. She went on to win a second America's Cup in 1977 with Ted Turner at the helm, and participated in three more Cup campaigns to become the first ever boat to be both defender and challenger. In 2000, she became the State Yacht of Rhode Island, in recognition of her contributions to yacht racing and her home state. After a long and varied career, she was purchased by Craig Millard for the Courageous Foundation, and underwent a major restoration back to her 1977 lines.

Courageous has an active racing schedule of national and international regattas with the reinvigorated 12 Metre class. Along with the America's Cup champion, Freedom, she hosts corporate match racing events for professional clients, focusing on team building and leadership development while recreating the heyday of America's Cup racing in Newport. She is also participating in a unique educational program that provides participants the opportunity to develop and teach sailing and boat maintenance skills while learning about 12 Metres, the America's Cup, and the rich local sailing heritage.

Flag:	US
Rig:	Sloop
Homeport/waters:	Newport, RI USA
Who sails?	Groups and individuals of all ages
Season:	April - October
Program type:	Sail training for volunteer trainees, private charters, day sails

Specifications:	Sparred length: 66' 6"	LOA: 66' 6"	LWL: 45' 6"
	Draft: 9'	Beam: 12'	Rig height: 90'
	Freeboard: 4'	Sail area: 1770 sq. ft.	
	Tons: 55 GRT		

Designer:	Olin Stephens
Built:	1974
Crew:	10. Trainees/passengers: 6 (day sails)
Contact:	Mr. Niccolo Porzio
	H2O Riders
	559 Thames St.
	Newport, RI 02840
	Tel: 401-845-2005; Fax: 401-845-2105
	E-mail: info@h2oriders.com
	Web site: http://www.h2oriders.com

Cutty Sark sails the waters of the State of Washington from historic Captain Whidbey Inn on the shores of Penn Cove, Whidbey Island. *Cutty Sark* operates as a commercial charter sailing ship, as well as offering volunteer educational opportunities for local school districts and scout groups. Charterers are encouraged, although not required, to lend a hand at running the ship as she slips past the sylvan shores of the San Juan Islands. School groups, however, stand watches, navigate the ship, and sing sea chanteys as they raise the sails, while learning the history, ecology, and lore of these enchanting islands. A ship provides an excellent platform for learning by experience: communication skills are honed and teamwork is established as the rule rather than the exception. The interdependence of shipboard life renders a microcosm of the world which gives the student sailors transferable skills.

Programs can be designed for groups of any type, from gourmet country inn cruises, small business retreats, overnight excursions for middle school, high school, and college students, to day sails for elementary school students.

Flag:	USA
Rig:	Gaff ketch
Homeport/waters:	Coupeville, Washington: Whidbey Island and San Juan Islands, Washington
Who sails?	School groups from elementary school through college. Individuals and families of all ages. Affiliated groups include the Coupeville, South Whidbey, and Sedro Wooley School Districts, and Troop 58 BSA.
Cost:	$500 group rate per day, $250 per day for schools
Program type:	Sail training for volunteer or paying trainees. Sea education in marine science, maritime history, ecology, and other subjects in cooperation with other groups and as informal, in-house programming.

Specifications:			
	Sparred length: 52'	Draft: 6' 6"	Sail area: 1,100 sq. ft.
	LOD: 40'	Beam: 13' 6"	Tons: 19 GRT
	LOA: 40'	Rig height: 55'	Hull: teak
	LWL: 33' 4"	Freeboard: 3' 6"	

Designer:	Hugh Angleman/Charlie Davies
Built:	1960; Hong Kong, American Marine
Contact:	Captain John Colby Stone
	Æolian Ventures, Ltd., SV *Cutty Sark*
	2072 West Captain Whidbey Inn Road
	Coupeville, WA 98239
	Tel: 800-366-4097, 360-678-4097; Fax: 360-678-4110
	E-mail: captjohn@whidbey.net
	Web site: http://www.captainwhidbey.com/cutty.htm

Dariabar

Dariabar, launched in 1992, is a custom-built sailing research vessel. Her lines are those of a John Alden schooner and her design incorporates both traditional and modern aspects. She is built from steel with watertight subdivisions and a double bottom. She has a generous lab and workspace amidships with lifting gear above deck. *Dariabar* is presently involved in bioacoustic research and marine mammal observation. She is associated with Pelagikos, a California-based marine research organization. Pelagikos, in conjunction with Mendocino College, conducts courses in marine mammal ecology and behavior aboard *Dariabar*. These classes offer students the opportunity to engage in active research while learning about sailing and life at sea. Pelagikos also employs *Dariabar* as a platform for research conducted by other college and scientific organizations.

Flag:	USA
Rig:	Schooner
Homeport/waters:	Sausalito, California: California and northeast Pacific
Who sails?	College students and adults involved in ocean research
Program type:	Sea education, marine science, ecology, and bioacoustic research in cooperation with accredited institutions.

Specifications:			
	LOA: 84'	Draft: 10'	Sail area: 3,000 sq. ft.
	LOD: 84'	Beam: 18'	Tons: 84 GRT
	LWL: 64'	Rig height: 90'	Power: diesel
	Freeboard: 6'	Hull: steel	

Designer:	John Alden
Built:	Oakland, California, E.A. Silva
Coast Guard certification:	Ocean Research Vessel (Subchapter U)
Crew:	4 (educators). Trainees: 30 (day); 10 (overnight)
Contact:	Dr. Urmas Kaldveer, Executive Director
	Pelagikos
	3020 Bridgeway # 155
	Sausalito, CA 94966
	Tel: 707-462-5671; Fax: 707-468-3120
	E-mail: silva@well.com

Denis Sullivan

The S/V *Denis Sullivan*, completed in year 2000, will operate its Great Lakes sailing season from May through September. She operates as a floating, traveling classroom and as a goodwill ambassador for the State of Wisconsin from her homeport of Milwaukee on Lake Michigan. She winters in Florida and the Bahamas.

The Association is committed to re-establishing the historical, cultural and environmental bonds between the community and one of its most valuable resources, the Great Lakes. The schooner offers education day sails and charters for people of all ages as well as LakeWatch and Dockside Discovery education programs from 5th through 12th graders, Multi-day Education Under sail programs in Great Lakes and Science Under Sail programs in the Bahamas and Florida.

Denis Sullivan

Flag:	USA
Rig:	Schooner, three-masted
Homeport/waters:	Milwaukee, Wisconsin: Great Lakes, Bahamas, Florida
Who sails?	Schools and other groups from elementary school through college, individuals, families and other interested groups
Cost:	Day sails starting at $50/person
Program type:	Sail training for crew and volunteers. Learning expeditions under sail in marine science, maritime studies, and ecology. LakeWatch and Dockside Discovery education programs from 5th through 12th graders. Multi-day Education Under sail programs in Great Lakes and Science Under Sail programs in Bahamas and Florida. Professional development for educators, and special "themed" sails. Passenger day sails and dockside interpretation.

Specifications:	Sparred Length: 138'	Draft: 8'9"	Sail area: 5,000 sq. ft.
	LOD: 98'	Beam: 24"	Tons: 97 GRT
	LOA: 99'	Hull: wood	Power: twin diesels
	LWL: 88'4"		

Designer:	Timothy Graul
Built:	2000; Milwaukee, Wisconsin, Rob Stevens
Coast Guard certification:	Sailing School Vessel (Subchapter R), Passenger Vessel (Subchapter T)
Contact:	Jeff Phillips
	Wisconsin Lake Schooner Education Association
	500 North Harbor Drive
	Milwaukee, WI 53202
	Tel: 414-276-7700; Fax: 414-276-8838
	E-Mail: info@lakeschooner.org
	Web site: http://www.lakeschooner.org

For generations, Nova Scotians have traveled the coast in small boats, learning wisdom and courage from the sea. The Nova Scotia Sea School takes young people to sea in small boats today for fun and personal challenge. The Sea School teaches traditional seamanship and navigation, and gives teenagers the chance to discover the Nova Scotia coast, and to discover themselves.

Young people 14-18 years old, male and female, from all over North America and Europe sail on voyages ranging from five days to three weeks, living in an open boat powered by sails and oars. They explore the coast, live with the elements, visit the islands, and learn to take command of the boat, and of their lives. As one student said, "I don't always understand things at home—out here they make sense."

Professional enrichment programs for experiential educators, sail trainers and outdoor leaders are also offered as well as programs exploring how to work with youth and the sea (or any demanding environment) in the most powerful way possible.

Flag:	Canada
Rig:	Ketch
Homeport/waters:	Halifax, Nova Scotia, Canada: coastal Nova Scotia
Who sails?	Individuals and groups associated with accredited schools and colleges as well as summer camps and other youth organization participation.
Cost:	$110 per person per day
Program type:	Sail training with paying trainees. Sea education programs in marine science, maritime history, and ecology, and informal, in-house programming.

Specifications:			
LOD: 28' 6"	Draft: 5'	Hull: wood
LOA: 28' 6"	Beam: 7'	Tons: 4 GRT

Designer:	E.Y.E. Marine
Built:	1995; Halifax, Nova Scotia, Canada
Crew:	2. Trainees: 10
Contact:	The Nova Scotia Sea School
	PO Box 546, Central CRO
	Halifax, Nova Scotia B3J 2S4 Canada
	Tel: 902-423-7284; Fax: 902-423-7241
	E-mail: info@seaschool.org
	Web site: http://www.seaschool.org

Dream Catcher is a 72-foot steel schooner built by Treworgy Yachts in Palm Coast, Florida in 1996. Designed by marine architects Woodin and Marean, from Maine, her conception, design factors and interior design came from Captain John Duke. John grew up on the waters of Biscayne Bay in Miami, Florida, has been USCG licensed since 1979, and has been sailing the waters of the lower Florida Keys, South Florida and the Bahamas for 30 years. During this time he has worked with scientific research groups, youth groups, and environmental groups, and has introduced hundreds of marine enthusiasts to the many wonders of the sea.

The *Dream Catcher* provides sailing adventures designed to be informative for both environmental professionals and individuals interested in marine habitat. Ideal for large families and groups (scouts, clubs, students) interested in participating in and learning all aspects of sailing and navigation,

Dream Catcher is looking for groups that want to be a part of the adventure! Starting in January of 2003, *Dream Catcher* will begin offering trips to the Bahamas.

Flag:	USA
Rig:	Schooner
Homeport/waters:	Oceanside Marina, Key West, Florida: Florida Keys, Bahamas
Who sails?	Students, individuals, families and groups of all ages.
Program type:	Sail training for volunteer crew and paying trainees. Sea Education in cooperation with accredited institutions and other organized groups. Longboat rowing aboard *Aida*, a 32' longboat that is used on *Dream Catcher's* extended voyages
Cost:	$75 per person per (8 hr) day. $850 group rate (charter) per day.

Specifications:		
Sparred length: 74'	Draft: 5'	Sail area: 1,700 sq. ft.
LOD: 65'	Beam: 20'	Tons: 49 GRT
LOA: 69'	Rig height: 73'	Power: 130 John Deere
LWL: 62'	Freeboard: 5'	Hull: steel
Hull color: turquoise	Spar material: aluminum	

Designer:	Woodin and Marean
Built:	1996; Hammocks, Florida, Treworgy Yachts
Cost Guard certification:	Passenger Vessel (Subchapter T)
Crew:	Trainees/passengers: 49 (day sails), 19 (overnight)
Contact:	Captain John Duke
	Coastal Sailing Adventures, Inc.
	28555 Jolly Roger Drive
	Little Torch Key, FL 33042
	Tel: 305-295-8844
	E-mail: saildreamcatcher@mindspring.com
	Web site: http://www.keywest.com/dreamcatcher/

Eagle (WIX 327)

One of five sister ships built for sail training in Germany in the 1930s, *Eagle* was included in reparations paid to the United States following World War II and the Coast Guard took her over as a training ship. Aboard the *Eagle*, cadets have a chance to put into practice the navigation, engineering, and other skills they are taught at the Coast Guard Academy. As underclassmen, they fill positions normally taken by the enlisted crew of a ship, including watches. They handle the more than 20,000 square feet of sail and more than 20 miles of rigging. Over 200 lines must be coordinated during a major ship maneuver, and the cadets must learn the name and function of each. As upperclassmen, they perform officer-level functions. For many, their tour of duty aboard *Eagle* is their first experience of life at sea; but it is here that they learn to serve as the leaders they will one day become in the Coast Guard.

Flag:	USA
Rig:	Barque, three-masted
Homeport/waters:	New London, Connecticut: Atlantic Ocean, Caribbean, and Pacific Ocean
Who sails?	US Coast Guard Academy Cadets, US Coast Guard Officer Candidates, and other Coast Guard personnel.
Season:	Year-round
Cost:	Included in school tuition
Program type:	Seamanship

Specifications:			
	Sparred length: 295'	Draft: 17'	Sail area: 22,245 sq. ft.
	LOA: 266' 8"	Beam: 40'	(23 sails)
	Tons: 2,186 GRT	Rig height: 147' 4"	Power: 1,000 HP diesel
	LWL: 231'		Hull: steel

Built:	1936; Hamburg, Germany, Blohm & Voss
Contact:	Commanding Officer
	USCGC EAGLE (WIX-327)
	45 Mohegan Avenue
	New London, CT 06320
	Tel: 860-444-8595; Fax: 860-444-8445
	E-mail: Kboda@cgceagle.uscg.mil
	Web site: http://www.cga.edu/eagle

The second-largest vessel of the Square Sail fleet was originally named *Orion* and built in Pukavik, Sweden, in 1945 as one of the last three-masted sailing schooners. She traded timber in the Baltic and British East Coast until being laid up in Thisted, Denmark in 1974. Square Sail purchased her in 1979 and she underwent a complete restoration, which commenced in 1985. In 1994 she was commissioned as the three-masted wooden barque that she is today.

All of Square Sail's ships are fully commissioned and work throughout the year. When not filming, they have a regular sailing program, giving people the chance to experience traditional square-rig sailing first-hand. These voyages typically run between four and seven days, and occasionally longer. They are either based from Square Sail's homeport of Charlestown, Cornwall, UK, or they work around the annual schedule offering voyages

between the various ports.

Square Sail runs an annual course from February to October where trainees are given the opportunity to learn the skills associated with sailing these ships, and in addition to maintenance and shore-based instruction, they form part of the regular crew throughout the season.

Flag:	UK
Rig:	Barque, three-masted, single topsail
Homeport/waters:	Charlestown Harbour, St. Austell, Cornwall, UK: UK and Europe
Who sails?	Individuals of all ages and families. Affiliated institutions include Falmouth Marine School and Cornwall College.
Cost:	$220 per person per day, $9000 group rate (charter) per day.
Program type:	Sail training for professional crew, volunteer and paying trainees. Sea education in maritime history in cooperation with accredited institutions and as informal, in-house programming. Worldwide film work and corporate charters.

Specifications:	Sparred length: 145'	Draft:10' 6"	Sail area: 9,500 sq. ft.
	LOD: 115'	Beam: 24'	Tons: 174 GRT
	LOA: 145'	Rig height: 93'	Power: 300 HP diesel
	LWL: 108'	Freeboard: 7'	Hull: oak on oak

Built:	1948, Pukavik, Sweden, Albert Svenson
Certification:	MCA Oceans (UK)
Crew:	15. Trainees/passengers: 50 (day sails), 12 (overnight)
Contact:	Chris Wilson, Marketing Manager, Square Sail
	Charlestown Harbour
	St. Austell, Cornwall PL25 3NJ, United Kingdom
	Tel: 44-1726-67526; Fax: 44-1726-61839
	E-mail: info@square-sail.com
	Web site: http://www.square-sail.com

Eastwind

Schooner *Eastwind*, built in Albion, Maine, is the sixth schooner built by Herb and Doris Smith. The other five were all named *Appledore*, two of which the Smiths sailed around the world. *Eastwind* is built of native white oak and planked with Port Orford cedar. She is fastened with copper rivets and bronze screws. In November of 1999, the Smiths left with *Eastwind* for South America. They have since returned to Boothbay Harbor, Maine, where they take passengers during the summer months.

Flag:	USA
Rig:	Topsail schooner
Homeport/waters:	Boothbay Harbor, Maine: Boothbay Harbor (summer), southern waters (winter)
Who sails?	Individuals of all ages
Cost:	$22 per person per two-hour sail
Program type:	Sail training for paying passengers. Dockside interpretation while in homeport.

Specifications:			
	Sparred length: 64'	Draft: 7'	Sail area: 1,600 sq. ft.
	LOD: 56'	Beam: 14'	Tons: 31 GRT
	LOA: 56'	Rig height: 75'	Hull: wood
	LWL: 47'	Freeboard: 4'	
	Hull color: white	Spar Material: wood	

Designer:	McIntosh
Built:	1999; Albion, Maine, Herb Smith
Coast Guard certification:	Passenger Vessel (Subchapter T)
Crew:	1 Trainees/passengers: 28 (day sails)
Contact:	Captain Herb Smith
	Eastwind Cruises
	20 Commercial St.
	Boothbay Harbor, ME 04538
	Tel: 207-633-6598
	Web site: http://www.fishermanswharfinn.com

In 1975, a rusted iron hulk lay in the waters of Piraeus, Greece. Nearly 100 years earlier, she had sailed the world's oceans as a proud square-rigged sailing ship. Cut down, leaking, and decrepit, she waited a cable's length from the scrap yard.

Today, *Elissa* remains one of the hallmarks of maritime preservation. Lovingly restored and maintained, she sails again, continuing a far longer life than most ships are ever granted. She tests her readiness annually in a series of sea trials amid the oilrigs and shrimpers off Galveston Island. Working under professional officers, her volunteer crew completes an extensive dockside training program. As funds allow, she makes

longer voyages, such as her journey to New York to participate in Operation Sail 1986/Salute to Liberty.

Elissa

Flag:	USA
Rig:	Barque, three-masted
Homeport/waters:	Galveston, Texas: coastal waters near Galveston
Who sails?	School groups from middle school through college and individuals of all ages.
Season:	April to November
Cost:	Volunteers and guests only
Program type:	Sail training for crew and apprentices. Sea education in maritime history based on informal, in-house training. Dockside interpretation.

Specifications:

Sparred length: 205'	Draft: 10'	Sail area: 12,000 sq. ft.
LOA: 155'	Beam: 28'	Tons: 411 GRT
LOD: 150'	Rig height: 110'	Power: 450 HP diesel
Freeboard: 10'	Hull: iron	

Built:	1877; Aberdeen, Scotland, Alexander Hall and Sons Yard
Coast Guard certification:	Cargo and Miscellaneous Goods (Subchapter I)
Crew:	40. Trainees: 85 (day)
Contact:	Kurt Voss, Director

Texas Seaport Museum/Galveston Historical Foundation
Pier 21, No. 8
Galveston, TX 77550
Tel: 409-763-1877; Fax: 409-763-3037
E-mail: elissa@galvestonhistory.org
Web site: http://www.tsm-elissa.org

Elizabeth II

and 1587. She probably carried marines, colonists, and supplies to establish a military garrison to support England's claim to the New World.

Elizabeth II's sail training program teaches volunteer crew about America's 16th-century maritime heritage. In addition to classroom instruction and dockside training, crew members participate in the care and maintenance of wooden vessels. The 24-foot ship's boat, *Silver Chalice*, is used for underway training and travels with *Elizabeth II* when she sails. Voyages are scheduled during the spring and fall seasons. Sponsorship for the volunteer crew program is provided by the nonprofit Friends of *Elizabeth II*, Inc.

Built with private funds to commemorate the English colonization of America's 400th anniversary, *Elizabeth II* is named for a vessel that sailed from Plymouth, England, on the second of the three Roanoke voyages sponsored by Sir Walter Raleigh between 1584

Flag:	USA
Rig:	Barque, three-masted (lateen mizzen)
Homeport/waters:	Manteo, North Carolina: inland sounds of North Carolina
Who sails?	Volunteer crew
Season:	Spring and fall
Cost:	$8 for adults, $5 students (dockside visits), free for children under 6 accompanied by an adult
Program type:	Sail training for volunteer crew and apprentices. Dockside interpretation.

Specifications:	Sparred length: 78'	Draft: 8'	Sail area: 1,920 sq. ft.
	LOA: 68' 6"	Beam: 16' 6"	Tons: 97 GRT
	LOD: 55'	Rig height: 65'	Hull: wood
	LWL: 59'		

Designer:	W.A. Baker and Stanley Potter
Built:	1983; Manteo, North Carolina, O. Lie-Nielsen, Creef-Davis Shipyard
Age:	16+
Contact:	Captain Horace Whitfield
	Roanoke Island Festival Park
	One Festival Park
	Manteo, NC 27954
	Tel: 252-475-1500; Fax: 252-475-1507
	E-mail: horace.whitfield@ncmail.net or rifp.information@ncmail.net
	Web site: http://www.roanokeisland.com

SAIL TALL SHIPS!

The *Ellida* was designed by John Alden and built in 1922 at the Morse Boat Yard in Thomaston, Maine for the renowned psychologist, Dr. Austin Briggs. For a great part of her life she remained in the Marble Head / Gloucester area. During the Second World War, *Ellida* served as a coastal patrol vessel.

Kristina and Paul Williamson purchased *Ellida* in 1999 and added her to their established Maine windjammer business, Maine Classic Schooners. She now operates as a windjammer cruise vessel entertaining 11 guests on 3 to 6 day cruises and private charters.

On board *Ellida* offers three cabins which feature double beds and private heads, two cabins which feature two twin berths and share a head. There is a fresh hot water shower on board. One of *Ellida's* nicest features is a fully

Photo By V. Thordike

enclosed, heated deck side awning with roll down sides for dining and entertaining in all weather. The comfort is enhanced by the plentiful elegant fare freshly prepared on board.

Ellida carries a licensed Captain, deck hand, and chef. Passengers are always welcome to participate. *Ellida* is fast and graceful and her beautiful lines turn heads everywhere she travels.

Flag:	USA
Rig:	Marconi Main Schooner
Homeport/waters:	Rockland, Maine: Midcoast Maine
Who sails?	Groups and individuals of all ages.
Season:	Late May to mid-October
Cost:	$400-$975 per person 3-6 day cruises, $1600/day private charter
Program type:	Sail training for paying trainees

Specifications:	Sparred length: 80'	LOD: 62'	LOA: 65'
	LWL: 49'	Draft: 8' 6"	Beam: 16'
	Rig height:70'	Freeboard: 3' 6"	Sail area: 2000 sq. ft.
	Tons: 30 GRT	Power: diesel	

Designer:	John Alden
Built:	1922; Thomaston, Maine: Morse
Coast Guard certification:	Passenger Vessel (Subchapter T)
Crew:	3. Trainees/passengers: 30 (day sails), 11 (overnight)
Contact:	Captain Paul & Kristina Williamson
	Maine Classic Schooners, Inc.
	178 East Pond Road
	Jefferson, ME 04348
	Tel: 888-807-6921, 207-549-3908; Fax: 207-549-4519 (call first)
	E-mail: schoonerff@aol.com
	Web site: http://www.maineclassicschooners.com

Endeavour

Endeavour is an exact museum standard replica of the ship Captain James Cook used on the first of his three famous voyages. On that voyage, from 1768 to 1771, Cook solved the geography of the Pacific, defeated scurvy, was the first to accurately calculate his longitude at sea, and successfully charted the islands of New Zealand and the east coast of Australia.

Built in Fremantle, Western Australia, from Australian hardwoods and American Douglas Fir, the ship is the result of over five years of painstaking research coordinated by the National Maritime Museum, Greenwich, UK. The original ship was very accurately recorded in the 18th century and hence the replica is virtually a reincarnation of that ship, not a 20th-century designer or historian's view of what she may have been like. The only concessions to the 20th century are modern heads and showers, and electric galley and mess, locker, machinery, and freezer spaces. All of these are housed in what was the capacious hold on the original ship. The crew live, sleep, and work the ship exactly as they did in the18th century.

Flag:	Australia
Rig:	Full-rigged ship
Homeport/waters:	Sydney, Australia: international
Who sails?	Adults of all ages
Program type:	Sail training for volunteer crew and trainees. Sea education in maritime history based on informal, in-house programming. Passenger day sails.
Cost:	Varies, average $100 per person per day

Specifications:			
	Sparred length: 145' 6"	Draft: 12' 6"	Sail area: 15,800 sq. ft.
	LOD: 105'	Beam: 29' 2'	Tons: 397 GRT
	LOA: 109' 3"	Rig height: 121' 4"	Power: diesel
	LWL: 101' 5"	Freeboard: 13' 6"	Hull: wood

Designer:	David White/Bill Leonard
Built:	1993; Fremantle, Western Australia, HM Bark Endeavour Foundation
Certification:	USL 2A Ocean
Crew:	16. Trainees/passengers: 70 (day sails), 40 (overnight)
Contact:	Dominic Hannelly, Sydney Manager
	HM Bark Endeavour Foundation
	Australian National Maritime Museum
	PO Box 4537, Sydney, NSW, 2001, Australia
	Tel: 61-2-9298 3872; Fax: 61-2-9298 3849
	E mail: crewman@attglobal.net
	Web site: http://www.barkendeavour.com.au

On February 5, 1894, a single line in a corner of the Gloucester Daily Times recorded an addition to the Massachusetts fishing fleet: "The new schooner for J.F. Wonson and Co. has been named *Effie M. Morrissey.*" This marked the birth of a schooner that would become famous as a Grand Banks fisher, an arctic expeditionary vessel under the command of Captain Robert Abrams Bartlett, and as a World War II survey vessel under Commander Alexander Forbes. After a fire in 1946, the *Morrissey* was raised and renamed *Ernestina* to serve in the transatlantic Cape Verdean packet trade. In 1982 she was gifted by the Republic of Cape Verde to the people of the United States as a symbol of the close ties between lands.

The essence of *Ernestina's* educational mission today extends from the vessel's phenomenal track through history. Aboard *Ernestina*, learners of all ages use the ship as a platform to study the marine environment and human impacts during structured underway and dockside programs. They gain confidence and self-esteem by learning how to orient themselves in the natural world while solving real-world problems.

Additionally, a membership program presents special sailing opportunities including both day sails as well as multiple day sails.

Flag:	USA
Rig:	Gaff topsail schooner, two-masted
Homeport/waters:	New Bedford, Massachusetts: East Coast US, Canada (summer); Caribbean and West Africa (winter)
Who sails?	School groups from elementary through college, and individuals of all ages.
Season:	Year-round
Cost:	$125 per person per day, $2,700 group rate or charter per day/$1,600 half-day
Program type:	Sail training for volunteer or paying trainees. Sea education in marine science, maritime history, and ecology in cooperation with accredited schools and colleges, Scouts, and other groups. Passengers carried on day and overnight sails. Dockside interpretation.

Specifications:			
	Sparred length: 156'	Draft: 13'	Sail area: 8,323 sq. ft.
	LOD: 106'	Beam: 24' 5"	Tons: 98 GRT
	LWL: 94'	Rig height: 115'	Power: 259 HP diesel
	LOA: 112'	Hull: wood	

Designer:	George M. McClain
Built:	1894; Essex, Massachusetts, Tarr and James Shipyard
Coast Guard certification:	Sailing School Vessel (Subchapter R), Passenger Vessel (Subchapter T)
Crew:	11. Trainees/passengers: 80 (day), 24 (overnight)
Contact:	Gregg Swanzey, Executive Director
	Schooner Ernestina Commission
	PO Box 2010
	New Bedford, MA 02741-2010
	Tel: 508-992-4900; Fax: 508-984-7719
	E-mail:gswanzey@ernestina.org
	Web site: http://www.ernestina.org

Esprit

Esprit was launched in 1995. Honored in 1997 for her work promoting international understanding with mixed 50:50 German/host country crews, she is the only German sail training vessel to win the Cutty Sark Trophy. Since then Esprit has sailed as a sail training vessel between England, Portugal, the Lofoten Islands in northern Norway, and Russia, taking part in all European Cutty Sark Tall Ships Races. In 2000 she took part in the Tall Ships 2000® Race Around the Atlantic, winning honors in class Southampton/ Cadiz, and Cadiz/ Bermuda, with mixed German/American/ Bermudan/Norwegian/Australian crew, several on scholarships from HANSA and ISTA. Esprit returns to Gulf of Maine in 2003.

Esprit is a "cold-molded" wooden boat. Built for safe sailing with good handling qualities and high speed potential, she is easily sailed by novice crews, with her modern rig: gaff fore, Bermuda main. Living on board is comfortable in a bright modern atmosphere - from the galley, mess, and state-of-the-art navigation area there is a panoramic view of the sea. Trainee berths are in three four-berth cabins, each with its private head. Esprit's owner, BBV seeks to teach teamwork and traditional and contemporary boat-building skills, to develop self confidence through experiential education, and to further international understanding through exchanges of young participants.

BBV's 95-foot sailing ship Franzius, new in 2000, is available on the Weser, Elbe and Baltic for up to 32 people. School groups, incentive and corporate training, as well as individuals are welcome.

Flag:	Germany
Rig:	Schooner, two-masted
Homeport/waters:	Bremen-Vegesack: North Sea, Baltic, and Atlantic
Who sails?	Youth trainees, individuals, and groups.
Cost:	$70 for youth trainees, $110 for trainees over 26 per day
Program type:	Sail training for students, apprentices, and adults as paying trainees.
Specifications:	LOA: 64' 9" Draft: 9' 9" Sail area: 1,800 sq. ft.
	Beam: 16' 6" Hull: wood Power: 212 HP diesel
Designer:	Volker T. Behr, N.A.
Built:	1995; Bremen, Germany, Bremer Bootsbau Vegesack
Certification:	Constructed to specifications of German Lloyd
Crew:	4. Trainees: 4 (day sails), 12 (overnight)
Contact:	BBV Sailing
	Teerhof 46
	D-28199 Bremen, Germany
	Tel: 49-421-50-50-37; Fax: 49-421-59-14-00
	E-mail: info@bbv-sailing.de
	Web site: http://www.bbv-sailing.de

The barque *Europa* was built for the City of Hamburg in 1911 at the Stulcken Shipyard. Between 1987 and 1994, she was restored into a fine square-rigger.

The ship represents the end of the famous clipper era and is one of the few ships in the world that carries a full set of studding sails. Below decks you will find a classic romantic interior with lounge, bar, and saloon. All cabins have their own shower and toilet, and modern necessities for safety and comfort are hidden by the historic appearance.

For part of the year, *Europa* is the official sail training vessel of the Enkhuizen Nautical College, which educates officers and masters for commercial oceangoing sailing vessels.

In 2000 she sailed the entire Tall Ships 2000® race and went to Antarctica for 4 expeditions. Upon her return in 2001 the *Europa* participated in the Cutty Sark Tall Ships race, before returning to the USA in October 2001. In November 2001 she started her long voyage to the Far East, where she will participate as the only European tall ship in the Sail Korea 2002 races, before crossing the Pacific again for the 2002 Pacific Coast TALL SHIPS CHALLENGE®. She will sail a classic Cape Horn Voyage from San Diego to the Falklands and will call at South Georgia and the Antarctic Peninsula before returning to her home waters.

Flag:	The Netherlands
Rig:	Barque, three-masted
Homeport/waters:	Amsterdam, The Netherlands: world wide
Who sails?	Youth trainees, individuals, families, and groups of all ages.
Cost:	From $ 110 per person per day (overnight). Special rates for youth trainees.
Program type:	Sail training for paying trainees. Fully accredited sea education in maritime history. Special expeditions. Dockside interpretation during port visits.

Specifications:

Sparred length: 185'	Draft: 12'	Sail area: 11,000 sq. ft.
LOD: 143'	Beam: 24'	Tons: 303 GRT
LOA: 150'	Rig height: 109'	Hull: steel
LWL: 132'	Freeboard: 4'	

Built:	1911; Hamburg, Germany, Stülcken
Certification:	Bureau Veritas Worldwide
Crew:	12. Trainees: 100 (day sails), 50 (overnight)
Contact:	Rederij Bark Europa B.V.
	Vissershavenweg 65-I
	NL-2583 DL The Hague, The Netherlands
	PO Box 17402
	NL-2502 CK The Hague, The Netherlands
	Tel: +31-70-331 7475; Fax: +31-70-354 2865
	E-mail: info@barkeuropa.com
	Web site: http://www.barkeuropa.com

Evangelyn

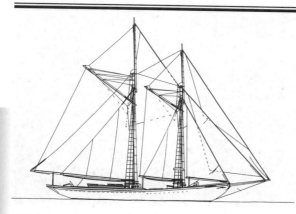

for sail training, maritime related courses, and private charters on the waters surrounding Narragansett Bay.

The students of the Aquidneck Island School of Boatbuilding, Newport, RI will conduct construction of these schooners, over the next two years beginning mid-2001.

Students enrolled in this full-time course will be involved in the design, displacement, and stability calculations, lofting, construction, commissioning, and certification of these schooners. Once in operation, there will be six paid sail training berths available.

The schooner *Evangelyn* and her sister ship *Narragansett* are an adaptation of the style of fast fishing schooner once common along the New England coast prior to the World War II. Designed for the Newport Schooner Project, these schooners will be used

Flag:	USA
Rig:	Schooner
Homeport/waters:	Newport, Rhode Island: Narragansett Bay and vicinity
Who sails?	Individuals and groups of all ages.
Program type:	Sail training for volunteer crew/trainees in cooperation with accredited institutions and other organized groups.

Specifications:

Sparred length: 86'	Draft: 9'	LOD: 57'6"
Beam: 15'4"	Tons: 40 GRT	LOA: 62'10"
Rig height: 65'	LWL: 46'10"	Hull: wood
Power: 100HP CAT		

Designer:	Jeff Szala
Built:	Fall 2000; Newport, Rhode Island, Aquidneck Island School of Boatbuilding
Coast Guard certification:	Passenger Vessel (Subchapter T) approved
Crew:	5. Trainees/passengers: 45 (day sails), 4 (overnight)
Contact:	Jeff Szala, Project Manager
	Newport Schooner Project
	c/o The Aquidneck Island School of Boatbuilding
	PO Box 913
	Newport, RI 02840
	Tel: 401-849-5034
	E-mail: Jeff@aisbinc.org
	Web site: http://www.aisbinc.org

The Los Angeles Maritime Institute is constructing two 90-foot brigantines named *Exy Johnson* and *Irving Johnson* in honor of the Johnsons and their life-long commitments to character-building sail training. The vessels were launched on April 27, 2002 and will be commissioned by the end of August.

The voyages of Irving (1905-1991) and Electa (b. 1909) Johnson aboard *Yankee* are well known by nearly everyone familiar with the sea.

When asked, "How does your wife feel about all this voyaging?" Captain Irving Johnson's reply was, "It was her idea!" As his extraordinary wife-mate, *Exy* distinguished herself as a full partner on their three *Yankees*. Her skills and talents complimented and completed the excellence of their joint endeavors. *Exy* is a multi-lingual, cultural ambassador extraordinaire, whether exploring remote islands of the vast Pacific, leading her pre-teen granddaughter out on the bowsprit of SEA's *Corwith Cramer*, or going aloft, at 85, when she sailed on the *Swift of Ipswich*.

Construction took place at the Los Angeles Maritime Museum in John Gibson Park, San Pedro, CA. The brigantine design, based on one developed in the 1930's, was adapted by W.I.B. Crealock to meet US Coast Guard and LAMI program requirements.

The shipyard is visitor-friendly, set up as a living history exhibit of the museum. Construction was carried out by professional, paid shipwrights, working with trained volunteers. Funding for this project has come from private donations, corporate sponsorships, and foundation grants.

Flag:	USA
Rig:	Brigantine
Homeport/waters:	Los Angeles, California: Southern California and offshore islands
Who sails?	Referred youth-at-risk and groups catering to students and adults
Season:	Year-round
Cost:	Based on ability to pay
Program type:	Educational sailing adventures for youth and adult groups.

Specifications:			
	Sparred length: 110' 8"	Draft: 11'	Sail area: 4,540 sq. ft.
	LOA: 90'	Beam: 21' 9"	Tons: 99 GRT
	LWL: 72' 6"	Rig height: 87' 8"	Power: diesel

Coast Guard certification:	Sailing School Vessel (Subchapter R), Passenger Vessel (Subchapter T)
Contact:	Captain Jim Gladson, President
	Los Angeles Maritime Institute
	Berth 84, Foot of Sixth Street
	San Pedro, CA 90731
	Tel: 310-833-6055; Fax: 310-548-2055

Eye of the Wind

Originally a topsail schooner, the *Eye of the Wind* was built for the South American hide trade in 1911. In 1923 she was sold to Swedish owners and for the next fifty years served as Baltic trader in the Baltic and North Seas.

In 1973, she was purchased by a private five-member syndicate that restored and furnished her to serve as the flagship of Operation Drake in the South Pacific. Along with an appearance in the First Fleet Reenactment to celebrate Australia's centenary, this brigantine again rounded Cape Horn in December 1991 to take place in the Grand Columbus Regatta of 1992. She starred in the movie *White Squall*. In 2000 she participated in Tall Ships 2000® making two transatlantic crossings, from Cadiz, Spain to Bermuda, and again from Halifax, Nova Scotia, Canada to Amsterdam, The Netherlands.

With her tanbark sails and colorful pennants flying from her mainmast, *Eye of the Wind* is an active and attractive addition to the international fleet of tall ships.

Flag:	United Kingdom			
Rig:	Brigantine			
Homeport/waters:	Faversham, Kent, United Kingdom			
Who sails?	Individuals of all ages			
Program type:	Sail training for paying trainees			
Specifications:	Sparred length: 127'	LOA: 105'	Draft: 10'	
	Beam: 24'	Rig height: 84'	Tons: 150 GRT	
	Hull: Iron	Hull color: black		
Built:	1911			
Crew:	4. Trainees/passengers: 30			
Contact:	Mr. Ole Johannessen			
	PO Box 22003			
	Los Angeles, CA 90022			
	Tel: 323-726-3503; Fax: 323-726-1005			
	E-mail: olewj@aol.com			

Built in 1982, *Fair Jeanne* is a 110-foot brigantine originally built by the late Captain Thomas G. Fuller as a private yacht. Carrying 4,000 square feet of sail, the ship is now in service as a sail training vessel carrying up to 30 youths aged 14 to 24. Programs are also available for adults and seniors. During the summer months, the ship operates in the Great Lakes, St Lawrence Seaway and the East Coast. During 2000, *Fair Jeanne* participated in a range of activities including the Boston to Halifax Race Leg of Tall Ships 2000®; and in 2001, Tall Ships Challenge 2001®. The program reflects Captain Fuller's belief in using sail training as a means of building confidence and resourcefulness in our youth. He was one of Canada's most decorated WW II naval war heroes, earning the name "Pirate of the Adriatic" and holding the distinction of the longest time served in offensive war action. His wartime experience taught him the value of instilling confidence and resourcefulness in our youth through adventure at sea. Bytown Brigantine, Inc. was established in 1983 by the Fuller family as a charitable foundation to provide opportunities for young people to experience adventure in the time-honored traditions inherent in square rigged sailing, aboard the family's donated brigantines *Fair Jeanne* and *Black Jack*.

Flag:	Canada
Rig:	Brigantine
Homeport/waters:	Ottawa, Ontario, Canada: Great Lakes, Maritime Provinces (summer), Caribbean (winter)
Who sails?	Students between 14 and 24, adults, seniors (June, September)
Season:	May to October
Cost:	$100 Canadian per person per day
Program type:	Sail training for paying trainees. Sea education in maritime history in cooperation with organized groups and as informal, in-house programming. Dockside interpretation during port visits.

Specifications:	Sparred length: 110'	Draft: 6'	Sail area: 4,000 sq. ft.
	Rig height: 80'	Beam: 24' 6"	Tons: 135 GRT
	Freeboard: 8'	Hull: steel & fiberglass	Power: 235 HP

Designer:	T.G. Fuller
Built:	1981; Ottawa, Ontario, Canada, T. G. Fuller
Crew:	6. Trainees/passengers: 50 (day sails), 24 (overnight)
Contact:	Simon A. F. Fuller, President
	or Robbin Zrudlo, Foundation Manager
	Bytown Brigantine, Inc.
	2700 Queensview Drive
	Ottawa, Ontario K2B 8H6 Canada
	Tel: 613-596-6258; Fax: 613-596-5947
	E-mail: tallshipinfo@tallshipsadventure.org
	Web site: http://tallshipsadventure.org

Fantasy

Planned in 1870, the *Fantasy* was not built until 1913. During that time, trees were planted and grown specifically for this ship, bent and bound during growth and earmarked for various parts of the vessel. In 1998, *Isla De Ibiza* became *Fantasy*, and a new era in her history began. Today's ship is an elegant mixture of old-world shipbuilding techniques and modern amenities.

Originally named *Isla De Ibiza*, the *Fantasy* has had a colorful history.

Flag:	USA
Rig:	Topsail schooner, two-masted
Homeport/waters:	Castries, St. Lucia: Caribbean
Who sails?	High school and college students, and individuals.
Program type:	Sail training for paying trainees. Sea education in marine science, maritime history, and culture and language studies in cooperation with accredited institution and as part of informal, in-house programming.
Cost:	$3,000 per person per month

Specifications:

Sparred length: 120'	Draft: 8' 10"	Sail area: 4,000 sq. ft.
LOD: 90'	Beam: 19'	Tons: 150 GRT
LOA: 96'	Rig height: 75'	Power: Caterpillar 342
LWL: 90'	Freeboard: 3'	Hull: wood

Built: 1912; Spain, Palma Sues Shipyard

Contact: Tom Gibbs
Experiential Learning
210 Dixon Street
Henderson, KY 42420
Tel: 502-827-8291; Fax: 502-827-8006
E-mail: tgibbs@cooltides.com
Web site: http://cooltides.com

The 65' sloop, *America II*, was the third boat built for the New York Yacht Club's 1987 America's Cup Challenge. She was featured in the movie "WIND". Acquired by Alfred B. Van Liew in the fall of 1993, she was re-named *Fiddler*.

Flag:	USA
Rig:	Sloop
Homeport/waters:	Newport, Rhode Island: Southern New England
Who sails?	Individuals of all ages.
Program type:	Sail training for volunteer crew/trainees from local colleges and universities. Training for Corinthian Racing and events in cooperation with the Newport Museum of Yachting's Courageous Program.

Specifications:		
Sparred length: 65'	Draft: 9'	Beam: 12'
LOA: 65'	LOD: 65'	LWL: 50'
Rig height: 90'	Tons: 28 GRT	Freeboard: 4'
Power: Volvo 100 HP		

Designer:	S & S
Built:	1986; Newport, Rhode Island, Williams & Manchester
Crew:	15. Trainees/passengers: 4
Contact:	Alfred B. Van Liew, Owner
	306 Indian Avenue
	Middletown, RI 02842
	Tel: 401-272-2510 ext. 106; Fax: 401-272-6590
	E-mail: avanliew@vanliewtrust.com

Formidable

Boston area in the summer. She hopes to be Subchapter T inspected by 2002. An extensive day charter schedule will be offered, including fundraising for nonprofit organizations. *Formidable* is rigged as a brig. Her main mast has main tops'l, main royal, main top gallant and main course square sails. Her foremast carries the fore tops'l , fore topgallant, fore royal, and fore course square sails. *Formidable* is one of the few maritime military reenactors.

Formidable has an active reenactment schedule in the St. Petersburg, Florida area in the winter, and the

Flag: USA
Rig: Brig
Homeport/waters: Gloucester, Massachusetts
Program type: Day charters including fund raising trips for non-profit organizations. Maritime military reenactments.
Specifications: Sparred length: 72'   Draft: 6'   Sail area: 3,000 sq. ft.
LOA: 55'   Beam: 18'   Rig height: 55'
LWL: 49'
Contact: Captain Keating Willcox
Longmeadow Way - Box 403
Hamilton, MA 01936-0403
Tel: 866-921-9674; Fax: 978-468-1954
E-mail: kwillcox@shore.net
Web site: http://www.tallshipformidable.com

Friendship, a full size replica of a Salem East Indiaman built for the National Park Service and berthed at Salem Maritime National Historic Site in Salem, Massachusetts, was launched in August 1998. Although she represents a specific vessel built in Salem in 1797, she is typical of a class of commercial carriers commonly employed in both the East India and trans-atlantic trades during the early years of the new American republic.

Friendship's historic predecessor is credited with 15 voyages to the Far East, South America, Mediterranean, and northern Europe. She had the misfortune of being taken as a prize of war by the Royal Navy on a return voyage from Archangel, Russia, in 1812. Sold by the British government in 1813, her ultimate fate remains a mystery.

Today's *Friendship* is built from wood laminates and solid timbers and was designed to meet all requirements as a passenger carrying and sail training vessel while exhibiting the look and function of an historic vessel.

While the National Park Service completes her remaining rigging, *Friendship* is accessible to the public for dockside tours. The National Park Service and the "Friends of Friendship" are developing interpretive and sailing programs jointly. Ongoing outfitting and rigging activities may be viewed from adjacent wharves at Salem Maritime National Historic Site.

Flag:	USA
Rig:	Full-rigged ship
Homeport/waters:	Salem, Massachusetts
Program type:	Dockside interpretation as an historic site exhibit. Port visitation. Informal sea education in maritime history.

Specifications:			
	Sparred length: 171'	Draft: 11' 3"	Sail area: 9,409 sq. ft.
	LOD: 104'	Beam: 30'	Tons: 99 GRT
	LOA: 116'	Rig height: 112'	Power: twin 300 HP diesels
	LWL: 99'	Freeboard: 10'	Hull: wood

Designer:	Bay Marine, Inc., Barrington, Rhode Island
Built:	1998; Port of Albany, New York, Scarano Boats: 1999-2000; Dion Yacht Yard, Salem, Massachusetts.
Contact:	Colleen Bruce, Project Manager
	Salem Maritime National Historic Site
	174 Derby Street
	Salem, MA 01970
	Tel: 978-740-1694; Fax: 978-740-1685
	E-mail: colleen_Bruce@nps.gov

There she met up with the Tall Ships 2000® fleet arriving from Europe. From Bermuda, *Fritha* raced to Charleston, South Carolina as part of ASTA's Bermuda to Charleston Race. She then cruised in company up the Eastern Seaboard to Boston, Massachusetts, where she participated in Sail Boston 2000. She completed the voyage with her arrival in Mackeral Cove, Maine, only a few nautical miles from her place of origin, the drawing board of her designer, Murray Petterson.

   Fritha is available for sail training charters on a weekly basis for groups of up to six. She is also available for special events.

Built in New Zealand in 1985, *Fritha* reached Bermuda in May of 2000.

Flag:	USA
Rig:	Brigantine
Homeport/waters:	Mackeral Cove, Maine
Who sails?	Groups and individuals of all ages. Private charters.
Season:	June to October
Cost:	$6000 per week, private charter
Program type:	Sail training for paying trainees. Private charters. Special event appearances.

Specifications:			
	Sparred length: 74'	LOD: 53'	LOA: 47'
	Draft: 7'	Beam: 14'	Rig height: 65'
	Freeboard: 5'	Tons: 40 GRT	Power: 175 HP diesel
	Hull: wood		

Designer:	Murray Petterson
Built:	1985; New Zealand, McMullan and Wing
Coast Guard certification:	Uninspected Vessel (6 passengers)
Crew:	3. Trainees/passengers: 12 (day sails), 6 (overnight)
Contact:	Philip Fuller, Captain/Owner
	304 Chestnut Street
	N. Andover, MA 01845
	Tel: 918-685-0061; Fax: 978-258-6808
	E-mail: lbpomeroy@aol.com

The brig *Fryderyk Chopin* is one of a series of modern tall ships designed by Zygmunt Choren, and built in Poland over the last twenty years. Since her maiden voyage as part of the 1992 transatlantic Columbus Race, she has proven to be a very fast vessel. Her sea worthiness was successfully tested when she voyaged around Cape Horn in the winter 1999/2000. She is a frequent and regular participant in the annual Cutty Sark Tall Ship races and other tall ship events.

The brig was designed to the specifications of Captain Krysztof (Chris) Baranowski to accommodate long-term, tall ship-based schooling for teenagers. Continuing in this service, the *Fryderyk Chopin* and Canadian-based Class Afloat (see *Concordia*) will celebrate their 10th Anniversary of working together to provide sail training and education under sail opportunities to young people of all nationalities.

The ship is presently owned by the European School of Law and Administration in Warsaw, Poland. When not engaged in providing semesters at sea to Polish students, she is available to groups of trainees of all ages, with or without previous experience.

PHOTO BY WOJTEK WACOWSKI

Fryderyk Chopin

Flag :	Poland
Rig:	Brig
Homeport/waters:	Szczecin, Poland: worldwide
Who sails?	Individuals and Groups of all ages
Season:	Year-round
Program type:	Sail training for paying trainees, semesters at sea, dockside receptions while in port

Specifications:

Sparred length: 182'	LOA: 151'	Draft: 12' 6"
Beam: 28'	Rig height: 122'	Sail area:12,912 SQ.FT.
Tons: 360 GRT	Power: 400 HP diesel	
Hull:steel		

Designer:	Zygmunt Choren
Built:	1992; Poland
Crew:	8. Trainees/passengers: 42
Contact:	European School of Law and Administration
	ul. Grodzienska 21/29
	03-750 Warszawa
	Tel: 011-22-6199011; Fax: 011-22-6195240

North American Representative:
Wojtek (Voytec) Wacowski
Tel: 440-775-3158
E-mail: voytec@tallshipharbor.com
Web site: http://www.tallshipharbor.com

Future Builders

Mr. Ted Kryzak
PO Box 291
Milton Mills, NH 03852
Tel: 207-477-2883

Fyrdraca is based on a small 10th-century warship found near Ralswiek on the German Island of Rugen in the Baltic Sea. The Longship Company seeks to rediscover the lost arts of early medieval sailing and navigation. To that end, *Fyrdraca* sails twice a month from March through November with a volunteer crew.

Fyrdraca also appears at waterfront and cultural festivals near the Potomac River and Chesapeake Bay and also participates in living history demonstrations in concert with the Markland Medieval Mercenary Militia's Viking reenactment camps. Voyage and demonstration schedules are published on the Longship Company's Web site.

Fyrdraca and her consort *Gyrfalcon* are both owned and operated by the Longship Company, Ltd., a member-supported nonprofit educational organization.

Flag:	USA
Rig:	Viking longship
Homeport/waters:	Oakley, Maryland: Potomac River and Chesapeake Bay
Who sails?	School groups from elementary school through college. Individuals of all ages.
Season:	March to November
Program type:	Sail training for volunteer crew and apprentices. Sea education in maritime history based on informal, in-house programming. Non-paying passengers for day sails. Dockside interpretation during port visits.

Specifications:	Sparred length: 34'	Draft: 2'	Sail area: 240 sq. ft.
	LOA: 32'	Beam: 9' 2"	Tons: 3 GRT
	LWL: 29'	Rig height: 25'	Hull: wood
	Freeboard: 2' 6"		

Designer:	Traditional Norse design
Built:	1979; Keyport, New Jersey, Hans Pederson & Sons
Coast Guard certification:	Uninspected Vessel
Crew:	18 (day sails), 12 (overnight). Trainees/passengers: 4 -12
Contact:	Bruce E. Blackistone, Registered Agent
	Longship Company, Ltd.
	21924 Oakley Road
	Avenue, MD 20609
	Tel: 301-390-4089
	E-mail: longshipco@hotmail.com
	Web site: http://www.wam.umd.edu/~eowyn/Longship/

(PHOTO BY AL OLZAUSKAS, JR.)

Gallant

Bay Schooner Races in 1994 and 1997, the 1986 salute to the Statue of Liberty, and OpSail 2000 in New York Harbor. *Gallant* is based on a Chesapeake Bay pilot schooner with quite a bit of coaster influence. Her designer described her as being a "main topmast flying jibboomer."

Gallant is of unusually rugged build by today's standards, using very traditional construction features such as standing rigging of iron cable, tarred, parceled and served, maintained with pine tar, and fastened to lignum vitae deadeyes. She has plenty of deck area to enjoy a stable sail. *Gallant* is privately owned and maintained, offering guests day trips on the lower Hudson and East River, teaching the workings of the schooner rig, safety, and traditional maintenance, among other subjects. Based at Liberty Landing Marina across from lower Manhattan, *Gallant* carries a 10-gauge cannon for saluting notable vessels.

Pete Cullers' schooner *Gallant* was designed and built for Richard Tilghman in 1966, who cruised her on the East Coast until 1983, at which time she was donated to the Chesapeake Bay Maritime Museum. In 1986 the present owners, Tuck and Anne Elfman, purchased her from the Museum and put her back into service sailing the Chesapeake Bay and coastal waters, participating in the Great Chesapeake

Flag:	USA
Rig:	Main topsail schooner, two-masted
Homeport/waters:	Jersey City, New Jersey; Hudson River, East River and East Coast
Who sails?	Individuals of all ages and families
Program type:	Sail training for volunteer crew or trainees. Informal, in-house programming in vessel maintenance. Dockside interpretation while in homeport.

Specifications:			
	Sparred length: 62'	Draft: 6' 6"	Sail area: 1,450 sq. ft.
	LOD: 40' 6"	Beam: 12' 6"	Tons: 20 GRT
	LOA: 43' 8"	Rig height: 62'	Power: 68 HP diesel
	LWL: 35'	Freeboard: 2'	Hull: wood

Designer:	Pete Culler
Built:	1966; South Dartmouth, Massachusetts, Concordia – Waldo Howland
Coast Guard certification:	Uninspected Vessel
Crew:	1. Trainees/passengers: 6
Contact:	A. Tuck Elfman, Owner 51 Elfman Drive Doylestown, PA 18901 Tel: 215-348-2731: Fax: 215-348-4178

SAIL TALL SHIPS!

The scow schooner was a unique type of working sailing craft developed to transport cargo around San Francisco Bay and its tributaries. These thoroughly effective and practical vessels combined a variety of desirable qualities: they navigated shallow rivers, were easy to work, handled well under different conditions, and maneuvered well in close quarters. *Gas Light* is a replica of the famous San Francisco bay scows that plied the bay during the nineteenth century, until the advent of the internal combustion engine.

The original *Gas Light* was built in the1870's. More than a century later, in 1991, the new *Gas Light* was launched. Billy Martinelli, the owner and primary craftsman, conceived and built the new schooner *Gas Light* as a window on the proud heritage of the original working scows.

The schooner *Gas Light* is available for special events and private parties seeking a sailing adventure on San Francisco Bay and its tributaries. This schooner's spacious, light, and airy 19 x 30 ft cabin, with a 12 ft buffet table, is ideal for parties of 25 to 35, although *Gas Light* can carry up to 49 passengers.

Sail back in time on a traditional working schooner designed for extreme stability while under sail on bay and delta waters. Overnight and extended excursions for smaller parties may be arranged.

Gas Light's crew would like to share their passion, knowledge, and skills of sailing aboard this remarkable gaff rigged schooner.

Flag:	USA
Rig:	San Francisco scow schooner
Homeport/waters:	Sausalito, California: San Francisco Bay
Who sails?	Groups and individuals of all ages. Private charters.
Program type:	Sail training for paying trainees in cooperation with organized groups and established non-profit organizations

Specifications:	Sparred length: 72'	LOD: 50'	LWL: 42'
	Draft: 3' 4" (centerboard up), 7' 6" (centerboard down)	Beam: 19'
	Rig height: 70'	Freeboard: 2' 6"	Sail area: 1,700 sq. ft.
	Tons: 48 GRT	Power: Detroit diesel 671	

Designer:	Billy Martinelli
Built:	1991; Sausalito, California, Billy Martinelli
Coast Guard certification:	Passenger Vessel (Subchapter T)
Crew:	3. Trainees/passengers: 49 (day sails) 10 (overnight)
Contact:	Billy Martinelli, Owner/Builder
	60C Liberty Ship Way
	Sausalito, CA 94965
	Tel: 415-331-2769
	E-mail: gaslightcharters@hotmail.com
	Web site: http://www.gaslightcharters.com

Gazela Philadelphia

and Camden, New Jersey. A new initiative is the maritime education of Philadelphia's disadvantaged youth. *Gazela* and her volunteer crew have also taken part in the filming of *Interview with the Vampire,* the documentary *The Irish in America,* and *The Widow of St. Pierre.*

The century-old *Gazela Philadelphia* was built as a Grand Banks fishing vessel. She is one of many Portuguese ships that fished for cod there for hundreds of years. Now owned and operated by the Philadelphia Ship Preservation Guild, a nonprofit organization, the *Gazela* sails as a goodwill ambassador for the City of Philadelphia, the Commonwealth of Pennsylvania, and the Ports of Philadelphia

Gazela is maintained and sailed by a very active and knowledgeable volunteer group participating in maintenance and sail training activities throughout the year. After 25 hours of work on the vessel, a volunteer is eligible for a crew position on the next available voyage.

Flag:	USA
Rig:	Barquetine, three-masted
Homeport/waters:	Philadelphia, Pennsylvania: Delaware River and Atlantic Coast
Who sails?	Volunteers who support the maintenance of the ship. Dockside visitors include school groups from elementary school through college, as well as individuals and families.
Program type:	Sail training for crew and apprentices. Sea education based on informal, in-house programming. Dockside interpretation during outport visits.

Specifications:			
	Sparred length: 178'	Draft: 17'	Sail area: 8,910 sq. ft.
	LOD: 140'	Beam: 27' 9"	Tons: 299 GRT
	LOA: 150'	Rig height: 100'	Power: diesel
	LWL: 133'	Hull: wood	

Built:	1883; Cacilhas, Portugal. Major rebuild 1901; Setubal, Portugal
Coast Guard certification:	Attraction Vessel and Uninspected Vessel
Crew:	35 (volunteer)
Contact:	Gay Burgiel, Volunteer Coordinator
	Philadelphia Ship Preservation Guild
	801 S. Columbus Blvd.
	Philadelphia, PA 19147-4306
	Tel: 215-218-0110; Fax: 215-463-1875
	E-mail: gazela@usa.net
	Web site: http://www.gazela.org

Geronimo makes three six-to-eight week trips during the school year, carrying students from St. George's School. Marine biology and English are taught on board, and the students continue their other courses by correspondence with the faculty at St. George's. Students receive full academic credit for their time on board. These cruises usually include operations along the eastern seaboard and in the waters of the Bahamas and northern Caribbean.

Geronimo's marine biology research has always included tagging sharks and collecting biological samples for the Apex Predator Investigation of the National Marine Fisheries Service. *Geronimo* also tags sea turtles in cooperation with the Center for Sea Turtle Research of the University of Florida. Their recent work has included the use of satellite transmitters on loggerhead turtles in Bahamian waters.

In the summer, *Geronimo* makes two three-week cruises, usually to the waters south of New England, to Bermuda, or to the Bahamas. Each summer cruise includes a series of lectures on marine biology and fisheries management as well as sail training, snorkeling, and the collecting of data on turtles and/or sharks.

Flag:	USA
Rig:	Sloop
Homeport/waters:	Newport, Rhode Island: North Atlantic and Caribbean
Who sails?	Enrolled students at St. George's School.
Season:	Year-round
Cost:	Regular school tuition (winter); inquire for summer 2001 cruise
Program type:	Full curriculum academics, marine biology, and environmental studies for high school students.

Specifications:			
	Sparred length: 69' 8"	Draft: 6' 8" 13' 5",	Sail area: 2,091 sq. ft.
	LOD: 68'	Beam: 18' 7"	Tons: 53 GRT
	LOA: 69' 8"	Rig height: 85' 6"	Power: diesel
	LWL: 53' 11"	Freeboard: 5'	Hull: fiberglass

Designer:	Ted Hood Design Group
Built:	1998; Portsmouth, Rhode Island, New England Boatworks
Coast Guard certification:	Sailing School Vessel (Subchapter R)
Crew:	2. Trainees: 8
Contact:	St. George's School
	372 Purgatory Road, PO Box 1910
	Newport, RI 02840
	Tel: 401-847-7565; Fax: 401-842-6696
	E-mail: geronimo@stgeorges.edu
	Web site: http://www.stgeorges.edu

Glenn L. Swetman

Ship Island. Walk-up day sailing trips are made when she is not under charter. Groups can learn about the maritime and seafood heritage of the Gulf Coast and about the vessels that began Biloxi's seafood industry. The *Glenn L. Swetman* is an integral part of the museum's Sea and Sail Summer Camp, and sailing classes are also offered through local colleges. *Glenn L. Swetman* also accommodates weddings, parties, and Elderhostel and school groups.

The *Glenn L. Swetman* is the first of two replica Biloxi oyster schooners built by the Biloxi Schooner Project under the auspices of the Maritime and Seafood Industry Museum. She is available for charter trips in the Mississippi Sound and to the barrier islands, Cat Island, Horn Island, and

Money for construction and equipping the *Glenn L. Swetman* and her sister ship, *Mike Sekul,* has come from donations by interested individuals, businesses, civic groups, and a variety of museum-sponsored fundraising events.

Flag:	USA
Rig:	Gaff topsail schooner, two-masted
Homeport/waters:	Biloxi, Mississippi: northern Gulf of Mexico
Who sails?	Individuals and groups of all ages. Affiliated institutions include William Carey College, Mississippi State University, J.L. Scott Marine Education Center, and Seashore Methodist Assembly.
Season:	Year-round
Cost:	$20 per adult or $10 per child (2-1/2 hours). Group rates: 20 passengers - $950 per day, $600 for half-day, $350 (2-1/2 hrs). Additional passengers $15 each.
Program type:	Sail training for volunteer and paying trainees. Sea education in maritime history, marine science, and ecology for college students and adults in cooperation with accredited institutions, organized groups, and as informal in-house programming. Children's summer camp, scouting groups, and private charters.

Specifications:			
	Sparred length: 76'	Draft: 4' 10"	Sail area: 2,400 sq. ft.
	LOD: 50'	Beam: 17'	Tons: 21 GRT
	LOA: 65'	Freeboard: 4' 6"	Power: 4-71 Detroit diesel
	LWL: 47'	Hull: Juniper	

Designer:	William Holland
Built:	1989; Biloxi, Mississippi, William T. Holland
Coast Guard certification:	Passenger Vessel (Subchapter T)
Crew:	3. Trainees: 49 (day sails)
Contact:	Robin Krohn, Executive Director
	Maritime and Seafood Industry Museum of Biloxi
	PO Box 1907
	Biloxi, MS 39533
	Tel: 228-435-6320; Fax: 228-435-6309
	E-mail: schooner@maritimemuseum.org
	Web site: http://www.maritimemuseum.org

Gloria

Built in Bilbao, Spain, and purchased in 1966 by the Colombian Navy, the three-masted barque *Gloria* is used today as a school ship for the Colombian Navy. She has proudly served for 33 years training more than 700 officers and 4,500 enlisted men and women.

Gloria carries a complement of 150 men and women, ranging from enlisted to midshipmen and officers. The cruise is aimed at training officers, in their third year at the Naval Academy, to imple- ment their academic knowledge in the areas of navigation, seamanship, leadership, and teambuilding. *Gloria* is a proud goodwill ambassador of the Colombian Navy.

Flag:	Colombia
Rig:	Barque
Homeport/waters:	Cartegena, Colombia
Who sails?	Colombian Naval Academy cadets and officers of the Colombian Navy.
Season:	Year-round
Program type:	Sail training for Colombian Naval Academy cadets.

Specifications:			
	Sparred length: 249' 4"	Draft: 14' 9"	Sail area: 15,075 sq. ft.
	LOD: 189'	Beam: 34' 9"	Tons: 934 GRT
	LOA: 212'	Rig height: 126' 4"	Power: twin 256 KV
	LWL: 184'	Freeboard: 21' 7"	Hull: steel

Designer:	Sener
Built:	1968; Bilbao, Spain, Celaga S. A. Shipyards
Certification:	Colombian Naval vessel
Crew:	160
Contact:	Naval Attaché, Colombia
	2118 Leroy Place NW
	Washington, DC 20008
	Tel: 202-387-8338; Fax: 202-232-8643
	E-mail: arcgloria@yahoo.com

Grand Nellie

Designers Parker Marean III and Russel Woodin of Boothbay, Maine balanced traditional Maine schooner lines with modern technology for comfort, safety and performance in creating the classic schooner *Grand Nellie*. Top quality materials and equipment were chosen throughout the building process to meet the highest standards of compliance with US Coast Guard Oceans and SOLAS International regulations for passenger vessels.

Owner operated *Grand Nellie* provides tall ship sailing experience for beginner to advanced sailors of all ages and abilities. Participation in all aspects of vessel operation is encouraged to allow passengers and trainees to gain experience and increase their abilities while on board. Offshore and multiple day voyages provide participants the opportunity to be an integral part of sail handling, navigation and watchkeeping.

On deck, *Grand Nellie* is free of clutter, providing plenty of room to move about or just lounge in the sun or the shaded cockpit. Below deck, the open interior is beautifully appointed with cherry and maple custom woodwork.

Grand Nellie, known as the Queen of her Fleet, participates in festivals, special events and races throughout the Caribbean and Western Atlantic. In 2001, *Grand Nellie* led ASTA's fleet in the Great Lakes TALL SHIPS CHALLENGE® and was awarded the Perry Bowl.

PHOTO BY TIM WRIGHT

Flag:	USA
Rig:	Topsail schooner
Homeport/waters:	St. Thomas, USVI: Caribbean and Western Atlantic
Season:	Year-round
Who sails?	Families and individuals of all ages.
Program type:	Sail training for paying trainees. Sea education in cooperation with accredited institutions and other organized groups. Dockside interpretation. Participation in festivals and special events.

Specifications:			
	Sparred length: 75'	Draft: 8'	Beam: 16'
	LOA: 60'	LOD: 57'	LWL: 49'
	Rig height: 75'	Freeboard: 5'	Sail area: 3,000 sq. ft.
	Hull: steel	Power: 140 HP Yanmar	Tons: 42 GRT
	Hull color: white	Spar material: aluminum	

Designer:	Parker Marean III and Russel Woodin
Built:	1998; Merritt, North Carolina, Custom Steel Boats
Coast Guard certification:	Passenger Vessel (Subchapter T)
Homeport/waters:	Caribbean and Western Atlantic
Crew:	4. Trainees/passengers: 49 (day sails), 6 (overnight)
Contact:	Jeff and Ellen Troeltzsch
	Schooner Grand Nellie
	525 Lake Avenue South, Suite 405
	Duluth, MN 55802
	Tel: 252-249-0290, Cell: 602-538-5949; Fax: 252-249-0945
	E-mail: ellen@grandnellie.com
	Web site: http://www.grandnellie.com

Guayas was built in the Celaya Shipyard in Bilbao, Spain, with construction beginning in 1974. She is named after the Chief of Huancavilcas, a native culture in the Ecuadorian coastal region. The general arrangement was the same as *Gloria* of Colombia, *Simon Bolivar* of Venezuela and *Cuahtemoc* of Mexico were also built using the same design. *Guayas* was commissioned on July 23, 1977, and since that date has proudly served for more than 20 years training more than 500 officers and 3,000 enlisted men.

Guayas has participated in many tall ship events over the years. This representation has led her to be referred to as Ecuador's Afloat Embassy. The ship carries a complement of 16 officers, 43 midshipmen, and 94 enlisted men, including the ship's band. During a cruise, considered one semester at the Ecuadorian Naval Academy, midshipmen apply—in a very challenging environment—theoretical principles of navigation, seamanship, and other subjects learned in the classroom.

Flag:	Ecuador
Rig:	Barque
Homeport/waters:	Guayquil, Ecuador: cruises to various destinations worldwide
Who sails?	Ecuadorian Naval Academy cadets.
Season:	Year-round
Program type:	Sail training for Ecuadorian Naval Academy cadets.

Specifications:	Sparred length: 257' 1"	Draft: 15' 4"	Sail area: 15,784 sq. ft.
	LOD: 218'	Beam: 34' 9"	Hull: steel
	LOA: 221'	Power: diesel	LWL: 184'

Designer:	Celaya
Built:	1976; Celaya Shiupyard, Bilbao, Spain
Certification:	Ecuadorian Naval Vessel
Crew:	76
Contact:	Naval Attaché, Ecuador and Captain, "Buque Escuela Guayas"
	2535 15th St. NW
	Washington, DC 20009
	Tel: 202-265-7674; Fax: 202-667-3482
	E-mail: Aembassyec@aol.com

Gyrfalcon

Gyrfalcon is a copy of the faering (four-oared boat) buried with the Gokstad ship in Norway in the 9th century. She was built by the boat building program at the Hampton Mariner's Museum (now the North Carolina Maritime Museum) in Beaufort, North Carolina under the direction of Geoffrey Scofield

Gyrfalcon is often seen at cultural, waterfront, community, and boat festivals, historic reenactment events, and school demonstrations. She also participates in living history events in concert with the Markland Medieval Mercenary Militia's Viking reenactment camps, where the public enjoys the spectacle of crews, dressed in costume and armor, offering historic interpretation.

As an enticement to school children and adults to discover more about the Viking Age, *Gyrfalcon* often spends off-season time on display at area libraries and schools. *Gyrfalcon* and her consort, *Fyrdraca,* are both owned and operated by the Longship Company, Ltd., a member-supported nonprofit educational organization.

Flag:	USA
Rig:	Viking faering boat
Homeport/waters:	Oakley, Maryland: East Coast and Chesapeake Bay
Who sails?	School groups from elementary school through college. Individuals of all ages.
Season:	March to November
Program type:	Sail training for volunteer crew and apprentices. Sea education in maritime history based on informal, in-house programming. Dockside interpretation at port visits and outport events.

Specifications:	Sparred length: 21'	LOA: 21'	Draft: 1'
	Beam: 5'	Rig height: 10'	Freeboard: 1'
	Sail area: 80 sq. ft.	Tons: 200 lbs.	Hull: wood

Designer:	Traditional Norse design
Built:	1981; Hampton Mariner's Museum (now the North Carolina Maritime Museum), Beaufort, North Carolina
Coast Guard certification:	Uninspected vessel
Crew:	4. Trainees/passengers: 1-3
Contact:	Bruce E. Blackistone, Registered Agent
	Longship Company, Ltd.
	21924 Oakley Road
	Avenue, MD 20609
	Tel: 301-390-4089
	E-mail: longshipco@hotmail.com
	Web site: http://www.wam.umd.edu/~eowyn/Longship/

One of the last skipjacks to be built, and still commercially dredging oysters during the winter months (November – March), the *H. M. Krentz* offers day sails on the Chesapeake's Eastern Shore waters near St. Michaels, Maryland from April through October.

Get the feel of a true working vessel and learn about the history of the working fleet of sailing vessels on the Chesapeake Bay. Experience dragging for oysters, and then explore the ecology and economic development of the Chesapeake region through discussing the past and present status of this once abundant natural resource.

What we can learn about ourselves and about our surrounding world through sailing is what makes the present the greatest age of sail. By working with the technologies and traditions of the past, perhaps we can have a better vision for the future. Since 1972, Captain Ed Farley has been a commercial oysterman and has worked to preserve several of the working skipjacks; since 1985, he has been sharing his life experience with school children, business leaders, politicians and family groups.

Flag:	USA
Rig:	Skipjack/sloop
Homeport/waters:	Potomac River, Maryland; Chesapeake Bay
Season:	Mid-April to late October
Who sails?	School groups from elementary through college as well as families and individuals of all ages.
Program type:	Sail training for professional and volunteer crew/trainees. Sea education in marine science, maritime history and ecology as informal in-house programming. Dockside interpretation while in port.
Cost:	$30 per person per 2-hour day sail ($15 children under 12)
	$400 per school group (3-hour day sail), Group rate: $25 per person per 2-hr day sail (12 person minimum)

Specifications:			
	Sparred length: 70'	Draft: 4'8"	Sail area: 1,850 sq. ft.
	LOD: 48'	Beam: 16'	Tons: 8 GRT
	LOA: 54'	Rig height: 65'	Hull: wood
	LWL: 45'	Hull color: white	Spar material: wood
	Power: 150 HP diesel; yawl boat		

Designer:	Krentz/Skipjack
Built:	1955; Harryhogan, Virginia, Herman M. Krentz
Coast Guard certification:	Passenger Vessel (Subchapter T)
Crew:	1 Passengers/trainees: 32 (day sails)
Contact:	Captain Ed Farley
	Chesapeake Skipjack Sailing Tours, LLC
	PO Box 582
	St. Michaels, MD 21663
	Tel: 410-745-6080
	E-mail: hmkrentz@bluecrab.org
	Web site: http://www.oystercatcher.com

Half Moon (Halve Maen)

The replica ship *Half Moon (Halve Maen)* was launched on June 20, 1989, to draw attention to the exploration and colonization of the Mid-Atlantic States. The 1609 voyage of the original *Halve Maen*, under the command of Henry Hudson, led to the first European settlements by the Dutch in what are now the States of New York, New Jersey, Connecticut, Delaware, and Pennsylvania. In 1614, the Dutch named the area "Nieu Nederlandt."

Since her launch, the replica *Half Moon* has visited over 40 ports along the eastern seaboard and the Great Lakes. She has been boarded by over 100,000 visitors and participated in port festivals and a yearly New Netherland Festival. The Half Moon is featured in the 1994 Walt Disney movie, *Squanto: An Indian Warrior's Tale.*

The ship's design is based on original Dutch East India Company documents, including the resolution of 1608 ordering the original ship's construction and Juet's Journal. Hudson sailed the *Halve Maen* up the Hudson River as far as present-day Albany in 1609.

The *Half Moon's* program offers the public both an active sail training program and instruction on the history of New Netherland. Thus, the crew is trained in both historical presentation and ship handling.

Flag:	USA
Rig:	Full-rigged ship
Homeport/waters:	Albany, New York: East Coast and Great Lakes
Who sails?	School groups from elementary school through high school, individuals and adults.
Program type:	Sail training and maritime history based on informal programs. Dockside interpretation.

Specifications:			
	Sparred length: 95'	Draft: 8' 5"	Sail area: 2,757 sq. ft.
	LOD: 64' 3"	Beam: 17' 6"	Tons: 112 GRT
	LOA: 65'	Rig height: 78'	Power: diesel
	LWL: 84'	Freeboard: 10' 5"	Hull: wood

Designer:	Nicholas S. Benton
Homeport/waters:	Albany, New York: East Coast and Great Lakes
Built:	1989; Albany, New York; constructed by The New Netherland Museum
Coast Guard certification:	Attraction Vessel
Crew:	7-12 (day sails), 8-15 (overnight)
Contact:	Dr. Andrew Hendricks, Chairman
	New Netherland Museum and Half Moon Visitor Center
	PO Box 10609
	Albany, NY 12201-5609
	Tel: 518-443-1609
	Web site: http://www.newnetherland.org

SAIL TALL SHIPS!

The schooner *Harvey Gamage* is owned by the Ocean Classroom Foundation. She sails on sea education programs ranging from four month semesters-at-sea to weeklong programs with schools and youth groups. All programs use the power of the sea and the challenge of traditional seafaring as the basis for the academic curriculum taught on board.

Ocean Classroom, a fully accredited high school semester-at-sea, is a true voyage of discovery for qualified sophomores, juniors, and seniors. Young people come from all over the US to join this outstanding learning adventure. The voyage covers more than 4,000 nautical miles, connecting South American shores to the Canadian Maritimes. Students live and work as sailors while they study maritime history, maritime literature, marine science, applied mathematics, and navigation. Ocean Classroom is offered fall, spring, and summer terms.

Some other programs include SEAmester (a complete semester-at-sea for college credit), Marine Awareness Research Expeditions (also for college credit), and Summer Seafaring Camp (for teens age 13-17).

The Ocean Classroom Foundation also owns and operates the schooner *Spirit of Massachusetts.*

Flag:	USA
Rig:	Gaff topsail schooner, two-masted
Homeport/waters:	Islesboro, Maine: Eastern US and Canada (summer), Caribbean and South America (winter)
Who sails?	School groups from middle school through college. Affiliated institutions include Proctor Academy, Long Island University, Franklin Pierce College, and other schools.
Season:	Year-round
Cost:	Varies with program
Program type:	Sail training with paying trainees/students. Fully accredited sea education in marine science, maritime history, maritime literature, marine applied mathematics and navigation.

Specifications:			
	Sparred length: 131'	Draft: 9' 7"	Sail area: 4,200 sq ft.
	LOD: 90'	Beam: 23' 7"	Tons: 94 GRT
	LOA: 95'	Rig height: 91'	Power: 220 HP diesel
	LWL: 85'	Hull: wood	

Designer:	McCurdy & Rhodes
Built:	1973; South Bristol, Maine, Harvey Gamage Shipyard
Coast Guard certification:	Sailing School Vessel (Subchapter R), Passenger Vessel (Subchapter T)
Crew:	7 – 11 (including instructors). Students: 27 (overnight)
Contact:	Bert Rogers, Director Ocean Classroom Foundation, Inc. PO Box 446 Cornwall, NY 12518 Tel: 800-724-7245 or 845-615-1412; Fax: 845-615-1414 E-mail: mail@oceanclassroom.org Web site: http://www.oceanclassroom.org

The *Hawaiian Chieftain* is a 103-foot square-rigged topsail ketch. A replica of an 18th century European trading vessel, she was built in Hawaii in 1988 with a contemporary interpretation of a traditional design. She utilizes a variety of programs designed to develop self-esteem for youth in a challenging environment.

The ship has toured Californian ports in company with the *Lady Washington* for the past six winters providing the "Voyages of ReDiscovery" sailing and dockside educational programs. This hands-on-history program teaches 4th & 5th grade students about the exploration of the west coast during the 1790's.

The summertime "Voyagers Camp", for youth ages 13 to 16 years, is an expeditionary longboat program. The boats, two 25 foot Crotch Island pinky schooners and a 23 foot Royal Navy launch, are sailed on the San Francisco Bay and the Sacramento / San Joaquin River Deltas. A Sausalito based, week-long day camp "Buccaneers & Explorers Camp" aboard the *Chieftain* is available for youth ages 9 to 12 years. These programs focus on empowering the students through education, experience and exploration.

The *Hawaiian Chieftain* also offers sail training and team building for adults, private charters, natural history cruises and naval battle reenactments with visiting vessels.

Flag:	USA
Rig:	Square topsail ketch
Homeport/waters:	Sausalito, California: San Francisco Bay (summer), southern California coast (winter)
Who sails?	Elementary and middle school groups, individuals and families.
Season:	Year-round
Cost:	$30 to $100 per person for day sails; $2,400 group rate per day
Program type:	Sail training for volunteer or paying trainees. Sea education in maritime history in cooperation with accredited schools and colleges. Passenger day sails. Dockside interpretation during port visits.

Specifications:			
	Sparred length: 103'	Draft: 6'	Sail area: 4,200 sq. ft.
	LOD: 65'	Beam: 22'	Tons: 64 GRT
	Rig height: 75'	Freeboard: 3'	Power: twin diesels
	LWL: 62'	Hull: steel	

Designer:	Raymond R. Richards
Built:	1988; Lahaina, Maui, Hawaii, Lahaina Welding Co.
Coast Guard certification:	Passenger Vessel (Subchapter T)
Crew:	8. Trainees: 47
Contact:	Captain Ian McIntyre
	Hawaiian Chieftain Inc.
	Suite #266, 3020 Bridgeway
	Sausalito, CA 94965
	Tel: 415-331-3214; Fax: 415-331-9415
	E-mail: tallship@hawaiianchieftain.com
	Web site: http://www.hawaiianchieftain.com

Heart's Desire is a scaled down version of a 1920s fishing schooner. She has been beautifully restored by Paul Rollins and is now maintained and managed by Pease Boat Works and Marine Railway. *Heart's Desire* sails out of Chatham, Massachusetts with a crew of two, taking individuals, families and small groups day sailing or on special overnight adventures.

Flag:	USA
Rig:	Gaff schooner
Homeport/waters:	Chatham, Massachusetts: New England
Who sails?	Groups and individuals of all ages
Season:	Spring, Summer, Fall
Cost:	$135 per person per day
Program type:	Sail training for paying trainees, sea education in traditional maritime skills, private charters

Specifications:	Sparred length: 53'	LOD: 43'	LOA: 43'
	LWL: 32' 6"	Draft: 6' 4"	Beam: 11' 6"
	Rig height: 48	Freeboard: 4'	Sail area: 940 sq. ft.
	Tons: 15 GRT	Power: 48 HP diesel	

Designer:	John Alden
Built:	1925; Freeport, Maine, T. H. Soule
Restored:	1980; Paul Rollins
Coast Guard certification:	Uninspected Vessel (6 passenger)
Crew:	2. Trainees/passengers: 6 (day sails), 6 (overnight)
Contact:	Brad Pease, Director
	Cape Cod Maritime Traditions
	43 Eliphamets Lane
	Chatham, MA 02633
	Tel: 508-945-7800; Fax: 508-945-2285
	E-mail: info@peaseboatworks.com
	Web site: http://www.peaseboatworks.com

The *R/V Heraclitus* (named after the Greek philosopher, Heraclitus) is an 84 ft, ferro-cement, Chinese junk designed and built by the Institute of Ecotechnics (UK), and outfitted as an ocean-going research vessel. Since her launch in March, 1975, *R/V Heraclitus* has traveled over 200,000 nautical miles, undertaking a series of voyages and expeditions to some of the most challenging, remote and exotic places on Earth.

Although the *R/V Heraclitus* has performed many different tasks during this time, perhaps the real meaning of the ship has been to introduce people who first arrive aboard - with little understanding of life at sea - to the classic explorer tradition and the ancient ways of sea-peoples. All who have voyaged on *R/V Heraclitus* have experienced this marvelous way of life, the adventure of the high seas, remote cultures and coral reefs.

R/V Heraclitus has been chartered by the Planetary Coral Reef Foundation, www.pcrf.org, since 1991 and is now completing its eighth year of an ongoing expedition dedicated to mapping, monitoring and preserving the world's coral reefs. *R/V Heraclitus* offers an innovative seamanship and coral reef field research educational program and to date is the only ship continually out in the field studying and monitoring coral reefs on a planetary basis.

Flag:	Belize
Rig:	Chinese Junk
Homeport/waters:	Raffles Marina Singapore: Worldwide
Who sails?	The Planetary Coral Reef Foundation's nine month seamanship and coral reef research expedition attracts an international team of students 18 years or older.
Season:	Year-round
Program type:	In this expedition program, the student "learns by doing" and fully integrates into ship life, diving expeditions, coral reef research, as well as cultural exchanges.

Specifications:		
LOA: 84'	LWL: 70'	Draft: 8' 6"
Beam: 19' 6"	Tons: 118 GRT	Sail Area: 2,500 sq. ft.
Hull: Ferro-cement	Power: 671 Detroit Diesel	

Designer:	Institute of Ecotechnics (UK)
Built:	1974; Oakland, California
Certification:	Motor auxiliary sailing vessel in Panama
Crew:	6-7 officers and up to 7 apprentices
Age:	Over 18 years of age; primarily from 18 to 40
Contact:	Planetary Coral Reef Foundation
	9 Silver Hills Road
	Santa Fe, NM 87505 USA
	Tel: 505-474-7444; Fax: 505-424-3336
	E-mail: alling@pcrf.org
	Web site: http://www.pcrf.org

The beautiful varnished-hulled *Heritage* was built in 1970, the last year of the wooden twelve-meters. Designed, built, and sailed by Charlie Morgan, her tank tests showed her to be a technological breakthrough. However, by the end of the summer's racing, the redesigned *Intrepid* won the right to defend the Cup.

Heritage avenged her earlier defeat to *Intrepid* when they met on the Great Lakes in the 1980s. There she dominated the Great Lakes racing circuit, scoring multiple wins in the Chicago to Mackinac, Port Huron to Mackinac, Trans-Superior, and Queen's Cup races. In 1988 she sailed from the Lakes to California and in 1991 returned to New England. She is now part of the America's Cup Charters twelve-meter fleet in Newport, Rhode Island. *Heritage* is available for charter in New England and New York and is a perfect platform for family outings and corporate entertaining or team building.

Flag:	USA
Rig:	Sloop
Homeport/waters:	Newport, Rhode Island: New England and Chesapeake Bay
Who sails?	Individuals and groups of all ages
Cost:	$2100 group rate per day, $75 per person for evening sails
Program type:	Sail training for paying trainees. Passenger day sails, corporate team building, corporate racing, individual and group charters

Specifications:	LOD: 65'	Draft: 10'	Sail area: 1,700 sq. ft.
	LOA: 65'	Beam: 12'	Power: diesel
	LWL: 46'	Rig height: 90'	Hull: wood

Designer:	Charles Morgan
Built:	1970; Clearwater, Florida, Morgan Custom Yachts
Coast Guard certification:	Passenger Vessel (Subchapter T)
Crew:	3. Trainees: 14
Contact:	George Hill/Herb Marshall
	America's Cup Charters
	PO Box 51
	Newport, RI 02840
	Tel: 401-849-5868; Fax: 401-849-3098
	Web site: http://www.americascupcharters.com

Heritage of Miami II

The *Heritage of Miami II* is an 83-foot square topsail schooner that is modern in materials and construction but traditional in style. Built specifically for crossing wide expanses of open water, she has a wide, spacious deck that provides ample room for working the sails, lounging in the sun, and sleeping in the evening. Her shoal draft makes even small islands accessible while her long bowsprit, topmasts, and yards allow extra sails for speed between them.

Heritage of Miami II's travels take her from her Miami home base down through the coral reefs of the Florida Keys to Garden Key and the famous Fort Jefferson in the Dry Tortugas. Sea Explorer cruises last for six days and five nights. Co-winner of the 1999 ASTA Sail Training Program of the Year, her professional captain and crew help the Explorers experience the life of the sea: setting and furling sails, manning the helm, and even catching, cleaning and cooking fish. The program offers a unique opportunity to explore a part of the Florida Keys while enjoying a hands-on sailing experience.

Flag:	USA
Rig:	Square topsail schooner, two-masted
Homeport/waters:	Miami, Florida: Biscayne Bay, Florida Keys, Gulf of Mexico
Who sails?	School groups from elementary school through college as well as individuals. Affiliated institutions include Dade County Schools, Broward County Schools, area private schools, and the Boy Scouts of America.
Season:	Year-round
Cost:	$1,000 group rate per day
Program type:	Sail training for crew, apprentices, and paying trainees. Sea education in maritime history and ecology in cooperation with accredited schools and colleges and other organized groups. Passenger day sails and overnight passages. Dockside interpretation.

Specifications:			
	Sparred length: 85'	Draft: 6'	Sail area: 2,200 sq. ft.
	LOD: 65'	Beam: 17' 9"	Tons: 47 GRT
	LOA: 68'	Rig height: 64'	Power: 140 HP diesel
	LWL: 62'	Freeboard: 8'	Hull: steel

Designer:	Merritt Walters
Built:	1988; Norfolk, Virginia, Howdy Bailey
Coast Guard certification:	Passenger Vessel (Subchapter T)
Contact:	Captain Joseph A. Maggio
	The Schooner Heritage of Miami, Inc.
	3145 Virginia St.
	Coconut Grove, FL 33133
	Tel: 305-442-9697; Fax: 305-442-0119
	E-mail: heritage2@mindspring.com
	Web site: http://www.heritageschooner.com

On May 12, 1792 Captain Robert Gray sailed his ship, *Columbia Rediviva,* over the bar of the "Great River of the West" and named it Columbia's River in honor of his ship. Robert Gray never would have entered that river had it not been for the information he received from the first American vessel to enter the river, *Columbia's* longboat.

Unnamed and unheralded, ship's boats were the workhorses of the 16th to 19th century. Powered by either oars or sails, these versatile seaworthy craft carried all manner of cargo from ship to shore and back again.

Grays Harbor Historical Seaport Authority built two 18th-century ship's longboat reproductions in 1993. The design for the Seaport longboats was painstakingly researched by noted maritime historian and artist Hewitt R. Jackson, who worked closely with naval architect Stuart Hoagland and Seaport Director Les Bolton to ensure both historical accuracy and the meeting of specific program needs.

Powered by ten oars or up to a three-masted dipping lugsail rig, these versatile vessels are ideal for exploring the protected inland waterways of Washington. Programs are customized to the needs and interests of specific groups. Half-day, full-day, and weeklong programs are available to organized groups as well as to individuals.

Flag:	USA
Rig:	Dipping lug
Homeport/waters:	Aberdeen, Washington: Western Washington, Grays Harbor, Washington
Who sails?	School groups from middle school through college, individuals under 25.
Program type:	Sail training for volunteer and paying trainees. Sea education in marine science, maritime history, ecology, and team building in cooperation with accredited institutions and as part of informal, in-house programming. Passenger day sails, dockside interpretation.
Cost:	$95 per person per day, $600 group rate per day. Residential programs, $55 per person per day (five-day minimum).

Specifications:	Sparred length: 36'	Draft: 20"	Sail area: 310 sq. ft.
	LOD: 25'	Beam: 7'	Tons: 3,800 lbs. (dsp)
	LOA: 26'	Rig height: 16'	Hull: wood
	LWL: 26'	Freeboard: 20"	

Designer:	Stuart Hoagsland/Hewitt Jackson
Built:	1993; Aberdeen, Washington, Grays Harbor Historical Seaport Authority
Coast Guard certification:	Sailing School Vessel (Subchapter R)
Crew:	2. Trainees: 8-13
Contact:	Les Bolton, Executive Director
	Grays Harbor Historical Seaport
	PO Box 2019
	Aberdeen, WA 98520
	Tel: 800-200-LADY (5239); Fax: 360-533-9384
	E-mail: ghhsa@techline.com
	Web site: http://www.ladywashington.org

Hibiscus

Polynesian multi-hull ships were among the earliest long distance travelers. A catamaran experience is unique and one of the longest-standing ways to sail the seas. The catamaran is stable and provides a more comfortable platform to learn sail handling skills.

Captain Larry and First Mate Nikki White share their experiences-traveling the Southeast Pacific, the US Pacific Coast and the Caribbean including extensive knowledge of the Bahamas. Each summer is spent training the Boy Scouts of America in their High Seas Adventure in the Abacos.

Flag:	USA
Rig:	Sloop
Homeport/waters:	Miami, Florida: Bahamas and Caribbean cruising areas.
Season:	Year-round
Who sails?	Families and individuals of all ages. Affiliated groups include the Boy Scouts of America.
Program type:	Sail training for paying trainees. Bareboat certification, corporate team building & charters. Day sailing for groups, overnight 3 queen berths and room for 6 on deck under the stars.
Cost:	$80-$150 per person per day. Group rates available.

Specifications:		
LOA: 39'	Draft: 3'8"	Sail area: 1,180 sq. ft.
LWL: 36'	Beam: 21'	Rig height: 59"
Power: 54 HP diesel	Freeboard: 6'	Hull: fiberglass

Designer:	Phillip Jeantot
Built:	1990
Coast Guard certification:	Uninspected Vessel
Contact:	Larry K. White, Captain
	8305 SW 39th Street
	Miami, FL 33155
	Tel: 305-793-4487; Fax: 242-367-2033
	E-mail: whibiscus@oii.net

This summer *Highlander Sea* begins her new role as flagship ambassador for Port Huron, Michigan and the Blue Water Area. Purchased by Acheson Ventures of Port Huron, the ship was repatriated as a US flag vessel in April 2002.

This gaff-rigged topsail schooner was built in 1924, in Essex, Massachusetts. Originally christened *Pilot,* she served 47 years as a Boston Harbor pilot ship. In the 1970s, she was purchased to circumnavigate the globe, got as far as Fiji, and was sold. In 1998, Secunda Marine Services of Nova Scotia, Canada, located the ship in San Diego, renamed her, *Highlander Sea,* conducted a multi-stage refit, and employed her for cadet sail training.

Dedicated to showcasing the marine lore of Port Huron and the Great

Lakes region, and providing educational experiences for the public, Acheson Ventures will further *Highlander Sea's* program. The ship will berth in Port Huron, sail the Great Lakes and Eastern Seaboard, and be available for public tours, educational programs and dockside events.

Flag:	USA
Rig:	Gaff topsail schooner, two-masted
Homeport/waters:	Port Huron, Michigan: Great Lakes and Eastern Seaboard
Who sails?	High school and college students, individuals of all ages, and marine institute students
Season:	Year-round
Program type:	Sail training for volunteer trainees and professional crew. Informal, in-house sea education. Dockside interpretation during port visits and in homeport.

Specifications:			
	Sparred length: 154'	LOD: 126'	LOA: 154'
	LWL: 100'	Draft: 14'	Beam: 25' 8"
	Rig height: 125'	Sail area: 10,000 sq. ft.	Tons: 140 GRT
	Power: twin 350 HP diesel	Hull: wood	Hull color: black

Designer:	Starling Burgess
Built:	1924; Essex, Massachusetts, F. W. James & Son
Crew:	7. Trainees/passengers: 12 - 14
Contact:	Pamela Thomas, Marketing Director
	S/V Highlander Sea
	Acheson Ventures, LLC
	PO Box 8049
	Port Huron, MI 48061
	Tel: 810-966-0900 x222; Fax: 810-966-0990
	E-mail: pamelathomas@advent.net

wooden vessel designed as a half-scale model of a 19th-century Grand Banks fishing schooner. In her long career she has been a private yacht, a cargo ship transporting spice from India, and as a US Navy U-boat tracker in World War II on the Eastern Seaboard. *Hindu* has also participated in many blue water races, including two of the Newport-Bermuda classics.

Hindu is Coast Guard inspected for coastwise navigation, carrying 49 passengers overnight. She is privately owned and available for charter. In the past, *Hindu* has called on such ports as Bermuda; Port Antonio, Jamaica; Grand Cayman; Havana, Cuba; Porta Plata, Dominican Republic; and Key West, Florida. Hindu has been conducting two-hour day sails out of Provincetown, Massachusetts for over fifty years.

Hindu was designed by William Hand, Jr. and built as a private yacht in 1925 in East Boothbay, Maine, by the Hodgdon Brothers. She is a 79-foot

Flag:	USA
Rig:	Gaff schooner
Homeport/waters:	Provincetown, Massachusetts: Provincetown, Massachusetts (summer), Caribbean (winter)
Who sails?	Elementary and middle school students, and individuals of all ages.
Season:	Year-round
Cost:	$60 per person per day, $1,500 group rate per day
Program type:	Sail training for paying trainees. Sea education as informal, in-house programming.

Specifications:			
	Sparred length: 73'	Draft: 9'	Sail area: 2,500 sq. ft.
	LOD: 61' 3"	Beam: 15'	Tons: 29 GRT
	LOA: 64'	Rig height: 60'	Power: 90 HP diesel
	LWL: 47'	Freeboard: 4'	Hull: wood

Designer:	William Hand, Jr.
Built:	1925; Boothbay Harbor, Maine, Hodgdon Brothers
Coast Guard certification:	Passenger Vessel (Subchapter T)
Crew:	3. Trainees/passengers: 49 (day sails), 6 (overnight)
Contact:	John Bennett, President
	Hindu of Provincetown, Inc.,
	333R Commercial Street
	Provincetown, MA 02657
	Tel: 508-487-3000
	E-mail: hindu@gis.net
	Web site: http://www.schoonerhindu.com

Howard Blackburn is a fine example of a classic John G. Alden design. Built in 1951 in Cristobal, Panama, her hull design and construction are reminiscent of the fishing vessels that sailed from New England in the 1900s. She is a very able and seaworthy vessel. Originally built as a private yacht, *Howard Blackburn* also spent some time in the charter trade, sailing in waters from South America to New England. She also did some campaigns for the Greenpeace organization.

In 1995 Mark Roesner and Terry Westhead took ownership and brought her to the Chesapeake Bay area. Mark and Terry both have years of experience sailing and teaching aboard sail training vessels. *Howard Blackburn can* take up to six trainees on day and overnight trips. During the summer

camp program, youths between the ages of 13-18 come aboard to learn all aspects of seamanship, marine science, and ecology of the Chesapeake Bay. The vessel is also available for individual, family, and group charters.

Flag:	USA
Rig:	Ketch
Homeport/waters:	Baltimore, Maryland: Chesapeake Bay, New England
Who sails?	Students from elementary school through college, individuals, and families.
Cost:	$100 per person per day
Program type:	Sail training for volunteer and paying trainees. Informal, in-house sea education in marine science and ecology.

Specifications:			
	Sparred length: 58'	Draft: 6' 6"	Sail area: 1,100 sq. ft.
	LOD: 45'	Beam: 14'	Tons: 22'
	LOA: 58'	Rig height: 57'	Power: 80 HP diesel
	LWL: 36' 6"	Freeboard: 4'	Hull: wood

Designer:	John G. Alden
Built:	1951; Cristobal, Panama Canal Zone
Crew:	1. Trainees: 6
Contact:	Captain Mark Roesner, Owner
	925 Bowleys Quarters Road
	Baltimore, MD 21220
	Tel/Fax: 410-335-7357
	E-mail: 4roesner@msn.com
	Web site: http://www.maritime_charters.com

Hurricane Island Outward Bound® School

For 35 years The Hurricane Island Outward Bound School's sailing expeditions aboard unique 30-foot ketch-rigged pulling boats modeled after traditional whaling vessels have challenged both novice and seasoned sailors. Students experience open-ocean adventure and island living sailing the coast of Maine, one of the world's greatest cruising grounds. Nearly 3,000 islands and 3,500 miles of shoreline make this one of the last intact coastal wildernesses in America. As trainees navigate rugged shores they rotate responsibilities, learning sail handling, navigation, and boat handling.

Founded in 1964, the Hurricane Island Outward Bound School is the largest Outward Bound School in the United States. From its headquarters in Rockland, Maine, the school operates in 14 locations stretching from Maine through Maryland and Philadelphia, all the way to the Florida Keys. The school is a nonprofit educational organization whose mission is to conduct safe, adventure-based courses structured to encourage growth and discovery, and to inspire confidence, self-reliance, concern for others, and care for the environment.

By combining the school's mission with Outward Bound's motto, "To serve, to strive, and not to yield," the school hopes to better society by providing people with positive experiences that can change their outlook, their attitudes, and their lives.

Flag:	USA
Rig:	Ketch-rigged pulling boat
Waters:	Maine Coast, Chesapeake Bay, and Florida Keys.
Who sails?	Students and individuals (age 14+, coed), corporations, educational, and civic organizations.
Program type:	Sail training and seamanship taught to impel students into confidence-building, life-enhancing experiences.

Specifications:	LOA: 30'	Draft: 18"	Sail area: 366 sq. ft.
	LWL: 28'	Beam: 8'	Freeboard: 2'
	Rig height: 20'	Hull: wood	

Designer:	Cyrus Hamlin, Kennebunk, Maine
Built:	1965-1988; Maine Coast and Maryland
Crew:	2. Trainees: up to 13
Contact:	Admissions/Hurricane Island Outward Bound School
	75 Mechanic Street
	Rockland, ME 04841
	Tel: 800-341-1744; Fax: 207-594-8202
	E-mail: admissions@hurricaneisland.org
	Web site: http://www.hurricaneisland.org

Launched in 1986, *Idea Due* is a custom-built schooner able to accommodate 12 passengers for overnight voyages and 25 for day sails. The design guarantees a high level of safety and comfort. *Idea Due* is operated by a specialized company as a school and charter vessel in the Mediterranean Sea. She participated in the 1992 Columbus Regatta and other international events. Fully certified by R.I.Na. (Registro Italiano Navale), *Idea Due* has been mentioned in the official publication for the celebration of "A Hundred Years of Lega Navale Italiana".

Flag:	Italy
Rig:	Schooner
Homeport/waters:	Otrano, Italy: Mediterranean Sea
Who sails?	High school and college students, individuals of all ages, and families.
Cost:	$1,000 - $1,500 group rate per day
Program type:	Sail training for volunteer crew and trainees. Sea education in marine science and ecology in cooperation with accredited institutions. Dockside interpretation while in homeport.

Specifications:	Sparred length: 78'	Draft: 10'	Sail area: 4,130 sq. ft.
	LOD: 73'	Beam: 15'	Tons: 49 GRT
	LOA: 75'	Rig height: 85'	Power: twin 145 HP
	LWL: 63'	Freeboard: 6'	Hull: steel

Designer:	Stefano Rossi
Built:	1986; Fano (Pesaro), Italy, Bugari
Certification:	R.I.Na. (Registro Italiano Navale)
Crew:	4. Trainees/passengers: 12
Contact:	Captain Pantaleo Coluccia
	Otranto Navigazione s.a.s.,
	Via G. Galilei, n. 2
	Casamassella, Lecce 73020, Italy
	Tel/Fax: 39-337-701451

Imagine.. !

The 76-foot schooner *Imagine…!* was built and put into service in 1997 to provide high quality leadership and team performance training programs to corporate executives and managers. Using two to five-day cruises, clients are challenged with a variety of "dock to destination" exercises, where their success is contingent upon operating individually as effective leaders and collectively as an efficient team. Ultimately the participants are expected to master the skills necessary to safely operate the vessel from point to point, using one another as resources. Facilitated debriefing sessions by professional corporate trainers transfer the experience from the "boat to the boardroom."

Imagine…! also operates educational sails for school groups, adjudicated youth, special need students, and other young people. These programs provide a wide spectrum of learning experiences, ranging from pure science-based curriculum to a full-fledged sail training offering. Cruises range from several hours to several days in duration.

Imagine…! operates primarily in the Baltimore/Annapolis, Maryland area, but throughout a March-November season travels as far north as Philadelphia, Pennsylvania and as far south as Norfolk, Virginia.

Flag:	USA		
Rig:	Gaff schooner		
Homeport/waters:	Annapolis, Maryland: Chesapeake Bay, eastern US		
Who sails?	School groups, individuals, and corporate groups.		
Program type:	Sail training for paying trainees. Corporate team building, charters.		
Specifications:	LOD: 65'	Draft: 7' 9"	Sail area: 1,900 sq. ft.
	LOA: 76'	Beam: 16'	Power: twin 50 HP diesels
	LWL: 55'	Hull: cedar	
Built:	1997; Port of Albany, New York, Scarano Boat Building		
Coast Guard certification:	Passenger Vessel (Subchapter T)		
Contact:	Captain Michael Bagley		
	Imagine Yacht, LLC		
	PO Box 1469		
	Annapolis, MD 21404		
	Tel: 410-897-9030		
	E-mail: mail@schoonerimagine.com		
	Web site: http://www.schoonerimagine.com		

Sailing out of Chatham, Massachusetts, *Infanta* has been lovingly restored. She is maintained and operated by Pease Boat Works & Marine Railway and charters day sails and overnight passages in and around New England waters. Youth sailing adventures are scheduled for summer months to teach traditional seamanship and life skills. *Infanta* participates in classic yacht racing and is well received and admired in every port.

Flag:	USA
Rig:	Yawl
Homeport/waters:	Chatham, Massachusetts: New England
Who sails?	Groups and individuals of all ages
Season:	Spring, Summer, Fall
Cost:	$135 per person per day
Program type:	Sail training for paying trainees. Sea education in traditional maritime skills. Private charters.

Specifications:	Sparred length: 54'	LOD: 45'	LOA: 47'
	LWL: 32'	Draft: 6' 8"	Beam: 15'
	Rig height: 58'	Freeboard: 4'	Sail area: 1,068 sq. ft.
	Tons: 15 GRT	Power: 42 HP diesel	

Designer:	Phillip Rhodes
Built:	1947; City Island, New York, Kretzer Boatworks
Coast Guard certification:	Uninspected Vessel; (6 passengers)
Crew:	2. Trainees/passengers: 6 (day sails), 6 (overnight)
Contact:	Brad Pease, Director
	Cape Cod Maritime Traditions
	43 Eliphamets Lane
	Chatham, MA 02633
	Tel: 508-945-7800; Fax: 508-945-2285
	E-mail: info@peaseboatworks.com
	Web site: http://www.peaseboatworks.com

The schooner *Inland Seas* is owned and operated by Inland Seas Education Association (ISEA). Now in its fourteenth year of operation, the ISEA Great Lakes Schoolship Program was named ASTA "Sea Education Program of the Year" in 2001. Since its founding in 1989, over 45,000 learners of all ages have studied the science and spirit of the Great Lakes through ISEA Education programs. Summer shipboard experiences for all ages include astronomy, history, and science programs on Grand Traverse Bay and Lake Michigan. The goal of every ISEA program is to foster an appreciation of the natural and cultural heritage of the Great Lakes.

Flag:	USA
Rig:	Gaff schooner, two-masted
Homeport/waters:	Suttons Bay, Michigan: Grand Traverse Bay, Lake Michigan
Who sails?	School groups and individuals of all ages.
Season:	May through early October.
Program type:	Sail training for volunteer and paying trainees. Sea education in marine science, maritime history, and ecology for students from elementary school through college, adults, and at-risk-youth. Dockside interpretation during port visits.

Specifications:

Sparred length: 77'	Draft: 7'	Sail area: 1,800 sq. ft.
LOD: 61' 6"	Beam: 17'	Tons: 41 GRT
LWL: 53'	Rig height: 66'	Power: 130 HP
Freeboard: 4'	Hull: steel	

Designer:	Charles W. Wittholz, Woodin & Marean
Built:	1994; Palm Coast, Florida, Treworgy Yachts
Coast Guard certification:	Passenger Vessel (Subchapter T)
Crew:	5. Trainees: 30 (day sails), 11 (overnight), 5 (volunteer instruction)
Contact:	Thomas M. Kelly, Executive Director
	Inland Seas Education Association
	PO Box 218
	Suttons Bay, MI 49682
	Tel: 231-271-3077; Fax: 231-271-3088
	E-mail: isea@traverse.com
	Web site: http://www.schoolship.org

Inland Seas

The incomparable two-time America's Cup winner *Intrepid* is close to the hearts of all sailors. Designed by Sparkman and Stephens and built by Minneford's in City Island, New York in 1967, *Intrepid* represents a tremendous breakthrough in twelve-meter design. She was the first twelve to separate the rudder from the keel, include a "bustle" or "kicker" and use a trim tab. *Intrepid's* underbody type, with relatively minor refinements, was used on every subsequent Cup boat until *Australia II's* winged keel of 1983.

After 32 years of hard sailing she has been rebuilt to "as new" condition. America's Cup Charters' George Hill and Herb Marshal worked with Sparkman and Stephens, Brewer's Cove Haven Marina, and master shipwright Louis Sauzedde to restore this landmark yacht. *Intrepid* proudly joins the twelve-meter fleet at America's Cup Charters, offering leisure sails, racing, and corporate team building charters from any port between Maine and the Chesapeake.

Flag:	USA
Rig:	Sloop
Homeport/waters:	Newport, Rhode Island: New England and Chesapeake Bay
Who sails?	Individuals and groups of all ages
Cost:	$2100 group rate per day, $75 per person for evening sails
Program type:	Sail training for paying trainees. Passenger day sails, corporate team building, corporate racing, individual and group charters.

Specifications:	Sparred length: 69'	Draft: 9'	Sail area: 1,850 sq. ft.
	LOD: 65'	Beam: 12'	Tons: 28 GRT
	LOA: 65'	Rig height: 90'	Power: diesel
	LWL: 46'	Hull: wood	

Designer:	Sparkman and Stephens
Built:	1967; City Island, New York, Minneford
Coast Guard certification:	Passenger Vessel (Subchapter T)
Crew:	3. Trainees/passengers: 12
Contact:	George Hill/Herb Marshall
	America's Cup Charters
	PO Box 51
	Newport, RI 02840
	Tel: 401-849-5868; Fax: 401-849-3098
	Web site: http://www.americascupcharters.com

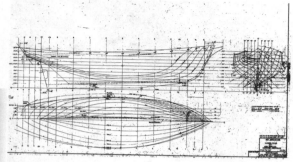

The Los Angeles Maritime Institute is constructing two 90-foot brigantines. Named *Irving Johnson* and *Exy Johnson* in honor of the Johnsons and their life-long commitments to character-building sail training, the vessels will be launched on April 27, 2002, and will be in commission by the end of August.

Irving McClure Johnson began training for a sailor's life as a teenager. In 1929 he sailed around Cape Horn on the four-masted barque *Peking,* a voyage he documented in a film entitled "Around Cape Horn."

Captain Johnson met Electa on his next voyage aboard the *Wander Bird.*

The Johnsons sailed around the world seven times in two different *Yankees* and cruised European and African waters in their third *Yankee,* a ketch, sharing their skill and knowledge of the sea with a hand-picked crew generally composed of four young women, 16 young men, a doctor, a cook, and a mate.

Construction is taking place at the Los Angeles Maritime Museum in John Gibson Park, San Pedro. The brigantine design, based on one developed in the 1930's, has been adapted by W.I.B. Crealock to meet US Coast Guard and LAMI program requirements.

The shipyard is visitor friendly, set up as a living history exhibit of the museum. Construction is carried out by professional, paid shipwrights, working with trained volunteers. Funding for this project has come from private donations, corporate sponsorships, and foundation grants.

Flag:	USA
Rig:	Brigantine
Homeport/waters:	Los Angeles, California: Southern California and offshore islands
Who sails?	Referred youth-at-risk and groups catering to students and adults.
Season:	Year-round
Cost:	Based on ability to pay
Program type:	Educational sailing adventures for youth and adult groups.

Specifications:	Sparred length: 110' 8"	Draft: 11'	Sail area: 4,540 sq. ft.
	LOA: 90'	Beam: 21' 9"	Tons: 99 GRT
	LWL: 72' 6"	Rig height: 87' 8"	Power: diesel

Coast Guard certification:	Sailing School Vessel (Subchapter R), Passenger Vessel (Subchapter T)
Contact:	Captain Jim Gladson, President
	Los Angeles Maritime Institute
	Berth 84, Foot of Sixth Street
	San Pedro, CA 90731
	Tel: 310-833-6055; Fax: 310-548-2055

Isaac H. Evans

The schooner *Isaac H. Evans*, designated a National Historic Landmark, was built in 1886, in the era when oystering was the biggest fishing industry in the country. She spent many years on the Delaware Bay, fishing and freighting. In 1973, she was completely rebuilt to suit her for her new trade of carrying passengers on 3, 4, and 6-day cruises in mid-coast Maine.

Her captain and crew (first mate, cook, and deck hand) provide hands-on training to eager passengers from late May through early October. She has a shallow draft for ghosting alongside Maine's granite islands. There is no engine on board, although a yawl boat is carried for windless days. The minimum age for passengers is six, and youngsters are encouraged to get involved in all aspects of running the vessel.

From the deck hand working toward a captain's license, to armchair sailors on vacation, to wide-eyed youth experiencing a turn at the helm, the *Isaac H. Evans* continues to provide historic maritime experiences.

Flag:	USA
Rig:	Gaff topsail schooner, two-masted
Homeport/waters:	Rockland, Maine: Penobscot Bay and surrounding area.
Season:	May to October
Who sails?	Families and individuals ages 6 and older.
Program type:	Sail training for paying trainees.
Cost:	$125 per person per day, $390-$780 (3, 4, and six day trips)

Specifications:			
	Sparred length: 99'	LOD: 65'	LOA: 65'
	LWL: 52'	Draft: 6'	Beam: 20'
	Tons: 53 GRT	Rig height: 82'	Sail area: 2,600 sq. ft.
	Hull: wood	Hull color: white	Spar material: wood
	Freeboard: 4'		

Builder:	1886; Mauricetown, New Jersey, George Vannaman
Coast Guard certification:	Passenger Vessel (Subchapter T)
Crew:	4. Trainees/passengers: 46 (day sails), 26 (overnight)
Contact:	Brenda Grace Walker, Captain/Owner
	PO Box 791
	Rockland, ME 04841
	Tel: 207-594-7956
	E-mail: evans@midcoast.com
	Web site: http://www.midcoast.com/evans

Mr. Mike Liese
79 Church Street
Northport, NY 11768
info@sailcaribbean.com
Tel: 800-321-0994; Fax: 631-754-3362

Windjamming is the best of both worlds: adventure and relaxation. We sail where the wind and tide take us and experience freedom from everyday noises and distractions. We throw itineraries to the wind, anchoring in a different harbor every night and even enjoying a traditional lobster bake on the beach, Maine-style! Winding our way through the islands of Penobscot Bay, the cacaphony of our home and work places slip away and enjoyment in a simpler life takes it's place. The sight of lighthouses, pink-granite islands and colorful sunrises, the smell of fresh bread just out of the wood stove or freshly brewed coffee from the wood stove, all are part of your trip on our windjammer.

The Schooner *J. & E. Riggin* is a family run business. The captain, Jon Finger, has almost two decades of professional experience on the water from Maine to the Mediterranean. His wife and the cook on board, Annie Mahle, also has her captains license and is a trained chef.

From May to October twenty-four people join us as our guests for a week of sailing, sightseeing and nature-watching. Our quiet adventures travel from Boothbay, Maine to Bar Harbor, Maine. The accommodations are simple and the fare, the best of new and old-world styles, is prepared by a trained chef. This traditional sailing vessel was built as an oyster dredger in 1927, and is now a National Historic Landmark.

Flag:	USA
Rig:	Schooner
Homeport/waters:	Rockland, Maine: New England
Who sails?	Groups and individuals of all ages
Program type:	Sail training for paying trainees, passenger day sails, group charters
Specifications:	Sparred length: 120' LOD: 89' LOA: 90'
	LWL: 78' Draft: 7' (centerboard up), 14' (centerboard down)
	Beam: 22' 6" Rig height: 74' Freeboard: 2' 6"
	Sail area: 4000 sq. ft. Tons: 61 GRT
Designer:	Charles Riggin
Built:	1927; Dorchester, New Jersey
Coast Guard certification:	Passenger Vessel (Subchapter T)
Crew:	6. Trainees/passengers: 24
Contact:	Captains Jon Finger and Anne Mahle
	Schooner J. & E. Riggin
	136 Holmes Street
	Rockland, ME 04841
	Tel: 800-869-0604; Fax: 207-594-4921
	Email: info@riggin.com
	Web site: http://www.riggin.com OR http://www.mainewindjammer.com

Jeanie Johnston

Over the past 3 years, a full size replica of the famous Irish immigrant ship, *Jeanie Johnston* (1847-58), has been under construction at Blennerville, Tralee, County Kerry, Ireland.

Upon completion, and following sea-trials, she will set sail on an historic North American voyage, visiting several ports in the United States and Canada. At each port the ship will be open to the public and the 'tween deck will recreate life on board an Irish immigrant ship of the 19th century. Under sail, the vessel will offer opportunities to individuals and groups for sail training on both the transatlantic crossings and the inter-city legs of the voyage.

The original *Jeanie Johnston* was built in Quebec. On over 16 transatlantic voyages she carried thousands of Irish immigrants to America and Canada. Unlike the infamous "Coffin-Ships" of the time, the *Jeanie Johnston* never lost a passenger or crewmember to disease or to the sea.

Young people from Ireland North and South have worked side-by-side with skilled shipwrights to build the *Jeanie Johnston*. A further 70 young trainees will help sail the ship throughout her North American voyage.

Flag:	Ireland
Rig:	Barque
Program type:	Sail training for volunteer and paying crew/trainees. Dockside interpretation during port visits.

Specifications:

Sparred length: 148'	LOD: 123'	LOA: 123'
Rig height: 94'	Beam: 26'3"	Draft: 14'
Sail area: 6,490 sq. ft.	Tons: 450 GRT	Freeboard: 6'
Hull: wood	Spar material: wood	Hull color: black
Power: 2/280 HP	Sail number: 18	

Designer:	Fred Walker
Built:	2000; Blennerville Shipyard, Tralee, County Kerry, Ireland, Jeanie Johnston Co.
Certification:	Department of Ireland Marine Sail Training Vessel
Crew:	11. Trainees: 29
Contact:	Ann Martin, Marketing Executive

The Jeanie Johnston Project
Blennerville Shipyard
Blennerville, Tralee, County Kerry, Ireland
Tel: +353-66-7129999; Fax: +353-66-7181888
Web site: http://www.jeaniejohnston.com

The *John E. Pfriem* is a classic Chesapeake Bay bugeye ketch design built in Gloucester, Massachusetts in 1964. She operates as a marine environmental education vessel sailing the waters of Long Island Sound from April through November.

Flag:	USA
Rig:	Chesapeake Bay bugeye ketch
Homeport/waters:	Bridgeport, Connecticut: Long Island Sound
Who sails?	Affiliated institutions include the University of Bridgeport, Housatonic Community College, and seven Connecticut school districts.
Season:	April to November
Program type:	Sail training for crew and apprentices. Sea education in marine science and ecology in cooperation with accredited institutions. Dockside interpretation.

Specifications:			
	Sparred length: 65'	Draft: 3'	Sail area: 1,200 sq. ft.
	LOA: 55'	Beam: 14' 6"	Tons: 14 GRT
	LWL: 47'	Rig height: 49'	Hull: wood
	Freeboard: 2' 6"		

Designer:	Russell Grinnell
Built:	1964; Gloucester, Massachusetts, Russell Grinnell
Coast Guard certification:	Research Vessel (Subchapter U)
Crew:	2-3. Trainees: 22
Contact:	Edwin T. Merritt, Executive Director
	The Aquaculture Foundation
	525 Antelope Trail
	Shelton, CT 06484
	Tel: 203-372-4406; Fax: 203-372-4407
	E-mail: tmerritt@pcnet.com
	Web site: http://www.tallshipblackpearl.org

Jolie Brise

Dauntsey's School Sailing Club was established in the mid-1970s by the boys and girls at Dauntsey's School. The Sailing Club operates *Jolie Brise,* a 1913 Le Havre Pilot Cutter in conjunction with the Exeter Maritime Museum. *Jolie Brise* became famous in 1925 when she won the first ever Fastnet Race. She again won the Fastnet Race in 1929 and 1930. In 1932 she rescued thirty crew from the American yacht *Adriana,* which had caught fire during the Bermuda Race, earning her the Blue Water Medal. *Jolie Brise* was also the last vessel to carry the Royal Mail under sail.

Jolie Brise sails with up to ten trainees, aged 13 and up, throughout northern Europe, with a different program each summer. In the year 2000 she came to Bermuda, Boston and Halifax as part of Tall Ships 2000®, then sailed back across the Atlantic to Amsterdam. Traditionally rigged, sailing her is very much a hands-on experience, requiring everyone to be involved. The atmosphere is very friendly, informal, and relaxed.

Flag:	UK
Rig:	Cutter
Homeport/waters:	Southampton, England: Northern Hemisphere, British South Coast
Who sails?	School groups from high school through college, as well as individuals of all ages.
Program type:	Sail training for volunteer and paying trainees. Dockside interpretation during port visits.

Specifications:	Sparred length: 76'	Draft: 11'	Sail area: 3,750 sq. ft.
	LOD: 56'	Beam: 15'	Tons: 44 GRT
	LOA: 60'	Rig height: 77'	Power: 60 HP
	LWL: 50'	Freeboard: 4'	Hull: oak

Designer:	Paumelle
Built:	1913; LeHavre, France, Paumelle
Certification:	British MCA Cat. '0' - Sail Training
Crew:	3. Trainees: 15 (day sails), 10 (overnight)
Contact:	Captain T.R. Marris, Head of Sailing
	Dauntsey's School Sailing Club
	West Lavington, Near Devizes
	Wiltshire, SN10 4HE, United Kingdom
	Tel: 44-1380-818-216; Fax: 44-1380-818-216
	E-mail: marrist@dauntseys.wilts.sch.uk

PHOTO BY RUSSELL A. FOWLER

For over 50 years young people have come to Mystic Seaport, our nation's leading maritime museum, to learn to sail and live on board the tall ship *Joseph Conrad*. Each morning, campers tackle the wind and current of the Mystic River and then set off for an active afternoon investigating the Museum's unique exhibitions. After a late-day sailing session, some "R and R" and dinner, campers spend their evenings with new friends, stargazing in a planetarium, climbing the rigging of the *Conrad* or enjoying a lively sea music sing-a-long.

The *Joseph Conrad* program is open to individual boys and girls and organized groups ages 10 through 15. Groups must have one adult leader per 10 participants. No prior experience is required for beginner sessions, only a desire to participate and learn. Intermediate sessions are for those who have attended a previous beginner session or have had sailing experience. All must hold current Red Cross swimmers certification or its equivalent.

Flag:	USA
Rig:	Ship, three-masted
Homeport:	Mystic, Connecticut
Who sails?	Individuals and organized groups ages 10 through 15.
Season:	June through August
Cost:	$525 per person per six-day program
Program type:	Sail training. Dockside visitation for school groups and individuals.

Specifications:			
	Sparred length: 118' 6"	Draft: 12'	Tons: 213 GRT
	LOA: 100' 8"	Beam: 25' 3"	Hull: iron
	Rig height: 98' 6"		

Designer:	Burmeister and Wain
Built:	1882; Copenhagen, Denmark, Burmeister & Wain
Trainees:	32-50
Contact:	Waterfront, Preservation and Programs Department
	Mystic Seaport
	PO Box 6000
	Mystic, CT 06355-0990
	Tel: 860-572-0711; Fax: 860-572-5355
	Web site: http://www.mysticseaport.org/sailing

Kajama

Kajama is a 165' three-masted schooner built in Rendsburg, Germany in 1930. She was launched as *Wifrid* and sailed under Captain Wilhelm Wilckens of Hamburg until 1960. The ship traded in general cargo throughout Europe and Scandinavia. In 1960 she was sold to Danish flag. In 1998 she made her last cargo voyage with a load of grain within Denmark.

In 1999 *Kajama* was purchased by Great Lakes Schooner Company and delivered to Toronto. After a ten-and-a-half month refit, the ship was re-launched as a three-masted schooner once again. Sailing from her berth at Toronto's Harbourfront, *Kajama* carries out a busy schedule of day sails, port visitation, pri-

vate charters, corporate team building, and day sail educational programs for elementary through high school students.

Great Lakes port visits include waterfront sail-pasts and interactive dockside activities. Private charters are fully catered parties under sail, with music, dancing and a licensed bar. Public day sails, departing from Toronto's Harbourfront Centre, maintain a regular schedule from June through to the end of September. Teambuilding events are custom designed intensive management training programs, often offered in cooperation with one of our management-consulting partners. The educational program, "A Sail Through Time", has a hands-on interactive curriculum emphasizing regional history, social science, and ecology. Since its inception in 1991 the 1-1/2 hour "A Sail Through Time" program has hosted over 55,000 students from both Canada and the United States.

Kajama begins her season in May and can be seen sailing the waters of Toronto Bay and Lake Ontario through early fall.

Flag:	Canada
Rig:	Gaff rig schooner, three-masted
Homeport/waters:	Toronto, Ontario, Canada: Lake Ontario
Who sails?	Individuals and groups of all ages. *Kajama* operates a day sail training program in conjunction with The Pier - Toronto's Waterfront Museum.
Season:	April to October
Program type:	Day sail training program, passenger voyages, corporate, charter, maritime events.

Specifications:			
	Sparred length: 165'	Draft: 9'	Sail area: 7000 sq. ft.
	LOD: 142'	Beam: 24'	Tons: 263 GRT
	Rig height: 100'	Hull: steel	Power: 400 HP
	Freeboard: 7'		

Designer:	Nobiskrug
Built:	1930; Rendsburg, Germany, Nobiskrug Shipyard
Certification:	Transport Canada Certified Passenger Vessel
Crew:	8. Trainees/passengers: 225 (day sails)
Contact:	Roger Nugent, President
	Great Lakes Schooner Company
	249 Queen's Quay West, Suite 111
	Toronto, Ontario M5J 2N5, Canada
	Tel: 416-260-6355; Fax: 416-260-6377
	E-mail: roger@greatlakesschooner.com
	Web site: http://www.greatlakesschooner.com

Kalaha

Designed by W.I.B. Crealock to be a world cruiser, the ketch *Kalaha* was built by the Westsail Corporation in 1975. Her cruising area is the Bahamas in the summer with the Sea Base program (Boy Scouts). Trainees learn sail handling, how to use ground tackle, prepare meals, and basic coastal navigation. *Kalaha* also travels to the Tortugas, Key West, and the Florida Keys. She day sails on the Gulf of Mexico and Pine Island Sound, and is available for charter for special events and overnight trips.

Flag:	USA
Rig:	Ketch
Homeport/waters:	Bokeelia, Florida: Bahamas (summer), Caribbean (winter)
Who sails?	Individuals and families of all ages. Affiliated groups include the Boy Scouts of America.
Season:	Year-round
Cost:	$80 per person per day, $480 group rate (charter)
Program type:	Sail training for paying trainees. Sea education in cooperation with Boy Scouts of America.

Specifications:			
	Sparred length: 47'	Draft: 6'	Sail area: 990 sq. ft.
	LOD: 42' 11"	Beam: 13'	Tons: 13 GRT
	LOA: 47'	Rig height: 56'	Power: 85 HP diesel
	LWL: 33' 4"	Freeboard: 6'	Hull: fiberglass

Designer:	W.I.B. Crealock
Built:	1975; California, Westsail
Coast Guard certification:	Uninspected Vessel
Crew:	1
Contact:	Captain Bill Misenheimer
	Pine Island Yacht Service
	11943 Oakland Dr.
	Bokeelia, FL 33922
	Tel/Fax: 941-283-7129

Kalmar Nyckel

her mission of goodwill.

With the support of a colonial ship-yard, Colonial History-Living Today™, *Kalmar Nyckel* transforms Delaware's history into hands-on educational opportunities for school children through adults. She provides economic development opportunities, tourism & convention development, corporate charters, public sails and statewide marketing initiatives on a national scale, fulfilling her role as Delaware's official tall ship ambassador. *Kalmar Nyckel* is quickly becoming a "film star", having participated in several films and documentaries.

The *Kalmar Nyckel* is a recreation of the first colonial Swedish settlement ship to arrive in America at what is now Wilmington, Delaware. Launched in the fall of 1997, commissioned in May 1998, and USCG-certified in June 2000, this ornately carved 17th century Dutch built pinnace sails seasonally, carrying out

The *Kalmar Nyckel* is manned by a professional captain, mates, engineer and volunteer crew. The vessel sails the Northern and Mid-Atlantic regions. She is available for charter to school groups, corporations, and private parties both underway and dockside. Kalmar Nyckel Foundation™ is planning a trip to Europe in the near future to recreate her historical voyages and re-connect with her European heritage.

Flag:	USA
Rig:	Full-rigged ship
Homeport/waters:	Wilmington, Delaware: Mid-Atlantic
Who sails?	School groups from elementary through college, as well as individuals and families. Affiliated institutions include the Challenge Program.
Cost:	$40 per person per day sail, $7000 group rate per day
Program type:	Sail training for volunteer or paying trainees. Dockside interpretation during port visits.

Specifications:

Sparred length: 139'	Draft: 12' 2"	Sail area: 7,600 sq. ft.
LOD: 93'	Beam: 24' 11"	Tons: 160 GRT
LOA: 97' 4"	Rig height: 65'	Power: diesel
LWL: 89' 2"	Freeboard: 8'	Hull: wood
Rig height: 105'	Hull color: natural/colonial blue	
Spar material: wood		

Designer:	Tom Gillmer
Built:	1997; Wilmington, Delaware, Allen C. Rawl
Coast Guard certification:	Passenger Vessel (Subchapter T)
Crew:	8. Trainees/passengers: 49 (day sails), 31 (overnight)
Contact:	Steven D. Luthultz, Executive Director
	Kalmar Nyckel Foundation™
	1124 East Seventh Street
	Wilmington, DE 19801
	Tel: 302-429-7447; Fax: 302-429-0350
	E-mail: execdir@kalnyc.org
	Web-site: http://www.kalnyc.org

The flagship of the Square Sail fleet, *Kaskelot* is a three-masted barque and one of the largest remaining wooden ships in commission. Built by J. Ring Andersen in 1948 for the Royal Greenland Trading Company, *Kaskelot* supplied the remote East Greenland coastal settlements. In the late 1960s *Kaskelot* then worked as a fisheries support vessel in The Faroes. Square Sail purchased her in 1981 and totally redesigned and re-rigged her to replicate the *Terra Nova,* returning to East Greenland to make a film about Captain Scott's ill-fated expedition to the South Pole.

All of Square Sail's ships are fully commissioned and work throughout the year. When not filming, they have a regular sailing program, giving people the chance to experience traditional square-rig sailing first-hand. These voyages typically run between four and seven days, and occasionally longer. They are either based from Square Sail's homeport of Charlestown, Cornwall, UK, or they work around the annual schedule offering voyages between the various ports.

Square Sail runs an annual course from February to October where trainees

are given the opportunity to learn the skills associated with sailing these ships, and in addition to maintenance and shore-based instruction, they form part of the regular crew throughout the season.

Flag:	UK
Rig:	Barque, three-masted
Homeport/waters:	Charlestown, Cornwall, UK: UK and Europe
Who sails?	Individuals of all ages and families. Affiliated institutions include Falmouth Marine School and Cornwall College.
Cost:	$220 per person per day. $9000 per day group rate, corporate charter
Program type:	Sail training for professional crew and volunteer and paying trainees. Sea education in maritime history in cooperation with accredited institutions and as informal, in-house programming. Worldwide film work and corporate charters.

Specifications:			
	Sparred length: 153'	Draft: 12'	Sail area: 9,500 sq. ft.
	LOD: 120'	Beam: 28'	Tons: 226 GRT
	LOA: 124'	Rig height: 105'	Power: 375 HP diesel
	LWL: 115'	Freeboard: 9'	Hull: oak on oak

Built:	1948; Denmark, J. Ring Anderson
Certification:	Bureau Veritas and MCA Class VI certificate (UK)
Crew:	14. Trainees/passengers: 50 (day sails), 12 (overnight)
Contact:	Chris Wilson, Marketing Manager, Square Sail, Charlestown Harbour, St. Austell, Cornwall PL25 3NJ, United Kingdom Tel: 44-1720-67526; Fax: 44-1726-61839, E-mail: info@square-sail.com Web site: http://www.square-sail.com

Kathryn M. Lee

The last working fishing schooner under sail in the Chesapeake Bay oyster dredging fleet, the *Kathryn M. Lee* is listed on the National Register of Historic Places. Pulled off a mud bank where she had been left to perish, this schooner was rescued by Captain Jim McGlincy a decade ago and, after much rebuilding and re-rigging, brought back to life. Originally built in 1923 in Dorchester, New Jersey for dredging on the Delaware Bay, the *Kathryn M. Lee* is back once more working under sail.

Recently purchased by Captain Ed Farley and Captain Steve Pagels, the schooner continues to oyster on the bay during dredge season (starting November 1). Currently undergoing a major rebuilding near Rock Hall, Maryland, the *Kathryn M. Lee* will rejoin the oyster fleet when the rebuilding is complete. She will also be offering day sails and educational cruises both on the Chesapeake Bay and in Atlantic City, NJ. Her rebuild is being led by Captain Ed Farley, who is a master shipwright. Follow her progress on our website, and if you would like to work on the restoration, please feel free to contact us.

Flag:	USA
Rig:	Schooner
Homeport/waters:	St. Michaels, Maryland: Chesapeake Bay
Season:	Year-round
Who sails?	Individuals and groups of all ages.
Program type:	Sail training for volunteer crew/trainees.

Specifications:			
	Sparred length: 85'	LOA: 62'	Rig height: 60'
	Draft: 6'	Beam: 20'	Sail area: 2,000 sq. ft.
	Hull: wood	Hull color: white	Spar material: wood
	Tons: 37 GRT	Power: Yawl boat	

Built:	1923; Dorchester, New Jersey, Harry Stowman & Sons
Coast Guard certification:	Passenger Vessel (Subchapter T)
Crew:	3. Trainees: 49 (day sails)
Contact:	Captain Steve Pagels
	Downeast Windjammer Cruises
	PO Box 28
	Cherryfield, ME 04622
	Tel: 207-546-2972 (winter); 207-288-4585 (summer); Fax: 207-546-2023
	Email: decruise@midmaine.com
	Website: http://downeastwindjammer.com

Keewatin is a sea-kindly, comfortable vessel with all of the classic features typical of 19th and 20th century schooners with the addition of modern conveniences. She is a great platform for educating young people in sail and line handling, knot work, helmsmanship, piloting and more. The activities aboard and the teamwork necessary to sail her promote not only strong physiques but also sterling character traits.

Her location in Abaco allows for controlled cruising in semi-protected waters abounding with marine mammals, fish, turtles, shellfish and bird life. Clean dry air and open horizons offer opportunities for astronomy. Uninhabited cays allow a first hand introduction to unique Bahamian flora. Abaco is home to settlements established in Loyalist times that present a very real insight into the historical narrative of that age.

A *"Keewatin"* has been in the Turner family since 1968. An identical schooner, built in Newfoundland, served until 1989, when she was sailed to Alabama where her hardware and rig were removed to outfit a new hull utilizing modern materials and building techniques in conjunction with traditional design. Her captain and crew delight in their opportunities to instruct and assist new sailing enthusiasts and to share the wonder of the Bahamas' unique marine environment.

Flag:	USA
Rig:	Gaff schooner
Homeport/waters:	Marsh Harbor, Abaco, Bahamas
Who sails?	Individuals, families, charter groups.
Season:	Year-round
Program type:	Sail training for volunteer and paying trainees. Sea education in marine science, maritime history and ecology in cooperation with accredited institutions and other organized groups. Passenger day sails, overnight voyages, dockside interpretation.

Specifications:			
	Sparred length: 72'	Draft: 6'	Sail area: 1,650 sq. ft.
	LOA: 56'	Beam: 16'	Tons: 60 GRT
	LWL: 48'	Rig height: 67'	Power: GM 125
	Freeboard: 6'6"	Hull: wood	Spar: spruce
	Hull color: white		

Designer:	John Alden
Built:	1992; Coden, Alabama, Zirlott
Certification:	Bahamian License
Crew:	3. Trainees: 16, Passengers: 8
Contact:	Captain Ron Turner
	Box AB20469, Marsh Harbour
	Abaco, Bahamas
	Tel: 242-367-5711 or 242-375-8317 (cell)
	E-mail: keewatin@batelnet.bs
	Web site: http://www.bahamasVG.com/keewatin.html

A Letter From The Chairman

It is safe to say that everything changed on the morning of September 11, 2001, and that the world will never be the same as it was before that awful morning in New York and Washington. Americans – indeed the entire world – will be struggling for the foreseeable future to come to grips with, and understand, why this terrible assault was unleashed. Was it about religion? Was it about culture? Was it about the gaping disparity between the haves and the have-nots of the world?

It would be easy to say at this moment that sail training, and events like the TALL SHIPS CHALLENGE®, are trivial and irrelevant. But the reality of sail training, and of tall ships events in general, is that they are terribly important in bridging gaps between nations and furthering understanding between peoples of different cultures and backgrounds.

This has been proven again and again in Europe with the Cutty Sark Tall Ships Races organized by the International Sail Training Association. The aim of those races has always been "to enable young people of all nations to race together at sea under sail", and it is noteworthy that some of the first cracks in the old Iron Curtain came in connection with those races when ships from Poland took part in them for the first time in 1972.

Sail training brings people together in a challenging situation, and forces them to summon all their resources to meet difficulty and danger alongside others they may not know at all, but with whom they share a common goal and a unique mutual interdependence. Tall ships events bring proud and substantial symbols of other places and cultures, crewed by enthusiastic representatives of those places and cultures, to port cities where they mingle in an atmosphere of friendship and celebration of both their differences and similarities.

Sail training, and ASTA's TALL SHIPS CHALLENGE®, will be only a small part of the coming effort to bridge the gulf that opened before us on September 11; that effort will take years, and require the efforts of millions of people around the world. But, as elements of the global effort to bring people together so that hatred and violence can be diminished in the world, they constitute an undertaking, which now seems more important than ever.

Fair Winds,

CAPTAIN David V.V. Wood, USCG (Ret.)
Chairman

September 10, 2001

Half Moon

Voyage of Discovery

By William T. "Chip" Reynolds

Our world was shattered the morning of September 11, 2001. As with the rest of our nation, we grieve the tragedy that has been inflicted on so many innocent lives. Out of respect, and to allow for a period of mourning, we cancelled the remainder of the first leg of our Voyage of Discovery, and postponed the final leg.

This Voyage of Discovery is the annual re-creation of the 1609 voyage of the Half Moon. We start in lower New York Harbor on September 8, and conclude in Albany on September 19, the date of Hudson's arrival at the limit of navigation. Along the way, we anchor on the dates and at the locations that Hudson did. During the Voyage, our student crew, comprised of middle school youth, pursues a rigorous educational program, and learns to operate the ship. This is why we found ourselves anchored two miles below the World Trade Center the morning of September 11, 2001, 392 years to the day from when the original Half Moon lay at much the same site.

Many have asked, "What did the children see?" This is a legitimate concern about the impact of the monumental events that unfolded right before our eyes. People are naturally inclined to assume that horrific images of destruction and evil are those that last. But other more profound images emerged at a deeper and stronger level.

First, the students saw themselves respond immediately, competently and maturely, working as a team to weigh anchor, get the ship underway, and organize the vessel for protracted operations in conditions that we could not predict. While we could have implemented these actions with only our adult crew, our students took the initiative in the manner in which they had been trained just the day before. Without any explicit statement to this effect, they shouldered these adult responsibilities and conducted them well. If one ever had any doubt about the future of our nation, let these outstanding young people serve as the beacon of hope for our ability to rise above any circumstance.

As we proceeded north, other powerful images unfolded before our eyes. Tens of thousands of people massed along the shoreline, where they had become trapped after evacuating buildings. Tugboats, ferries and commercial vessels from all parts of the harbor moved immediately to their aid. The vessels, overladen with people, moved back and forth from the Battery to New Jersey and Brooklyn. As each tower of the World Trade Center collapsed with a massive explosion, clouds of debris obscured lower Manhattan and reduced visibility on the nearby waters to zero. Yet we watched these vessels move deliberately from safety into the fog, putting themselves at grave risk in order to aid those on the shores.

Farther along, we could see a river of people and cars fleeing Manhattan. Every movement of people was north except for the countercurrent of fire trucks, ambulances, and emergency vehicles of all types moving at maximum speed, carrying rescue workers into the area of maximum danger and need. During the hours it took us to reach the George Washington Bridge, the flow of rescue workers moving south into the danger zone never ceased.

While we had gotten a message through to the schools in the morning that we were safe, it was about 1:30 PM before we were finally able to establish direct contact with the schools, both to confirm our safety and to learn that our own families and communities were safe. About 5:30PM we reached our own home port and the safety of King Marine in Verplanck, NY; never have dock lines felt as secure as those put down that afternoon by Randy King.

We were met by Karen Urbanski, the Rensselaer Middle High School principal, who came with a school bus and counselors from Rensselaer, Philip Livingston Magnet Academy, and Bethlehem Central Middle School. By 9:30PM our students and their families were rejoined in a reunion joyful for our personal return, yet somber for the tragedy inflicted upon our country.

After a period of mourning and reflection, we determined to resume our Voyage of Discovery on September 15. The second group of students boarded the ship under very different circumstances than the first, and faced their own unique challenges, which they met with aplomb. We arrived in Albany on September 19, the very date of Hudson's arrival in the area. Our return touched the community in a manner deeper than we could have anticipated. In recognition of our roots as immigrants, we conducted a naturalization ceremony for a group of children ready to become United States citizens. All present joined in reciting the oath of citizenship, a powerful catalyst to reflect on our unique rights and responsibilities as citizens. Our school tours and general public visits proceeded as planned over the next three weeks.

Realize that the resumption of our Voyage and school tours was not a return to business as usual. We resumed our daily activities with a clear vision of what the students saw. They saw the best demonstration of what makes our country strong: Values that animate people of all backgrounds, faiths and nationalities to work together for the common good; Values that compel rescue workers to walk into the heart of the flame to help those they do not know; Values that drive ordinary people to operate tugs and ferries through a shroud of smoke and debris to rescue stranded citizens; Values that allow children to handle themselves as maturely and competently as any adult could ever wish.

This is the vision that we carry with us as we rebuild our lives and move forward from this moment.

KRI Dewaruci, the beautiful barquentine flying the red and white (the colors of Indonesia's flag), is the largest tall ship in the Indonesian Navy. *KRI Dewaruci* was built in 1952 by H.C. Stulchen and Son, Hamburg, Germany. After being launched in 1953, she was sailed to Indonesia by the Indonesian Navy. Since then the ship has served the Indonesian Navy as a sail training vessel and a successful ambassador of goodwill for the people of Indonesia. *Dewaruci's* name comes from a Hindu epic play: Dewa Ruci is the name of a character representing the god of truth and courage.

Flag:	Indonesia
Rig:	Barquentine
Homeport/waters:	Surabaya, Indonesia: Indonesian waters, Indian Ocean, Pacific Ocean
Who sails?	Cadets of the Indonesian Naval Academy
Season:	Year-round
Program type:	Sail training and sea education for Indonesian Naval cadets.

Specifications:	Sparred length: 191'	Draft: 13'	Sail area: 11,738 sq. ft.
	LOD: 163' 1"	Beam: 31'	Tons: 847 GRT
	LOA: 165'	Rig height: 119' 7"	Power: 986 HP diesel
	LWL: 138' 4"	Freeboard: 15' 1"	Hull: steel

Built:	1952; Hamburg, Germany, H.C. Stulchen & Sohn
Certification:	Indonesian Sailing School Vessel
Crew:	70. Trainees: 80
Contact:	Leutenant Colonel H. Drs. Didin Zainal Abidin, Commanding Officer
	KRI Dewaruci-Satban/Ronban-Armatim-Ujung
	Surabaya 60155, Indonesia
	Tel: +62-31-329-4000; Fax: +62-31-329-4171
	Indonesian Naval Attaché, Defense Attaché Office
	2020 Massachusetts Avenue NW
	Washington, DC 20036

Kruzenshtern

homeport of Hamburg to Port Lincoln in Australia in only 67 days. At the end of World War II she was handed to the USSR and converted into a sail training ship.

Since 1990, up to 40 trainees of all ages have been welcomed on board to sail along with the Russian students of the Baltic Academy in Kalingrad, Russia, learning the ropes, manning the helm, or climbing the rigging to set more than 30,000 square feet of sail. No previous experience is necessary.

Kruzenshtern is supported by Tall Ship Friends, a nonprofit organization in Hamburg, Germany. The goals of Tall Ship Friends are to promote sail training on square-riggers, to contribute to the further existence of these beautiful ships, and to provide an unforgettable experience for the participants. Members of Tall Ship Friends receive the quarterly Tall Ships News (English/German) and a personal sailing log.

Kruzenshtern was built as *Padua* in 1927 in Bremerhaven, Germany. The sister ship to *Peking,* she is the last of the "Flying P" liners still under sail. These vessels were engaged in the grain trade from Australia to Europe. In 1933 *Kruzenshtern* sailed from her

Flag:	Russia
Rig:	Barque, four-masted
Homeport/waters:	Kalingrad, Russia: Western European waters (summer), Southern European waters (winter)
Who sails?	Individuals and groups of all ages.
Cost:	$50-$100 per person per day. Group charters by appointment
Program type:	Sail training for paying trainees. Fully accredited sea education in traditional seamanship.

Specifications:	Sparred length: 376'	Draft: 19	Sail area: 36,380 sq. ft.
	LOA: 346'	Beam: 46'	Power: twin 600 HP
	LOD: 329'	Rig height: 176'	Hull: steel
	LWL: 311' 6"	Freeboard: 27' 9"	

Built:	1927; Bremerhaven, Germany, J.C. Tecklenborg
Certification:	Special Purpose (School Vessel), Russia
Crew:	45-70. Trainees: 250 (day sails), 60 (overnight)
Contact:	Wulf Marquard, Managing Director
	Tall Ship Friends Germany
	Schweriner Str. 17
	Hamburg, D22143, Germany
	Tel: 49-40-675 635 97; Fax: 49-40-675 635 99
	E-mail: tallship1@aol.com
	Web site: http://www.tallship-friends.de

Lady Maryland is an authentic pungy schooner, an elegant boat designed to haul cargo, fish, dredge for oysters, and carry luxury items quickly from port to port on Chesapeake Bay and along the Atlantic Coast. Instead of carrying watermelons and oysters, her mission today is to provide students with the opportunity to experience sailing a historic vessel while studying history, sailing, seamanship, marine science, and ecology on her traditional waters from Maryland to Maine.

The Living Classrooms Foundation has developed a flexible educational program that can fit the needs of a variety of school and community groups. More than 50,000 students participate in LCF programs each year. The *Lady Maryland* operates educational day experiences for 32 trainees and extended live-aboard sail training and marine science programs for up to 14 people.

Flag:	USA
Rig:	Pungy schooner (gaff rigged), two-masted
Homeport/waters:	Baltimore, Maryland: Chesapeake and Delaware Bays, East Coast between Maryland and Maine
Who sails?	Student and other organized groups, individuals, and families.
Season:	March through November
Cost:	Rates vary depending on program, please call
Program type:	Sail training with paying trainees. Sea education in marine science, maritime history, and ecology for school groups from elementary school through colleges as well as adults.

Specifications:	Sparred length: 104'	Draft: 7'	Sail area: 2,994 sq. ft.
	LOD: 72'	Beam: 22'	Tons: 60 GRT
	LWL: 64' 3"	Rig height: 85'	Power: twin 80 HP diesels
	Freeboard: 3'		

Designer:	Thomas Gilmer
Built:	1986; Baltimore, Maryland, G. Peter Boudreau
Coast Guard certification:	Passenger Vessel (Subchapter T)
Crew:	6 (day sails), 8 (overnight). Trainees: 32 (day sails), 12-14 (overnight)
Contact:	Christine Truett, Director of Education
	Living Classrooms Foundation
	802 South Caroline Street,
	Baltimore, MD 21231-3311
	Tel: 410-685-0295; Fax: 410-752-8433
	Web site: http://www.livingclassrooms.org

Lady Washington

Lady Washington

As a privateer during the American Revolution, the original *Lady Washington* fought to help the colonies gain their independence from England. In 1788 she became the first American vessel to visit the West Coast of North America, opening trade between the colonies and the native peoples of the Northwest Coast. As the first American vessel to visit Honolulu, Hong Kong, and Japan, she played a key role in developing American involvement in Asian Pacific trade.

Built at Grays Harbor Historical Seaport in Aberdeen, Washington and launched in 1989 as a Washington State Centennial project, the reproduction *Lady Washington* sails the waters of Washington State and the West Coast of North America as the tall ship ambassador for the state of Washington. With a busy year-round sailing schedule, *Lady Washington* regularly tours the West Coast, providing shipboard education programs for schools in 89 port communities in Washington, Oregon, California, British Columbia, and Alaska. More than 15,000 school children visit *Lady Washington* each year to learn about the rich and colorful maritime heritage of our nation.

Crew are both paid professionals and volunteer trainees. The Historical Seaport regularly partners with a number of entities to provide unique shipboard education opportunities for trainees with independent learning contracts.

Flag:	USA
Rig:	Brig
Homeport/waters:	Aberdeen, Washington: Grays Harbor, Washington, West Coast of North America
Who sails?	School groups from elementary school through college, individuals and families.
Season:	Year-round
Cost:	$35 per person for a three-hour sail, $105 per person per day, $3,500 for a full-day charter.
Program type:	Sail training for crew, apprentices, and paying trainees. Sea education in maritime history in cooperation with accredited institutions, based on informal, in-house programming. Passenger day sails overnight passages and family camps. Dockside interpretation.

Specifications:			
	Sparred length: 112'	Draft: 11'	Sail area: 4,400 sq. ft.
	LOD: 66' 9"	Beam: 24'	Tons: 99 GRT
	LOA: 87'	Rig height: 89'	Power: diesel
	LWL: 58'	Freeboard: 6'	Hull: wood

Designer:	Ray Wallace
Built:	1989; Aberdeen, Washington, Grays Harbor Historical Seaport Authority
Coast Guard certification:	Passenger Vessel (Subchapter T)
Crew:	12. Trainees: 48 (day sails), 8 (overnight)
Contact:	Grace Hagen, Operations Director
	Grays Harbor Historical Seaport
	PO Box 2019, Aberdeen, WA 98520
	Tel: 800-200-LADY (5239); Fax: 360-533-9384
	E-mail: ghhsa@techline.com, Web site: http://www.ladywashington.org

Designed and built as a modified replica of a 1767 Boston Schooner, *Larinda* is a unique sailing vessel with modern safety features yet she retains traditional wood appointments and museum quality. Much of her construction is done with recycled 100-year old hard pine. A restored seven ton 1928 Wolverine 100 HP diesel provides auxiliary power. 300-pound bronze cannons add period excitement. *Larinda* was launched from Falmouth, Massachusetts in 1996. While completing the rigging, she visited many East Coast ports covering over 4000 miles. Participating in Tall Ships 2000® festivals, and the Great Lakes TALL SHIPS CHALLENGE® in 2001, *Larinda* sailed over 6300 miles to events that drew millions of people to witness and admire the unique gathering of distinguished national and international tall ships.

Featured in publications worldwide, *Larinda* has also starred in several documentaries shown on national and local television. Awards have been won at boat shows including the 1997 Wooden Boat Show and 2000 Antique and Classic Boat Show. Private charters are welcomed and *Larinda* is available for special events. Seaport festivals and other maritime gatherings have enjoyed her unique presence.

Larinda

Flag:	USA
Rig:	Schooner
Homeport/waters:	Cape Cod, Massachusetts: Canada to the Caribbean
Who sails?	School groups from elementary through college and individuals of all ages
Cost:	Varies with program
Program type:	Sail training for volunteer and paying trainees. Sea Challenges for challenged youth. Sea education in marine science, maritime history and ecology in cooperation with organized groups and as informal in-house programming.

Specifications:	Sparred length: 86'	Draft: 8'	Sail area: 3,000 sq. ft.
	LOD: 56'	Beam: 16' 6"	Tons: 46 GRT
	LOA: 64'	Rig height: 62'	Power: 100 HP diesel
	LWL: 52'	Freeboard: 5'	Hull: wood and ferrocement

Designer:	Hallowell/Mahan
Built:	1996; Marstons Mills, Massachusetts, Wolverine Motor Works and Shipyard, LLC
Coast Guard certification:	Attraction Vessel
Crew:	6-8
Contact:	Captain Lawrence Mahan, President
	26 Redmond Avenue
	No. Reading, MA 01864
	Tel: 508-648-0797, 508-428-8728
	E-mail: SailLarinda@aol.com
	Web site: http://www.larinda.com

Lettie G. Howard

The *Lettie G. Howard* is a Fredonia model fishing schooner, a type of vessel once widely used along the Atlantic seaboard from Maine to Texas. She was built in 1893 at Essex, Massachusetts, where the majority of the schooners for the fishing fleets of Gloucester, Boston, and New York were produced. She operated out of Gloucester for her first eight years. The fishing would have been done with hand lines set either from the vessel's deck or from small boats called dories. The *Howard* was similar to the schooners that carried their Long Island and New Jersey catches to New York City's Fulton Fish Market.

In 1901 the *Howard* was purchased by Pensacola, Florida owners for use off Mexico's Yucatan Peninsula. Completely rebuilt in 1923, she was fitted with her first auxiliary engine a year later. She remained in the Gulf of Mexico until 1968, when she was sold to the South Street Seaport Museum.

The *Lettie G. Howard* was designated a National Historic Landmark in 1988. Between 1991 and 1993 the museum completely restored her to her original 1893 appearance, while outfitting her to accommodate trainees on educational cruises.

Flag:	USA
Rig:	Gaff topsail schooner, two-masted
Homeport/waters:	New York City: Northeast United States
Who sails?	School groups, Elderhostel, individual adults, and families.
Program type:	Sail training for volunteer and paying trainees. Sea education in marine science, maritime history, and ecology in cooperation with accredited institutions and other groups.

Specifications:		
Sparred length: 129'	Draft: 11'	Sail area: 5,017 sq. ft.
LOD: 83'	Beam: 21'	Tons: 52 GRT
LWL: 71'	Rig height: 91'	Power: twin 85 HP diesels
Hull: wood		

Built:	1893; Essex, Massachusetts, A.D. Story (restored at South Street Seaport Museum in 1993).
Coast Guard certification:	Sailing School Vessel (Subchapter R)
Crew:	7. Trainees: 14 (overnight)
Contact:	Captain Stefan Edick, Marine Education South Street Seaport Museum 207 Front Street New York, NY 10038 Tel: 212-748-8596; Fax: 212-748-8610 Web site: http://www.southstseaport.org

The frigate A.R.A. *Libertad* was built in 1963 as a training ship for the Argentine Navy. As a training ship, her mission is to enhance the maritime knowledge and cultural background of her midshipmen while integrating them to life at sea and instructing them on the fundamentals of the art of sailing. *Libertad* also serves as a floating ambassador representing the Argentine Republic, establishing professional and friendly ties with navies around the world while preparing her cadets academically, physically and spiritually.

In 1966 *Libertad* established the world record for speed crossing the North Atlantic sailing from Cape Race (Canada) to Dursey Island (Ireland) in six days and 21 hours. This record is officially recognized by the International Sail Training Association (ISTA), and *Libertad* flies a pennant commemorating this achievement.

Her figurehead was made by a Spanish sculptor and depicts Liberty, for which the ship is named. *Libertad* has sailed the seven seas and participates in regattas and port visits around the world, most recently winning ISTA's Boston Teapot Trophy (an award she's garnered seven times) as part of her voyage during Tall Ships 2000®.

Flag:	Argentina
Rig:	Full-rigged ship
Homeport/waters:	Buenos Aires, Argentina: worldwide
Who sails?	Argentinian Naval cadets
Specifications:	LOA: 356' Beam: 45' 3" Draft: 21' 9"
	Sail area: 28,546 sq. ft. Power: 2/1,200 HP diesel
	Hull: steel
Built:	1956:
Contact:	Fragata A.R.A. LIBERTAD
	Estado Mayor General de la Armada
	Comodor Py 2055
	1104 Buenos Aries, Argentina
	E-mail: libertad@interar.com.ar
	Web site: http://www.fragatalibertad.ar
	http://www.ara.mil.ar

Fragata A.R.A. LIBERTAD
Apostadero Naval Buenos Aries
Avenida Antartida Argentina No. 401
1104 Buenos Aires, Argentina

Liberty

Liberty is modeled on early 1800s coastal schooners used by New England fisherman and as cargo vessels along the East Coast to the Florida Keys. She is based in Key West, where she offers three two-hour sails each day. *Liberty* is kept "shipshape and Bristol fashion" and is available for charter day and evening for every occasion.

Flag:	USA
Rig:	Gaff topsail schooner
Homeport/waters:	Boston, Massachusetts (summer), Key West, Florida (winter): East Coast US
Who sails?	School groups from elementary through high school, individuals and families.
Cost:	$25-$35 per person per two-hour harbor cruise, $175 per person per day, $3,600 group charter rate per day.
Program type:	Passenger day sails and overnight passages. Corporate and private charters.

Specifications:			
	Sparred length: 80'	Draft: 7'	Sail area: 1,744 sq. ft.
	LOD: 61'	Beam: 17'	Tons: 50 GRT
	LOA: 64'	Rig height: 65'	Power: diesel
	LWL: 53'	Freeboard: 5'	Hull: steel

Designer:	Charles Wittholz
Built:	1993; Palm Coast, Florida, Treworgy Yachts
Coast Guard certification:	Passenger Vessel (Subchapter T).
Crew:	3 (day sails), 4 (overnight). Trainees: 49 (day sails), 8 (overnight)
Contact:	Gregory E. Muzzy, President
	The Liberty Fleet of Tall Ships
	Hilton Resort & Marina
	Key West, FL 33040
	Tel: 305-295-0095; Fax: 305-292-6411
	Web site: http://www.libertyfleet.com

The *Liberty Clipper* is a replica of the mid-19th century Baltimore Clippers famous for their fast passages around Cape Horn on their way to California and other Pacific ports. The *Liberty Clipper* joined the *Liberty* in Boston in the summer of 1996. She is available for charter, with up to 110 passengers, in Boston Harbor and Key West, for day and evening cruises. Her spacious decks and on-board hospitality create an ambiance under sail that will meet the expectation of the most discriminating clients. Guests are invited to join in hoisting the sails, steering the boat, and otherwise joining in the fun. During the winter, *Liberty Clipper* joins *Liberty* in Key West, offering day sails, dinner sails, and charters. Traveling to Key West in October, *Liberty Clipper* offers four one way trips along the East Coast and two one week trips in the spring as she returns to Boston.

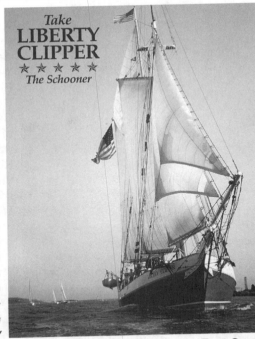

Take
LIBERTY CLIPPER
★ ★ ★ ★ ★
The Schooner

Flag:	USA
Rig:	Gaff topsail schooner
Homeport/waters:	Boston, MA (summer), Key West, FL (winter); East Coast US
Who sails?	School groups from elementary through high school, individuals, and families.
Cost:	$175 per person per day; $8,000 group charter rate per day.
Program type:	Passenger day sails and overnight passages. Corporate and private charters.

Specifications:			
	Sparred length: 125'	Draft: 8' (min.), 13' (max.)	Sail area: 4,300 sq. ft.
	LOD: 86'	Beam: 25'	Tons: 99 GRT
	LWL: 76'	Rig height: 78'	Power: diesel
	Freeboard: 5'	Hull: steel	

Designer:	Charles Wittholz
Built:	1983; Warren, Rhode Island, Blount Marine Corporation
Coast Guard certification:	Passenger Vessel (Subchapter T)
Crew:	5 (day sails), 10 (overnight). Trainees/passengers: 115 (day sails), 24 (overnight)
Contact:	Gregory E. Muzzy, President
	The Liberty Fleet of Tall Ships
	67 Long Wharf
	Boston, MA 02210
	Tel: 617-742-0333; Fax: 617-742-1322
	Web site: http://www.libertyfleet.com

Lily

The *Lily* was originally built as a working cargo sloop to haul freight out to Martha's Vineyard. After hauling cargo under sail for almost five years with her skipper and builder Rick Brown, she was sold north to the Maine Coast. At the time of her purchase by Captain Steven Pagels in the summer of 2001, the *Lily* had been out of the water for more than a dozen years. Relaunched in the summer of 2001, the *Lily* has been re-rigged as a schooner. During the 2002 season, the *Lily* will once again be sailing, offering both day sails and educational cruises.

Flag:	USA
Rig:	Schooner
Homeport/waters:	Cherryfield, Maine: Bar Harbor, Maine
Who sails?	Groups and individuals of all ages
Season:	Summer
Program type:	Sail training for volunteer and paying trainees. Dockside interpretation during port visits. Passenger day sails.

Specifications:

Sparred length: 55'	LOD: 40'	LOA: 40'
Draft: 3'	Beam: 15'	Sail area: 1,000 sq. ft.
Tons: 13 GRT	Power: two 20 HP diesels	Hull: wood
Hull color: white		

Designer:	Rick Brown
Built:	1979; Tisbury, Massachusetts, Rick Brown
Coast Guard certification:	Passenger Vessel (Subchapter T)
Crew:	2. Trainees/passengers: 6 (day sails)
Contact:	Captain Steven F. Pagels, owner
	Downeast Windjammer Cruises
	PO Box 28
	Cherryfield, ME 04622
	Tel: 207-546-2927; Fax: 207-546-2023
	E-mail: decruise@midmaine.com
	Web site: http://www.downeastwindjammer.com

One of the oldest surviving examples of a Chesapeake Bay Bugeye, the *Little Jennie* was built in 1884 and is listed on the National Register of Historic Places.

Originally built for oystering and freighting, the *Little Jennie,* once restored, will carry passengers on educational trips designed to highlight out maritime history and the ecology of coastal waters.

The *Little Jennie* is awaiting a major rebuild which will be required before she can ever again show her distinctive profile on the waters between Maine and the Chesapeake Bay. Anyone wanting to be involved in her restoration is invited to contact us.

Little Jennie

Flag:	USA
Rig:	Bugeye ketch
Homeport/waters:	Cherryfield, Maine: Bar Harbor, Maine (summer), Chesapeake Bay (winter).
Program type:	Sail training for volunteer or paying trainees. Dockside interpretation during port visits

Specifications:	Sparred length: 86'	Draft: 4'6"	Sail area: 1,600 sq. ft.
	LOA: 62'	LOD: 62'	LWL: 57'
	Beam: 17'	Tons: 22 GRT	Rig height: 60'
	Hull: wood	Hull color: white	Power: 100 HP diesel

Designer:	J.T. Marsh
Built:	1884; Solomons, Maryland, J.T. Marsh
Coast Guard certification:	Passenger Vessel (Subchapter T)
Crew:	2. Trainees/passengers: 32 (day sails), 6 (overnight)
Contact:	Captain Steven F. Pagels, Owner
	Downeast Windjammer Cruises
	PO Box 28
	Cherryfield, ME 04622
	Tel: 207-546-2927; Fax: 207-546-2023
	E-mail: decruise@midmaine.com
	Web site: http://downeastwindjammer.com

Lord Nelson

cally disabled people by offering them the opportunity to experience the excitement of tall ship sailing together.

Voyages last from 4 to 11 days, departing from a wide variety of ports and sailing in the English Channel and the North and Irish Seas. A winter season of voyages based in the Canary Islands is also available.

Above deck the ship's equipment enables physically disabled crew to work alongside their able-bodied crewmates. Features include power steering, wide decks to accommodate wheelchairs, a speaking compass, powered lifts between decks, and Braille marking. Below are specially designed wheelchair-accessible cabins, showers, and heads.

Voyages are open to anyone between 16 to 70+ with or without sailing experience. 20 people with physical disabilities, including eight wheelchair users, serve alongside an equal number of able-bodied people. There is a permanent crew of 10, including a medically trained person and a cook.

The 180-foot, three-masted barque *Lord Nelson* was built in 1986 for the Jubilee Sailing Trust to encourage integration between able-bodied and physically

Flag:	UK
Rig:	Barque, three-masted
Homeport/waters:	Southampton, United Kingdom: United Kingdom (summer), Canary Islands (winter)
Who sails?	Physically disabled and able-bodied people, aged 16 to 70+.
Cost:	Ranges from $65 to $133 per person per day, plus insurance
Program type:	Sail training for paying trainees. Integration of physically disabled and able-bodied people through the medium of tall ship sailing.

Specifications:			
	Sparred length: 180'	Draft: 13' 6"	Sail area: 11,030 sq. ft.
	LOD: 133'	Beam: 29' 6"	Tons: 368 GRT
	LOA: 140' 5"	Rig height: 108'	Power: twin 260 hp
	LWL: 121' 5"	Freeboard: 6' 8"	Hull: steel

Designer:	Colin Mudie
Built:	1986; Wivenhoe, UK, James W. Cook & Co., Ltd.
Certification:	Lloyds 100A1
Crew:	10. Trainees: 40
Contact:	Mrs. Lindsey Neve
	Jubilee Sailing Trust
	Jubilee Yard, Hazel Road, Woolston
	Southampton, Hampshire S019 7GB, United Kingdom
	Tel: 44-23-8044-9108; Fax: 44-23-8044-9145
	E-mail: jst@jst.org.uk
	Web site: http://www.jst.org.uk

SAIL TALL SHIPS!

The square topsail schooner *Lynx* has been designed and built to interpret the general configuration and operation of a privateer schooner or naval schooner from the War of 1812, the original *Lynx* being a "letter of marque" Baltimore Clipper commissioned during the opening days of the war. Serving effectively as a blockade runner and offensive weapon of war, she was among the first ships to defend American freedom.

LYNX

Dedicated to all those who cherish the blessings of America, *Lynx* sails as a living history museum, providing inspiration and resolve at this time in our nation's history. She is fitted with period ordnance and flies flags and pennants from the 1812 era. To complement her historic character, the *Lynx* crew wears period uniforms and operates the ship in keeping with the maritime traditions of early 19th Century America.

Lynx also operates as a sail training vessel to serve as a classroom for the study of historical, environmental and ecological issues. In addition, she undertakes "cruises of opportunity" that lead to personal growth and awareness through the experience of life at sea aboard a traditional sailing vessel.

Lynx is guided by the maxim, "Be Excellent to Each Other and To Your Ship."

Flag:	USA
Rig:	Square topsail schooner
Homeport/waters:	Portsmouth, New Hampshire
Who sails?	School groups from elementary age through college; individuals and families
Season:	Year-round
Program type:	Sail training for volunteer and paying trainees. Sea education in maritime history in cooperation with accredited institutions and other organized groups. Passenger day sails and overnight voyages; dockside interpretation.

Specifications:	Sparred Length: 122'	LOD: 76'	LOA: 78'
	LWL: 72'	Draft: 8' 6"	Beam: 23'
	Freeboard: 3' 6"	Sail Area: 4,669 square feet	
	Hull: wood	Hull color: Black with White Gunport Stripe	
	Power: Cat 3306B - 290 hp, Hundested Variable Pitch Propeller		

Designer:	Melbourne Smith - International Historical Watercraft Society
Built:	Rockport Marine, Rockport, Maine; Project Supervisor: Taylor Allen, Project Foreman: Eric Sewell Launched July 28, 2001 in Rockport, Maine
Coast Guard certification:	Passenger Vessel (Subchapter T)
Crew:	5. Trainees/passengers: 40 (day sails), 6-8 (overnight)
Contact:	Woodson K. Woods, Executive Director
	Woods Maritime LLC
	509 29th Street
	Newport Beach, California 92663
	Tel: 914-723-7814; Fax: 914-723-7815
	E-mail: whiskeykng@aol.com
	Website: http://www.privateerlynx.org

Mabel Stevens

The ketch *Mabel Stevens* offers charter services in the Washington, DC, and Chesapeake Bay areas. Sail training cruises, group and individual charters, and other tailored sailing and maritime education programs are offered by Captain Chalker aboard the *Mabel Stevens.*

Built by Captain Dick Hartge of Galesville, Maryland, the *Mabel Stevens* holds a special place in the Washington metropolitan area. During the 1980s, the *Mabel Stevens* officially represented the District of Columbia at the tall ships events in Boston (350th anniversary) and New York (Statue of Liberty centennial), and in 1992 in New York at the Christopher Columbus Quincentennial Celebrations. She is the District of Columbia's goodwill ambassador vessel at major historic events. The *Mabel Stevens* competes in ASTA rallies and has in the past raced with the best of the Class C tall ships. In 1986, she led the fleet of sail training vessels engaged in friendly competition en route to New York's Statue of Liberty festivities and participated in Philadelphia and Tall Ships® Newport '92.

Flag:	USA
Rig:	Ketch
Homeport/waters:	Cobb Island, Maryland: Lower Potomac River, Chesapeake Bay.
Who sails?	Individuals and groups
Season:	April to October
Cost:	$70 per person per day; inquire for group rates
Program type:	Maritime history and environmental studies.
Specifications:	Sparred length: 47' 6" Draft: 4' 6" Sail area: 1,200 sq. ft.
	LOA: 35' Beam: 11' 6" Sail number: TS-US 159
	LWL: 31' 9" Rig height: 45' Tons: 17 GRT
	Freeboard: 3' Hull: wood Power: 52 HP diesel
Built:	1935; Galesville, Maryland, Ernest H. Hartge
Coast Guard certification:	Uninspected Vessel
Crew:	1. Trainees: 4
Contact:	Captain Ned Chalker
	Ketch *Mabel Stevens*
	119 Fifth St. NE
	Washington, DC 20002
	Tel: 202-543-0110, 301-259-4458; Fax: 202-554-3949
	E-mail: Nchalker@aol.com

The *Madeline* is a reconstruction of a mid-19th-century schooner, typical of the trading schooners that once sailed the upper Great Lakes. The original *Madeline* was once the first Euro-American school in the Grand Traverse region and for a short time served as a lightship in the Straits of Mackinac.

The modern *Madeline*, launched in 1990, was built over period of five years by volunteers of the Maritime Heritage Alliance (MHA), using traditional methods and materials. From her homeport, Traverse City, Michigan, she has sailed with her volunteer crew on all five Great Lakes, visiting over 60 ports with dockside tours and historical interpretation. *Madeline* is the State of Michigan's official tall ship and is designated as the City of Traverse City's goodwill ambassador.

Madeline's dockside programs bring visitors on board to learn about schooners and Great Lakes history first-hand. Crewmembers, trained as historical interpreters, share their knowledge of history, marlinespike skills, and wooden boat building. School programs with special

hands-on activities are also available.

The Maritime Heritage Alliance, a nonprofit organization, fosters the study and practice of upper Great Lakes's maritime history. MHA programs, focusing on building and operating indigenous crafts, include crew training, traditional boat carpentry, and other wooden boat maintenance skills.

Flag:	USA
Rig:	Gaff topsail schooner, two-masted
Homeport/waters:	Traverse City, Michigan: upper Great Lakes
Who sails?	Trained crewmembers of the Maritime Heritage Alliance. *Madeline* is associated with the Association for Great Lakes History.
Program type:	Adult sail training and maritime history.

Specifications:	Sparred length: 92'	Draft: 7' 7"	Sail area: 2,270 sq. ft.
	LOA: 55' 6"	Beam: 16' 2"	Tons: 42 GRT
	LWL: 52'	Rig height: 71'	Freeboard: 2' 2"

Designer:	Robert Core
Built:	1990; Traverse City, Michigan, Maritime Heritage Alliance
Coast Guard certification:	Uninspected Vessel
Crew:	9
Contact:	Mr. Richard Brauer, President of the Board, Maritime Heritage Alliance
	322 Sixth Street
	Traverse City, MI 49684
	Tel: 231-946-2647; Fax: 231-946-6750
	E-mail: mhatc@bignetnorth.net
	Web site: http://www.traverse.com/maritime/

Makani Olu

The *Makani Olu* is owned and operated by the Marimed Foundation which has been involved in sail training since its inception in 1988. In July 2001, Marimed Foundation purchased the sail training ship in Florida and spent five months doing a major refit to prepare the private vessel for sail training in Hawaiian waters. Ten additional berths were added and the galley and engine room were equipped with the latest equipment. An exterior helm was added to the pilot house for warm weather operations. The 96-foot, three-masted staysail schooner arrived in Kaneohe Bay in March 2002 and began service with Marimed's Kailana Youth Program.

The *Makani Olu* (Gracious Wind) is the primary experiential educational component of the Kailana Program. Special-needs adolescents sail the ship year round in Hawaiian waters. From its base on Oahu, the *Makani Olu* makes six-day trips throughout the Hawaiian chain. Cadets from the Kailana Program learn marine skills, navigation and team building. They participate in service learning projects at ports of call.

In addition to providing the key component of the Kailana Program, the *Makani Olu* is available for group sail training and team building to youth, families and community organizations of all kinds. Day, weekend and six-day sail training trips are available.

Flag:	USA
Rig:	Staysail schooner, three masted
Homeport/waters:	Kaneohe Bay, Hawaii: Hawaiian Islands
Who sails?	Groups and individuals of all ages
Season:	Year-round
Cost:	$1000 to $1600 group rate (charter) per day, $900 to $1200 per person per six-day cruise
Program type:	Sail training for paying trainees. Fully accredited sea education in marine science, maritime history, and ecology, as well as service learning, in cooperation with accredited institutions and other organized groups, and as informal in-house programming.
Specifications:	Sparred length: 96' LOD: 75' LOA: 85'
	Draft: 8' Beam: 20' Rig height: 65'
	Freeboard: 5' Sail area: 2,000 sq. ft.
Designer:	Thomas Kolvin
Built:	1998; St. Augustine, Florida, Schrieber
Coast Guard certification:	Sailing School Vessel (Subchapter R)
Crew:	5. Trainees/passengers: 30 (day sails), 20 (overnight)
Contact:	Matthew Claybaugh, Ph.D., President and CEO
	Marimed Foundation
	45-021 Likeke Place
	Kaneohe, HI 96744
	Tel: 808-236-2288; Fax: 808-235-1074
	E-mail: kailana@marimed.org
	Web site: http://www.marimed.org

Named for Captain Mallory Todd, who served as master on American vessels during the Revolutionary War, the *Mallory Todd* is a modern 65-foot schooner built in the classic style with fireplaces and exceptionally fine woodwork. Designed for long distance voyages, she has sailed the West Coast from Mexico to Alaska for 18 years. When at homeport in Seattle, she relieves the tedium of long term cancer treatment with recreational outings for hospital patients and their caregivers under the auspices of the nonprofit Sailing Heritage Society.

Sail training trips to the San Juan Islands, Canada, and Alaska via the Inside Passage are blessed with the full bounty of nature. Humpback whales, Orcas, sea lions, dolphins, and sea otters cavort while bears forage ashore, eagles soar the winds, and fjord hillsides entice the naturalist with breathtaking wildflowers. These trips are open to anyone between 18 and 80 with or without sailing experience. Together, part time volunteers, trainees, and pro-fessionals get the job done. Hands on tending the sails, steering, scrubbing, navigating, fishing, or clamming, each contributes where a need fits their abilities.

Schooner *Mallory Todd* also offers corporate and private charters that provide a unique and delightful venue for business or recreational activities—be it exclusive executive meeting or picnic outing.

Flag:	USA
Rig:	Staysail schooner
Homeport/waters:	Seattle, Washington: Pacific Northwest, Canada, and Alaska
Who sails?	All ages for volunteers, paying trainees, and apprentices.
Cost:	Based on ability to pay
Program type:	Sail training for crew volunteers, trainees, and apprentices. Sea education based on programmed and day to day events. Passenger day sails for corporate team building or recreational events.

Specifications:	Sparred length: 65'	Draft: 5' (min.), 8' (max.)	Sail area: 1,545 sq. ft.
	LOD: 65'	Beam: 16'	Tons: 38 GRT
	LOA: 60'	Rig Height: 65'	Power: diesel
	LWL: 50'	Freeboard: 5'	Hull: composite

Designer:	Perry & Todd
Built:	1981; Seattle, Washington
Coast Guard certification:	Passenger Vessel (Subchapter T).
Crew:	2. Trainees: 6 (overnight), 25 (day sails)
Contact:	Captain George Todd
	Sailing Heritage Society
	10042 NE 13th Street
	Bellevue, WA 98004
	Tel: 425-451-8160; Fax: 425-451-8119
	E-mail: mallorytodd@email.msn.com
	Web site: http://www.sailseattle.com

Manitou

Owned and operated by Traverse Tall Ship Company, the schooner *Manitou* is one of the largest sailing vessels on the Great Lakes. She can accommodate 24 overnight guests and 56 passengers for day excursions. *Manitou* is fully certified by the US Coast Guard and offers 3, 4, and 5-day windjammer cruises to the islands, bays, and coastal villages of Lakes Michigan and Huron.

In conjunction with Inland Seas Education Association, *Manitou* offers the Schoolship Program, which provides an environmental, historical, and sail training education for students during the spring. Three day family packages are also available on two separate cruises during the regular season. Primarily offered as adult vacation, the windjammer season runs from June through October 1.

Flag:	USA
Rig:	Gaff topsail schooner, two-masted
Homeport/waters:	Northport, Michigan: Great Lakes
Who sails?	Science and marine biology student groups from elementary school through junior high. Individual, family, and corporate groups for multi-day windjammer cruises.
Season:	May to October
Program type:	Sail training for crew. Sea education in marine science, maritime history and ecology. Corporate team-building workshops. Individual and group windjammer cruises.

Specifications:

Sparred length: 114'	Draft: 7' (min.), 11' (max.)	Sail area: 3,000 sq. ft.
LOD: 77'	Beam: 21'	Tons: 82 GRT
LWL: 65'	Rig height: 80'	Power: 150 HP diesel
Freeboard: 6'	Hull: steel	Rig height: 75' 6"
Hull color: white	Spar material: wood	

Designer:	Woodin & Marean.
Built:	1982; Portsmouth, New Hampshire, Roger Gagnon Steel Ship Company
Coast Guard certification:	Passenger Vessel (Subchapter T)
Crew:	5. Trainees/passengers: 56 (day sails), 24 (overnight)
Contact:	Captain David P. McGinnis, Senior Captain
	Traverse Tall Ship Company
	13390 SW Bay Shore Drive
	Traverse City, MI 49684
	Tel: 231-941-2000; Fax: 231-941-0520
	E-mail: tallship@traverse.com
	Web site: http://www.tallshipsailing.com

Maple Leaf

The *Maple Leaf* is a 92 ft classic wooden schooner. With a rich history of operation along the north pacific coast.

Launched in 1904 as a private yacht for a lumber baron who spared no expense on her construction, she was overbuilt with large timbers of the finest local wood, details glinted with gold and bronze, and she even boasted new-fangled 'electric' lights.

A second life in the middle of the century as a halibut schooner on the stormy North Pacific saw *Maple Leaf* out-fish every other boat in the fleet. Vessel and crew became legendary-with the result being a loving rebuild of their prized *Maple Leaf;* again no expense was spared. *Maple Leaf* fished another 20 years and then underwent an award-winning, six-year restoration and was re-launched in 1986.

Her third incarnation now has her proudly offering sail training and eco-tourism adventures.

Since 1988 *Maple Leaf* has been part of the Royal Canadian Sea Cadets sail training program. While experiencing the opportunity to sail the beautiful British

Columbia coast, cadets gain an appreciation for the age-old traditions of sailing a tall ship and the inherent life and leadership skills that come from meeting new challenges.

In addition to youth sail training, *Maple Leaf* offers 5 to 11 day eco-tourism adventures on the B.C. and Alaska coasts. The trips explore the coast's natural and cultural history and are accompanied by expert naturalists and a gourmet chef. *Maple Leaf* is also available for private charter. Her beautiful form and maple-leaf-printed main sail are known and loved up and down the coast.

Flag:	Canada		
Rig:	Gaff schooner		
Homeport/waters:	Victoria, British Columbia: British Columbia & Alaska coasts		
Who sails?	Sea cadets (sail training) and Charter guests		
Season:	Sail Training: April, July, August Eco-tourism: April, May, June, September, October		
Program type:	Youth sail training / Eco-tourism		
Specifications:	Sparred Length: 92'	LOD: 75'	LOA: 77'
	LWL: 59'	Draft: 11'	Beam: 15'
	Rig height: 96'	Sail area: 3,300 sq. ft.	Tons: 40.75 GRT
	Freeboard: 5'	Power: 260 HP diesel	Hull: wood
Designer:	William Watts		
Built:	1904; Vancouver, British Columbia, Canada		
Certification:	Inspected passenger carrying vessel, Home Trade 3		
Crew:	5. Trainees/passengers: 30 (day sails), 18 (overnight) Adult eco-tourism guests: 9		
Contact:	Kevin J. Smith		
	Mapleleaf Adventures		
	2087 Indian Crescent		
	Duncan, B.C., V9L 5L9 Canada		
	Tel: 250-746-0906 (outside North America),		
	888-599-5323 (inside North America)		
	E-mail: mapleleaf@mapleleafadventures.com		
	Web site: http://www.mapleleafadventures.com		

Margaret Todd

Harbor, adjacent to Acadia National Park, the *Margaret Todd* can accommodate groups of up to 150 on day sails, educational, and sail training cruises.

Captain Pagels built the *Margaret Todd* (named after his grandmother) to replace his 3-masted schooner *Natalie Todd,* which he ran for ten years. The *Margaret Todd* routinely sails by some of the most spectacular scenery on the Maine coast. With her tandem center-boards and shallow draft this schooner also has a good turn of speed and offers her crew, trainees, and guests a unique and memorable experience under traditional sail.

Launched new in 1998, the 4-masted schooner *Margaret Todd* is the first 4-master to be based and operate in New England in over half a century. With her distinctive tanbark sails, this 151-foot schooner is becoming a legend on the Maine coast. Based in Bar

Flag:	USA
Rig:	Schooner, four-masted
Homeport/waters:	Cherryfield, Maine: Bar Harbor, Maine.
Program type:	Sail training for paid or volunteer crew or trainees. Passenger day sails. Dockside interpretation during port visits.

Specifications:

Sparred length: 151'	Draft: 5' 9"	Sail area: 4,800 sq. ft.
LOD: 121'	Beam: 23'	Tons: 99 GRT
LOA: 121'	Hull: steel	Power: diesel
Power: 400 HP diesel	Hull color: white	Spar material: steel/wood

Designer:	Woodin and Marean
Built:	1998; St. Augustine, Florida, Schreiber Boats
Coast Guard certification:	Passenger Vessel (Subchapter T)
Crew:	8. Trainees/passengers: 150
Contact:	Captain Steve F. Pagels, Owner
	Downeast Windjammer Cruises
	PO Box 28
	Cherryfield, ME 04622
	Tel: 207-546-2927; Fax: 207-546-2023
	E-mail: decruise@midmaine.com
	Web site: http://www.downeastwindjammer.com

Built in 1962 by Harvey Gamage, *Mary Day* combines the best aspects of the New England centerboard coaster with modern design thinking. *Mary Day* operates out of Camden, Maine, in the windjammer trade from late May to early October. She carries 30 passengers on weeklong vacation cruises in mid-coast Maine. *Mary Day* is a pure sailing vessel. She has no engine and depends on a small yawl boat when winds fail. She has a large and powerful rig and exhibits outstanding sailing abilities.

Mary Day carries a professional crew of six, including captain, mate, cook, two deckhands, and one galley hand. The galley and one deck position are considered entry-level positions, and a great many sailing professionals have started out or gained valuable experience on board the schooner *Mary Day*.

Flag:	USA
Rig:	Gaff topsail schooner, two-masted
Homeport/waters:	Camden, Maine: Mid-Coast and Downeast Maine
Who sails?	Individuals and families.
Season:	May to October
Cost:	$129 per person per day
Program type:	Sail training for crew and apprentices. Passenger overnight passages. Dockside interpretation in homeport.

Specifications:			
	Sparred length: 125'	Draft: 7' 6"	Sail area: 5,000 sq. ft.
	LOD: 90'	Beam: 22'	Tons: 86 GRT
	LOA: 92'	Rig height: 102'	Hull: wood
	LWL: 81'	Freeboard: 5'	

Designer:	H. Hawkins
Built:	1962; South Bristol, Maine, Harvey Gamage
Coast Guard certification:	Passenger Vessel (Subchapter T)
Crew:	7. Trainees: 49 (day sails), 29 (overnight)
Contact:	Captains Barry King and Jen Martin
	Penobscot Windjammer Company
	PO Box 798
	Camden, ME 04843
	Tel: 800-992-2218
	E-mail: captains@schoonermaryday.com
	Web site: http://www.schoonermaryday.com

Megan D

The *Megan D* will conduct a mixture of sail training programs, including middle school and junior high school programs, as well as offering adventure vacation opportunities. Programs will focus on team building while teaching traditional seamanship and the sailor's arts in the unique setting of a traditional square-rigged vessel. In port and underway, the ship will simulate the atmosphere of the early American Navy, depicting the life aboard ships of that era and passing on sea-going military tradition and heritage within a fun and challenging historical framework.

Designed and built by James D. Rosborough in his Nova Scotia yard, *Megan D* (formerly the *Distant Star*) was launched in 1978. She completed minor repairs in Port Townsend, Washington, and during the summer of 1999, she voyaged to her new home-port of San Diego.

All who sail aboard her are involved in sailing her. If you've ever dreamed of sailing aboard a traditional square-rigger, this is your chance!

Flag:	USA
Rig:	Brigantine
Homeport/waters:	San Diego, California: Eastern Pacific of Southern California
Season:	Year-round
Who sails?	School groups from elementary through high school and individuals of all ages.
Program type:	Sail trainng for paying trainees. Team building within a framework of maritime history, sea education, and naval science programs. Education programs featuring traditional seamanship and tailored multi-disciplinary subjects as requested.

Specifications:			
	Sparred length: 56'	LOA: 46'	LOD: 45'
	LWL: 36'6"	Draft: 7'	Beam: 14'
	Rig height: 55'	Sail area: 1,490 sq. ft.	Tons: 27 GRT
	Power: 84 HP diesel	Hull: wood	Hull color: white

Designer:	James D. Rosborough
Built:	1978: Parrsboro, Nova Scotia, James D. Rosborough
Crew:	2-4. Trainees: 6-10 (day sails), 4 (overnight)
Contact:	Tom Wing
	Continental Navy Foundation
	11054 Melton Court
	San Diego, CA 92131
	Tel/Fax: 858-271-4883
	E-mail: tmwing@sprintmail.com
	Web site: http://home.sprintmail.com/-tmwing/

The *Mike Sekul* is one of the two Biloxi oyster schooner replicas built as part of the Biloxi Schooner Project under the auspices of the Maritime and Seafood Industry Museum. She was launched in April of 1994 as part of the effort to preserve the maritime and seafood industry of the Mississippi Gulf Coast. Money for construction and fitting out of the *Mike Sekul* and her sister ship, *Glenn L. Swetman,* has come from donations and fundraising events.

The *Mike Sekul* is available for charter for two-and-a-half hours, half-day, and full-day trips in the Mississippi Sound and to the barrier islands, Cat Island, Horn Island, and Ship Island. Walkup day sailing trips are made when she is not under charter. Groups of up to 45 passengers learn about the maritime and seafood heritage of the Gulf Coast and about the vessels working in Biloxi's seafood industry.

Sailing classes are offered through local colleges and the museum's Sea and Sail Adventure summer camp. Wedding parties, Elderhostel, and school groups are also accommodated.

Flag:	USA
Rig:	Gaff topsail schooner, two-masted
Homeport/waters:	Biloxi, Mississippi: coastwise Gulf of Mexico
Who sails?	Elementary students through college age, adults, and families. Affiliated institutions include William Carey College, Seashore Methodist Assembly, J.L. Scott Marine Education Center, and Mississippi State University
Season:	Year-round
Cost:	$20 per adult or $10 per child (2-hour sail). Group rate $950 (full day) $600 (half-day). half-day, $750 per day.
Program type:	Sail training for paying and volunteer trainees. Sea education in marine science, maritime history, and ecology in cooperation with accredited institutions and organized groups and as informal, in-house programming.

Specifications:	Sparred length: 78'	Draft: 5' 10"	Sail area: 2,499 sq. ft.
	LOD: 50'	Beam: 17'	Tons: 24 GRT
	LOA: 78'	Hull: wood	Power: 4-71 Detroit diesel
	LWL: 43'		

Designer:	Neil Covacevich
Built:	1994; Biloxi, Mississippi, Neil Covacevich
Coast Guard certification:	Passenger Vessel (Subchapter T)
Crew:	3. Trainees: 45 (day). Age: 15+
Contact:	Robin Krohn, Executive Director
	Maritime and Seafood Industry Museum of Biloxi
	PO Box 1907
	Biloxi, MS 39533
	Tel: 228-435-6320; Fax: 228-435-6309
	E-mail: schooner@maritimemuseum.org
	Web site: http://www.maritime museum.org

Minnie V.

The skipjack *Minnie V.*, built in Wenona, Maryland, was used to dredge oysters on the Chesapeake Bay for many years. The vessel was rebuilt by the City of Baltimore in 1981 and is now owned and operated by the Living Classrooms Foundation. The Foundation uses the vessel for educational programs and as a tourist attraction offering interpretive tours of the historic port of Baltimore. While on board the *Minnie V.*, students learn about the oyster trade, its importance to the economy of Maryland, and the hard life of a waterman as they relive history by raising the sails on one of the Chesapeake's few remaining skipjacks.

Flag:	USA
Rig:	Sloop
Homeport/waters:	Baltimore, Maryland: Baltimore Harbor
Who sails?	School groups from middle school through college as well as individuals and families.
Season:	April through October
Cost:	Rates vary depending on program. Please call for more information.
Program type:	Sea education in marine science, maritime history, and ecology in cooperation with accredited schools, colleges, and other organized groups. Passenger day sails. Dockside interpretation.

Specifications:

Sparred length: 69'	Draft: 3'	Sail area: 1,450 sq. ft.
LOD: 45' 3"	Beam: 15' 7"	Tons: 10 GRT
Rig height: 58'	Freeboard: 2'	Hull: wood

Built:	1906; Wenona, Maryland, Vetra
Coast Guard certification:	Passenger Vessel (Subchapter T)
Crew:	2. Trainees: 24
Contact:	Christine Truett, Director of Education

Living Classrooms Foundation
802 South Caroline Street
Baltimore, MD 21231-3311
Tel: 410-685-0295; Fax: 410-752-8433
Web site: http://www.livingclassrooms.org

Mir is regarded by many as the fastest Class A sail training ship in the world. She was the overall winner of the 1992 Columbus Race and the winner of the Cutty Sark Tall Ship Races in 1996, 1997, and 1998 under the command of Captain Victor Antonov. *Mir* was launched in 1989 at the Lenin shipyard in Gdansk, Poland, the builders of five more of the M 108 type ships: *Dar Mlodziezy, Pallada, Khersones, Druzhba,* and *Nadezhda.*

Mir is the school ship of the Makaroz Maritime Academy in St. Petersburg, Russia, training future navigators and engineers for the Russian merchant fleet. Since 1990 up to 60 trainees of all ages are welcomed on board to sail along with the Russian students, learning the ropes, manning the helm, or climbing the rigging to set the sails. No previous experience is necessary.

Mir is supported by Tall Ship Friends, a nonprofit organization in Hamburg, Germany. The goals of Tall Ship Friends are to promote sail training on square-riggers, to contribute to the

further existence of these beautiful ships, and to provide an unforgettable experience for the participants. Members of Tall Ship Friends receive the quarterly Tall Ships News (English/German) and a personal sailing log.

Flag:	Russia
Rig:	Full-rigged ship
Homeport/waters:	St. Petersburg, Russia: west and southwest European waters
Who sails?	Students and individuals of all ages. Affiliated with Tall Ship Friends clubs in France, UK, Switzerland, Austria, Ireland, and Italy.
Cost:	$50-$100 per person per day
Program type:	Sail training for paying trainees. Fully accredited sea education in traditional seamanship. Dockside interpretation during port visits.

Specifications:	Sparred length: 345' 9"	Draft: 18'	Sail area: 29,997 sq. ft.
	LOA: 328'	Beam: 44' 9"	Tons: 2,856 GRT
	LOD: 300' 9"	Rig height: 149'	Power: twin 570 HP diesels
	LWL: 254'	Freeboard: 34' 6"	Hull: steel

Designer:	Z. Choren
Built:	1987; Gdansk, Poland, Stocznia Gdanska
Certification:	Russian registered Sailing School Vessel
Crew:	45-70. Trainees/passengers: up to 250 (day sails), 60 (overnight)
Contact:	Wulf Marquard, Managing Director, Tall Ship Friends Germany Schweriner Str. 17 Hamburg, D22 143, Germany Tel: 49-40-675 635 97; Fax: 49-40-675 635 99 E-mail: tallship1@aol.com Web site: http://tallship-friends.de

Miss Mavis

Make your own itinerary or follow one of ours. We make your dream vacation come true! Sail, snorkel, and dive while you explore the islands of the Florida Keys, the Abacos, the Dry Tortugas, and beyond. Let us help design a trip for you.

Flag:	USA
Rig:	Ketch
Homeport/waters:	Fort Lauderdale, Florida: Abaco, Bahamas (summer); Florida Keys (winter)
Who sails?	Families and adults of all ages.
Program type:	Sail training for paying trainees. Sea education in marine science and ecology as informal in-house programming.
Season:	May through August

Specifications:

Sparred length: 42'	Draft: 4'2"	Sail area: 880 sq. ft.
LOD: 40'	LOA: 41'3"	LWL: 34'
Beam: 13'10"	Rig height: 63'	Freeboard: 5'
Power: diesel	Hull: fiberglass	Hull color: white
Sail number: 3	Spar material: aluminum	

Designer:	Charles Morgan
Built:	1981; Florida, Morgan Co.
Crew:	1 Passengers/trainees: 6
Contact:	Captain Barry Stanley, Owner
	7464 Charleston Run Cove
	Memphis, TN 38125
	Tel: 901-757-7895; Fax: 901-757-1278
	E-mail: capbarry@mindsouth.rr.com

The *Mist of Avalon* began her life in 1967 as the motor vessel *Liverpool Bay.* She was built of strong native timber, and by the skilled hands of shipwrights of MacLean Shipbuilding, Mahone Bay, Nova Scotia, Canada. Her captain and crew worked the banks off Nova Scotia and Newfoundland, fishing for the cod that was her reason for being.

After 20 years working in the harsh environment of the North Atlantic, with fish stock declining and her machinery and equipment well past their prime, this once proud vessel was left abandonded at a Halifax pier in 1987. Another five years of neglect added to her decline, but under layers of old paint and algae, behind the rotting timber and planks, was a gracious schooner hull waiting to return her to the sea.

In 1992 she began a new life as the *Mist of Avalon,* named for the mystic Celtic island of rebirth. She was brought from Nova Scotia to her new homeport at Holiday's Afloat Museum in

Ivy Lea, Ontario, Canada in the summer of 1993. There work continued on the conversion from motor vessel to fully rigged tall ship in the tradition of the late 19th century Grand Banks schooners.

Flag:	Canada
Rig:	Gaff schooner
Homeport/waters:	Ivy Lea, Ontario, Canada
Who sails?	Groups and individuals of all ages
Program type:	Sail training for paying trainees, corporate & social events, festivals, boat shows, tall ship events. Passenger day sails and overnight passages.

Specifications:	Sparred length: 100'	LOD: 83'	LOA: 84'
	Draft: 10'	Beam: 20' 1"	Rig height: 92'
	Sail area: 3,668 sq. ft.	Tons: GRT	Power: 3306 Cat diesel
	Hull: wood		

Built:	1967; Mahone Bay, Nova Scotia, Canada, MacLean Shipbuilding
Crew:	3. Trainees/passengers: 8
Contact:	George Mainguy
	29 Ivy Lea Road
	Lansdowne, Ontario K0E 1L0
	Tel: 613-659-3207; Fax: 613-382-7710
	E-mail: mistofavalon@1000island.net
	Web site: http://www.mistofavalon.ca

Momentum

The Friendship Sloop *Momentum* was built by the Lash Brothers of Friendship, Maine as one of the last working Friendships built of wood. She was launched with the name *Dirigo* and represented the State of Maine at the 1964 World's Fair in New York City. She has appeared in numerous print advertisements including a national ad for Kodakis.

Momentum is owned by Pittsburgh businessman Ronald Esser and operated by the Bayfront Center for Maritime Studies (BCMS). BCMS is a community based non-profit corporation whose mission is to design and deliver unique, hands-on maritime related educational, vocational and recreational opportunities for everyone.

Momentum provides numerous on the water experiences for students including the award winning Environmental Rediscoveries program during the day and serves as a passenger vessel providing sightseeing tours of historic Presque Isle Bay during the evenings and on weekends.

Flag:	USA
Rig:	Friendship sloop
Homeport/waters:	Erie, Pennsylvania: Presque Isle Bay, Lake Erie
Who sails?	Students, elementary school through college. Groups of all ages.
Season:	April 15 through November 15
Program type:	Sail training for volunteer and paying trainees. Sea education in marine science, maritime history and ecology in cooperation with accredited institutions , other organized groups, and as informal in-house programming. Affiliated schools and organizations include Pennsylvania Sea Grant, Penn State Erie, Mercyhurst College, Northwest Tri-County Intermediate Unit, Perseus House, Inc., Cornell ABRAXAS, and Sarah Reed Children's Center

Specifications:			
	Sparred length: 42'	LOD: 30'	LOA: 32'
	LWL: 28'	Draft: 7'	Beam: 8'
	Rig height: 45'	Tons: 9 GRT	Power: 18 HP diesel

Designer:	Winfield Lash
Built:	1964; Friendship, Maine, Lash Brothers
Coast Guard certification:	Passenger Vessel (Subchapter T)
Crew:	1. Trainees/passengers: 12 (day sails)
Contact:	Jim Stewart, Executive Director
	Bayfront Center for Maritime Studies
	7 East Dobbins Landing
	Erie, PA 16507
	Tel: 814-456-4077; Fax: 801-640-5140
	E-mail: eriesailing@hotmail.com
	Web site: http://www.goerie.com/bcms

Built in 1967 and rebuilt in 1994, the *Mystic Whaler* carries passengers and trainees on a variety of cruises, ranging from one day to one week. In April and May, the schooner will be on the Hudson River, conducting environmental education programs in conjunction with the *Clearwater*. Sailing from Mystic, CT throughout the summer months, the Mystic Whaler offers great sailing opportunities for both novice and experienced passengers. In September and October, the Mystic Whaler will sail the Chesapeake Bay and take part in the Great Chesapeake Bay Schooner Race. Some of the two-day and three-day cruises during the season focus on specific topics, such as lighthouses, sea music, art, and photography. Lobster cruises are popular during the summer. Two-week apprenticeship programs run throughout the season.

Flag:	USA
Rig:	Gaff-rigged schooner
Homeport/waters:	Mystic, Connecticut: southeast New England
Who sails?	School groups from elementary school through college, as well as individuals and families.
Program type:	Sail training for crew and apprentices. Sea education in maritime history and ecology based on informal programming with organized groups such as Scouts. Passenger day sails and overnight passages.

Specifications:			
	Sparred length: 110'	Draft: 7' 6" (min.), 13' (max.)	Sail area: 3,000 sq. ft.
	LOD: 83'	Beam: 25'	Tons: 97 GRT
	LOA: 83'	Rig height: 90'	Power: 6-71 diesel, 175 HP
	LWL: 78'	Freeboard: 7'	Hull: steel

Designer:	"Chub" Crockett
Built:	1967; Tarpon Springs, Florida, George Sutton
Coast Guard certification:	Passenger Vessel (Subchapter T)
Crew:	5. Trainees: 65 (day), 36 (overnight)
Contact:	Captain John Eginton
	Mystic Whaler Cruises, Inc.
	PO Box 189
	Mystic, CT 06355-0189
	Tel: 860-536-4218; Fax: 860-536-4219
	E-mail: mysticwhaler@earthlink.net
	Web site: http://www.mysticwhaler.com

Anderson Syndicate at the Graves yard in Marblehead, Massachusetts for the 1962 America's Cup. She was designed and skippered by Ted Hood, who ousted both *Easterner* and *Columbia* before being eliminated by Bus Mosbacher's *Weatherly* in the defender's finals.

Following her Cup challenge, *Nefertiti* was converted for cruising and traversed the globe. She crossed the Atlantic to the Mediterranean and chartered out of Greece for several years. By 1983 she was back in Newport as a spectator of the last America's Cup series held in Newport. *Nefertiti* then traveled down to the West Indies, to Fremantle, Australia in 1987, and crossed the Indian Ocean to South Africa where she remained until September 1997. She has been restored to racing trim by America's Cup Charters.

The 1962 12-meter class sloop *Nefertiti* has returned to Newport, Rhode Island. Brought back by America's Cup Charters' George Hill and Herb Marshall, owners of the America's Cup defender, *Weatherly* and Ted Turner's former *American Eagle, Nefertiti* is part of their charter fleet of former cup contenders.

Nefertiti was built for the Ross

Flag:	USA
Rig:	Sloop
Homeport/waters:	Newport, Rhode Island: New England and Chesapeake Bay
Who sails?	Individuals and groups of all ages
Cost:	$2100 group rate per day, $75 per person for evening sails
Program type:	Sail training for paying trainees. Passenger day sails, corporate team building, corporate racing, individual and group charters

Specifications:	Sparred length: 69'		Draft: 9'		Sail area: 1,850 sq. ft.
	LOD: 67'		Beam: 13' 6"		Tons: 28 GRT
	LOA: 67'		Rig height: 90'		Power: diesel
	LWL: 46'		Freeboard: 4'		Hull: wood

Designer:	Ted Hood
Built:	1962; Marblehead, Massachusetts, Graves
Coast Guard certification:	Passenger Vessel (Subchapter T)
Crew:	3. Trainees/passengers: 14
Contact:	George Hill/Herb Marshall, America's Cup Charters
	PO Box 51
	Newport, RI 02840
	Tel: 401-849-5868; Fax: 401-849-3098
	Web site: http://www.americascupcharters.com

Crosscurrent Voyages is a sail training program operated onboard the Class C tall ship *Nehemiah.* Emulating the training style used on such vessels as the USCG Barque *Eagle,* the program attempts to awaken and cultivate leadership skills by challenging students to learn various disciplines and to manage different types of information and technical matters. Traditional knowledge and skills are used to integrate educational disciplines such as math, reasoning, English, and history. The object is to utilize the pace and style of administering a large sailing vessel as a tool for equipping trainees to develop personal styles for dealing with the sea of information, knowledge, and options which saturate their daily lives. The program rounds out the training by enhancing personal character development in the areas of family and community values.

The primary target age is 12 through 18. The training personnel often come from the USCG and profes-

sional maritime fields. The sailing vessel *Nehemiah* has circumnavigated the globe a number of times under previous ownership, thus adding a context to the learning.

Flag:	USA
Rig:	Ketch
Homeport/waters:	Richmond, California: San Francisco Bay and Pacific Coast
Who sails?	Groups from elementary school through college, youth organizations, individuals, and families. Court referrals are also accepted. Emphasis is on at-risk youth.
Program type:	Sail training emphasizing character and community building. Sea education in marine science, maritime history, and ecology. Passenger day sails and overnight passages.

Specifications:	Sparred length: 57'	Draft: 6' 5"	Tons: 23 GRT
	LOD: 46' 8"	Beam: 14' 3"	Power: Perkins 4-236
	LOA: 50'	Rig height: 58'	Hull: wood
	LWL: 39'	Freeboard: 5'	

Designer:	William Garden (modified)
Built:	1971; Santa Barbara, California, Joseph Meyr
Coast Guard certification:	Passenger Vessel (Subchapter T)
Crew:	2. Trainees: 25 (day sails), 12 (overnight)
Contact:	Captain Rod Phillips
	Crosscurrent Voyages
	92 Seabreeze Drive
	Richmond, CA 94804-7410
	Tel/Fax: 510-234-5054
	E-mail: captain@sailingacross.com
	Web site: http://www.sailingacross.com

PHOTO BY BOB LOWRY

The present *Niagara* has auxiliary power and modern navigation equipment, but lacks modern amenities such as warm water, showers and privacy. She is sailed by a crew of 18-20 professionals supplemented by 20 volunteers willing to live under Spartan conditions such as hammock berthing and living out of a duffel bag. Volunteers do not need to have experience, but a minimum sign-on of three weeks is required.

Niagara is inspected as an Attraction Vessel in port, and sails as an Uninspected Vessel. During "home summers" (odd numbered years) there are typically two day sails per week from early May to late September/early October, with a short voyage of three to four weeks sometime in the season. In the even years, the ship is away from seven to eighteen weeks on voyages to ports in the Great Lakes, US East Coast, and Canadian Maritimes. A typical schedule is public visitation in port for three days and four-day passage between ports. When not on extended voyages, she makes her home at the Erie Maritime Museum in Erie, Pennsylvania.

The US Brig *Niagara* was built in 1988 as a reconstruction of the warship aboard which Oliver Hazard Perry won the Battle of Lake Erie in 1813 during the War of 1812. Her mission is to interpret War of 1812 history, promote the Commonwealth of Pennsylvania and the Erie Region, and preserve the skills of square-rig seafaring.

Flag:	USA		
Rig:	Brig		
Homeport/waters:	Erie, Pennsylvania: Coastwise and Great Lakes		
Who sails?	School groups from middle school through college, as well as individuals and families.		
Program type:	Sail training for crew and apprentices. Sea education based on informal, in-house programming. Dockside interpretation.		
Specifications:	Sparred length: 198'	Draft: 11'	Sail area: 11,600 sq. ft.
	LOD: 116'	Beam: 32' 6"	Tons: 162 GRT
	LOA: 123'	Rig height: 121'	Power: twin 200 HP diesels
	LWL: 110'	Hull: wood	
Designer:	Melbourne Smith		
Built:	1988; Erie, Pennsylvania		
Coast Guard certification:	Uninspected Vessel and Attraction Vessel		
Crew:	40		
Contact:	Captain Walter P. Rybka		
	Pennsylvania Historical and Museum Commission		
	150 East Front Street, Suite 100		
	Erie, PA 16507		
	Tel: 814-452-2744; Fax: 814-455-6760		
	E-mail: sail@brigniagara.org		
	Web site: http://www.brigniagara.org		

Built in 1980 as a replica of a 19th-century coastal schooner, *Nighthawk* sails the waters of the Chesapeake Bay and its tributaries from April 1 through November 1 each season. She voyaged to the Caribbean, Mexico, and South America prior to arriving in Baltimore in 1986.

Nighthawk operates as a private charter vessel as well as offering basic sail training to local school and scout groups. Docked in the historic Fells Point section of Baltimore's Inner Harbor, the *Nighthawk* and her captain and crew provide an ideal opportunity for character and team building through hands-on exploration.

Nighthawk is also available for wide variety of corporate and private charters and celebrations, as well as public excursions. "Murder Mystery" and other theme cruises are featured. Weddings are performed aboard by the captain and catering is available.

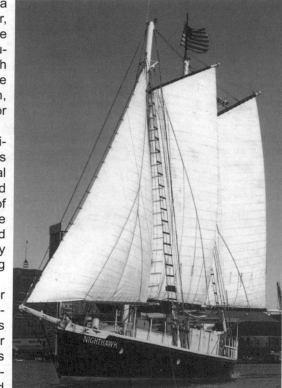

Flag:	USA
Rig:	Schooner
Homeport/waters:	Baltimore, Maryland: Chesapeake Bay
Who sails?	Students from middle school through college. Affiliated institutions include Girl Scouts and church and youth organizations.
Season:	April through November
Program type:	Sail training for paying trainees based on informal, in-house programming.

Specifications:	Sparred length: 82'	Draft: 5'	Sail area: 2,000 sq. ft.
	LOD: 65'	Beam:20'	Tons: 45 GRT
	LWL: 60'	Rig height: 55'	Power: twin diesels
	Freeboard: 6'	Hull: steel	

Designer:	Haglund
Built:	1980; Florida, Haglund Schooner Company
Coast Guard certification:	Passenger Vessel (Subchapter T)
Crew:	4. Trainees/passengers: 49 (day sails), 6 (overnight)
Contact:	Captain Martin D. Weiss, President
	Schooner Nighthawk Cruises, Inc.
	1715 Thames St., Box 38153
	Baltimore, MD 21231
	Tel: 410-276-7447; Fax: 410-327-7245
	E-mail: schoonernighthawk@erols.com
	Web site: http://www.a1nighthawkcruises.com

Niña (Santa Clara)

The *Niña* is a historically accurate replica of a 15th century caravel. John Sarsfield, the leading authority on caravels, was designer and builder until his death halfway through the project. Jonathon Nance, a noted British designer and archaeologist, finished the vessel and designed the sailplan and rig.

She was built in Valenca, Bahia, Brazil, using only traditional tools and techniques of the 15th century. Her mission today is to educate the public on the "space shuttle" of the 15th century, and over one million students and teachers have visited the *Niña* since her completion in 1992. Starting in 2001, the *Niña* will be in Grand Cayman Island taking passengers on day sails from December through May. She is available for films, documentaries, and charters.

Flag:	USA
Rig:	15th century caravel redonda
Homeport/waters:	Salvador, Brazil: Pacific Coast of US and Canada (summer)
	Cayman Islands (winter)
Who sails?	School groups from elementary through college. Families and adults of all ages.
Program type:	Sail training for professional and volunteer crew and trainees. Sea education in maritime history as informal in-house programming. Dockside interpretation while in port.

Specifications:			
	Sparred length: 92'	Draft: 7'	Sail area: 1,919 sq. ft.
	LOD: 65'	Beam: 18'	Tons: 37 GRT
	LOA: 68'	Rig height: 54'	Power: 128 HP diesel
	LWL: 58'	Freeboard: 5'	Hull: wood
	Hull color: brown/black	Spar material: wood	

Designer:	John Sarsfield/Jonathon Nance
Built:	1988-1991; Valenca, Brazil, John Sarsfield/Jonathon Nance/Ralph Eric Nicholson
Coast Guard certification:	Attraction Vessel
Crew:	6. Trainees/Passengers: 45-50 (day sails)
Contact:	Morgan P. Sanger, Captain/Director
	Columbus Foundation
	Box 5179
	St. Thomas, VI 00803
	Tel: 284-495-4618; Fax: 284-495-4616
	E-mail: columfnd@surfbvi.com
	Web site: http://www.thenina.com

Captain Lane Briggs' "tugantine" is a favorite flagship for sail-assisted working vessels and is credited with a 1984 "circumnavigation of Virginia." The *Norfolk Rebel* is a familiar site to all involved in sail training and tall ships events up and down the Chesapeake. In 2000 she participated in Tall Ships 2000®, traveling as far as Halifax, Nova Scotia from her homeport of Norfolk, Virginia. In 2001 she participated in the TALL SHIPS CHALLENGE® in the Great Lakes.

A long-time supporter of sail training, Captain Lane Briggs was the 2001 recipient of the ASTA Lifetime Achievement Award (see page 26).

Flag:	USA
Rig:	Gaff schooner, 2-masted
Homeport/waters:	Norfolk, Virginia; East Coast from Canada to the Gulf of Mexico
Season:	Year round
Who sails?	Individuals of all ages
Program type:	Sail training for crew and apprentices. Sea education in local maritime history and ecology based on informal, in-house programming. Dockside interpretation.

Specifications:	Sparred length: 59'	LOA: 51'	LOD: 51'
	LWL: 48'	Draft: 6'6"	Beam: 15'3"
	Rig height: 50'	Freeboard: 4'6"	Sail area: 1,700 sq. ft.
	Tons: 38 GRT	Power: diesel	Hull: steel

Designer:	Merritt N. Walter
Built:	1980; Howdy Bailey, Norfolk, Virginia
Crew:	3 (day), 6 (overnight) Trainees: 3
Contact:	Captain Lane Briggs, Owner/Master
	Rebel Marine Service, Inc.
	1553 Bayville Street
	Norfolk, VA 23503
	Tel: 804-588-6022; Fax: 804-588-7102
	E-mail: tugantine@aol.com

Norseman

Built in 1992, the *Norseman* offers people a glimpse of Viking culture and reminds everyone of the first discovery of North America by Europeans; Leif Ericson and his fellow Vikings, who sailed from Greenland in about the year 1000 to explore the new lands to the west.

Crewmembers appear in full Viking costume, share their interests in Viking culture and their Scandinavian heritage, and practice their sailing and rowing skills. The *Norseman* has appeared in sailing events on the East Coast of the US, in Sweden and, in 2000, sailing from Labrador's south coast to L'anse aux Meadows, Newfoundland to celebrate the Millennium of Leif Ericson's voyage to North America!

In 2001, among other events, the *Norseman* assisted the North Shore Vikings in the Cleveland, Ohio area in celebrating the placement of a bust of Leif Ericson on the waterfront of the Cuyahoga River, to commemorate the Millennium of his coming to North America.

This year our schedule will see us going to favorite haunts in NJ, NY, MD, PA and making a trip to Mentor, Ohio, to help the city celebrate their "Ships Festival on the Lagoons" in July. Our season runs from March to November, beginning with clean-up and training, continuing our training among our events and culminating with our Leif Ericson Day Celebration in Philadelphia on October 9th each year. "Celebrate America's First Hero – take a Viking to Lunch"!

Flag:	USA
Rig:	Viking longship (single square sail)
Homeport/waters:	Wilmington, Delaware: Chesapeake Bay, Delaware River, Jersey Shore, New York Bay, Hudson River, and Long Island Sound
Who sails?	Students and individuals of all ages.
Program type:	Sail training for volunteer crew and apprentices. Sea education in maritime history relevant to Viking period. Dockside interpretation during port visits.
Specifications:	Sparred length: 40' (same as LOA)

Draft: 3'	Sail area: 297 sq. ft.	LOD: 32'
Beam: 9'	Tons: 2 GRT	LOA: 40'
Rig height: 30'	LWL: 30'	Freeboard: 3'
Hull: fiberglass		
Power: 19 HP Volvo Penta diesel sail drive		

Designer:	Applecraft, Inc.
Built:	1992; Isle of Man, UK, Applecraft, Inc.
Crew:	7-12. Trainees: 7-12
Contact:	Jim Thornton, President or Dave Segermark, Captain
	Leif Ericson Viking Ship, Inc.
	4919 Township Line Rd. #303, Drexel Hill, PA 19026-5017
	Tel: 302-656-3257; Fax: 302-656-8414 (Jim Thornton)
	Tel: 410-275-8516: Fax: 410-275-2633 (Dave Segermark)
	E-mail: info@vikingship.org
	Web site: http://www.vikingship.org

Ocean Classroom Foundation Schooner Project

The Ocean Classroom Foundation is working to build a new steel ship, to meet the growing demand for the Ocean Classroom program. TriCoastal Marine Architects have completed the design, and the project has been sent out to bid at several US shipyards. The new vessel (as yet unnamed) will be a superb platform for teaching, as well as an excellent sailer for global voyages. Fundraising for the project continues in earnest, with more than 1/3 of the needed funds already secured. Keel laying and launch dates to be announced.

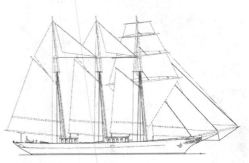

Ocean Classroom is a fully accredited term at sea for high school students. Young people come from all parts of the country to join this award-winning program, and gain an unparalleled learning and growth experience. The new ship, conceived specifically to fulfill the mission of Ocean Classroom, will enable us to include more students, to teach them better, and to increase the amount of financial aid we can award each term.

As a non-profit organization, we gratefully accept contributions of equipment, materials, or funds for this project or the Scholarship Endowment. For information about Ocean Classroom, or to make a contribution, please contact our office.

Flag:	USA
Rig:	Square topsail schooner, three masted
Homeport/waters:	Islesboro, Maine: Eastern US and Canada (summer), Caribbean and South America (winter)
Who sails?	School groups from middle school through college. Affiliated institutions include Proctor Academy, Long Island University, Franklin Pierce College, and other schools.
Season:	Year-round
Cost:	Varies with term
Program type:	Sail training with paying trainees/students. Fully accredited sea education in marine science, maritime history, maritime literature, marine applied mathematics and navigation.

Specifications:			
	Sparred length: 158'	Draft: 12' 6"	Sail area: 8,000 sq. ft.
	LOD: 112' 6"	Beam: 27'	Tons: 99 GRT
	LOA: 124'	Rig height: 108'	Power: 500 HP diesel
	LWL: 100'	Hull: steel	

Designer:	TriCoastal Marine
Coast Guard certification:	(planned) Sailing School Vessel (Subchapter R), Passenger Vessel (Subchapter T)
Crew:	10-15, including instructors. Trainees: 30 (overnight)
Contact:	Bert Rogers, Director
	Ocean Classroom Foundation, Inc.
	PO Box 446
	Cornwall, NY 12518
	Tel: 800-724-7245 or 845-615-1412; Fax: 845-615-1414
	E-mail: mail@oceanclassroom.org
	Web site: http://www.oceanclassroom.org

Ocean Star

PHOTO BY MAURICIO HANDLER

Launched in 1991 as the school ship for Ocean Navigator magazine, *Ocean Star* now sails under the banner of Sea-mester programs as a college-level semester voyage. Sea-mester programs offer 35 and 80-day semesters aboard and are based on principles of experiential and adventure education. Learning through interaction and practical activities, the primary academic foci of oceanography, marine science, communication, and leadership skills development are brought from the textbook into real-life application. Under the guidance of professional staff, including Ph.D. and Masters graduates, our students earn college credits for both academic and vocational activities, while piloting *Ocean Star* throughout the islands of the Lesser Antilles. Along the way, the crew visits up to 20 individual Caribbean islands, undertaking research and service projects with local government and private organizations while simultaneously working toward certifications in sailing and scuba diving. No experience is necessary. Programs are available to high school seniors (Argo Academy), high school graduates and college-aged students. Sea-mester programs are coeducational and non-competitive. The activities are not physically demanding, yet are challenging enough to teach the crew to work together. In the stimulating environment of the Caribbean islands, the expedition becomes the vehicle for gaining knowledge and understanding, confidence and skills.

Flag:	UK
Rig:	Schooner, two-masted
Waters:	Eastern Caribbean
Who sails?	12th grade high school students (fall semester), high school graduates and college-age students (fall, spring and summer).
Season:	Year-round
Program type:	Experiential education semesters for high school graduates and college students. Accredited academics with sail and scuba training, service projects and adventure travel.

Specifications:	LOA: 88'		Draft: 9'		Sail area: 4,600 sq. ft.
	LOD: 73'		Beam: 20'		Tons: 70 GRT
	LWL: 65'		Rig height: 92'		Power: 210 HP diesel
	Freeboard: 5'		Hull: steel		

Designer:	Bill Peterson
Built:	1991; Norfolk, Virginia, Marine Metals
Crew:	4. Trainees: 14
Contact:	Sea-mester / Argo Academy
	PO Box 5477
	Sarasota, FL 34277
	Tel: 941-924-6789, 800-317-6789; Fax: 941-924-6075
	E-mail: info@seamester.com
	Web site: http://www.seamester.com

Ocean Star

The *Odyssey* is one of the largest boats designed by Sparkman Stevens and was designed as a family yacht in 1938. She was commandeered by the United States Navy for use during WW II. The Navy changed her name to the *Saluda.* After the war the Navy assigned her first to Woods Hole, Connecticut and later, to San Diego, California. The boat won the Newport to Ensenada race in 1950. She spent four years at Whidbey Island before being sold to the Scouts. She is currently a Sea Scout training vessel, spending two months every summer in the San Juan Islands where, each week, a youth crew teach twelve youth and adults how to sail and handle a large boat. The remainder of the year the *Odyssey* is used for training

Sea Scouts. Graduates of our program are employed in the marine industry and several have gone to the maritime academies. Each summer we need an adult, lady, cook for our summer program. If interested call 253-925-0956.

Flag:	USA
Rig:	Yawl
Homeport/waters:	Tacoma, Washington: San Juan Islands (July – August)
Who sails?	High School age Sea Scouts.
Season:	Year-round
Program type:	Sail training for volunteer trainees. Sea Education in maritime history, ecology, and marine science in cooperation with other organized groups (Sea Scouts).

Specifications:			
	Sparred length: 96'	LOD: 88' 6"	LOA: 89'
	Draft: 12'	Beam: 18'	Rig height: 105'
	Freeboard: 5'	Sail area: 4,000 sq. ft.	Tons: 63 GRT

Designer:	Sparkman and Stevens
Built:	1938; City Island, New York, Nevins Shipyard
Coast Guard certification:	Passenger Vessel (Subchapter T)
Crew:	Trainees/passengers: 35 (day sails), 12 (overnight)
Contact:	Dick Clayton, Skipper
	Pacific Harbors Council BSA
	5346 Frances Avenue NE
	Tacoma, WA 98422
	Tel: 253-927-2787; Fax: 253-952-6592
	E-mail: claytonodyssey@aol.com

OMF Ontario

On July 2, 1994, the hull of the schooner *OMF Ontario* was launched amidst the cheers of over 2,500 people from as for away as Florida and California. They came to applaud a six-year commitment by an all-volunteer crew to stimulate interest in and awareness of the Great Lakes. In 1998 all welding was completed, the final ballast in place, and spar construction begun. She will resemble many of the ships built at this location in the 19th century, except that she is built of welded steel to modern standards and will have backup diesel power. When complete, the schooner will serve as a floating classroom for the Education Through Involvement program. Participants of all ages will have a hands-on learning experience about the history, heritage, resources, ecology, and the future of the Great Lakes.

Flag:	USA
Rig:	Topsail schooner
Homeport/waters:	Oswego, New York: Great Lakes
Who sails?	School children, community groups, and senior citizens.
Program type:	Passenger day sails for organized groups such as schools, community organizations, and businesses. Dockside interpretation.

Specifications:			
	Sparred length: 85'	Draft: 8'	Sail area: 2,000 sq. ft.
	LOD: 60'	Beam: 16'	Power: 100 HP diesel
	LOA: 65'	Rig height: 70'	Tons: 42 GRT
	Freeboard: 6'	Hull: steel	

Designer:	Francis MacLachlan
Built:	1994; Oswego, New York
Coast Guard certification:	Passenger Vessel (Subchapter T)
Crew:	2, 4 instructors. Trainees: 25
Contact:	Dr. Henry Spang, Director

Education Through Involvement Program Oswego Maritime Foundation
41 Lake Street
Oswego, NY 13126
Tel: 315-342-5753

One and All was built to fulfill the dream of a dedicated group of South Australians to provide sail training in South Australia. This dream came to fruition on April 5, 1987 on her commissioning day. Since her commissioning, *One and All* has carried many thousands of trainees from South Australia and further afield from all states and territories of Australia and overseas.

One and All also caters to many other groups, including half and full-day educational trips for school groups, recreational day trips to the public, and adventure voyages of two to ten days for those who wish to experience the wonders of sailing on a square-rigged vessel.

One and All has participated in three Sydney to Hobart Races, a Darwin to Ambon Yacht Race, has been chartered to carry out scientific studies on the East Coast of Australia, and has participated in a number of tall ship events in Australia. *One and All* spends her time sailing the Australian coastline, but is equipped and certified to the highest Australian survey standard, which has allowed her to sail internationally in the past. No previous experience is needed to sail on board *One and All,* only a desire to experience sailing a square-rigger in Australian waters.

Flag:	Australia
Rig:	Brigantine
Homeport/waters:	Port Adelaide, Adelaide, South Australia, Australia: East Coast of Australia (summer), Gulfs of South Australia (winter)
Who sails?	High school students and individuals of all ages.
Season:	Year-round
Cost:	$3,000 AUS group rate per day, $120 AUS per person per day on extended voyages
Program type:	Sail training for paying trainees. Sea education based on informal, in-house programming. Dockside interpretation during port visits.

Specifications:			
	Sparred length: 140'	Draft: 9' 4"	Sail area: 6,251 sq. ft.
	LOD: 98' 7"	Beam: 26' 11"	Tons: 121 GRT
	LWL: 86' 11"	Rig height: 88' 7"	Power: 380 HP diesel
	Hull: wood		

Designer:	Kell Steinman
Built:	1985, North Haven, South Australia, Australia, W.G. Porter and Sons Pty. Ltd.
Certification:	Australian Maritime Safety Authority Certificate for Australian and International Waters
Crew:	10. Trainees: 50 (day sails), 24 (overnight)
Contact:	Captain Ian Kuhl, CEO
	Sailing Ship Trust of South Australia, Inc.
	PO Box 222
	Port Adelaide, South Australia, 5015, Australia
	Tel: 61-8-8447-5144; Fax: 61-8-8341-0167
	E-mail: tallship@oneandall.org.au
	Web site: http://www.oneandall.org.au

Pacific Grace

schooner *Pacific Swift,* in providing youth sail training programs along the coast of British Columbia. During the summer months of July and August 10-day trips are available to anyone aged 13 - 25. In the spring and fall shorter school programs are offered.

Each year over one thousand young people participate aboard *Pacific*

Built over seven winters, *Pacific Grace* was launched in her homeport of Victoria, British Columbia on October 9, 1999. She replaces the *Robertson II,* one of Canada's last original Grand Banks fishing schooners, and is built along the lines of the old ship using traditional methods.

Her maiden voyage began on May 31, 2001, when she joined the topsail

Grace in an experience which combines all aspects of shipboard life from galley chores to helmsmanship, with formal instruction in navigation, pilotage, seamanship and small boat handling. S.A.L.T.S. is a registered charitable organization that seeks to develop to the full, through shipboard life in a Christian context, the spiritual, mental and physical potential of young people.

Flag:	Canadian
Rig:	Gaff topsail schooner
Homeport/waters:	Victoria, British Columbia, Canada: coastal waters of British Columbia
Who sails?	Students and young adults ages 13 – 25.
Season:	March through October
Cost:	$90 (CDN) per person per day, $65 (CDN) group rate (charter) per person
Program type:	Sail training for paying trainees.

Specifications:			
	Sparred length:	138' 7"	LOD: 108' 7"
	LOA: 102' 6"	LWL: 89' 6"	Draft: 11' 6"
	Beam: 22' 2"	Rig height: 115'	Freeboard: 3' 7"
	Sail area: 7,564 sq. ft.	Tons: 175 GRT	Power: Twin diesels
	Hull: wood		

Built:	1999; Victoria, British Columbia, Canada, SALTS
Canadian Coast Guard certification:	Passenger Vessel, Sailing School Vessel
Crew:	5. Trainees/passengers: 40 (day sails), 30 (overnight)
Contact:	Mr. Ron Howatson, Executive Director
	Sail and Life Training Society (SALTS)
	PO Box 5014, Station B
	Victoria, British Columbia V8R 6N3 Canada
	Tel: 250-383-6811; Fax: 250-383-7781
	E-mail: info@salt society.com
	Web site: http://www.saltsociety.com

Built as a working exhibit at Expo '86 in Vancouver, British Columbia, the *Pacific Swift* has sailed over 100,000 deep-sea miles on training voyages for young crewmembers. Her offshore travels have taken her to Australia and Europe, to remote communities on Easter and Pitcairn Islands, and to many other unusual and far-flung ports of call.

When not offshore, the *Swift* provides coastal sail training programs among the cruising grounds of the Pacific Northwest which include shorter school programs in the spring and fall and 10-day summer trips open to anyone aged 13 to 25.

Each year over one thousand young people participate in an experience which combines all aspects of shipboard life, from galley chores to helmsmanship, with formal instruction in navigation, pilotage, seamanship, and small boat handling. Rooted in Christian values, SALTS believes that training under sail provides the human

spirit a real chance to develop and mature. SALTS received the 1998 Sail Training Program of the Year Award from the American Sail Training Association.

Flag:	Canada
Rig:	Square topsail schooner, two-masted
Homeport/waters:	Victoria, British Columbia, Canada: Coastal waters of British Columbia
Who sails?	Individuals and groups.
Season:	March through October
Cost:	$90 CDN per person per day, $65 CDN per person group rate
Program type:	Offshore and coastal sail training.

Specifications:

Sparred length: 111'	Draft: 10' 8"	Sail area: 5,205 sq. ft.
LOD: 77' 3"	Beam: 20' 6"	Tons: 98 GRT
LOA: 81'	Rig height: 88'	Power: 220 HP diesel
LWL: 73'	Freeboard: 3' 6"	Hull: wood

Built:	1986; Vancouver, British Columbia, Canada, SALTS
Canadian Coast Guard certification:	Passenger vessel, Sailing School Vessel
Crew:	5. Trainees/passengers: 35 Age: 13 - 25
Contact:	Mr. Ron Howatson, Executive Director
	Sail and Life Training Society (SALTS)
	PO Box 5014, Station B
	Victoria, British Columbia V8R 6N3 Canada
	Tel: 250-383-6811; Fax: 250-383-7781
	E-mail: info@salt society.com
	Web site: http://www.saltsociety.com

Palawan

ocean racer under the CCA rating rule, *Palawan* is a landmark in yacht design. She led the move from the full keel, with a fin and skeg configuration, though she retains the wineglass sections of more traditional boats. Olins Stephens declared her "perhaps the easiest steering boat I ever drew."

Maine Maritime Academy used her in their sailing program for over 10 years, as *Omega,* and many have learned offshore sailing and buoy racing under her tutelage.

Palawan has operated as a passenger vessel since 1988, in Portland, Maine. She serves both individuals and groups, and is easy to find at the Long Wharf, by DiMillo's Floating Restaurant.

Winters may be spent in the Caribbean, with up to 6 crew aboard.

Designed in 1965, built by Derecktor's for Thomas Watson as an

Flag:	USA
Rig:	Cutter
Homeport/waters:	Portland, Maine: Casco Bay, Caribbean
Who sails?	Students, adults, and groups.
Cost:	$20 to $40 for 2 or 3-hour day sail, $95 for all-day sail, with lunch and island landing, $150 per person on multi-day trips possible Spring and Fall, Winter. Group rates on application.
Program type:	Sail training with team-building activities for paying trainees. Passenger day sails and overnight passages.

Specifications:	Sparred length: 58'	Draft: 8' 1"	Sail area: 1,308 sq. ft.
	LOD: 58'	Beam: 12' 4"	Tons: 24 GRT
	LOA: 58'	Rig height: 68'	Power: 60 HP
	LWL: 40'	Freeboard: 4' 4"	Hull: aluminum

Designer:	Olin Stephens
Built:	1965; New York, New York, Derecktor
Coast Guard certification:	Passenger Vessel (Subchapter T)
Crew:	2 (day sails), 3 (overnight). Trainees: 24 (day sails), 6 (overnight)
Contact:	Captain Tom Woodruff
	Palawan Services, Inc.
	PO Box 9715-240
	Portland, ME 04104
	Tel: 207-773-2163; Fax: 207-781-8281
	E-mail: palawan@nlis.net
	Web site: http://www.sailpalawan.com

Pallada is the fifth ship of the Dar Mlodziezy-class built in Poland during the 1980s. Unlike her white-hulled sisters, *Pallada* has a black hull with false gunports and resembles the great Russian barque *Kruzenshtern*. She is named for the Greek goddess Pallas Athena. She is owned by Dalryba, a conglomerate of fishing companies, and offers sail training to foreign marine-college cadets.

Though her home port is in Vladivostok, which is on the far eastern coast of Russia, *Pallada* voyages widely. She visited the West Coast of the United States in 1989 and Europe in 1991; participated in the European Columbus Regatta in 1992; completed a circumnavigation to celebrate the 500th anniversary of the Russian navy in 1996; and sailed in the 1997 Hong Kong to Osaka race.

Pallada sails with a compliment of 143 cadets and a permanent crew of 56 officers, teachers, and professionals. With twenty-six sails and masts soaring 162 feet above the deck, *Pallada* combines traditional sail training with a modern maritime college curriculum.

PHOTO AND TEXT BY THAD KOZA

Flag:	Russia
Rig:	Full-rigged ship
Homeport/waters:	Vladivostok, Russia: worldwide
Who sails?	Marine-college cadets
Season:	Year-round
Program type:	Sail training and sea education for marine-college cadets
Specifications:	Sparred length: 356' 4" Draft: 22' 4" Beam: 45' 9"
	Hull: steel
Designer:	Zygmunt Choren
Built:	1989; Gdansk, Poland
Crew:	56. Trainees/passengers: 143
Contact:	Evgeny N. Malyavin
	Far Eastern State Technical Fisheries University
	52-B, Lugovaya Street
	Vladivostok 690950 Russia
	Tel: +0117 42 32 44-03-06; Fax: +011 7 42 32 44-24-32
	E-mail: tuof@marine.ru

Youth between the ages of 14 and 18 become the working crew on one or two-week adventures, making 24-hour passages from ports all over the Great Lakes. The program is delivered by youth officers between the ages of 15 and 18, trained and qualified during Tall Ship Adventures' Winter Training Programs. The captain and first mate are the only adults on board. Every year each ship sails over 4,000 miles, spends over 40 nights at sea, and introduces 300 trainees to the tall ship experience. *Pathfinder* is owned and operated by Toronto Brigantine, Inc., a registered charity.

Tall Ship Adventures conducts sail training on board *Pathfinder,* a square-rigged ship designed specifically for youth sail training on the Great Lakes. Since 1964 over 15,000 young people have lived and worked aboard *Pathfinder* and her sister ship, *Playfair.*

Flag:	Canada
Rig:	Brigantine
Homeport/waters:	Toronto, Ontario, Canada: Great Lakes
Who sails?	In July and August, youth programs for ages 14-18; in May, June, and September, school groups from middle school through college, and interested adult groups.
Cost:	$675 CDN for one week, $1,175 CDN for two weeks. Call for spring and fall group rates.
Program type:	Sail training for paying trainees, including seamanship and leadership training based on informal, in-house programming. Shoreside winter program. Dockside interpretation. Affiliated institutions include the Canadian Sail Training Association and the Ontario Camping Association.

Specifications:			
	Sparred length: 72'	Draft: 8'	Sail area: 2,600 sq. ft.
	LOD: 58'	Beam: 15' 3"	Tons: 31.63 GRT
	LOA: 60'	Rig height: 54'	Power: 150 HP diesel
	LWL: 45'	Freeboard: 4'	Hull: steel

Designer:	Francis A. Maclachlan
Built:	1963; Kingston, Ontario, Canada, Kingston Shipyards
Crew:	10. Trainees: 25 (day sails), 18 (overnight)
Contact:	Catharine McLean, Executive Director
	Toronto Brigantine, Inc.
	370 Queen's Quay West, Ste. 203
	Toronto, Ontario, M5V 3J3, Canada
	Tel: 416-596-7117; Fax: 416-596-9119
	E-mail: mail@tallshipadventures.on.ca
	Web site: http://www.tallshipadventures.on.ca

Peking was launched in 1911 at Hamburg, Germany by the Blohm & Voss shipyard. She was owned by the F. Laeisz Company of that port, who used her to carry fuel and manufactured goods to the West Coast of South America, around Cape Horn, and return to European ports with nitrate mined in northern Chile.

With her four-masted barque rig, steel hull and masts, and mid-ship bridge deck, *Peking* represents the final generation of sailing ships built for world trade. Though a product of the 20th century, she still sailed in the traditional way, with few labor-saving devices or safety features. Her crew followed the standard sailing vessel routine of four hours on duty and four hours off duty, around the clock, seven days a week.

Peking was retired in 1933, when steamers using the Panama Canal took over what was left of the nitrate trade. She served as a nautical school for boys, moored on a British River, until she was acquired by the South Street Seaport Museum in 1974. She now serves as a floating dockside exhibit. Educational programs for children and young adults take place on board, with a wet lab on the ship interpreting the biology of New York harbor.

Flag:	USA
Rig:	Barque, four-masted
Homeport/waters:	New York, New York
Cost:	$3 per person
Program type:	Sea education in marine science, maritime history, and ecology based on informal, in-house programming.

Specifications:	Sparred length: 377' 6"	Draft: 16'	Sail area: 44,132 sq. ft.
	LOD: 320'	Beam: 45' 8"	Tons: 3,100 GRT
	Rig height: 170' 5"	Hull: steel	

Built:	1911; Hamburg, Germany, Blohm & Voss
Contact:	Paula Mayo, Director of Programs
	South Street Seaport Museum
	207 Front Street
	New York, NY, 10038
	Tel: 212-748-8681; Fax: 212-748-8610
	Web site: http://www.southstseaport.org

the mid-1980s the Nassau County Board of Cooperative Services used her as a platform for their marine biology public school education program. The vessel was later sold and moved to the Bahamas.

In 1993 *Phoenix* returned to Long Island and was acquired by the Coastal Ecology Learning Program, a nonprofit educational corporation. C.E.L.P. offers shipboard environmental education programs for schoolchildren, families, and adults. *Phoenix* is the training ship for the Long Island US Naval Sea Cadets. The vessel is also available for private functions, children's birthday parties, corporate events, etc. *Phoenix* travels the length of Long Island Sound, offering programs throughout the region.

The coastal schooner *Phoenix* was built on Long Island, New York and launched in 1984 as a replica of the type of vessels plying the waters of Long Island Sound at the turn of the century. *Phoenix* was first used as a cargo vessel between Port Jefferson, New York and Bridgeport, Connecticut, before carrying passengers over the same route for day trip excursions. In

Flag:	USA
Rig:	Gaff schooner, two-masted
Homeport/waters:	Glen Cove, New York: Long Island Sound
Who sails?	Students of all ages, individuals and families.
Cost:	$220 per person per day, $7,000 group rate (charter) per day
Program type:	Sail training for volunteer and paying trainees. Sea education in marine science, ecology, and maritime history. Affiliated with the Long Island US Naval Sea Cadets.

Specifications:	Sparred length: 71'	Draft: 6'	Sail area: 1,600 sq. ft.
	LOD: 56'	Beam: 16'	Tons: 40 GRT
	LOA: 59'	Rig height: 60'	Power: 80 HP
	LWL: 54'	Freeboard: 4'	Ford/Lehman
	Hull: steel	Hull color: white	Spar material: aluminum

Designer:	Walter Merrit
Built:	1984; Patchogue, New York, Greg Brazier
Coast Guard certification:	Passenger Vessel (Subchapter T)
Crew:	3. Trainees/passengers: 2
Contact:	Captain Dennis F. Watson
	Coastal Ecology Learning Program, Inc.
	PO Box 473
	Huntington, NY 11743
	Tel: 631-385-CELP; Fax: 631-385-2357
	E-mail: celp@optonline.net
	Web site: http://www.coastalecology.org

Built in Denmark in 1929 as a missionary schooner, *Phoenix* retired from missionary work after 20 years and carried cargo until her engine room was damaged by fire in 1972. In 1974 she was purchased and converted into a brigantine, before being purchased by Square Sail in 1988. In 1991 she was converted into a 15th-century Caravel, to replicate the *Santa Maria,* Christopher Colombus' flagship, for Ridley Scott's film "1492: Conquest of Paradise". In 1996 her name was changed back to *Phoenix* and she was converted into a two-masted brig.

All of Square Sail's ships are fully commissioned and work throughout the year. When not filming, they have a regular sailing program, giving people the chance to experience traditional square-rig sailing first-hand. These voyages typically run between four and seven days, and occasionally longer. They are either based from Square Sail's homeport of Charlestown, Cornwall, UK, or they work around the annual schedule offering voyages between the various ports.

Square Sail runs an annual course from February to October where trainees are given the opportunity to learn the skills associated with sailing these ships, and in addition to maintenance and shore-based instruction, they form part of the regular crew throughout the season.

Flag:	UK
Rig:	Brig, two-masted
Homeport/waters:	Charlestown Harbour, St. Austell, Cornwall, UK: UK and Europe
Who sails?	Individuals and families of all ages.
Season:	Year-round
Cost:	$220 per person per day, $7,000 group rate (charter) per day
Program type:	Sail training for professional crew, volunteer and paying trainees. Sea education in maritime history in cooperation with accredited institutions and as informal, in-house programming. Worldwide film work and corporate charters.

Specifications:	Sparred length: 112'	Draft: 8' 6"	Sail area: 4,000 sq. ft.
	LOD: 76'	Beam: 21'	Tons: 79 GRT
	LOA: 86'	Rig height: 81'	Power: 235 HP diesel
	LWL: 70'	Freeboard: 6'	Hull: oak on oak

Built:	1929; Frederickshavn, Denmark, Hjorne & Jakobsen
Certification:	MCA and MECAL (UK)
Crew:	10. Trainees: 12
Contact:	Chris Wilson, Marketing Manager, Square Sail
	Charlestown Harbour, St. Austell
	Cornwall PL25 3NJ, United Kingdom
	Tel: 44-1720-67526; Fax: 44-1726-61839
	E-mail: info@square-sail.com
	Web site: http://www.square-sail.com

Picara

The Nauset Sea Scouts have just celebrated more than 50 years of sail training. This program teaches seamanship and sailing to young people between the ages of 14 and 20 through education and annual cruises along the New England Coast. While on cruises, each scout takes part in every aspect of the voyage, including planning, cooking, navigation, sail repair, and sailing the vessel. The Nauset Sea Scouts have participated in such tall ships gatherings as the New York World's Fair 1964, Montreal's Expo '67, OpSail '76, Boston's 350th anniversary in 1980, and the Grand Regatta 1992 Columbus Quincentenary in both New York and Boston.

Flag:	USA
Rig:	Sloop
Homeport/waters:	Eastham, Massachusetts: New England coast
Who sails?	Sea Explorers, middle school and high school students.
Program type:	Sail training for crew and apprentices. Sea education in maritime history and ecology in cooperation with Sea Scouts. Dockside interpretation during outport visits.

Specifications:

Sparred length: 36'	Draft: 5' 6"	Sail area: 750 sq. ft.
LOA: 36'	Beam: 12'	Tons: 15 GRT
LWL: 28'	Rig height: 49'	Power: 4,108 diesel
Freeboard: 4'	Hull: fiberglass	

Designer:	S-2 Yachts
Built:	1982; Holland, Michigan, S-2 Yachts
Crew:	2. Trainees: 20 (day sails), 11 (overnight). Age: 14-20
Contact:	Captain Michael F. Allard
	Nauset Sea Explorers
	PO Box 1236
	Orleans, MA 02653
	Tel: 508-255-8150
	E-mail: mallard@capecod.net

Picton Castle

The 300-ton Barque *Picton Castle* is a traditionally operated sail training ship dedicated to making square-rig sailing ship voyages around the world in the tradewinds. In June of 2003 the *Picton Castle* will cast off from Lunenburg, Nova Scotia, on her third global circumnavigation, returning in June 2004. On this ocean odyssey, this ship and her crew will sail over 28,000 deep-sea miles and put into 20 or so remote islands and tropical ports including Galapagos, Pitcairn Island, Rarotonga, Fiji, Vanuatu, Bali, Mauritius, and Cape Town. As a training ship, all on board work, stand watch, and learn the way of a tall ship. Workshops are conducted in rigging, sail making, boat handling, navigation, and practical seamanship.

On her last world voyage, in cooperation with WorldWise Inc., the crew of the *Picton Castle* delivered 30 tons of donated used textbooks and educational supplies, including wall maps contributed by the National Geographic Society, to remote and under-supplied schools in the South Pacific, Bali and South Africa.

In Summer 2002, the *Picton Castle* will undertake a six-week sail training voyage in the North Atlantic after her return from her 2nd world voyage, departing from Lunenburg about July 1, visiting St. Pierre, Miquelon, and Bermuda, and returning to Lunenburg in mid-August.

The *Picton Castle* is rigged following Germanischer Lloyds' rules for Cape Horners and outfitted to the highest standard with safety gear. She is a strong, seaworthy home for adventurers devoted to learning the art of square-rig seafaring.

Flag:	Cook Islands
Rig:	Barque, 3-masted
Homeport/waters:	Lunenburg, Nova Scotia, Canada. Rarotonga, Cook Islands, South Pacific; worldwide. Worldwide service with refits in Lunenburg, Nova Scotia, Canada
Who sails?	Those over 18 years old on the world voyage, 16 years and up on shorter training cruises
Program type:	Deep water sail training for expense-sharing trainees. Maritime education in cooperation with various institutes and organized groups. Comprehensive instruction in the arts of seafaring under sail. Dockside school visits and receptions. Charitable/educational outreach and supply to isolated islands.
Specifications:	Sparred length: 176' LOD: 135' LOA: 148' Draft: 14'6" Beam: 24' Rig height: 100' Freeboard: 6' Sail area: 12,450 sq. ft. Tons: 284 GRT Power: 130' Hull: steel
Designer:	Masting and rigging, decks and layout: Daniel Moreland, MM Stability, calculations and ballasting: Daniel Blachley, NA/ME Webb Institute
Certification:	Registered and certified as a Sail Training Vessel for worldwide service by the Cook Islands Ministry of Transportation
Crew:	Permanent crew 10. Trainees: 38. Sex: Co-ed
Contact:	David Robinson Barque PICTON CASTLE Voyages 1 Woodbine Lane Amherst, NH 03031-2102 Tel: 603-424-0219; Fax: 603-424-1849 E-mail: wissco@juno.com, info@picton-castle.com Web sites: http://www.picton-castle.com, http://www.worldwise.org

Pierius Magnus

The *Pierius Magnus* is a handcrafted wooden vessel, engineless by design, sailing to exemplify a new millennium socio-technological paradigm: responsibly using the best of available tradition, geochronology, and human interaction. Captain "Longhair Boogie" Arjen van der Veen expresses respect for life, freedom, and the responsibilities necessary to maintain those with ship operations and voyage quests.

Most of the wood used in the construction of the *Pierius Magnus* was cut from a Michigan forest by builder Captain van der Veen. Many varieties of wood were cut and used, chosen for particular applications. Captain van der Veen's knowledge for these choices was gained at Maritime College in The Netherlands. The harvested wood, 4000-board feet, was cut on a low energy usage portable sawmill. Many volunteers assisted in the construction and shop space was donated by Mr. Al Weener. The facility was a defunct , old, energy- guzzling, manufactory. After the ship was constructed, Mr. Weener converted the building into the "Blue Star Music Camp," to encourage and develop young talent. Mr. Weener and Captain van der Veen are both professional caliber musicians.

The ship uses traditional technology such as oil lanterns, and naturally occurring resources like wood in combination with modern devices such as wind electric generators that greatly increase human productivity and comfort without damaging the environment.

The aura surrounding the ship has developed friendships, created poetry writings, song compositions, and changed lives. *Pierius Magnus* is the only sailing ship we know of fitted with a piano. The keyboard hand and voice of Captain "Longhair Boogie" perform concerts both dockside and at sea as well as educational and motivational speech presentations for youth in public schools or dockside, encouraging them on life's journey. Sail training is available.

Flag:	USA
Rig:	Dutch gaff topsail schonker
Homeport/waters:	South Haven, Michigan
Who sails?	Groups and individuals of all ages
Program type:	Sail training for paying trainees, dockside interpretation.

Specifications:`		
Sparred length: 52'	LOD: 34'	Draft: 4'
Beam: 11' 6"	Rig height: 12'	Sail area: 1,200 sq. ft.
Power: sail only	Hull: wood	

Built:	2001; South Haven, Michigan, Captain Arjen van der Veen
Contact:	Captain Arjen van der Veen
	League Atlantis World Wide
	PO Box 99
	Forked River, NJ 08731
	Tel: 205-525-5100; Fax: 205-525-5300
	E-mail: hig77@aol.com or atlantis_contacts@hotmail.com
	or ronprichep@aol.com
	Web site: http://www.atlantiscrewing.com

The *Pilgrim* is a full-scale replica of the ship immortalized by Richard Henry Dana in his classic book *Two Years Before the Mast.* Owned and operated by the Ocean Institute, *Pilgrim* is dedicated to multidisciplinary education. During the school year, the Ocean Institute offers an 18-hour, award-winning living history program that offers a hands-on exploration of literature, California history, and group problem solving in which crewmembers recreate the challenge of shipboard life. Students live like sailors of the 1830s as they hoist barrels, row in the harbor, stand night watches, swab the decks, and learn to cope with a stern captain.

On summer evenings, audiences are treated to the sights and sounds of the sea as the *Pilgrim's* decks come alive with theatrical and musical performances. In late summer the *Pilgrim* sails on her annual cruise with an all-volunteer crew to ports along the California coast as a goodwill ambassador for the City of Dana Point. She returns in September to lead the annual tall ship parade and festival.

Flag:	USA
Rig:	Snow brig
Homeport/waters:	Dana Point, California: Point Conception to Ensenada, Mexico
Season:	Year-round
Who sails?	Student groups and individual volunteers.
Program type:	Maritime living history and volunteer sail training.

Specifications:

Sparred length: 130'	Draft: 9'	Sail area: 7,600 sq. ft.
LOD: 98'	Beam: 24' 6"	Tons: 99 GRT
Freeboard: 8'	Rig height: 104'	Power: diesel
Hull: wood		

Designer:	Ray Wallace
Built:	1945; Holbaek, Denmark, A. Nielsen
Coast Guard certification:	Uninspected Vessel
Crew:	35. Dockside visitors: 50
Contact:	Daniel Stetson, Director of Maritime Affairs
	Ocean Institute
	24200 Dana Point
	Dana Point, CA 92629
	Tel: 949-496-2274; Fax: 949-496-4296
	E-mail: dstetson@ocean-institute.org
	Web site: http://www.ocean-institute.org

Pilgrim

mission lies in creating an interest and appreciation of the Great Lakes maritime heritage and environment. The *Pilgrim* offers adult sail training, private charters, and participation in historical reenactments and festivals.

The captain and crew welcome the challenge of fulfilling your dreams through unique hands-on opportunities designed especially for you or your group.

The *Pilgrim* sails primarily the waters of Lake Ontario and the Thousand Islands area of the St. Lawrence River. This schooner's main

Flag:	USA
Rig:	Gaff schooner, two-masted
Homeport/waters:	Oak Orchard River, New York: Lake Ontario, Thousand Islands area of St. Lawrence River
Who sails?	High school students, adults, and families.
Season:	May to October
Cost:	$100 per person per day, $600 group rate per day
Program type:	Sail training for paying trainees. Sea education in cooperation with organized groups and as part of informal, in-house programming.

Specifications:			
	Sparred length: 68'	Draft: 6'	Sail area: 1,850 sq. ft.
	LOD: 52'	Beam: 15'	Tons: 33 GRT
	LOA: 52'	Rig height: 58'	Power: 85 HP diesel
	LWL: 44' 3"	Freeboard: 3' 6"	Hull: steel

Designer:	William Wood
Built:	1987; Norfolk, Virginia, Marine Metals
Coast Guard certification:	Uninspected Vessel
Crew:	3. Trainees: 6
Contact:	Captain Gary Kurtz
	Pilgrim Packet Company
	PO Box 491
	Kendall, NY 14476
	Tel: 716-682-4757

The first iron sloop built in the United States, *Pioneer* is the only surviving American iron-hulled sailing vessel. Built in 1885 by the Pioneer Iron Foundary in Chester, Pennsylvania, she sailed the Delaware River, hauling sand for use in the iron molding process. Ten years later *Pioneer* was converted to a schooner rig for ease of sail handling. In 1966, the then abandoned vessel was acquired and rebuilt by Russell Grinnell, Jr. of Gloucester, Massachusetts. In 1970 the fully restored schooner was donated to the South Street Seaport Museum.

Today historic *Pioneer* serves as a vital education platform. Students of all ages can come on board and experience New York history and other curricular subjects during the hands-on program. *Pioneer* also offers corporate and private charters, Elderhostel day programs, and public sails.

Flag:	USA
Rig:	Gaff topsail schooner, two-masted
Homeport/waters:	New York, New York: New York Harbor, Hudson River, and Atlantic Coast
Who sails?	School groups from elementary school through college, charter groups, museum members, and general public.
Season:	April through October
Program type:	Sail training for crew and volunteers, hand-on education sails designed to augment school curriculums in history, ecology, marine science, physics, and math. Corporate and private charters, Elderhostel programs, and public sails.

Specifications:	Sparred length: 102'	Draft: 4' 8" (min.), 12' (max.)	Sail area: 2,700 sq. ft.
	LOD: 65'	Beam: 21' 6"	Tons: 43 GRT
	LOA: 65'	Rig height: 79'	Power: diesel
	LWL: 58' 11"	Hull: steel	

Built:	1885; Marcus Hook, Pennsylvania, Pioneer Iron Works (rebuilt 1968; Somerset, Massachusetts)
Coast Guard certification:	Passenger Vessel (Subchapter T)
Crew:	3
Contact:	Captain Malcom Martin
	South Street Seaport Museum
	207 Front Street
	New York, NY 10038
	Tel: 212-748-8684; Fax: 212-748-8610
	Web site: http://www.southstseaport.org

Playfair

Tall Ship Adventures conducts sail training on board *Playfair,* a square-rigged ship designed specifically for youth sail training on the Great Lakes. Since 1964 over 15,000 young people have lived and worked aboard *Playfair* and her sister ship, *Pathfinder.*

Youth between the ages of 14 and 18 become the working crew on one or two-week adventures, making 24-hour passages from ports all over the Great Lakes. The program is delivered by youth officers between the ages of 15 and 18. Our youth officers are trained and qualified during Tall Ship Adventures' Winter Training Programs. The captain and first mate are the only adults on board. Every year each ship sails over 4,000 miles, spends over 40 nights at sea, and introduces 300 trainees to the tall ship experience. *Playfair* is owned and operated by Toronto Brigantine, Inc., a registered charity.

Flag:	Canada
Rig:	Brigantine
Homeport/waters:	Toronto, Ontario, Canada: Great Lakes
Who sails?	In July and August, youth programs for ages 14-18; in May, June, and September, school groups from middle school through college, and interested adult groups.
Cost:	$675 CDN for one week; $1,175 CDN for two weeks (summer youth rate). Call for spring and fall group rates. Also day sails and group rates.
Program type:	Sail training for paying trainees, including seamanship and leadership training based on in-house programming. Shoreside winter program. Dockside interpretation. Affiliated institutions include the Canadian Sail Training Association and the Ontario Camping Association.

Specifications:

Sparred length: 72'	Draft: 7' 6"	Sail area: 2,600 sq. ft.
LOD: 58'	Beam: 16'	Tons: 32.98 GRT
LOA: 60'	Rig height: 54'	Power: 110 HP diesel
LWL: 45'	Freeboard: 4'	Hull: steel

Designer:	Francis A. Maclachlan
Built:	1973; Kingston, Ontario, Canada, Canada Dredge and Dock Co.
Crew:	10. Trainees: 25 (day sails), 18 (overnight)
Contact:	Catharine McLean, Executive Director
	Toronto Brigantine, Inc.
	370 Queen's Quay West, Ste. 203
	Toronto, Ontario, M5V 3J3, Canada
	Tel: 416-596-7117; Fax: 416-596-9119
	E-mail: mail@tallshipadventures.on.ca
	Web site: http://www.tallshipadventures.on.ca

Pride of Baltimore II

The *Pride of Baltimore II* is a topsail schooner built to the lines of an 1812-era Baltimore Clipper. Owned by the State of Maryland and operated by Pride of Baltimore, Inc., her primary mission is to promote tourism and economic development for Maryland and the Port of Baltimore internationally. She also serves as a unique electronic platform for Maryland's students through specially designed curricula used via the Internet. *Pride II* is available for charter and for dockside and sailing receptions in each of her destinations. She can accommodate up to six paying passengers for hire as "working guest crew" between ports of call.

The *Pride of Baltimore II* sails year-round with two full-time rotating captains and a crew of 11. Crew positions are open to qualified individuals. The *Pride of Baltimore II* maintains an international sailing schedule, most recently completing a tour of Asia. The 2001 tour schedule included participation in ASTA's Tall Ships Challenge® race series in the Great Lakes.

Flag:	USA
Rig:	Square topsail schooner, two-masted
Homeport/waters:	Baltimore, Maryland: Global
Who sails?	Corporate clients and residents of the State of Maryland and the City of Baltimore.
Season:	Year-round
Cost:	$150 per person per day (working guest crew); $750 per hour (dockside reception); $1,000 group rate per hour (sailing reception)
Program type:	Sea education and marketing development in cooperation with the State of Maryland. Passenger day sails and overnight passages, dockside school tours.
Specifications:	Sparred length: 170' Draft: 12' 4" Sail area: 10,442 sq. ft.
	LOD: 96' 6" Beam: 26' Tons: 97 GRT
	LOA: 108' Rig height: 107' Power: twin 165 HP diesels
	Freeboard: 6' Hull: wood
Designer:	Thomas C. Gillmer
Built:	1988; Baltimore, Maryland, G. Peter Boudreau
Coast Guard certification:	Passenger Vessel (Subchapter T)
Crew:	12. Trainees: 35 (day sails), 6 (overnight). Age: 18+
Contact:	Linda Christenson, Esq., Executive Director
	Pride of Baltimore, Inc.
	401 East Pratt Street, Suite 222
	Baltimore, MD 21202
	Tel: 410-539-1151; Fax: 410-539-1190
	E-mail: pride2@pride2.org
	Web site: http://www.pride2.org

Providence

The *Providence* is a replica of one of the first ships of the American Navy. Built as a merchant ship in the 1760s, the *Providence* (ex-*Katy*) went on to become the first command of John Paul Jones and one of the most successful American ships to fight in the Revolutionary War. After a successful career in which she sank or captured 40 British ships, she earned the nick-name *"Lucky Sloop."* John Paul Jones said of her, "She was the first and she was the best."

The Continental Sloop *Providence* is a statewide resource administered by the Providence Maritime Heritage Foundation and the City of Providence, Rhode Island. The primary mission of the *Providence* is to inspire and educate the thousands of Rhode Islanders served each year and to keep Rhode Island's rich maritime heritage alive. As Rhode Island's Flagship, the Sloop *Providence* serves youth and adults through the "Classroom Under Sail" programs, which illuminate Rhode Island's maritime history and the importance of the city of Providence in our nation's early development.

The Sloop *Providence* also serves as the Ocean State's sailing ambassador, representing Rhode Island at waterfront festivals along the East Coast. The *Providence* is available for charter for education, special events, corporate outings, documentary and film use, and historic reenactments.

Flag:	USA
Rig:	Square topsail sloop
Homeport/waters:	Providence, Rhode Island: East Coast US
Who sails?	School groups from elementary school through college, individuals, and families.
Program type:	Sail training for crew and volunteers. Passenger day sails. Dockside interpretation at homeport and during port visits. Sea education in marine science, maritime history, Cadet program, and more for school groups of all ages.

Specifications:

Sparred length: 110'	Draft: 10'	Sail area: 3,470 sq. ft.
LOD: 61' 1'	Beam: 20'	Tons: 59 GRT
LOA: 65'	Rig height: 94'	Power: 170 HP diesel
LWL: 59'	Freeboard: 8'	Hull: fiberglass and wood

Designer:	Charles W. Wittholz
Built:	1976; Melville, Rhode Island
Coast Guard certification:	Passenger vessel (Subchapter T)
Crew:	5-8. Trainees: 24-40 (day sails), 4-6 (overnight)
Contact:	Robert Hofmann, Executive Director
	Providence Maritime Heritage Foundation
	PO Box 1261
	Providence, RI 02901
	Tel: 401-274-7447; Fax: 401-751-0121
	E-mail: info@sloopprovidence.org, Web site: http://www.sloopprovidence.org

Built in 1984 for the passenger service, *Quinnipiack* now serves as the primary vessel for Schooner Sound Learning, an organization dedicated to teaching about the ecology of Long Island Sound. Since 1975, Schooner Sound Learning has taught in classrooms, on the shores, and aboard a variety of vessels. Participants of all ages study under sail and explore the ecology of the estuary while getting an introduction to maritime heritage and seamanship. Students work alongside the crew, learning the lessons in teamwork, self-reliance, flexibility and interdependence that only sailing vessels can teach.

Quinnipiack programs complement traditional classroom studies in sciences, mathematics, geography, history, literature, folklore, and social studies. Hands-on learning activities include collection, identification, and interpretation of estuarine organisms, land use, plankton study, piloting, sail handling, seamanship, sediment analysis, water chemistry, and weather.

During the summer Schooner offers weeklong programs for grades K - 12. The

Seafaring Scientists program is conducted aboard the *Quinnipiack* for grades 6-8 and teaches basic seamanship and marine ecology. Internships are available for high school and college students to learn the operation and care of a traditional sailing vessel while sailing as crew. The *Quinnipiack* is also available for corporate charters and special events.

Flag:	USA
Rig:	Two masted, gaff schooner
Homeport/ waters:	New Haven, Connecticut: Long Island Sound
Who Sails?	School groups from middle school through college, individuals, and families.
Season:	April – November
Program type:	Sail training for crew, apprentices, and trainees. Sea education in marine science, maritime history, and ecology in cooperation with accredited schools and colleges and as informal, in-house programming. Dockside interpretation during port visits. Passenger day sails.

Specifications:	Sparred length: 91'	Draft: 4'5" – 11'	Sail area: 2400 sq.ft.
	LOD: 62'	Beam: 20'	Tons: 41 GRT
	LOA: 65'	Rig height: 77'	Power: 135 HP diesel
	LWL: 58'	Freeboard: 5' 2"	Hull: wood

Designer:	Philip Sheldon
Built:	1984; Milbridge, Maine, Philip Sheldon
Coast Guard certification:	Passenger vessel (subchapter T)
Crew:	5 professional, Trainees: 40 (day sails), 4-6 (overnight)
Contact:	Beth McCabe, Executive Director / Captain Jonathan Wisch
	Schooner Sound Learning
	60 South Water Street, New Haven, CT 06519
	Tel: 203-865-1737; Fax: 203-624-8816
	E-mail: SSL@schoonersoundlearning.org
	Web site: http://www.schoonersoundlearning.org

Quissett (Coaster II)

and sometime in the 1950's was a winner of the Transpac race from San Francisco to Honolulu where she remained until the middle nineties. She returned to the mainland and was restored to her present condition by shipwrights in Port Townsend, Washington. In 1998 she was designated a Historic Site by the Department of the Interior.

Quissett, originally christened as *Coaster II,* is a 1/2 scale nineteenth century style Grand Banks fishing schooner. She was designed and built by Murray Peterson at Booth bay, Maine in 1933 and was his personal yacht. She was later sold and moved to the west coast rounding Cape Horn. Legend has it that she was once owned by 1950's movie actor Rory Calhoun

Quissett is based in Tacoma, WA and is primarily used for the benefit of young people as a sail training vessel. She is also available for day sails and overnight charters by the general public. More information can be obtained by writing to the Classic Schooner Institute, 1112 Alexander Ave, Tacoma, WA 98421, or by calling her Skipper, Kevin Porter at 253-468-9607.

Flag:	USA
Rig:	Gaff schooner
Homeport/waters:	Tacoma, Washington: Puget Sound
Who sails?	Groups and individuals of all ages
Season:	April through October
Cost:	$35 per person per half-day, $450 Group rate per day, $300 per person per 4-day sea camp
Program type:	Sail training for paying trainees. 4-day sea camps include basic sail training, first aid, and camping on shore

Specifications:	Sparred length: 58'	LOD: 43'	LOA: 43'
	LWL: 35' 6"	Draft: 7'	Beam: 12'
	Rig height: 57'	Power: 65 hp	

Designer:	Murray Peterson
Built:	1930; Maine, Goudy
Crew:	3. Trainees/passengers: 6 (day sails), 3 (overnight)
Contact:	Captain Kevin W. Porter
	Classic Schooner Institute
	9724 Eckerstam-Johnson
	Anderson Island, Washington 98303
	Tel: 253-884-1142; Fax: 253-272-6241
	E-mail: akporter5@aol.com

The *R.H. Ledbetter* is the flagship of the Culver Summer Naval School, located on Lake Maxinkuckee in Culver, Indiana. The three-masted square-rigger, named in honor of Georgia philanthropist and Culver alumnus Robert H. Ledbetter, was built in 1983-84 by the T.D. Vinette Co. of Escanaba, Michigan.

Dedicated July 7, 1984, the *Ledbetter* replaced the wooden-hulled *O.W. Fowler,* which had served as the flagship from 1941-83. The masts, spars, and sails from the *Fowler* were used on the *Ledbetter.*

During spring 2002, the 100th anniversary of Culver Summer Camps, which began with the founding of the Naval School in 1902, was celebrated with the *R.H. Ledbetter* navigating the Intracoastal Waterway from Palm Beach, Fla., to Washington, D.C. The six-week voyage included eight ports-of-call, at which Culver alumni and friends had the opportunity to celebrate the centennial

before the boat was trucked back to its home port.

Culver Summer Camps offer two simultaneous coed six-week camps from mid-June to early August (Woodcraft for ages 9-13, and Upper Camp for 13-17) and 10 two-week specialty camps from early to mid-August.

Administered by The Culver Educational Foundation, which also operates the Culver Academy, the camps use the facilities of the 1,800-acre wooded campus along the north shore of Indiana's second-largest lake.

Flag:	USA
Rig:	Full rigged ship
Homeport/waters:	Culver, Indiana: Lake Maxinkuckee in Culver, Indiana
Who sails?	Students and Alumni of Culver Academy
Program type:	Sail training for students of Culver Academy. Sea education in cooperation with organized groups such as the American Camping Association. Dockside interpretation while in home port.

Specifications:	Sparred length: 65'	LOD: 50'	LOA: 54'
	Draft: 5'	Beam: 13'	Rig height: 49'
	Freeboard: 5'	Tons: 25 GRT	Power: diesel

Designer:	Marine Power
Built:	1984; Escanoba, Michigan, T. D. Vinette
Contact:	Anthony Mayfield, Director Culver Summer Camps
	Culver Summer Camps
	1300 Academy Road, RD# 138
	Culver, IN 46511
	Tel: 800-221-2020; Fax: 574-842-8462
	E-mail: mayfiea@culver.org
	Web site: http://www.culver.org

R. Tucker Thompson

The traditional gaff-rigged schooner, *R. Tucker Thompson* was started by R. Tucker Thompson in the late 1970s as a project to embody the best features of a traditional design, married to the materials of today. After Tucker's death, the *R. Tucker Thompson* was completed by Tucker's son Tod Thompson and Russell Harris. The ship was built in Mangawhai, New Zealand and launched in 1985.

Her design is based on the Halibut schooners of the North West American coast which were considered fast and sea kindly and easily manned. She has a lofty rig of varnished Oregon spars. Kwila decks and bulwarks with flashes of brasswork to make her look as she should, a working ship of the 18th Century, purposeful and square–shouldered, but with a touch of style and speed – sufficient to out-run the law!

Most of her voyages take place during winter seasons of the years. During summer she operates as a day charter ship and has carried over 60,000 visitors around the Bay of Islands.

The ship has taken part in five film productions. These were the *Adventurer* series for TVNZ, *Red* – a Sommerset Maugham story set in Tonga for a German film company and *Rite of Passage* for the Australian First Fleet Re-enactment Company. We have also featured in the BBC's David Attenborough *Life of Mammals* (to be shown 2003) as well as the *Captain's Log* a TVNZ documentary about the Voyage of Captain James Cook around New Zealand.

The ship's current survey is class seven foreign vessel which means that she can carry passengers around the coast of New Zealand as well as off shore. She has been built and maintained to the highest standards and is professionally manned and equipped to go anywhere in the world at any time. In 2002 she will voyage to Korea for Sail Korea 2002 and onwards to the Pacific Coast of the United States where she will participate in the TALL SHIPS CHALLENGE®.

Flag:	New Zealand
Rig:	Gaff rigged schooner
Homeport/waters:	Whangarei, New Zealand: worldwide
Who sails?	Individuals and groups of all ages
Season:	Year-round

Specifications:	Sparred length: 85'	LOD: 60'	Draft: 6'
	Beam: 16'	Sail area: 3,000 sq. ft.	Power:180 HP Ford diesel
	Hull: steel	Hull color: black	

Built	1985; Mangawhai, New Zealand, Tod Thompson and Russell Harris
Crew:	15. Trainees/passengers: 45 (day sails)
Contact:	Russell Harris
	c/o Opuu P.C.
	Bay of Islands
	New Zealand
	Tel: +64-9-402-8430; Fax: +64-9-402-8565
	E-mail: r.tucker@clear.net.nz

The *Rachel B. Jackson* is a one off design of an 1890s coastal schooner by Burt Frost. The keel was laid in Jonesport, Maine in 1974. She was planked and floated in Southwest Harbor where she sat unfinished at a mooring until 1979. The hull was purchased by George Emery and towed to Freeport, Maine. George, his brother Jim, and their father took the next three years to complete the *Rachel B. Jackson,* and launched her in 1982. George and Jim operated the boat out of Mystic Seaport as a sail training vessel. In 1984 she was sold and embarked on a three-year circumnavigation. She was sold again in 1990 and was put into the charter trade in Maine and the Virgin Islands. The *Rachel B.* was chartered by the National Geographic Society to do whale research off the coast of the Dominican Republic. The current owners, Steve and Andrew Keblinsky, just completed a two-year refit in May 1999. The *Rachel B. Jackson* now operates in Boston and Maine.

Flag:	USA
Rig:	Schooner, two-masted
Homeport/waters:	Southwest Harbor, Maine: Maine
Who sails?	School groups from elementary school through high school, individuals, and families.
Cost:	$2,000 group rate per day (charter)
Program type:	Sail training for volunteer and paying trainees. Sea education in marine science, maritime history, and ecology in cooperation with organized groups. Passenger day sails, dockside interpretation during port visits.

Specifications:			
	Sparred length: 75'	Draft: 8'	Sail area: 2,500 sq. ft.
	LOD: 52'	Beam: 17'	Tons: 52 GRT
	LOA: 52'	Rig height: 75'	Power: 108 HP diesel
	LWL: 43'	Freeboard: 4'	Hull: wood

Designer:	Burt Frost
Built:	1982; Freeport, Maine, George Emery
Coast Guard certification:	Passenger Vessel (Subchapter T)
Crew:	3. Trainees/passengers: 30
Contact:	Captain Steven Keblinsky
	Downeast Sailing Adventures, LLC
	PO Box 1252
	Southwest Harbor, ME 04679
	Tel: 207-244-7813
	E-mail: downeastsail@acadia.net
	Web site: http://www.downeastsail.com

Rainbow Chaser

Rainbow Chaser is a cutter rigged ketch, owned and operated by Rainbow Chaser Ltd. as a training and charter vessel. She was built by Gulfstar in 1976 as part of the Independence series. After several years of neglect, she was bought by the present owners and has been lovingly restored.

During the summer months, she takes part in the Boy Scouts of America High Adventure Program in the Abacos. Here, young people learn basic sailing and navigation skills as well as the traits of responsibility and cooperation.

In the fall, *Rainbow Chaser* is available for charter in her homeport of Melbourne, Florida, just south of Cape Canaveral Space Center. In the winter and spring she is available for charters in the Bahamas.

Flag:	USA
Rig:	Ketch
Homeport/waters:	Melbourne, Florida; Bahamas
Who sails?	Families, groups and individuals of all ages.
Program type:	Sail training for paying trainees. Sea education in cooperation with other organized groups.
Season:	Year-round

Specifications:

Sparred length: 56'	LOD: 50'	LOA: 52'
LWL: 46'	Draft: 5'	Beam: 14'
Tons: 29 GRT	Rig height: 59'	Power: Perkins 130 HP
Freeboard: 5'	Hull: Fiberglass	diesel
Hull color: white	Spar material: aluminum	

Built:	1976; Tampa, Florida, Gulfstar
Crew:	2. Trainees/passengers: 12 (day sails), 12 (overnight)
Contact:	Captain Jack Leahy
	Rainbow Chaser Ltd.
	4 East Hill Drive
	Doylestown, PA 18901
	Tel: 267-880-0418
	E-mail: charter@rchaser.com
	Web site: http://www.rchaser.com

Raindancer II is a unique modern classic. Fashioned from rare Angelique teak, she was finely crafted in Lunenburg, Nova Scotia, in 1981. *Raindancer II* was refurbished in 1997/98 and currently sails the Caribbean (including Cuba) and the East Coast of Canada. She is comfortably appointed with private cabins to serve six guests on weekly eco-sailing adventures combining hands-on shipboard activities with shore excursions and exploration.

Flag:	Canada		
Rig:	Staysail schooner		
Homeport/waters:	Lunenburg, Nova Scotia, Canada		
Who sails?	Individuals, families, and corporate groups.		
Season:	Year-round		
Program type:	Sail training for paying trainees. Passenger day sails and overnight voyages.		
Specifications:	LOA: 75'	Draft: 8'	Sail area: 2,700 sq. ft.
	Rig height: 76'	Tons: 45 GRT	Power: 225 HP diesel
	Hull: teak		
Designer:	Stevens		
Built:	1981; Nova Scotia, Canada, Stevens		
Contact:	Captain Ron Lipscombe		
	Raindancer Sailing		
	10 Daleview Court		
	Peterborough, Ontario K9J 8E5 Canada		
	Tel: 613-542-6349		
	E-mail: info@raindancerii.com		
	Web site: http://www.raindancerii.com		

Ranger (Work in Progress)

The Ranger Foundation, Inc. was established in March 1999 to undertake one of the most exciting ventures in American maritime history—the rebuilding of John Paul Jones' famous warship, the *Ranger*. In 1777, no one expected that John Paul Jones and the Continental Sloop of War *Ranger* would help turn the tide of the American Revolution—no one but Jones himself. It was unthinkable for a lone ship to take on the world's mightiest navy in its own home waters, but that's exactly what Jones did.

It was the *Ranger* that first carried the new American flag into harm's way. When the French acknowledged that flag at Quiberon Bay off the coast of France, *Ranger* became the first ship under American colors to be recognized by a foreign power. Not long after, Jones and the *Ranger* crew initiated a guerilla naval campaign against Britain that is the subject of books and ballads to this day. The Ranger Foundation is dedicated to bringing that story alive by creating a sailing and maritime education program around a full-size replica of the famous ship.

Flag:	USA
Rig:	Full-rigged ship, three-masted
Homeport/waters:	Portsmouth, New Hampshire: worldwide
Program type:	Planned: Sail training and an extensive maritime education program integrated with other historical and maritime organizations throughout the region.
Coast Guard certification:	Planned: Sailing School Vessel (Subchapter R), Passenger Vessel (Subchapter T)
Crew (projected):	12 (fulltime, including instructors) Trainees/passengers: 24
Contact:	Tom Cocchiaro, Chair
	The Ranger Foundation
	PO Box 6578
	Portsmouth, NH 03802-6578
	Tel: 603-436-2808; Fax: 603-436-2808
	Email: info@rangerfoundation.org
	Web site: http://www.rangerfoundation.org

The *Red Witch*, designated as the official Flagship of the 2003 Ohio Bicentennial, is a living tribute to US maritime history and her designer, John G. Alden. She was built in the tradition of the vessels that were the workhorses of America's 19th-century transportation system. True to her ancestors, her block and tackle, wooden hull, and gaff rig capture the romance and adventure of sail.

Built expressly for chartering, she worked in San Diego and Hawaii from 1987 through 1996. In 1997 the *Red Witch* started plying the waters of western Lake Erie. From her new home in Sandusky, she visits various ports in Ohio, Michigan, Pennsylvania and New York. These ports include Toledo, Detroit, Cleveland, Erie and Buffalo. Available for walk-on day sails or private group charters, the *Red Witch* also offers sail training programs for youth groups. The *Red Witch* offers dockside interpretations, two-hour hands-on sails and all-day island excursions.

Flag:	USA
Rig:	Gaff schooner
Homeport/waters:	Sandusky, OH: Great Lakes
Who sails?	School groups from elementary school through college, individuals, and families.
Season:	May through October
Program type:	Sail training for volunteer or paying trainees. Sea education in marine science and maritime history in cooperation with accredited institutions and organized groups. Passenger day sails.

Specifications:
Sparred length: 77' Draft: 6'6" Sail area: 2,100 sq. ft.
LOD: 54' Beam: 17'6" Tons: 41 GRT
LOA: 57' Rig height: 73' Power: 125 HP diesel
LWL: 49' Hull: wood Hull color: red
Spar material: wood Freeboard: 4'6"

Designer: John Alden
Built: 1986; Bayou La Batre, Alabama, Nathaniel Zirlott
Coast Guard certification: Passenger Vessel (Subchapter T)
Crew: 4. Trainees/passengers: 49
Contact: Captain Karl A. Busam
Red Witch Charters
PO Box 386
Port Clinton, OH 43452
Tel: 419-734-0734; Fax: 419-734-9339
E-mail: schooner@redwitch.com
Web site: http://www.redwitch.com

Resolute

Resolute was an active participant in intercollegiate and club racing circuits on the East Coast.

Resolute now finds her home on the West Coast. Purchased for one dollar by the Evergreen State College in 1972, she currently provides sail training opportunities and access to Pacific Northwest waters for students and volunteers. *Resolute* and her companion vessel *SeaWulff* are used to teach a wide range of interdisciplinary programs, which vary from year to year. All of these classes are built around the fundamentals of sailing, seamanship, and navigation. Previous programs include Wooden Boat Building and Repair, Marine Biology and Field Work Methods, Native American Culture Studies, Pacific Northwest History and Development, and Maritime Literature.

Resolute was built in 1939 for the US Naval Academy at Annapolis, Maryland. She was the third of twelve Luders yawls built for the Navy, and over the course of twenty years it is estimated that some seventy thousand midshipmen trained aboard these yawls. During this time

Academic programs are available to students enrolled at Evergreen only, though outside charters are considered on a case by case basis. Student and community volunteers assist in maintaining *Resolute* and *SeaWulff* in exchange for sailing opportunities.

Flag:	USA
Rig:	Yawl
Homeport/waters:	Olympia, Washington: Puget Sound and inland waters of British Columbia
Who sails?	Enrolled students at Evergreen State College. Outside charters on a case by case basis.
Cost:	$225 group rate per day
Program type:	Sail training for volunteer trainees. Fully accredited sea education in marine science, maritime history, ecology, and maritime studies.

Specifications:	Sparred length: 44'	Draft: 6'	Sail area: 1,050 sq. ft.
	LOD: 44'	Beam: 11'	Tons: 12 GRT
	LOA: 44'	Rig height: 60'	Power: diesel
	LWL: 30'	Freeboard: 3'	Hull: wood

Designer:	Luders
Built:	1939; Stamford, Connecticut, Luders Marine Construction Company
Coast Guard certification:	Passenger Vessel (Subchapter T)
Crew:	2. Trainees: 10 (day sails), 5 (overnight)
Contact:	Greg Buikema, Marine Operations Manager
	The Evergreen State College
	2700 Evergreen Parkway NW
	Olympia, WA 98505
	Tel: 360-866-6000; Fax: 360-867-5430
	E-mail: buikemag@evergreen.edu
	Web site: http://www.evergreen.edu

A recreation of the Chebacco boats and pinky schooners of New England of the early 1800's, *Resolution* is based in Annapolis, Maryland and sails the waters of the Chesapeake Bay. *Resolution* is operated by Ship's Company, a maritime living history not-for-profit which provides period-dressed docent support for numerous historical sites and maritime events in the Baltimore - Washington DC - Annapolis region. Ship's Company's six sections include Circa 1800 (Navy and Marines), Civil War (Navy and Marines), the singing Chanteymen, and the new (1999) Boat Group. *Resolution* is a Class C tall ship and combined with historical re-enactors can be engaged for dockside interpretation of circa 1800 (1775-1825) shipboard life and tours within a day or two sail of Annapolis, Maryland.

Resolution is supported by Ship's Company's other vessels...*Circuitous,* a 1934 sloop and *Enterprize Jollyboat*, a 14-foot recreation of ship's lapstrake. *Resolution* and her crew can interpret a

wide variety of periods. However, her baseline representation is as an 1800 pinky schooner taken up by the early United States Navy as an armed tender despatch schooner, supporting the USS ENTERPRIZE. Ship's Company supports the activities of National Maritime Heritage Foundation (www.spiritofenterprize.org) to build and operate a full scale representation for youth education in Washington DC.

Flag:	USA
Rig:	Topsail Schooner; gaff fore and marconi main with square 'great sail'
Homeport/waters:	Annapolis, Maryland and the Chesapeake Bay
Who sails?	Members of Ship's Company (www.shipscompany.org) a maritime living history group
Season:	April through November
Cost:	$500 for a visit within half a day sail; $2000 for a visit within 2 days sail (adjusted by distance/time); additional interpretation (encampment, tavern, crafts, musical performances, etc) can be added.
Program type:	Sail training for members. Dockside interpretation and offshore demonstrations in support of waterside living history and traditional maritime events.

Specifications:

Sparred length: 45'	Draft: 6.2'	Sail area: 900 sq ft
LOD: 34'	Beam: 11.2'	Tons: 11 GRT
LOA: 38'	Rig height: 50'	Power: 60 hp diesel
LWL: 30'	Hull: Wood carvel	

Built:	1988-1995; hull by James Rosbourough Yard in Nova Scotia; completed Ontario, NY
Coast Guard certification:	Uninspected vessel
Crew:	2 to 14. Coed.
Contact:	Michael Bosworth Ship's Company Boat Coordinator 357 Ayr Hill Ave, NE Vienna, VA 22180 Tel: 703-864-4174 E-mail: michael.bosworth@verizon.net Web site: http://www.shipscompany.org

or Captain Steven Deatherage
Ship's Company RESOLUTION
Tel: 703-765-8889

The *Richard Robbins* is a genuine two-masted, gaff-rigged schooner with canvas sails. She was built entirely of white oak and yellow pine in 1902, just after the Spanish American War. She has a long and colorful history, beginning with her launching at Greenwich, New Jersey, near Cape May. She sailed for many years with a fleet of schooners dredging for oysters in Delaware Bay. She was owned by the Robbins family until 1967, when she was sold and taken to Rockland, Maine where she entered the charter trade. In 1978 she went to Lake Champlain, offering week-long sailing vacations. In 1984 she returned to New Jersey and now sails from Weehawken, where she offers sail training, corporate dinner charters, Sunday brunch sails, and private birthday parties. She is a registered historic tall ship and participated in Operation Sail 1986, and Operation Sail 1992 and OpSail 2000. Share in the sense of wonder and discovery felt by Sir Henry Hudson from the deck of an authentic sailing ship!

Flag:	USA
Rig:	Gaff schooner, two-masted
Homeport/waters:	Weehawken, New Jersey: Hudson River, New York Harbor, Sandy Hook Bay, Long Island Sound.
Who sails?	Students of all ages, individuals, families, clubs, corporations
Program type:	Sail training for groups arranging a private charter. Ecologists and scientists can be included for an additional cost. Dinner parties for fundraisers, corporations, and individuals. Sea chantey singers available at an additional cost.

Specifications:

Sparred length: 80'	LOD: 60'	LOA: 75'
LWL: 50'	Draft: 5'	Beam: 18' 6"
Rig height: 50'	Freeboard: 4'	Sail area: 1,800 sq. ft.
Tons: 45 GRT	Power: diesel	Hull: wood

Designer:	William Parsons
Built:	1902; Greenwich, New Jersey, Greenwich Marine Piers and Railway
Coast Guard certification:	Passenger Vessel (Subchapter T)
Crew:	3. Trainees/passengers: 49 (day sails), 20 (overnight)
Contact:	Captain Alan Jadro Classic Sail Windjammer Co., Inc. PO Box 459 Madison, NJ 07940 Tel: 973-966-1684

The brig *Roald Amundson* was originally built in 1952 as a motor-tanker for the East German Navy, but on the plans of a sailing logger. After the German reunification she was bought and transformed into her present shape.

Since 1993, *Roald Amundson* has sailed between Iceland, St. Petersburg, and the Canary Islands on voyages mainly dedicated to the education and understanding of young people. Since 2000, she has worked in cooperation with the Hurricane Island Outward Bound School in Rockland, Maine providing sail training opportunities as part of an international youth exchange program.

Roald Amundson is designed to sail with all hands onboard helping to sail the ship. Her permanent crew undertakes the challenge of forming the new trainees into a group of enthusiastic sailors.

While the rig of the *Roald Amundson* is designed like it was in the 19th century, the interior is built to high standards, with wood paneling and private heads.

The vessel was built under the surveillance of Germanischer Lloyd and fully complies with the German "Traditionsschiffsverordnung" (safety standards for traditional sail training vessels). Her safety standards are the highest available and she is licensed for worldwide voyaging.

Flag:	Germany
Rig:	Brig
Homeport/waters:	Wolgast, Germany: Baltic Sea, Canary Islands, Caribbean Sea
Who sails?	Youth trainees, school groups, families, and individuals over 16.
Program type:	Sail training for apprentices and paying trainees. Accredited sea education. Day sails and overnight passages.

Specifications:	Sparred length: 165'	Draft: 15'	Sail area: 9,265 sq. ft.
	LOD: 139'	Beam: 25'	Tons: 252 GRT
	LOA: 140'	Rig height: 112'	Power: 300 HP
	LWL: 130'	Freeboard: 8' 6"	Hull: steel

Designer:	Detlev Löll
Built:	1952: Ro ss lau, Germany. 1992/93: Wolgast, Germany, LebenLernen auf Segelschiffen e.V.(Learning to Live on Sailing Ships) .
Certification:	German Lloyd Traditionsschiffsverordung
Crew:	16 overnight, 20 day sails Trainees: 32 day sails, 60 overnight
Contact:	LlaS
	Jungfernstieg 104
	24340 Eckernförde
	Germany
	Tel: +49-4351+726074; Fax: +49-4351-726075
	E-mail: office@sailtraining.de
	Web site: http://www.sailtraining.de

Robert C. Seamans

SEA's newest vessel, launched in the spring of 2001, was built at JM Martinac Shipbuilding in Tacoma, Washington. Designed by Laurent Giles of Hampshire, England, the 134-foot steel brigantine is the most sophisticated sailing research vessel ever built in the United States. Improvements in design and equipment, including a wet/dry laboratory and a large library, classroom, and computer laboratory, will enhance the SEA academic program. The new vessel is slated for SEA Semesters in the Pacific for two years. Cruise tracks include Hawaii, Costa Rica, Alaska, and Tahiti.

Robert C. Seamans

Flag:	USA
Rig:	Brigantine
Homeport/waters:	Woods Hole, Massachusetts; worldwide
Season:	Year-round
Who sails?	Educators and students who are admitted by competitive selection. Over 150 colleges and universities award credit for SEA programs.
Program type:	Marine and maritime studies including oceanography, nautical science, history, literature, and contemporary maritime affairs. SEA programs include SEA Semester (college level, 12 weeks long, 17 credits), SEA Summer Session (college level, 8 weeks long, 12 credits), and SEA Seminars for high school students and K-12 teachers. All programs include a seagoing component on board one of the sailing school vessels.
Specifications:	Sparred length: 134'6" LOA: 119' Draft: 13'
	Sail area: 8,200 sq. ft. LWL: 87'6" Beam: 26'6"
	Power: Caterpillar 3408, 455 HP Hull: steel
	Displacement: 300 tons median load
Designer:	Laurent Giles, Hampshire, England
Built:	Tacoma, Washington, JM Martinac Shipbuilding
Coast Guard certification:	Sailing School Vessel (Subchapter R)
Crew:	6 professional mariners and 4 scientists. Trainees: Up to 25 in all programs
Contact:	Sea Education Association, Inc.
	PO Box 6
	Woods Hole, MA 02543
	Tel: 508-540-3954; Fax: 508-540-0558
	E-mail: admissions@sea.edu
	Web site: http://www.sea.edu

One of the last original Canadian Grand Banks fisherman built, the *Robertson II* was launched at Shelburne, Nova Scotia in 1940. Fishing up to 1974, she was brought through the Panama Canal to Victoria, British Columbia, where for the last 20 years she has provided sail training programs for young people.

Officially retired in 1995 from active service, the *Robertson II* is open to the general public from May until September. The City of Victoria has provided a permanent dock in the inner harbor where the historic schooner is prominently exhibited.

Flag:	Canada		
Rig:	Gaff schooner, two-masted		
Homeport:	Victoria, British Columbia, Canada		
Program type:	Interpretive programs.		
Specifications:	Sparred length: 130'	Draft: 11' 1"	Sail area: 5,500 sq. ft.
	LOD: 105'	Beam: 22' 1"	Tons: 170 GRT
	Rig height: 105'	Hull: wood	Power: GM diesel
Built:	1940; Sherburne, Nova Scotia, Canada, McKay and Sons		
Contact:	Mr. Ron Howatson, Executive Director		
	Sail and Life Training Society (SALTS)		
	PO Box 5014, Station B		
	Victoria, British Columbia V8R 6N3 Canada		
	Tel: 250-383-6811; Fax: 250-383-7781		
	E-mail: info@saltsociety.com		
	Web site: http://www.saltsociety.com		

"HMS" Rose

The tall ship *Rose* is a three-masted full-rigged ship designed after an 18th-century colonial-era British frigate of the same name. Until 2001 she was the only Class A size ship certified by the US Coast Guard as a Sailing School Vessel, and carried groups as large as 100 for day sailing or as many as 49 for overnight passages and live-aboard programs.

She carried 19 professional crew and educators and specialized in adventure-under-sail, experience-based education for youth groups, but also included a number of sessions in her itinerary each year that were open to the public for general admission. Corporate training, civic events, and other private functions were also scheduled by groups or individuals.

At press time *Rose* was in the Pacific preparing for her role in the Peter Weir-directed film version of Patrick O'Brian's *The Far Side of the World*. The film is scheduled for a June 2003 release. You might also catch an occasional glimpse of *Rose* in one of her many appearances in television documentaries and feature films both here and abroad.

Post film plans for the ship are uncertain at present, but a New England based nonprofit organization is committed to returning her to sail training if she is de-accessioned by her current film studio owners.

Flag:	USA.
Rig:	Full-rigged ship, 3-masted.
Homeport/waters:	Newport, RI.
Who sails?	Actors, extras, Russell Crowe, etc.
Season:	Year-round.
Cost:	Not available at present.
Program type:	Fundamental sail training with additional education modules tailored for specific programs for middle and high school, college and university, adults and families, corporate team building, and more.

Specifications			
Sparred length: 179'	LOD: 125'	LOA: 135'
LWL: 105'	Draft: 13'	Beam: 32'
Rig height: 130'	Freeboard: 13'	Sail area: 13,000 sq. ft.
Tons: 500 GRT	Power: twin diesels	Hull: wood

Designer:	Original design by Hugh Blades, British Admiralty, in 1757; revised by Phil Bolger, 1970.
Built:	1969/70; Lunenburg, Nova Scotia, Smith & Rhuland (rebuilt: 1985-87; Bridgeport, CT and Fairhaven, MA).
Coast Guard certification:	Sailing School Vessel (Subchapter R).
Crew:	18. Trainees: 85 (day sails), 31 (overnight). Age: junior high school to adult Sex: coed.
Contact:	Commander Production Marine Department
	6341 Arizona Circle
	Los Angeles, CA 90045
	Tel: 310-338-1234; Fax: 310-338-1116

The training program aboard *Rose of Sharon* is intended to provide the trainees with character-building experiences, hauling lines, trimming sails, serving the vessel's needs as a cruise progresses. The bugeye rig provides opportunities for handling tackle in a classic manner, in turn demonstrating how such experience enriches one in forming strengthened character and enhanced self-esteem. The *Rose of Sharon* program is being developed in the Pacific Northwest with primary objectives: to provide local area youth with an introduction to the joys, challenges, and traditions of sailing; and for those who wish to go further, to provide advanced skills preparatory to crewing with larger vessels in the waters of Washington State and British Columbia.

The platform for the program, the bugeye ketch (3-sail bateau) *Rose of Sharon* (ex *Cristobal*), is currently undergoing restoration. She was built on the banks of the Chesapeake by local hands and materials, and launched in 1965.

After cruising Eastern waters, she was trucked to the Northwest, and has sailed in the Strait of Juan de Fuca and northward to Alaskan waters in her more recent years.

The sail training program will be made available to church youth groups. There is no cost to participants as the Ministry is a member of a 501(c)(3) corporation, Homestead Ministries, and is wholly supported by donations from local businesses and individuals.

Flag:	USA
Rig:	Ketch
Homeport/waters:	Port Angeles, WA: San Juan Islands (Summer), Straits of Juan de Fuca (Winter)
Who sails?	High School and College students
Season:	Year-round
Program type:	Sail training opportunities for volunteer crew and trainees, day sails and overnight trips, sea education as informal in-house programming, dockside interpretation during port visits and while in home port.

Specifications:			
	Sparred length: 63'	LOD: 44' 6"	LOA: 46'
	LWL: 39'	Draft: 4' 6"	Beam: 13' 2"
	Rig height: 55'	Freeboard: 2' 6"	Sail area: 969 sq. ft.
	Tons: 15 GRT	Power: diesel	Hull: wood

Designer:	J.F. Gregory of Yorktown, VA
Built:	1965; Fairport, Virginia by E.C. Rice
Coast Guard certification:	Uninspected Vessel
Crew:	2. Trainees/passengers: 6 (day sails), 4 (overnight)
Contact:	Captain Bob Riggs, Helmsman
	Rose of Sharon Sailing Ministry
	P.O. Box 386
	Port Angeles WA 98362
	Tel: 360-681-5732; Fax: 360-452-0809
	E-mail: captbobriggs@hotmail.com
	Web site: http://www.rosesmin.org

Sagres II

Sagres II sails under the Portuguese flag as a naval training ship. She was built in 1937 at the Blohm & Voss shipyard in Hamburg, Germany, and is virtually a sister ship to *Eagle, Mircea, Tovarishch,* and *Gorch Fock II.* Originally named *Albert Leo Schlageter,* she served under American and Brazilian flags before being acquired by Portugal in 1962. At that time she replaced the first *Sagres,* which was built in 1896 as the *Rickmer Rickmers.* The original *Sagres* has now been restored and serves as a museum ship in Hamburg, Germany.

The name *Sagres* derives from the historic port that sent forth many famed Portuguese explorers and navigators. It served as the home and base for Prince Henry the Navigator (1394-1460). His court in Sagres was responsible for the geographic studies and practical explorations that made Portugal master of the seas in the early 15th century. A bust of Prince Henry serves as the figurehead on the bow of *Sagres II,* and the ship is easily identified by the traditional Portuguese crosses of Christ (Maltese crosses) that mark the square sails on her fore- and mainmasts.

Flag:	Portugal
Rig:	Barque
Homeport/waters:	Lisbon, Portugal: worldwide
Who sails?	Cadets of the Portuguese navy
Season:	Year-round
Program type:	Training vessel for the Portuguese navy
Specifications:	Sparred length: 293' 6" Draft: 17' Beam: 39' 6"
	Hull: steel
Built:	1937; Hamburg, Germany, Blohm & Voss Shipyard
Contact:	Portuguese Defense and Naval Attaché
	Embassy of Portugal
	2310 Tracy Place
	Washington, DC 20008
	Tel: 202-234-4483; Fax: 202-328-6827
	E-mail: ponavnir@mindspring.com

The School of Ocean Sailing operates in the North Atlantic Ocean off the coast of Maine, offering courses in offshore ocean sailing and ocean navigation in a live-aboard setting. *Samana* is a modern, well-found, romantic, beautiful, fast, and very seakindly vessel. Built in 1975 in The Netherlands, she has circumnavigated the globe and completed several noteworthy offshore passages.

Captain Larry Wheeler and Letty Wheeler are professional teachers with more than 25 years of classroom teaching experience and over 10 years of sail training experience. Based in Portland, Maine, courses span the Maine coast and reach the coastline of Nova Scotia. The curriculum is a rich blend of technical skills, confidence building, and common sense coupled with a spirit of adventure and romance.

The school offers courses in Advanced Ocean Sailing and Navigation, Celestial Navigation, and Offshore Passage Making. In each course, the trainees handle all offshore sailing operations. All instruction is delivered by mature, professional, Coast Guard-licensed teachers.

Flag:	USA
Rig:	Ketch
Homeport/waters:	Portland, Maine: Gulf of Maine to Nova Scotia (summer), Caribbean (winter)
Who sails?	Individuals of all ages
Cost:	$200 per person per day, $995 per person per five days
Program type:	Sail training for paying trainees. Ocean sailing, celestial navigation, offshore passage making.

Specifications:			
	Sparred length: 63'	Draft: 7'	Sail area: 1,500 sq. ft.
	LOD: 53'	Beam: 16'	Tons: 34 GRT
	LOA: 63'	Rig height: 85'	Power: Ford Lehman 135
	LWL: 45'	Freeboard: 4'	Hull: steel

Designer:	Van de Wiele
Built:	1975; The Netherlands
Crew:	3. Trainees: 6
Contact:	Captain Larry Wheeler
	School of Ocean Sailing
	PO Box 7359
	Portland, ME 04112
	Tel: 207-871-1315, 888-626-3557; Fax: 207-871-1315
	E-mail: svsamana@nlis.net
	Web site: http://www.sailingschool.com

The *SeaWulff* was originally conceived in 1974 by the faculty of The Evergreen State College as a sailing fishing vessel. Three years into its construction the vessel burned to the ground. Tremendous community support resulted in the project beginning anew. The design of the second vessel, launched in 1980, was revised to more fully meet the mission of the college. The fish hold was turned into laboratory space and sampling equipment was added. This gear enables the *SeaWulff* to provide all the teaching opportunities afforded by a sailing vessel and to be used as a platform for marine research and education.

The *SeaWulff* and her companion vessel *Resolute* are fundamental to a full range of academic programs at Evergreen. Previous classes have included Wooden Boat Design, Building, and Repair, Marine Biology and Fieldwork Methods, Native American Culture Studies, Pacific Northwest History, and Maritime Literature. Regardless of the focus of the class, students are always involved in all aspects of outfitting, operating, maintaining, and living aboard the college's sailing vessels.

Academic programs using the *SeaWulff* and *Resolute* change from year to year and are available to Evergreen State College students only. Student and community volunteers help maintain the vessels in exchange for sailing opportunities.

Flag:	USA
Rig:	Sloop
Homeport/waters:	Olympia, Washington: Puget Sound and inland waters of British Columbia
Who sails?	Evergreen State College students. Outside charters considered on a case by case basis.
Cost:	$225 group rate per day
Program type:	Sail training for volunteer trainees. Fully accredited sea education in marine science, maritime history, ecology, and maritime studies.

Specifications:	Sparred length: 39'	Draft: 6'	Sail area: 800 sq. ft.
	LOD: 36'	Beam: 12'	Tons: 12.5 GRT
	LOA: 36'	Rig height: 56'	Power: diesel
	LWL: 31'	Freeboard: 4'	Hull: wood

Designer:	Robert Perry and The Evergreen State College
Built:	1980; Olympia Washington, The Evergreen State College
Coast Guard certification:	Passenger Vessel (Subchapter T)
Crew:	2. Trainees: 10 (day sails), 4 (overnight)
Contact:	Greg Buikema, Marine Operations Manager
	The Evergreen State College
	2700 Evergreen Parkway NW
	Olympia, WA 98505
	Tel: 360-866-6000; Fax: 360-867-5430
	E-mail: buikemag@evergreen.edu
	Web site: http://www.evergreen.edu

The *Serenity* is a two-masted, gaff rigged schooner designed by Tom Colvin and built by Custom Steel Boats in 1986. The Low Sea Company purchased her in the spring of 2000 and brought her to Cape Charles, on Virginia's Eastern Shore. *Serenity* is USCG certified to carry 34 passengers.

The Low Sea Company offers day sails and group charters designed to foster an understanding and appreciation of the maritime history and ecology of the Chesapeake Bay. She also offers birding trips every October, in conjunction with the Eastern Shore Birding Festival. Aboard the *Serenity,* a customized educational program, catering to groups of all ages interested in sail training, maritime history, the history of the Chesapeake seafood industry, and the ecology of the Chesapeake Bay, is available.

Serenity sails out of historic Cape Charles harbor, located on the Eastern Shore of Virginia, 10 miles from the mouth of the Chesapeake Bay.

Flag:	USA
Rig:	Gaff Schooner, 2-masted
Homeport/waters:	Cape Charles, Virginia; Chesapeake Bay
Who sails:	Individuals and groups of all ages
Season:	April to November
Cost:	$1000 - $2000 per day for group charters, $30 per person for day sails
Program type:	Sail training for crew and apprentices. Sunset sails and eco-tour charters for groups and individuals of all ages.

Specifications:	Sparred length: 63'	Draft: 5'6"	Sail area: 1,544 sq. ft.
	LOD: 50'	Beam: 14'	Tons: 26 GRT
	LOA: 63'	Rig Height: 55'	Power: 66 hp Yanmar
	LWL: 40'	Freeboard: 4'	Diesel
	Hull: steel		

Designer:	Tom Colvin
Built:	1986; Arapaho, North Carolina, Custom Steel Boats
Coast Guard certification:	Passenger Vessel (Subchapter T)
Crew:	3. Trainees/passengers: 34
Contact:	Laura and Greg Lohse, Owners
	Low Sea Company
	505 Monroe Avenue
	Cape Charles, VA 23310
	Tel: 757-331-4361 or 757-710-1233
	E-mail: lowsea@msn.com
	Web site: www.schoonerserenity.com

Shearwater

Join us aboard *Shearwater* for the experience of a lifetime. This stunning vessel impeccably maintained and in pristine condition, offers the opportunity for you and your clients, guests or friends to enjoy pure luxury and elegance. She is USCG certified to carry 49 passengers. We specialize in corporate and private charters, from 2 to 7 hours, sailing out of New York and Long Island Sound including Stamford. *Shearwater* spends the winters in the Caribbean offering week-long charters in the U.S. Virgin Islands and the British Virgin Islands. Corporate entertainment for either your clients or staff can take the form of fine dining, buffet style lunch or dinner sails, cocktail sunset sails, staff team building day sails or just fun days in the sun. Other specialties include wedding, anniversary and birthday parties or friend and family reunions.

Whether that special occasion you are planning is business or pleasure, *Shearwater* will create a positive, elegant atmosphere that only a 1920s era yacht can deliver. As she heels over and puts her shoulder into the breeze and the wake fans out astern, you will cherish the moment and remember it forever.

Flag:	USA
Rig:	Schooner
Homeport/waters:	New York, New York: New England
Who sails?	Individuals and groups of all ages
Season:	Year-round
Program type:	Sail training for paying trainees, passenger day sails, corporate teambuilding, group charters, dockside interpretation while in port.

Specifications:			
	Sparred length: 82'	LOA: 67' 6"	LWL: 48"
	Draft: 10"	Beam: 16' 6"	Rig height: 70'
	Freeboard: 3'	Tons: 36 GRT	Power: diesel

Designer:	Theodore Wells
Built:	1929; East Boothbay, Maine
Coast Guard certification:	Passenger Vessel (Subchapter T)
Crew:	Trainees/passengers: 39 (day sails), 12 (overnight)
Contact:	Tom Berton, President
	Shearwater Holdings, Ltd.
	333 Pearl Street, Suite 19M
	New York, NY 10030
	Tel: 212-619-0885
	E-mail: manager@shearwater.com
	Web site: http://www.sail-shearwater.com

While the *Shenandoah* is not a replica, the vessel's design bears a strong resemblance to that of the US Revenue Cutter *Joe Lane* of 1851. For her first 25 years, the rakish square topsail schooner was painted white, but she now wears the black and white checkerboard paint scheme of the 19th century Revenue Service. She is the only non-auxiliary power square rigged vessel operating under the American Flag. Her hull form and rig, anchors, and all materials of construction adhere closely to mid-19th century practice.

Every summer *Shenandoah* plies the waters of southern New England visiting the haunts of pirates and the homeports of whaling ships. *Shenandoah* runs 6-day sailing trips for kids ages 9-14 from late June through August, and day sails in early September. She is also available for private charter.

Flag:	USA
Rig:	Square topsail schooner, two-masted
Homeport/waters:	Vineyard Haven, Massachusetts: Southern New England
Who sails?	School groups from elementary through college and individuals of all ages.
Season:	June to September
Cost:	Students: $650 per person per week, Adults: $750 per person per week (Sunday night through Saturday noon)
Program type:	Sail training for paying trainees ages 9-14. Private charters and day sails are also available.

Specifications:		
Sparred length: 152'	Draft: 11'	Sail area: 7,000 sq. ft.
LOA: 108'	Beam: 23'	Tons: 85 GRT
LWL: 101'	Rig height: 94'	Freeboard: 3' (amidships)

Coast Guard certification:	Passenger Vessel (Subchapter T)
Crew:	9. Trainees: 35 (day sails), 30 (overnight)
Contact:	Captain Robert S. Douglas
	Coastwise Packet Co., Inc.
	PO Box 429
	Vineyard Haven, MA 02568
	Tel: 508-693-1699; Fax: 508-693-1881
	Web site: http://www.coastwisepacket.com

Sigsbee

The skipjack *Sigsbee* was built in 1901 in Deale Island, Maryland and worked as an oyster dredge boat until the early 1990s. She was named after Charles D. Sigsbee, who was the Commanding Officer of the battleship *Maine*. The vessel was rebuilt by the Living Classrooms Foundation in 1994, and now sails Chesapeake Bay with students on board. While sailing on board the *Sigsbee*, students learn the history of skipjacks and the oyster industry, marine and nautical science, and gain an appreciation of Chesapeake Bay and the hard work of the watermen of a bygone era.

Flag:	USA
Rig:	Sloop
Homeport/waters:	Baltimore, Maryland: Chesapeake Bay and the Delaware River
Who sails?	Students and other organized groups, individuals, and families.
Season:	March through September
Program type:	Sail training with paying trainees. Sea education in marine and nautical science, maritime history, and ecology for school groups from elementary through college.

Specifications:

Sparred length: 76'	Draft: 3' 5"	Sail area: 1,767 sq. ft.
LOD: 50'	Beam: 16'	Tons: 14 GRT
Rig height: 68'	Freeboard: 2' 5"	Power: 150 HP diesel

Built: 1901; Deale Island, Maryland

Coast Guard
  certification: Passenger Vessel (Subchapter T)

Crew: 4. Trainees: 30 (day sails), 15 (overnight). Age: 13+. Dockside visitors: 30

Contact: Christine Truett, Director of Education
Living Classrooms Foundation
802 South Caroline Street
Baltimore, MD 21231-3311
Tel: 410-685-0295; Fax: 410-752-8433
Web site: http://www.livingclassrooms.org

Silva was built at Karlstads Mekaniska Verksta, Sweden as a three-mast steel schooner. During the first 2 decades of her life, she was used in the Scandinavian fishing industry, with regular trips to Iceland. In the 1960's, *Silva* was refitted as a bulk freighter, having her sailing rig removed. *Silva* continued coastal trading until 1994 and remained in Sweden until the summer of 2001 when Canadian Sailing Expeditions bought her and delivered her, for the first time, to North America.

This will be *Silva's* first year offering sailing tours of Halifax Harbour. She will be running educational programs for students, day trade for general public, and private and corporate charters. Canadian Sailing Expeditions is dedicated to providing opportunities for people of all ages to experience and explore our seacoast the traditional way.

Flag:	Canada
Rig:	3-masted schooner
Homeport/waters:	Halifax, Nova Scotia, Canada: Halifax Harbour, Nova Scotia Coast
Who sails?	Groups and individuals of all ages
Season:	April through October
Program type:	Sail training for paying trainees, passenger day sails, private charters

Specifications:	Sparred length: 130'	LOA: 115'	Draft: 9'
	Beam: 24'	Rig height: 75'	Freeboard: 4'
	Tons: 199 GRT	Power: 350 cummins	

Built:	1939; Verksta, Sweden, Karlstads Mekani
Certification:	Transport Canada
Trainees/ Passengers:	150 (daysails)
Contact:	Captain Doug Prothero, Owner/operator
	Canadian Sailing Expeditions
	PO Box 2613
	Halifax, NS B3J 3N5 Canada
	Tel: 902-429-1474; Fax: 902-429-1475
	E-mail: doug@canadiansailingexpeditions.com
	Web site:http://www.canadiansailingexpeditions.com

Soren Larsen

his family in the late 1970s, she initially starred in a number of films which helped to raise funds to fit her out to the high standards required by the British Maritime Coastguard Agency (MCA).

In 1982 the Davies realized their dream of taking people of all ages to sea under a three-year charter with the British Jubilee Sailing Trust, pioneering sailing for the disabled. In 1986 Soren Larsen embarked on a circumnavigation, rounding Cape Horn in 1991 and visiting New York and Boston for the Columbus Regatta.

In 1993 *Soren Larsen* sailed on a second world voyage to New Zealand via the Panama Canal. In 1999 she cruised the Pacific islands and was in New Zealand for millennial celebrations and the America's Cup races. In April 2000, *Soren Larsen* departed for Europe via the Pacific, Panama Canal, Caribbean, US, and Canada, participating in Tall Ships 2000® and OpSail 2000 events.

Soren Larsen is one of the last wooden sailing ships built in Denmark. Restored by Captain Tony Davies and

Flag:	United Kingdom
Rig:	Brigantine
Homeport/waters:	Auckland, New Zealand: New Zealand coastal waters (summer), southwest Pacific islands (winter)
Who sails?	Families and individuals of all ages.
Cost:	$100 per person per day for overnight voyages.
Program type:	Sail training for paying trainees. Sea education in marine science, maritime history, and ecology as informal, in-house programming.

Specifications:			
	Sparred length: 140'	Draft: 11'	Sail area: 6,500 sq. ft.
	LOD: 98'	Beam: 25' 6"	Tons: 125 GRT
	LOA: 105' 6"	Rig height: 100'	Power: 240 HP diesel
	LWL: 90'	Freeboard: 3' 7"	Hull: wood

Designer:	Soren Larsen
Built:	1949; Denmark, Soren Larsen and Sons
Certification:	UK Maritime and CG Agency Loadline; Bureau Veritas Class Certificate.
Crew:	12. Trainees: 80 (day sails), 22 (overnight)
Contact:	Tallship *Soren Larsen*
	Squaresail Pacific, Ltd.
	PO Box 310, Kumeu
	Auckland, New Zealand
	Tel: +649-411-8755; Fax: +649-411-8484
	E-mail: escape@sorenlarsen.co.nz
	Web site: http://www.sorenlarsen.co.nz

SoundWaters, Inc. is a non-profit education organization dedicated to protecting Long Island Sound and its watershed through education. Annually *SoundWaters* offers shipboard and land-based programs to 25,000 children and adults from Connecticut and New York. The schooner *SoundWaters* is the platform for a variety of programs including:

- **The Floating Classroom** A three-hour marine science and sail training experience for schools, camps, and other groups.
- **SoundCamp** Summer--five days with overnights for children 10-14 years old.
- **Journeys** A five-day leadership and teambuilding workshop. Students take over operation of the vessel and are encouraged to challenge themselves as leaders.
- **Charters, Public Sails, and Sunset Sails** Opportunities for the public to experience the Sound firsthand.

Instruction includes seamanship, navigation, helmsmanship, and field exploration of marine ecosystems.

SoundWaters crew includes environmental educators, biologists, naturalists, and a licensed captain.

In addition, SoundWaters, Inc. operates the SoundWaters Community Center for Environmental Education, featuring educational exhibits and displays, classroom and community meeting space, a wet lab, and cutting-edge "green" construction. The organization also conducts many free outreach programs, which are offered through public schools and community centers.

SoundWaters

Flag:	USA
Rig:	Gaff schooner, three-masted
Homeport/waters:	Stamford, Connecticut: Long Island Sound
Who sails?	School groups from elementary through college, individuals and families.
Season:	April to November
Cost:	$25 per person per two-hour sail, $700-$2,000 group rate for three-hour sail
Program type:	Sea education in marine science and ecology in cooperation with accredited institutions and other groups, and as informal, in-house programming.
Specifications:	Sparred length: 80' Draft: 3' (centerboards up), 8' (centerboards down)
	Sail area: 1,510 sq. ft. LOD: 65' Beam: 14'
	Tons: 32 GRT Rig height: 60' Hull: steel
	Power: diesel Freeboard: 3' 6"
Designer:	William Ward
Built:	1986; Norfolk, Virginia, Marine Metals, Inc.
Coast Guard certification:	Passenger Vessel (Subchapter T)
Crew:	3, 5 instructors. Trainees: 42 (day sails), 15-20 (overnight)
Contact:	Captain Jonathan Boulware, Director of Marine Education

SoundWaters, Inc.
Cove Island Park, 1281 Cove Road
Stamford, CT 06902
Tel: 203-323-1978; Fax: 203-967-8306
E-mail: connect@soundwaters.org
Web site: http://www.soundwaters.org

Spanish Rake

The *Spanish Rake* (formerly *Marguerite*) was constructed in 1932 by George H. Chaney who, at the time, was a well known saw mill manager in Coquille, Oregon. He was assisted by Herb Ellington of Gold Beach, Oregon. The vessel was built along the lines of a traditional Norwegian coastal sailing cargo vessel. The *Spanish Rake* is a traditionally constructed (plank on frame) bluewater gaff ketch sailing vessel. We are currently working on her inspected vessel statis.

Flag:	USA
Rig:	Gaff ketch
Homeport/waters:	Marina del Rey, California: California Coast
Who sails?	Individuals and groups of all ages.
Specifications:	Sparred length: 82' LOD: 61' LOA: 63'
	LWL: 52' 8" Draft: 8' 6" Beam: 14' 7"
	Tons: 28 GRT Power: 185 HP single diesel
Built:	1932; Coquille, Oregon, George H. Chaney
Contact:	Carrie Baer, Charter Manager
	5015 Pacific Avenue
	Marina del Rey, CA 90292
	Tel: 310-827-4105; Fax: 310-827-0381
	E-mail: charterconnection@filmboats.com
	Web site: http://www.filmboats.com

Spirit of Dana Point

A young colony in a new land dreamed of independence and built some of the fastest and best sailing ships in the world. These ships were the result of ingenuity, independence and a strong desire to accomplish something. It was Dennis Holland's life dream to build an accurate replica from the period when America fought for independence and world recognition. Armed with talent, determination, little money and plans he purchased from the Smithsonian Institute, he laid the keel in his yard on May 2, 1970. Thirteen years later this fast privateer was launched and his vision became reality.

Today at the Ocean Institute this dream continues as young students step aboard and back in time. During their voyages students re-live the challenges and discoveries of early ocean exploration. Through a series of national award winning living history programs, the *Spirit of Dana Point* serves as an excellent platform for our youth to directly experience life at sea, as it has been for hundreds of years. She sails throughout Southern California for more than 150 days a year.

Flag:	USA
Rig:	Schooner
Homeport/waters:	Dana Point, California; Southern California
Who sails?	School groups from elementary school through college, adult education groups, and individuals and families of all ages.
Season:	Year-round
Program type:	Sail training for volunteer crew or trainees. Sea education in marine science, maritime history, and ecology based on informal in-house programming and in cooperation with other organizations. Day sails and overnight passages. Affiliated institutions include the Ocean Institute, other school education programs, and museums.

Specifications:

Sparred length: 118'	LOD: 86'	LWL: 79'
Draft: 10'	Beam: 24'	Rig height: 100'
Freeboard: 6'	Sail area: 5,000 sq. ft.	Tons: 64 GRT
Power: HP diesel	Hull: wood	Designer: Howard Chapelle

Built:	1983; Costa Mesa, California, Dennis Holland
Coast Guard certification:	Passenger Vessel (Subchapter T)
Crew:	7. Trainees/passengers: 75 (day sails), 30 (overnight)
Contact:	Adam Himelson, Program Director
	Ocean Institute
	24200 Dana Point Harbor Drive
	Dana Point, CA 92612
	Tel: 949-496-2274; Fax: 949-496-4715
	E-mail: ahimelson@ocean-institute.org
	Web site: http://www.ocean-institute.org

Spirit of Massachusetts

The schooner *Spirit of Massachusetts* is owned by the Ocean Classroom Foundation. She sails on sea education programs ranging from 4 month semesters-at-sea to weeklong programs with schools and youth groups. All programs use the power of the sea and the challenge of traditional seafaring as the basis for the academic curriculum taught on board.

Ocean Classroom, a fully accredited high school semester-at-sea, is a true voyage of discovery for qualified sophomores, juniors and seniors. Young people come from all over the US to join this outstanding learning adventure. The voyage covers more than 4,000 nautical miles, connecting South American shores to the Canadian Maritimes. Students live and work as sailors while they study maritime history, maritime literature, marine science, applied mathematics, and navigation. Ocean Classroom is offered fall, spring, and summer terms.

Some other programs include SEAmester (a complete semester-at-sea for college credit), Marine Awareness Research Expeditions (also for college credit), and Summer Seafaring Camp (for teens age 13-17). The Ocean Classroom Foundation also owns and operates the schooner *Harvey Gamage*.

Flag:	USA
Rig:	Gaff topsail schooner, two-masted
Homeport/waters:	Boston, Massachusetts; Eastern US and Canada (summer), Caribbean and South America (winter)
Who sails?	School groups from middle school through college. Affiliated institutions include Proctor Academy, Long Island University, Franklin Pierce College and other schools.
Season:	Year-round
Program type:	Sail training with paying trainees/students. Fully accredited sea education in marine science, maritime history, maritime literature, marine applied mathematics, and navigation.

Specifications:

Sparred length: 125'	Draft: 10' 6"	Sail area: 7,000 sq. ft.
LOD: 100'	Beam: 24'	Tons: 90 GRT
LOA: 103'	Rig height: 103'	Power: 235 HP diesel
LWL: 80'	Freeboard: 7'	Hull: wood

Designer:	Melbourne Smith and Andrew Davis
Built:	1984; Boston, Massachusetts, New England Historic Seaport
Coast Guard certification:	Sailing School Vessel (Subchapter R), Passenger Vessel (Subchapter T)
Crew:	7 – 11 including instructors. Students/trainees: 22 (overnight)
Contact:	Bert Rogers, Director
	Ocean Classroom Foundation, Inc.
	PO Box 446
	Cornwall, NY 12518
	Tel: 800-724-7245, 845-615-1412; Fax: 845-615-1414
	E-mail: mail@oceanclassroom.org
	Web site: http://www.oceanclassroom.org

St. Christopher

The *St. Christopher* is a classic 3-masted schooner built (1932) just as the age of sail came to a close. Built in Delfzijl, Netherlands under the Germanischer Lloyd Certification, she is designed to operate in the roughest sea conditions in the world, the North Sea.

She has unfortunately been allowed to slide into very poor condition. Blown 4-1/2 miles from her mooring by Hurricane Georges into an estuary (saltmarsh), St. Christopher Services, LLC has acquired her and recovery is underway. Through volunteers and donations, we will rebuild and upgrade her to full U.S. Coast Guard passenger carrying certification. We have a strong shipbuilding community here on the Gulf Coast, the best in the world. Individuals and companies are stepping forward with their contributions toward the restoration. Our purpose is a service of Christian love and evangelism, to provide for medical missions, storm recovery, etc. We are not sponsored by any particular church organization, but relying on God's provisions and our volunteers.

What could be more fun than to be able to experience this piece of sailing history and to participate in a gift of Christian love with your own hands. Indications are that our schedule will be full, and *St. Christopher* will be well maintained and active far into this century.

Flag:	USA
Rig:	Schooner
Homeport/waters:	Mobile, Alabama; US and Caribbean
Season:	Summer
Who sails?	Groups and individuals of all ages.
Program type:	Christian missionary work/mercy ship

Specifications:

Sparred length: 149'	LOD: 118'	LOA: 121'
LWL: 108'	Draft: 6'6"	Power: Two GM 671
Tons: 149 GRT	Rig height: 118'	diesel
Freeboard: 4'	Beam: 19'	Hull: riveted steel
Hull color: white and blue	Spar material: wood	

Built:	1932; Delfzijl, Netherlands, Niestern Delfzijl
Coast Guard certification:	Mercy Ship
Crew:	5
Contact:	Mr. Bryan Leveritt, Chief Steward
	St. Christopher Services, LLC
	9275 Old Highway 43 South
	Creola, AL 36525
	Tel: 334-442-3247; Fax: 334-824-7768
	E-mail: bryan@stchristopherservices.org.
	Web site: http://www.stchristopherservices.org

work provided by sail training are especially applicable to teenagers. With 42 years of operation, Brigantine, Inc. is one of the pioneering sail training programs in North America.

Cruises in this hands-on program range from six to ten days or more in length. *St. Lawrence II's* crew complement of 28 comprises 18 new trainees, plus a crew of watch officers, petty officers, cook, and bosun, all aged 13 to 18. The captain is usually the only adult onboard.

The *St. Lawrence II* is a purpose-built sail training vessel in operation since 1957, primarily on the Great Lakes. She was designed to be manageable by a young crew, yet complex enough with her brigantine rig to introduce teenagers to the challenge of square-rig sailing.

The ship is owned and operated by Brigantine, Inc., a nonprofit charity staffed by local volunteers who share the conviction that the lessons of responsibility, self-reliance, and team-

The ship's teenage officers are graduates of Brigantine, Inc.'s winter training program, involving lessons in seamanship, navigation, and ship's systems, as well as the ongoing maintenance of the ship. Every year the *St. Lawrence II* sails over 4,000 miles, spends more than 40 nights at sea, and introduces over 300 trainees to the rigors of life aboard ship on the Great Lakes.

Flag:	Canada
Rig:	Brigantine
Homeport/waters:	Kingston, Ontario, Canada: Lake Ontario and adjacent waters
Who sails?	School groups and individuals of all ages
Season:	April to November (sailing); October to March (winter program)
Cost:	$75 (US) per person per day. Scholarships available.
Program type:	Sail training with paying trainees.

Specifications:			
	Sparred length: 72'	Draft: 8' 6"	Sail area: 2,560 sq. ft.
	LOD: 57'	Beam: 15'	Tons: 34 GRT
	LOA: 60'	Rig height: 54'	Power: 165 HP diesel
	LWL: 46'	Freeboard: 4' 6"	Hull: steel

Designer:	Francis McLachlan/Michael Eames
Built:	1953; Kingston, Ontario, Canada, Kingston Shipyards
Crew:	10. Trainees: 36 (day sails), 18 (overnight)
Contact:	Carol Jeffrey, General Manager
	Brigantine, Inc.
	53 Yonge Street
	Kingston, Ontario K7M 6G4, CANADA
	Tel: 613-544-5175; Fax: 613-544-5175
	E-mail: briginc@kos.net
	Web site: http://www.brigantine.ca

The Clipper *Stad Amsterdam* is absolutely unique: a modern 'extreme' clipper built on historic lines. The final design for the *Stad Amsterdam* combines the best characteristics of historic clippers with state of the art technology and the level of comfort expected in this day and age.

Construction of the Clipper started in December 1997, in Amsterdam, The Netherlands. During the construction period she served as a training opportunity for unemployed youngsters to gain valuable working experience. The Clipper is designed to fulfill the requirements of luxury charters, day trips, harbor receptions, conferences and seminars.

Owned by the city of Amsterdam and Randstad Group, the world's third largest employment agency, the Clipper provides opportunities for young people to gain work experience, while working alongside a professional crew. The ship takes part in STA-races, giving up to 60 youngsters the chance to experience sailing on a tall ship. *Stad Amsterdam* won the second leg of the Cutty Sark Tall Ship's Races 2001.

The Clipper *Stad Amsterdam* can be found in European waters in summer. In winter the ship sails the Caribbean with the possibility to visit the East Coast of the US or Canada.

Stad Amsterdam is part of the Nicholson fleet. For charter information please look on www.nicholsonyachts.com or contact newport@nicholsonyachts.com.

Flag:	The Netherlands
Rig:	Full rigged ship, 3-masted
Homeport / waters:	Amsterdam, The Netherlands
Who sails?	Groups and individuals of all ages
Program type:	Charters (coastal and passage), public relations activities, STA Races, sail training, harbor parties, seminars, meetings
Specifications:	Sparred length: 250' LOD: 199' Beam: 34'5"
	Rig height: 152' Sail area: 23,700 sq.ft. Tons: 723 GT
	Power: Caterpillar 1000 HP, diesel Hull: welded steel
Designer:	Gerard Dijkstra, Naval Architects and Marine Engineers, NBJA, Amsterdam
Built:	Damen Oranjewerf, Amsterdam
Certification:	Sailing Passenger Vessel
Crew:	25. Trainees / passengers: 120 (day trips), 32-64 (cruises)
Contact:	Cees Rosman, Hospitality Manager RCSA
	Rederij Clipper Stad Amsterdam
	P.O. Box 12600
	1100 AP Amsterdam
	The Netherlands
	Tel: +31 (0)20 569 5839; Fax: +31 (0)20 569 1720
	E-mail: mail@stadamsterdam.nl
	Web site: http://www.stadamsterdam.nl

The oldest active square-rigger in the world, *Star of India* has been around the globe 21 times and has never had an engine. Built as the full-rigged ship *Euterpe,* this former merchant ship has survived countless perils of the sea to survive as a fully restored square-rigger and National Historic Landmark. She embodies the term "tall ship" both in looks and spirit.

Star of India is the flagship of the San Diego Maritime Museum fleet. She sails on an annual basis. *Star* is host to thousands of schoolchildren each year, many of whom participate in overnight living history programs on board. *Star's* decks are also used for highly acclaimed cultural events from theatrical performances of *Two Years Before the Mast* and sea chantey festivals, to Gilbert & Sullivan comic operas and "Movies Before the Mast." Volunteer sail handling is held every other Sunday, with the best sailors being selected to sail the tall ship when she goes to sea.

Flag:	USA
Rig:	Barque, three-masted
Homeport/waters:	San Diego, California: Coastal waters between San Diego, California, and northern Baja California, Mexico
Who sails?	Selected volunteers, permanent crew, and invited passengers.
Program type:	Sail training for crew and apprentices. Sea education in maritime history based on informal, in-house programming. Dockside interpretation.

Specifications:			
	Sparred length: 278'	Draft: 21' 6"	Sail area: 18,000 sq. ft.
	LOD: 210'	Beam: 35'	Tons: 1,197 GRT
	LWL: 200'	Freeboard: 15'	Hull: iron
	Rig height: 140'		

Designer:	Edward Arnold
Built:	1863; Ramsey, Isle of Man, United Kingdom, Gibson, McDonald & Arnold
Coast Guard certification:	Museum Attraction Vessel
Trainees:	50. Dockside visitors: 300
Contact:	Erninia Taranto, Office Manager
	San Diego Maritime Museum
	1492 North Harbor Drive
	San Diego, CA 92101
	Tel: 619-234-9153; Fax: 619-234-8345
	E-mail: info@sdmaritime.org
	Web site: http://www.sdmaritime.org

The Schooner Sultana Project is a non-profit, 501(c)(3) organization based in the historic port of Chestertown, Maryland. The Sultana Project provides unique, hands-on educational opportunities for children and adults that focus on the history and natural environment of the Chesapeake Bay and its watershed. The principal classroom for the Sultana Project is a full-sized reproduction of the 1767 schooner *Sultana* launched in March of 2001.

Built as a cargo schooner in Boston, the original *Sultana* was purchased by the Royal Navy and used to enforce the notorious "Tea Taxes" on the Chesapeake, Delaware, and Narragansett Bays. *Sultana* is notable as one of the most thoroughly documented vessels from the time of the American Revolution. The schooner's original logbooks, crew lists, correspondence, and design drawings have all survived intact to the present day. Together these documents tell a vivid story of life along the coast of Revolutionary America - a story that has been incorporated into the schooner's educational programs.

Sultana's educational programs are designed to compliment and support national, state and local curriculum goals - but just as importantly, they are meant to excite students about the process of learning. Again and again teachers have found that a day on *Sultana* can help to bring subjects like history, science, math and reading alive.

Rig:	Square topsail schooner, two-masted
Homeport/waters:	Chestertown, Maryland: Chesapeake Bay & Mid-Atlantic.
Who sails?	School & adult groups as well as individuals of all ages.
Season:	April to November
Program type:	Under-sail educational experiences in environmental science and history, including both day trips and live-aboard programming.

Specifications:			
	Sparred length: 97'	LOD: 53'	LWL: 53'
	Draft: 8'	Beam: 17'	Rig height: 72'
	Freeboard: 5'	Tons: 50 GRT	Power: single screw diesel
	Hull: wood		

Designer:	Benford Design Group, St. Michael's, Maryland
Built:	2001; Millington, Maryland, Swain Boatbuilders, LLC
Coast Guard certification:	Passenger Vessel (Subchapter T)
Crew:	5. Students: 32 (day sails), 11 (overnight)
Contact:	Drew McMullen, Executive Director
	Sultana Projects Inc.
	P.O. Box 524
	Chestertown, MD 21620
	Tel: 410-778-5954; Fax: 410-778-4531
	E-mail: dmcmullen@schoonersultana.com
	Web site: http:// www.schoonersultana.com

Susan Constant

Susan Constant is a full-scale re-creation of the flagship of a small fleet that brought America's first permanent English colonists to Virginia in 1607. Together with the smaller *Godspeed* and *Discovery*, *Susan Constant* is on exhibit at Jamestown Settlement, a living history museum of 17th-century Virginia, and hosts nearly a half-million visitors every year. Jamestown Settlement is administered by the Jamestown-Yorktown Foundation, an agency of the Commonwealth of Virginia.

Built on the museum grounds and commissioned in 1991, *Susan* *Constant* replaced a vessel built for the 1957 Jamestown Festival commemorating the 350th anniversary of the colony's founding. While no plans or renderings of the original *Susan Constant, Godspeed,* and *Discovery* have ever been located, the replicas are based on the documented tonnages of the 17th-century ships, and *Susan Constant's* design incorporates research information that emerged after the first replicas were built.

With a crew of staff and volunteers, *Susan Constant* and *Godspeed* periodically sail to other ports in the Chesapeake Bay region to participate in commemorative and community events and host educational programs. A volunteer sail training program is offered to individuals of all ages. Participants are trained in sailing a 17th-century merchant vessel, including handling square sails, marlinespike seamanship, navigation, safety procedures, watch standing, and maritime history.

Flag:	USA
Rig:	Barque, three-masted (lateen mizzen)
Homeport/waters:	Jamestown Settlement, Virginia: Chesapeake Bay
Who sails?	Crew consisting of Jamestown Settlement staff and volunteers.
Program type:	Sail training for crew and apprentices. Dockside interpretation.

Specifications:			
	Sparred length: 116'	Draft: 11' 6"	Sail area: 3,902 sq. ft.
	LOD: 83'	Beam: 24' 10'	Tons: 180 GRT
	LOA: 96'	Rig height: 95'	Power: twin diesels
	LWL: 77'	Freeboard: 11'	Hull: wood

Designer:	Stanley Potter
Built:	1991; Jamestown Settlement, Virginia, Allen C. Rawl
Crew:	25
Contact:	Eric Speth, Maritime Program Manager
	Jamestown Settlement
	PO Box 1607
	Williamsburg, VA 23187
	Tel: 757-229-1607; Fax: 757-253-7350
	Web site: http://www.historyisfun.org

The *Swan fan Makkum,* the largest brigantine in the world, was constructed in 1993, inspired by her 19th century predecessors. Present-day standards of safety and comfort are incorporated in a classical design that carries on the tradition of a ship type which made history in the previous century.

With her stylish and representative interior, the *Swan* offers countless possibilities. A day trip (as an incentive, for a presentation, a party or a reception, etc.) can be made for groups of up to 120 persons. For multiple day trips or cruises (individual or group travel), the *Swan* has 17 two-berth cabins, each with its own private bathroom.

As proud as her 19th century predecessors, the *Swan fan Makkum* sails the seven seas. During the summer in Europe, her sailing area extends from the Mediterranean Sea to Scandinavian waters. She calls in at events such as the Kieler Woche, Sail Amsterdam, Cannes Film Festival, the Rally of Monte Carlo and the starts of the Fastnet and Whitbread races. The *Swan* herself takes part in the Cutty Sark Tall Ships Races, where she has built up a formidable reputation. She sets out for sunnier waters in the wintertime and visits such Caribbean destinations as the Grenadines and Virgin Islands as well as the Seychelles in the Indian Ocean.

Everyone who climbs aboard the *Swan* desires to simply push off at once. The towering masts and endless rope only need a pair of enthusiastic human hands and…wind, lots of wind. And the *Swan fan Makkum* is only in her element once the wind finds her sails and she cleaves the waves heeling over to starboard or port side.

Flag:	The Netherlands
Rig:	Brigantine
Homeport/waters:	Makkum, The Netherlands; world wide
Who sails?	Groups and individuals of all ages.
Program type:	Luxury cruises (coastal and passage), sail training for paying trainees, corporate team building, private charters.
Season:	Year round

Specifications:		
Sparred length: 196'	LOD: 150'	LOA: 164'
LWL: 128'	Draft: 12'	Beam: 30'
Rig height: 145'	Freeboard: 5'	Tons: 404 GRT
Sail area: 14,500 sq. ft.	Hull: steel	Hull color: black
Power:	Caterpillar 470 HP	Spar material: steel/wood

Designer:	Oliver van Mear
Built:	1993; Gdansk, Poland
Certification:	Passenger Vessel, Ocean
Crew:	10. Trainees/passengers: 120 (day sails), 36 (ovenight)
Contact:	Willem Sligting, Captain/Owner
	Swan fan Makkum
	Achterdijkje 8
	NL 8754 EP Makkum
	The Netherlands
	Tel: +31 (0) 515 231712; Fax: +31 (0) 515 232998
	E-mail: swanfan@wxs.nl Web site: http://www.swanfanmakkum.nl

Topsail is the basic outreach program, with participants recommended by people who work with youth, including educators, youth leaders, and clergy. Cost is on an ability-to-pay basis. The program begins with a five-day series of day sails followed by a five-day voyage planned and organized by the participants. Participants are encouraged to continue as active members of the "*Swift* Family."

The Los Angeles Maritime Institute (LAMI), the educational affiliate of the Los Angeles Maritime Museum, operates the square topsail schooner *Swift of Ipswich* and the gaff topsail schooner *Bill of Rights.* LAMI staff use the ship to teach trainees how to sail and how to develop personal and "human skills" such as communication, cooperation, teamwork, persistence, self-reliance, and leadership in three different programs.

Swift Expeditions are more advanced and challenging voyages with specific purposes, goals, and durations. Cooperative programs afford organizations such as youth, church, school, and community groups to voyage on *Swift of Ipswich.* The Los Angeles Maritime Museum and its affiliates take pleasure in offering assistance to visiting tall ships and other "educationally significant" vessels.

Flag:	USA
Rig:	Square topsail schooner, two-masted
Homeport/waters:	Los Angeles, California: Coastal California and offshore islands
Who sails?	Referred youth-at-risk and groups catering to students and adults.
Season:	Year-round
Program type:	Educational sailing adventures for "at-risk" youth and other youth or adult groups.

Specifications:			
	Sparred length: 90'	Draft: 10'	Sail area: 5,166 sq. ft.
	LOD: 66'	Beam: 18'	Tons: 46 GRT
	LOA: 70'	Rig height: 74'	Power: diesel
	LWL: 62'	Freeboard: 5'	Hull: wood

Designer:	Howard I. Chappelle
Built:	1938; Ipswich, Massachusetts, William A. Robinson
Coast Guard certification:	Passenger Vessel (Subchapter T)
Crew:	6. Trainees: 49 (day sails), 31 (overnight). Age: 12+
Contact:	Captain Jim Gladson
	Los Angeles Maritime Institute
	Berth 84, Foot of Sixth Street
	San Pedro, CA 90731
	Tel: 310-833-6055; Fax: 310-548-2055
	Web site: http://www.tollway.com/swift/

Tabor Boy has been engaged in sail training as a seagoing classroom for Tabor Academy students since 1954. Offshore voyaging and oceanographic studies go together in the curriculum, with cruises to destinations as distant as Mexico and Panama adding adventure to the experience. Many Tabor Academy graduates go on to the US Merchant Marine, Naval, or Coast Guard academies.

The schooner also offers seven summer orientation voyages for newly enrolled freshmen and sophomore students. During this time, trainees are fully involved in sail handling while studying Gulf of Maine marine wildlife and ecology. Winter programs feature sailing and snorkeling in the US and British Virgin Islands to observe and study coral reef ecosystems.

Flag:	USA
Rig:	Gaff schooner, two-masted
Homeport/waters:	Marion, Massachusetts: Coastal New England (summer), offshore Atlantic Ocean (school year)
Who sails?	Enrolled students at Tabor Academy.
Program type:	Seamanship and oceanography for high school students.

Specifications:

Sparred length: 115'	Draft: 10' 4"	Sail area: 3,540 sq. ft.
LOD: 84' 6"	Beam: 21' 8"	Tons: 99.9 GRT
LOA: 92' 10"	Rig height: 95'	Power: 295 HP diesel
LWL: 78' 8"	Hull: iron	

Built:	1914; Amsterdam, The Netherlands, Scheepswerven & Machinefabrik
Coast Guard certification:	Sailing School Vessel (Subchapter R)
Crew:	6. Trainees: 23. Age: 14-18
Contact:	Captain James F. Geil, Master
	Tabor Boy, Tabor Academy
	66 Spring Street
	Marion, MA 02738-1599
	Tel: 508-748-2000; Fax: 508-748-0353
	E-mail: jgeil@taboracademy.org
	Web site: http://www.taboracademy.org

The original warship *HMS Tecumseth* was built at Chippewa on Lake Erie to be a part of Britain's defense fleet during the War of 1812. *HMS Tecumseth* spent two years as a supply ship on Lake Erie before her eventual transfer to the Naval Establishment at Penetanguishene, Ontario.

The *Tecumseth* replica is patterned from the original British Admiralty plans; built to appear as close to the original as possible, she is equipped to meet today's safety standards.

Owned by the Province of Ontario, and operated by the staff and volunteers of the Marine Heritage Association, the *Tecumseth* takes visitors back to the days of Nelson's Navy and England's "wooden walls." During port visits the officers and crew dress in historic uniform and interpret and present the life of a 19th century vessel to the public. Sail training in the art of 1812 seamanship for the crew of *HMS Tecumseth* is an intrinsic part of the vessel's operation.

The schooner *Tecumseth* is proud of her role as an ambassador for the Province of Ontario as she visits Canadian and American ports throughout the Great Lakes.

Flag:	Canada
Rig:	Square topsail schooner, two-masted
Homeport/waters:	Discovery Harbour, Penetanguishene, Ontario, Canada: Georgian Bay, Lake Huron
Who sails?	Marine Heritage Association volunteers
Season:	June through September
Program type:	Sail training and attraction vessel. New programs currently being developed.

Specifications:

Sparred length: 125'	Draft: 8'	Sail area: 4,700 sq. ft.
LOD: 70'	Beam: 29'	Tons: 146 GRT
LOA: 80'	Rig height: 90'	Power: 360 HP diesel
LWL: 63'	Hull: steel	
Hull color: black	Spar material: wood	

Designer:	Bob Johnston
Built:	1992; St. Thomas, Ontario, Canada, Kanter Yachts
Crew:	20
Contact:	The Marine Heritage Association
	PO Box 353
	Midland, Ontario L4R 4L1 Canada
	Tel: 705-549-5575 or 866-MHA-5577; Fax: 705-549-5576
	E-mail: marineheritage@on.aibn.com
	Web site: http://www.marineheritage.ca

The 213-foot, three-masted barque *Tenacious* is the Jubilee Sailing Trust's (JST) new, second ship. She is the largest wooden tall ship of her kind to be built in Great Britain this century.

JST promotes the integration of able-bodied and disabled people though the mediums of tall ship sailing and building. Such has been the success of the JST's first ship, *Lord Nelson,* that that JST decided to build *Tenacious.*

Bringing the ethos of integration ashore, the JST has developed the concept of Shorewatch, weeklong shipbuilding holidays. Professional shipwrights and mixed-ability volunteers have worked side-by-side as part of this amazing project.

Like the *Lord Nelson, Tenacious* enables all members of her crew to sail together on equal terms. Features include signs in Braille, power-assisted hydraulic steering, and points throughout the ship that enable wheelchairs to be secured during rough weather.

Voyages are open to anyone between 16 – 70+ and no previous expe-

rience is required. The crew of 40 is split 50/50 between able-bodied and physically disabled people, with eight wheelchair users. There is a permanent crew of 10, including a medical purser and cook.

Flag:	United Kingdom
Rig:	Barque, three-masted
Homeport/waters:	Southampton, United Kingdom: Northern Europe (summer), Canary Islands and Southern Europe (winter)
Who sails?	Physically disabled and able-bodied people, aged 16 to 70+.
Season:	Year-round
Cost:	$135 per person per day
Program type:	Sail training for paying trainees. Integration of physically disabled and able-bodied people through the medium of tall ship sailing.

Specifications:			
	Sparred length: 213' 3"	Draft: 14' 9"	Sail area: 12,956 sq. ft.
	LOD: 163' 6"	Beam: 34' 9"	Rig height: 129' 9"
	LOA: 177' 3"	Hull: wood/epoxy	Power: twin 400 HP
	LWL: 151' 3"	Freeboard: 7' 3"	

Designer:	Tony Castro, Ltd.
Built:	1996-2000; Woolston, Southampton, United Kingdom
Crew:	8. Trainees: 40
Contact:	Mrs. Lindsey Neve, Jubilee Sailing Trust
	Jubilee Yard, Hazel Road, Woolston,
	Southampton, Hampshire, SO19 7GB United Kingdom
	Tel: 44-23-8044-9108; Fax: 44-23-8044-9145
	E-mail: jst@jst.org.uk
	Web site: http://www.jst.org.uk

Tole Mour

Tole Mour is a 156-foot three-masted square topsail schooner owned and operated by the non-profit organization Guided Discoveries. With her incredibly seaworthy construction, fifteen sails, hands-on science equipment, professional crew dedicated to teaching, and close proximity to Southern California's biologically rich Channel Islands, she is the ultimate platform for sail training and marine science education.

Tole Mour was purchased in 2001 to carry out the work of the Catalina Island Marine Institute (CIMI). CIMI Tall Ship Expeditions, founded in 1998, is a Guided Discoveries program that is dedicated to "taking young people to sea in order to build character and minds." CIMI Tall ship Expeditions offers live-aboard voyages during the school year, summer, and winter, that focus on sail training and marine science education and range from 2 to 21 days in length. *Tole Mour* accommodates groups of up to 36 and ages 10 to adult. She sails the waters of Southern California's eight off-shore islands and beyond.

Her name *Tole Mour* means gift of life and health – and was bestowed upon her by the school children of the Marshall Islands where she was originally commissioned as a health care support ship.

Set sail with us for the experience of a lifetime!

Flag:	USA
Rig:	Square topsail schooner, 3-masted
Homeport/waters:	Long Beach, California: Channel Islands and beyond
Who sails?	School groups 4th grade through college, individuals, and educational adult groups.
Season:	Spring and Fall, 2-7 day expeditions
Program type:	Live-aboard educational voyages focusing on sail training and marine science

Specifications:			
	Sparred length: 156'	LOD: 123'	LWL: 101'
	Draft: 13' 6"	Beam: 31'	Rig height: 110'
	Freeboard: 6'	Sail area: 8,500 sq. ft.	Tons: 229 GRT
	Power: 575 HP Deutz diesel	Hull: steel	

Designer:	Ewbank, Brooke, and Associates
Built:	1988; By Nichols Brothers on Whidbey Island, Washington
Coast Guard certification:	Sailing School Vessel (Subchapter R)
Crew:	13. Trainees/passengers: 53 (day sails), 36 (overnight)
Contact:	Tim Hatler
	CIMI Tall Ship Expeditions
	PO Box 1360
	Claremont, CA 91711
	Tel: 1-800-645-1423; Fax: 909-625-7305
	E-mail: thatler@guideddiscoveries.org
	Web site: http://www.guideddiscoveries.org
	http://www.tolemore.org

SAIL TALL SHIPS!

The schooner *Tree of Life,* launched in 1991, was built in Nova Scotia, Canada and Jacksonville, Florida. She sleeps 12 in three cabins and the foc'sle. Powered by 4,500 square feet of sail, she cruises at 8 to 10 knots. Her hull is a composite of strip planked clear fir and kevlar saturated in epoxy and sheathed in fiberglass. Her deck is fir, spars are spruce, and brightwork is Honduran mahogany. The interior is paneled in koa and teak.

The *Tree of Life*, her owners and a crew of four plus two trainees sailed out of Newport Harbor October 2002 on a six year circumnavigation. Sailing to Bermuda, St. Martin thru the Caribbean to Grenada and west to Venezuela, Colombia, the San Blas Islands, Panama, Ecuador, Galapagos, Easter Island, Pitcairn Island, the Gambier Islands and presently in Tahiti. The *Tree* will spend five months in Auckland, New Zealand via Bora Bora, the Southern Cooks and Fiji for the America's Cup challenge.

Permanent crew includes Captain, First Mate-Engineer, Bosun, Chef and two trainees. The owners are on board for the duration of the voyage.

Tree of Life was chosen as one of the top ten yachts in North America by Sail magazine (1993), and in 1997 won the Bay of Islands Race. She is the 1995 and 2000 winner in her class at the Antigua Classic Yacht Race Week. The *Tree of Life* also won first place, "Best Schooner in Fleet" at the 2001 Newport Classic Yacht Race and Festival.

Flag:	USA
Rig:	Gaff schooner
Homeport/waters:	Newport, Rhode Island
Who sails?	Adult individuals and families.
Program type:	Sail training for volunteer and paying trainees. Sea education in marine science and maritime history.

Specifications:			
	Sparred length: 93'	Draft: 8' 5"	Sail area: 4,200 sq. ft.
	LOD: 70'	Beam: 18' 6"	Tons: 70 GRT
	LOA: 70'	Rig height: 85'	Power: diesel
	LWL: 58'	Freeboard: 4' 5"	Hull: wood/epoxy

Designer:	Ted Brewer
Built:	1991; Covey Island, Canada
Crew:	4. Trainees: 6
Contact:	Sheri and John Laramee, Owners
	447 Bellevue Avenue
	Newport, RI 02840
	Tel: 401-847-0444 or 401-732-6464
	E-mail: JohnGL@aol.com
	Web site: http://www.schoonertreeoflife.com

True North of Toronto was built in 1947 as a North Sea Trawler. She was converted to sail in 1979 and has spent her years since then world voyaging for sail training and charter. *True North* is dedicated to promoting the preservation of traditional maritime life. This is accomplished by creating opportunities for people of all ages to participate in sail training voyages, fulfill professional crew positions, dockside visitations, and film work. *True North* was the proud recipient of the overall 1st place ranking for the 1998 ASTA Great Lakes Tall Ships® Race.

Flag:	Canada
Rig:	Topsail schooner
Homeport/waters:	Halifax, Nova Scotia: Great Lakes, Atlantic, Caribbean
Who sails?	Individuals of all ages.
Program type:	Sail training for groups and individuals. Nautical curriculum, waterfront festivals, and film work.

Specifications:

Sparred length: 118'	Draft: 10'	Sail area: 9,688 sq. ft.
LOD: 90'	Beam: 22'	Tons: 98 GRT
LWL: 83'	Freeboard: 3' 6"	Power: 350 HP diesel
Rig height: 90'	Hull: steel	

Built:	1947; Alphen, The Netherlands, Gouwsluis
Crew:	8. Trainees: 50 (day sails), 25 (overnight)
Contact:	Captain Doug Prothero, Owner/operator
	Canadian Sailing Expeditions
	PO Box 2613
	Halifax, NS B3J 3N5 Canada
	Tel: 902-429-1474; Fax: 902-429-1475
	E-mail: doug@canadiansailingexpeditions.com
	Web site:http://www.canadiansailingexpeditions.com

The Uncommon School presents a new model for teaching and learning. People in the 1800's created common schools to teach children by prescribing what they must know and by giving them formal instruction. This schooling is still given to young people today. Common schools work as if ideally everyone would learn the same things at the same time and in the same way. The Uncommon School works differently.

The Uncommon School is devoted to education, not schooling. We believe that it is best, as Mark Twain said, not to let your schooling interfere with your education. We provide you with a way to do this. Education—learning who you are and what you can do as an individual and as a member of the human race—doesn't necessarily result from schooling. The two aren't mutually exclusive, but they are different. And you can have one without the other.

The Uncommon School helps students educate themselves. Our students learn by asking questions and seeking answers. You learn from everything as you experience life, explore the world, and exercise your capabilities. Our teachers understand what you are trying to do and enjoy helping you realize your goals.

In our sailing program you learn to sail, earn an American Sailing Association certificate, explore some of the great literature of the sea (fiction and non-fiction), and explore Long Island Sound as you sail from Milford, Connecticut to Mystic, Connecticut and back. You spend the first five days of the two week program learning to sail the school's four J-22's. Then you sail the boats on the trip to Mystic. The fleet of students' sailboats is accompanied by a power boat and a thirty foot sailing auxiliary operated by the three teachers presenting the program.

Along the way, participants read and discuss works by Conrad, Melville, and others. It's interesting to read what these writer-sailors have to say while you're sailing yourself. In addition to these activities, you study nautical sciences like weather forecasting and navigation, and you have a close look at the marine ecology and environment of Long Island Sound. Participants live on board their sailboats, and plans each day include activities on shore. Accomodations are quite basic but adequate to meet your needs. You can anticipate living conditions like those you'd experience on a backpacking trip except with showers — sometimes! Admission to the program is open to students aged 15 and older.

Contact: Mr. Jamie Baldwin
The Uncommon School
173 Sunset Hill Road
Redding, CT 06896
Tel: 203-938-9297
E-mail: uncommonschool@snet.net.
Web site: http://www.uncommonschool.org

USS Constellation

The *USS Constellation,* the last all-sail warship built by the US Navy, was launched in 1854 at the Gosport Naval Shipyard in Portsmouth, Virginia. *Constellation* served the country for over ninety years in both military and non-military roles. Before the Civil War, she was flagship of an international squadron charged with the mission of intercepting vessels engaged in the illegal slave trade along the coast of West Africa. While on patrol in these waters, *Constellation* captured three vessels and set free over seven hundred men, women, and children, landing them safely back in Africa. During the Civil War, *Constellation* saw duty in the Mediterranean Sea protecting American interests there, and as part of the Gulf Coast Blockading Squadron.

During her later years the *Constellation* sailed as a training or "practice" ship for the US Naval Academy and then as a stationary training ship at the Naval War College in Newport, Rhode Island. She was last under sail in 1896. Her final role as a commissioned vessel came during World War II when *Constellation* served as Flagship of the Atlantic Fleet.

In 1955, *Constellation* was brought to Baltimore to be preserved as a national shrine. The ship recently has undergone a $9 million reconstruction that has restored the ship to her original 1854 configuration. The ship made her triumphant return to Baltimore's Inner Harbor on July 2, 1999 and she is now open for public tours, offering a wide array of living history and education programs under the management of the Living Classrooms Foundation.

Flag:	USA
Rig:	Full-rigged ship
Homeport/waters:	Baltimore, Maryland
Program type:	Dockside interpretation and educational programming.

Specifications:

Sparred length: 282'	Draft: 21'	Sail area: 20,000 sq. ft.
LOD: 176'	Beam: 42'	Hull: wood
LOA: 200'	Rig height: 165'	Freeboard: 16'
LWL: 179'		

Designer:	John Lenthall
Built:	1854; Portsmouth, Virginia, US Navy
Contact:	Christy Schmitt, Visitor Services Coordinator
	The Constellation Foundation
	Pier 1, 301 East Pratt Street
	Baltimore, MD 21202
	Tel: 410-539-1797; Fax: 410-539-6238
	E-mail: rowsom@constellation.org
	Web site: http://www.constellation.org

SAIL TALL SHIPS!

"*Old Ironsides*" is the oldest commissioned warship afloat in the world. One of six ships ordered by President George Washington to protect America's growing maritime interests in the 1790s, *Constitution* earned widespread renown for her ability to punish French privateers in the Caribbean and thwart Barbary pirates of the Mediterranean. The ship's greatest glory came during the War of 1812 when she defeated four British frigates. During her first engagement, against *HMS Guerriére* in 1812, seamen nicknamed her "*Old Ironsides*" when they saw British cannonballs glance off her 21-inch-thick oak hull.

In the 1830s, the ship was slated to be broken up, but a public outcry sparked by the publication of a poem by Oliver Wendell Holmes saved her. Over the following century, the ship undertook many military assignments and served as a barracks and as a training ship. She was restored in 1927, and after a coast-to-coast tour, *Constitution* was moored in the Charlestown Navy Yard in 1934 where she is now open year-round for free public tours. She again underwent an extensive restoration from 1992-96, and on July 21, 1997, launching a year-long celebration of her bicentennial, *Constitution* sailed under her own power for the first time in 116 years. As flagship of the Sail Boston celebration, she led the Tall Ships 2000® fleet into Boston Harbor during the Grand Parade of Sail on July 11, 2000.

Flag:	USA
Rig:	Full-rigged ship
Homeport/waters:	Charlestown, Massachusetts: Boston Harbor
Program type:	US naval history

Specifications:			
	Sparred length: 306'	Draft: 22'	Sail area: 42,710 sq. ft.
	LOD (gun deck): 174' 10"	Beam: 43' 6"	Tons: 2,200 GRT
	LOA: 204'	Rig height: 189' 2"	Hull: wood
	LWL: 175'	Freeboard: 15'	

Built:	1797; Boston, Massachusetts, US Navy, Edmond Hartt Shipyard
Certification:	Commissioned US Navy ship
Crew:	75
Contact:	Commander Randall A. Neal, USN, Commanding Officer
	USS Constitution, Charlestown Navy Yard
	Charlestown, MA 02129-1797
	Tel: 617-242-5670; Fax: 617-242-2308
	Web site: http://www.ussconstitution.navy.mil

Victory Chimes

Built in Bethel, Delaware, in 1900, the schooner *Victory Chimes* is the largest commercial sailing vessel under the American flag and the only original three-master still working in America. Recently nominated for National Historic Landmark status, the *Victory Chimes* has been quietly supporting herself and a succession of private owners for the past 95 years. She has never been supported by foundations, grants, or endowments, and continues to be a well-maintained working vessel. Her current caretakers/owners, Captain Kip Files and Captain Paul DeGaeta, offer Windjammer style vacations on Penobscot Bay. At over 200 gross tons, the *Victory Chimes* attracts career-minded professional crew and carries a crew of nine.

Flag:	USA
Rig:	Gaff schooner, three-masted
Homeport/waters:	Rockland, Maine: Coastal Maine
Who sails?	High school and college groups as well as individuals and adults of all ages. Affiliated institutions include Baylor Academy.
Season:	June through September
Cost:	$100 per person per day
Program type:	Sail training for crew, apprentices, and paying trainees. Sea education in marine science, maritime history, and ecology based on informal, in-house programming. Paying passengers on overnight passages.

Specifications:			
	Sparred length: 170'	Draft: 7' 5" (min.)	Sail area: 7,100 sq. ft.
	LOD: 132'	Beam: 25'	Tons: 208 GRT
	LOA: 140'	Rig height: 87'	Power: yawl boat
	LWL: 127'	Freeboard: 11'	with engine
	Hull: wood		

Designer:	J.M.C. Moore
Built:	1900; Bethel, Delaware, Phillips & Co.
Coast Guard certification:	Passenger Vessel (Subchapter T)
Crew:	10. Trainees: 44. Age: 16-75
Contact:	Captain Kip Files
	Victory Chimes, Inc.
	PO Box 1401
	Rockland, ME 04841
	Tel: 207-265-5651
	E-mail: kipfiles@aol.com
	Web site: http://www.victorychimes.com

Viking is a sailing whaleboat, an open boat designed to be launched from a larger ship while at sea, and was built at Puget Sound Naval Shipyard in 1939 for use in the Navy's fleet sailing program. As the US prepared for war, the Navy stripped its ships and whaleboats were sent ashore. The sailing program was never reinstated, and surplus Navy whaleboats found their way to Sea Scout units around the country, offering thousands of youth the opportunity to learn sailing, seamanship, and teamwork on the water. Of those boats, only a handful remain.

The Sea Scout Ship *Viking* has been serving the youth of the Bay Area for over 60 years, offering programs that teach sailing, seamanship, and leadership to young women aged 14-21. Her sister ship, *Corsair,* offers similar programs for young men. The two ships participate in many joint activities. In addition to the annual two-week summer cruise in the Sacramento Delta, the Sea Scouts organize day sails, races, weekend outings, dances, and regattas. New members are always welcomed, both young and adult.

Flag:	USA
Rig:	Cutter
Homeport/waters:	San Francisco, California: San Francisco Bay and tributaries
Who sails?	High school students and individuals. Affiliated institutions include Sea Scouting, Boy Scouts of America, San Francisco Bay Area Council.
Program type:	Sail training for female trainees, aged 14-21. Sea education in marine science and maritime history in cooperation with other groups.

Specifications:	Sparred length: 30'	Draft: 4' 6"	Sail area: 600 sq. ft.
	LOD: 30'	Beam: 8'	Tons: 8 GRT
	LOA: 30'	Rig height: 35'	Hull: wood
	LWL: 28'	Freeboard: 2'	

Designer:	US Navy
Built:	1939; US Navy, Puget Sound Naval Shipyard
Coast Guard certification:	Uninspected Vessel
Crew:	6-18
Contact:	Nick Tarlson, Skipper
	Sea Scout Ship Viking
	220 Sansome Street, Ste. 900
	San Francisco, CA 94104
	Tel: 415-956-5700; Fax: 415-982-2528
	E-mail: seascouts@dictyon.com
	Web site: http://www.tbw.net/~chriss/scouts

the convoy movements transiting in and out of Chesapeake Bay.

The Schooner Virginia Project, a 501(c) 3 not for profit corporation, seeks to build a replica of this historic ship along the Norfolk, Virginia waterfront. *Virginia's* "living shipyard" will provide a unique educational experience, focusing on traditional wood ship construction, maritime history, and the vital role ship pilots and their vessels played throughout the history of the Commonwealth of Virginia.

A topsail schooner, *Virginia* will accommodate up to ten passengers in addition to eight full-time crew on overnight voyages. Day excursions will be limited to 35 passengers. In her mission as a goodwill ambassador for the Commonwealth, *Virginia* will maintain a international sailing schedule with crew positions open to qualified individuals.

The last of the great pilot schooners, the 118-foot *Virginia* served the Virginia Pilot Association from 1917 to 1926. Fast and seaworthy, *Virginia* remained in service long into an age where power vessels became the preferred platform for pilot station ships. *Virginia* was recognized in WW I for outstanding piloting services rendered to

Flag:	USA
Rig:	Gaff topsail schooner, two-masted
Homeport/waters:	Hampton Roads, Virginia: worldwide
Who sails?	Students from elementary through college and individuals of all ages.
Season:	Year-round
Program type:	Sail training for volunteer crew and trainees. Sea education in marine science, maritime history, and ecology in cooperation with accredited institutions. Dockside interpretation during port visits.

Specifications:			
	Sparred length: 126'	Draft: 13'	Sail area: 7,000 sq. ft.
	LOD: 118'	Beam: 22'	Tons: 97 GRT
	LOA: 118'	Rig height: 105' 4"	Power: twin diesels
	LWL: 80'	Freeboard: 6'	Hull: wood

Built:	Construction to begin in 2002
Coast Guard certification:	Passenger Vessel (Subchapter T)
Crew:	8. Trainees: 35 (day sails), 10 (overnight)
Contact:	Captain Robert C. Glover III, Executive Director
	Virginia Maritime Heritage Foundation
	5000 World Trade Center
	Norfolk, VA 23510
	Tel: 757-627-7400; Fax: 757-627-8300
	E-mail: execdir@schoonervirginia.org
	Web site: http://www.schoonervirginia.org

302

Wavertree (Work in Progress)

Wavertree was built in Southampton, England in 1885. She was first employed to carry jute for use in making rope and burlap bags, voyaging between India and Scotland. Within two years, she entered the tramp trade, taking cargoes anywhere in the world. After 25 years, she limped into the Falkland Islands in 1911, having been almost dismasted in a gale off Cape Horn. Rather than re-rigging her, her owners sold her for use as a floating warehouse at Punta Arenas, Chile.

Wavertree was converted into a sand barge at Buenos Aires, Argentina in 1947, and was acquired there by the South Street Seaport Museum in 1968 for eventual restoration to her appearance as a sailing vessel. By the time *Wavertree* was built, she was nearly obsolete, being replaced by ocean-crossing steam ships. At the same time, iron—long the choice of ship-builders in iron-producing countries such as England—was giving way to steel. *Wavertree* was one of the last large sailing ships built of wrought iron, and today is the largest afloat. Currently undergoing restoration, the *Wavertree* is expected to begin a limited sail training program in 2001.

Wavertree

Flag:	USA
Rig:	Full-rigged ship
Homeport/waters:	New York, New York
Program type:	Sea education in marine science, maritime history, and ecology in cooperation with accredited schools and other groups. Other education programs focused toward restoration.

Specifications:

Sparred length: 325'	Draft: 11' (min.),	Sail area: 31,495 sq. ft.
LOD: 263'	22' (max.)	Beam: 40'
Tons: 2,170 GRT	Rig height: 167'	Hull: iron

Built:	1885; Southampton, England, Oswald Mordaunt & Co.
Contact:	Paula Mayo, Director of Programs
	South Street Seaport Museum
	207 Front Street
	New York, NY 10038
	Tel: 212-748-8681; Fax: 212-748-8610
	Web site: http://www.southstseaport.org

Weatherly

very close racing she defeated the first Australian challenger, *Gretel,* and won the Cup.

Weatherly is a classic; her mahogany hull has been restored by owner George Hill to her original lines and her varnished interior make her a beauty. She is part of America's Cup Charters' 12-meter fleet in Newport, Rhode Island, and is available

The fast and beautiful *Weatherly* is the only yacht in history to win the America's Cup without doing so when new. The legendary Emil "Bus" Mosbacher skippered her in 1962. In for racing, corporate team building, and casual sails at the port of your choice from Maine down to the Chesapeake. Sail aboard an America's Cup winner— no sailing experience is necessary.

Flag:	USA
Rig:	Sloop
Homeport/waters:	Newport, Rhode Island: New England and Chesapeake Bay
Who sails?	Individuals and groups of all ages
Cost:	$2100 group rate per day, $75 per person for evening sails
Program type:	Sail training for paying trainees. Passenger day sails, corporate team building, corporate racing, individual and group charters

Specifications:			
	Sparred length: 69'	Draft: 9'	Sail area: 1,850 sq. ft.
	LOD: 69'	Beam: 12'	Tons: 28 GRT
	LOA: 69'	Rig height: 90'	Power: diesel
	LWL: 46'	Freeboard: 4'	Hull: wood

Designer:	P. Rhodes
Built:	1958; Stamford, Connecticut, Luders
Coast Guard certification:	Passenger Vessel (Subchapter T)
Crew:	3. Passengers/trainees: 12
Contact:	George Hill/Herb Marshall
	America's Cup Charters
	PO Box 51
	Newport, RI 02840
	Tel: 401-849-5868; Fax: 401-849-3098
	Web site: http://www.americascupcharters.com

The *Welcome* is a 55-foot sloop, a replica of the original *Welcome* built in 1775 at Fort Michimackinac during the Revolutionary War, which later became a British military vessel. The current *Welcome* is under construction on a pier at the Heritage Harbor in Traverse City, Michigan.

The Mackinac Island State Park Commission built the *Welcome* for the 200th anniversary of Independence Day. The vessel sailed the Great Lakes for a number of years before serving as a dockside museum in Mackinac City. In December of 1992, the Maritime Heritage Alliance (MHA), a nonprofit organization located in Traverse City, Michigan, was awarded the vessel for reconstruction.

Volunteers of the MHA, having built the schooner *Madeline,* are using their traditional boat building skills to restore this magnificent vessel. A target date for launching has been set for 2004.

Welcome

Flag:	USA
Rig:	Square topsail sloop
Homeport/waters:	Traverse City, Michigan: Upper Great Lakes
Who sails?	Students from elementary school through high school and adult individuals.
Program type:	Sail training for volunteer trainees. Dockside sea education in maritime history during port visits.

Specifications:	Sparred length: 90'	Draft: 8'	Tons: 45 GRT
	LOA: 56'	Beam: 16'	Power: diesel
	LWL: 49'	Rig height: 96'	Hull: wood
	Freeboard: 6'		

Designer:	Ted McCutcheon
Built:	1976; Mackinaw City, Michigan, State of Michigan
Coast Guard certification:	Attraction Vessel
Crew:	5. Trainees: 11. Age: 13+
Contact:	Richard Brauer, Maritime Heritage Alliance
	322 Sixth Street
	Traverse City, MI 49684
	Tel: 231-946-2647; Fax: 231-946-6750
	E-mail: mhatc@bignetnorth.com
	Web site: http://www.traverse.com/maritime/

Western Union

Western Union Telegraph Company.

When launched in 1939, *Western Union* was among the last "working schooners" to be built in the United States. She was homeported in Key West during her 35 years of active service for *Western Union* as a cable repair vessel. In 1974 she was about to be converted into a barge when she was purchased by Captain John Krause and put into passenger service. *Western Union* was acquired by Vision Quest in 1984 and renamed *New Way* for the important role she would play in redirecting troubled youth.

The *Western Union* is patterned after the schooners of the turn of the century that once roamed the high seas in the age of sail. Constructed of long leaf yellow pine with a Spanish Madeira mahogany-framed hull, the ship was built in Key West by the order of the Thompson Fish Company for operations they conducted on behalf of the

In February 1997 the *Western Union* returned to Key West and was designated the flagship of the city. Already a national landmark, plans are underway to create a museum recalling the vessel's origins. She is now available for dockside tours, day sails, and special charters.

Flag:	USA
Rig:	Gaff topsail schooner, two-masted
Homeport/waters:	Key West, Florida
Who sails?	School groups from elementary school through high school and individuals of all ages.
Season:	Year-round
Program type:	Passenger day sails. Dockside interpretation while in port.

Specifications:			
Sparred length: 130'		Draft: 7' 9"	Sail area: 5,000 sq. ft.
LOD: 92'		Beam: 23'	Tons: 91 GRT
LWL: 85'		Rig height: 103'	Power: twin diesels
Hull: wood			

Built: 1939; Key West, Florida, Herbert Elroy Arch

Coast Guard
  certification: Passenger Vessel (Subchapter T)

Contact: Harry Bowman, General Manager
202 (R) William Street
Key West, FL 33040
Tel: 305-292-9830; Fax: 305-292-1727
E-mail: keywu@attglobal.net
Web site: http://www.historictours.com/keywest/wunion.htm

Owned and operated by Traverse Tall Ship Company, the schooner *Westwind* sails the spectacular waters of the Great Lakes. Able to accommodate 29 passengers for day sails, *Westwind* is fully certified by the US Coast Guard.

In conjunction with Inland Seas Education Association, *Westwind* offers the Schoolship Program, which provides an environmental, historical, and sail training education for students during the spring. The schooner offers partial as well as private charter service to family, company, motor coach, and corporate team building groups.

Flag:	USA
Rig:	Gaff topsail schooner, 2-masted
Homeport/waters:	Traverse City, Michigan; Great Lakes
Who sails?	Science and marine biology student groups from elementary school through junior high for educational programs; individual, family, and corporate groups on two-hour sails.
Program type:	Sail training for crew. Sea education in marine science, maritime history, ecology and corporate team-building workshops. Passenger day sails.
Season:	May to October

Specifications:		
Sparred length: 65'	LOD: 58'	LWL: 49'
Beam: 14'	Draft: 8'6"	Rig height: 63'6"
Tons: 34 GRT	Freeboard: 4"	Power: 90 HP diesel
Hull: steel	Hull color: white	Spar material: wood

Designer:	Bud McIntosh
Built:	1992; Palm Coast, Florida, Treworgy Yachts
Coast Guard certification:	Passenger Vessel (Subchapter T)
Crew:	3. Trainees/passengers: 29 (day sails)
Contact:	Captain David P. McGinnis, Senior Captain
	Traverse Tall Ship Company
	13390 SW Bay Shore Drive
	Traverse City, MI 49684
	Tel: 231-941-2000; Fax: 231-941-0520
	E-mail: tallship@traverse.com
	Web site: http://www.tallshipsailing.com

When and If

"When the next war is over, and if I live through it, Bea and I are going to sail her around the world." So said George S. Patton about the 63-foot Alden schooner he had commissioned in 1939. Built in Wicasset, Maine, *When and If*, as she was named, was perhaps the strongest Alden built. General Patton's dream was not to be, however—he was killed in an automobile accident shortly after the end of the war.

When and If remained in the Patton family until the 1970s, when Patton's nephew made a gift of her to the Landmark School in Pride's Crossing, Massachusetts, where she was the centerpiece of a sail training program for dyslexic children. In a storm in 1990, her mooring pennant broke and she was driven onto the rocks. Although the damage was extensive, the structural integrity of the boat was unaffected. She passed into private ownership, was rebuilt over the next three years, and relaunched in 1994.

When and If can now be seen cruising up and down the East Coast. With her majestic black hull and powerful rig, she turns heads wherever she goes.

Flag:	USA
Rig:	Schooner
Homeport/waters:	Vineyard Haven, Massachusetts: New England
Who sails?	School groups from elementary school through college, individuals, and families.
Program type:	Sail training for paying trainees. Sea education in cooperation with accredited schools and other groups. Special education arrangements are available. Dockside interpretation during port visits.

Specifications:	Sparred length: 85'	Draft: 9'	Power: GM 4-71
	LOD: 63' 5"	Beam: 15'	Hull: wood
	LOA: 63' 5"	LWL: 43' 3"	

Designer:	John G. Alden
Built:	1939; Wicasset, Maine, F.F. Pendleton. Rebuilt by Gannon and Benjamin, Vineyard Haven, Massachusetts.
Coast Guard certification:	Passenger Vessel (Subchapter T)
Crew:	3. Passengers/trainees: 15 (day sails), 6 (overnight)
Contact:	Virgina C. Jones
	Gannon and Benjamin Marine Railway
	Beach Road Box 1095
	Vineyard Haven, MA 02568
	Tel: 508-693-4658; Fax: 508-693-1818
	E-mail: gandb@gannonandbenjamin.com
	Web site: http://www.gannonandbenjamin.com

In an era when the Atlantic crossing is measured in hours rather than weeks and most people's occupations anchor them to a desk, counter, or workbench, Sea Exploring offers a learning-by-doing environment. Lessons of character building and teamwork apply to all facets of one's life. The Sea Explorer program requires that each trainee exert and extend him or herself physically, morally, and mentally to perform duties which contribute to the ship. The reward, over and above the experience of a world of beauty and challenge, is the satisfaction and self-assurance that contributes to self-discipline. The *William H. Albury's* Sea Explorer Program offers lessons in ecology and international cooperation, as well as history, science, literature, and art. Subject to the dictates of nature, the Sea Explorer program is adventuresome while also a developer of character and a molder of lives. The

William H. Albury is now in it's 28th year of sailing under the command of Captain Joe Maggio and was co-winner of the 1999 ASTA Sail Training Program of the Year Award.

Flag:	USA
Rig:	Gaff topsail schooner, two-masted
Homeport/waters:	Miami, Florida: Biscayne Bay, Florida Keys, and Bahamas
Who sails?	School and other groups and individuals. Affiliated institutions include Boy Scouts and schools in Dade County, Broward County and Abaco, Bahamas.
Cost:	$800 per day
Program type:	Sail training with crew, apprentices, and paying trainees. Sea education in maritime history and ecology in cooperation with accredited schools and colleges and other groups. Passenger day sails and overnight passages.

Specifications:	Sparred length: 70'	Draft: 6'	Sail area: 2,100 sq. ft.
	LOD: 56'	Beam: 14'	Tons: 24 GRT
	LOA: 60'	Rig height: 64'	Power: 150 diesel
	LWL: 49'	Freeboard: 6'	Hull: wood

Built:	1964; Man o' War Cay, Abaco, Bahamas, William H. Albury
Coast Guard certification:	Uninspected Vessel
Crew:	3. Trainees: 30 (day sails), 14 (overnight)
Contact:	Captain Joseph A. Maggio, Marine Superintendent
	Inter-Island Schooner
	3145 Virginia St.
	Coconut Grove, FL 33133
	Tel: 305-442-9697; Fax: 305-442-0119
	E-mail: heritage2@mindspring.com
	Web site: http://www.heritageschooner.com

William H. Thorndike

The *William H. Thorndike* sails the coast of Maine in the summer. She has received several awards, including the "Most Photogenic" at the 1994 Antigua Wooden Boat Regatta. Formerly the schooner T*yrone,* the *William H. Thorndike* is the fourth ship to be named for Dr. William H. Thorndike of Boston. Voyages feature traditional sailing with a spirit of lighthearted competition and camaraderie.

Flag:	USA
Rig:	Gaff schooner, two-masted
Homeport/waters:	Maine
Who sails?	Individuals and families
Season:	Year-round
Program type:	Sail training and seamanship for trainees of all ages.
Specifications:	Sparred length: 75'

Sparred length: 75'	Draft: 8' 6"	Sail area: 2,200 sq. ft.
LOD: 65'	Beam: 15'	Tons: 43 GRT
LOA: 75'	Rig height: 80'	Hull: wood
LWL: 50'	Power: Cummings B210 diesel	

Designer:	Sam Crocker
Built:	1939; Sims Brothers
Coast Guard certification:	Uninspected Vessel
Crew:	2. Trainees: 4
Contact:	Townsend D. Thorndike

222 Whiteface Intervale Road
North Sandwich, NH 03259
Tel: 603-284-7174; Fax: 603-284-9258
E-mail: tdtfarm@worldpath.net

Built as modern interpretations of the last days of commercial sail, the *Windy* and the *Windy II* are true to function while using modern materials and safety features. In 1996, *Windy* was the first four-masted commercial sailing vessel built since 1921, and *Windy II* was completed in 2001. They have many features not found on older tall ships like hot water showers, private bunks, great cabin, furling topsails, as well as bowthruster, shoal draft, and wing keel. Although sister ships, *Windy* is rigged as a schooner and *Windy II* as a barquentine with three square sails. With their divided and easily managed multi-sail designs, there are ample opportunities for persons of all walks of life to participate in the sailing experience. During the summer at Navy Pier, Chicago, both vessels offer hands on sailing experiences to the public as well as private charters for corporations, weddings, team building, and private parties. In the fall and spring one of the vessels makes a voyage south through the Great Lakes, Erie Canal, Eastern Seaboard and south visiting any interesting port along the way.

Windy sail training programs include short introductory programs for schools and scouts which focus on maritime heritage and nautical science. The planned longer course will focus on the whole student in the four areas of nautical science, American heritage, social dynamics, and spiritual growth during a 6 to 8 week voyage including port visits to see Capitol Hill, the Liberty Bell, the Statue of Liberty, and more. Home-schoolers will have a particular interest in this program. Visit the Web site for details on all the programs and cruises.

Flag:	USA
Rig:	Gaff topsail schooner, 4-masted
Homeport/waters:	Chicago, IL; Great Lakes, Eastern Seaboard, and Caribbean.
Who sails?	5th grade and up, Adults and Seniors of all ages
Cost:	From $10/student program, $25 for Adults for short cruises.
Season:	Spring and Fall

Specifications:			
	Sparred Length:148'	Draft: 8' 6"	Sail area: 4800' sq. ft.
	LOD: 109'	Beam 25'	Displacement: 142 tons
	LOA: 109'	Rig height: 85'	Power: 300 HP diesel
	LWL: 95'	Freeboard: 8'	Hull: steel

Designer:	R. Marthai
Built:	1996/2001; Detyens Shipyard/Southern Windjammer, Ltd.
Coast Guard certification:	Passenger Vessels (Subchapter T)
Trainees:	150 (day sails), 26 (overnight). Coed.
Contact:	In season:

Captain Bob Marthai
Windy of Chicago, Ltd.,
600 E. Grand Avenue, Navy Pier
Chicago, IL 60611
Tel: 312-595-5472
Web site: http://www.tallshipwindy.com

Off Season:
2044 Wappoo Hall Road
Charleston, SC 29412
Tel: 843-762-1342

Wolf

The *Wolf* is a classic 74-foot topsail schooner built in 1982-1983 in Panama City, Florida by Master Builder Willis Ray and Finbar Gittleman. Designed by Merrit Walter, the *Wolf* is a Norfolk Rover class steel-hulled schooner.

Homeported in Key West, Florida, the vessel is owned and operated by Captain Finbar Gittleman of Key West Packet Lines, Inc. She is patterned after the blockade runners that plied the waters of the Florida Straits, Caribbean Sea, and Atlantic Ocean in the 19th century. The *Wolf* provides an ideal setting for dockside receptions, day sails, and sunset cruises.

The *Wolf* has been operating in Key West for more than 16 years and has come to symbolize the essence of that "island spirit" which draws visitors from all parts of the world. She often serves as the lead vessel in local harbor parades and traditional events.

With Captain Gittleman at the helm, the *Wolf* has sailed extensively the waters of the Caribbean, Bahamas, and Gulf of Mexico, and is known for her humanitarian missions. She is showcased in many films and documentaries and is available for private charters, long-term voyages, and special events, including overnight Boy Scout excursions, weddings, and fundraising events..

Flag:	USA
Rig:	Square topsail schooner
Homeport/waters:	Key West, Florida: Caribbean, Atlantic, Gulf of Mexico
Who sails?	Elementary and middle school groups, individuals, and families.
Cost:	$25 per person for two-hour sail, $800-$1,900 group rate per day
Program type:	Sail training for crew and volunteer trainees. Sea education in cooperation with organized groups and as informal, in-house programming. Passenger day sails and overnight passages. Dockside interpretation at home and during port visits.

Specifications:			
	Sparred length: 74'	Draft: 7'	Sail area: 2,500 sq. ft.
	LOD: 63'	Beam: 15'	Tons: 37 GRT
	LOA: 63'	Rig height: 56'	Power: 216 HP diesel
	LWL: 49'	Freeboard: 5'	Hull: steel

Designer:	Merrit Walter
Built:	1983; Panama City, Florida, Willis Ray/Captain Finbar Gittleman
Coast Guard certification:	Passenger Vessel (Subchapter T)
Crew:	4-5. Trainees: 44 (day sails), 6 (overnight)
Contact:	Captain Finbar Gittleman
	Wolf/Key West Packet Lines, Inc.
	PO Box 1153
	Key West, FL 33041
	Tel: 305-296-9653; Fax: 305-294-8388
	Web site: http://www.schoonerwolf.com

The Schooner *Woodwind* and her sister ship the *Woodwind II* are identical 74-foot wooden schooners that sail out of Annapolis, Maryland and can accommodate up to 48 passengers each. These staysail-rigged schooners do a variety of different activities based out of the Annapolis Marriott Waterfront Hotel.

The *Woodwind's* offer 2-hour public cruises that depart up to four times daily from downtown Annapolis and sail into the Chesapeake Bay. These schooners also offer private charters for special events, family gatherings and corporate events. One of our specialties is our team building program where the clients Match Race both schooners and really learn what it is like to work as a team to get around the race course (hopefully first).

Another specialty is our Boat & Breakfast Package. *Woodwind* has four staterooms where couples can stay aboard on Friday & Saturday nights including a sunset sail, accommodations, and breakfast in the morning.

In mid-October, there are four cabins available to cruise the Chesapeake for five days on a one-way cruise from Norfolk, Virginia to Annapolis, Maryland. A beautiful time of the year to sail to many coves and quaint towns on the Bay! All meals, instruction, accommodations, sailing lore and plenty of lighthouse history are included on this 130-mile journey.

Flag:	USA
Rig:	Staysail schooner
Homeport/waters:	Annapolis, Maryland: Chesapeake Bay
Who sails?	School groups from elementary through college, individuals of all ages
Season:	April through November
Cost:	$25 - $29 per person per 2-hour cruise, $2500 - $4000 group rate (charter) per day, "Boat and Breakfast Package" $235 per evening, 5-day cruise - $1300 per couple.
Program type:	Sail training for paying trainees, informal sea education, Team building (including match racing), passenger day sails, group charters, special sailing packages available.

Specifications:		
Sparred length: 74'	LOD: 61'	LOA: 61'
LWL:51'	Draft: 7'	Beam: 16'
Rig height: 65'	Freeboard: 5'	Sail area: 1,800 sq. ft.
Tons: 25 GRT	Power: 100 HP diesel	

Designer:	John Scarano, Scarano Boat Builders
Built:	1993; Albany, New York, Scarano Boat Builders
Coast Guard certification:	Passenger Vessel (Subchapter T)
Crew:	10. Trainees/passengers: 49 (day sails), 8 (overnight)
Contact:	Jennifer Brest, Captain and Director of Marketing
	Running Free, Inc.
	1930 A Lincoln Drive
	Annapolis, MD 21401
	Tel: 410-263-8619; Fax: 410-280-6952
	E-mail: woodwind@pipeline.com
	Web site: http://www.schoonerwoodwind.com

Jersey to Spain in 1928. The crash of 1929 forced her sale to the San Francisco Pilots Association in 1931.

Renamed *California,* she served forty years off the Golden Gate as the largest schooner ever operated by the Bar Pilots. She was bought in 1975 by a group of young craftsmen experienced in wooden boat restoration and was renamed *Zodiac.*

In 1982 she was placed on the National Register of Historic Places. Certified by the Coast Guard as a Passenger Vessel, she sails Puget Sound, the San Juan Islands, and the Canadian Gulf Coast. *Zodiac's* spaciousness and amenities make her the ideal boat for sail training and education programs enjoyed by a wide range of people.

In early spring and late fall *Zodiac* hosts Elderhostel sessions, offering courses on sailing, navigation, Northwest Native American culture, legends of the Pig War Island, and geology and natural resources of the San Juan Islands. Summer sessions are open to sailing enthusiasts sixteen years and older.

Designed to reflect the highest achievement of naval architecture under working sail, *Zodiac* was fundamentally a yacht. Built in 1924 for the Johnson & Johnson Pharmaceutical Company, she raced the Atlantic from Sandy Hook, New

Flag:	USA
Rig:	Gaff schooner, two-masted
Homeport/waters:	Seattle, Washington: Puget Sound, San Juan Islands, Canadian Gulf Islands
Who sails?	High school through college age students, adults, and families.
Season:	March to November
Cost:	$3200 per group per day
Program type:	Sail training for trainees sixteen and older, learning by standing watches on the helm, on sailing stations, and in the chart house.

Specifications:			
	Sparred length: 160'	Draft: 16'	Sail area: 7,000 sq. ft.
	LOD: 127'	Beam: 26'	Tons: 147 GRT
	LOA: 127'	Rig height: 101'	Power: diesel
	LWL: 101'	Freeboard: 5'	Hull: wood

Designer:	William Hand, Jr.
Built:	1924; East Boothbay, Maine, Hodgdon Brothers
Coast Guard certification:	Passenger Vessel (Subchapter T)
Crew:	8. Trainees/passengers: 49 (day sails), 24 (overnight)
Contact:	June Mehrer, Vice President
	Vessel Zodiac Corporation
	PO Box 322
	Snohomish, WA 98291-0322
	Tel: 425-483-4088; Fax: 360-563-2469
	Web site: http://www.nwschooner.org

Dolphin

Dolphin is a traditional Baltic Trader design staysail schooner built during WW II in 1943 at the German Naval Shipyards at Schweinemünde which was the center for U-Boat and other vessel construction. She and six sister ships are believed to have been built to clandestinely carry V2 rocket motors and parts from the Schweinemünde fabrication site to the Peinemunde assembly site disguised as a fishing vessel.

After the war she was auctioned to a British yachtsman who refitted the boat into her cruising yacht configuration at Hatra-Werfp shipyards, completing the refit in 1963. Rechristened *Dolphin*, she was a very popular and successful char-ter/dive vessel in the Caribbean from 1964 through the 1980s.

Since retirement from charter service, the boat has been dismasted in a gale and sent to the bottom in a vain attempt to collect on the insurance, but has survived it all in remarkable condition. She will begin undergoing a complete refit in 2002.

When ready for service she will sleep 24 in modern comfort and undertake a number of missions including: Provide educational training programs for teenagers and young adults in marine restoration, repair & maintenance, sailing, seamanship, navigation, ocean sciences, ecology and the environment; provide humanitarian missions around the world by delivering free health care and medical services to people living in small coastal villages lacking modern medical care and facilities; provide inspirational and empowering daysail experiences for economically, physically, medically, mentally of otherwised challenged individuals in partnership with other charitable and humanitarian organizations; as well as charter service for Traditional Dive Charter / Ocean Adventure Packages, Eco-Tours and Adventure Travel, Health and Fitness Spa Cruises.

Flag:	USA
Rig:	Staysail schooner
Homeport/waters:	Norwalk, Connecticut: New England and Caribbean
Who sails?	Groups and individuals of all ages
Specifications:	Sparred length: 90' LOD: 80' LWL: 70'
	Draft: 9' Beam: 21' Rig height: 85'
	Sail area: 3,000 sq. ft. Tons: 79 GRT Power: 230 HP single diesel
	Hull: wood on steel frames
Designer:	Grubee
Built:	1943; Schweinemünde, Germany
Contact:	John Edmister/Sequoia Sun
	Schooner *Dolphin*
	Adventures in Paradise LLC
	48 Beach Road # F 13
	East Norwalk, CT 06855
	E-mail: sequoia@schoonerdolphin.com
	Web site: http://www.schoonerdolphin.com

Freedom was the last, and fastest, 12 Metre to spring from the drawing board of Olin Stephens, the world-famous designer of America's Cup champions *Ranger, Columbia, Constellation, Intrepid,* and *Courageous.* Designed for the 1980 America's Cup, she dominated the defender series, winning 37 of 40 races before going on to defeat the challenger, *Australia,* 4-0.

Owned by Ernest Jacquet since 2000, he has meticulously restored *Freedom* to her original 1980 specifications. In 2001, *Freedom* won 1st place in the International 12 Metre Modern Class World Championships at Cowes, which celebrated the America's Cup Jubilee honoring the 150th Anniversary of the original America's Cup race in 1851.

Freedom is now participating in the "Newport Performance Twelves" educational program run by H2O Riders. The boat is maintained and sailed by team members as part of a program focusing on teamwork, leadership, and service. Participants have the opportunity to develop and teach sailing and boat maintenance skills while learning about 12 Metres and the rich sailing heritage of Newport, Rhode Island and the America's Cup. The volunteer-led program is free for members in return for their commitment of time and effort.

The program also hosts Corporate Match Racing seminars for professional clients interested in teambuilding and leadership development.

Flag:	US
Rig:	Sloop
Homeport/waters:	Newport, Rhode Island
Who sails?	Groups and individuals of all ages
Season:	April through October
Program type:	Sail training for volunteer trainees, private charters, day sails

Specifications:	Sparred length: 62'	LOA: 62'	LWL: 45'
	Draft: 9'	Beam: 12'	Rig height: 90'
	Freeboard: 4'	Sail area: 1807 sq. ft.	Tons: 57 GRT

Designer:	Olin Stephens
Built:	1979
Crew:	10. Trainees/passengers: 6 (day sails)
Contact:	Mr. Niccolo Porzio
	H2O Riders
	559 Thames St.
	Newport, RI 02840
	Tel: 401-845-2005; Fax: 401-845-2105
	E-mail: info@h2oriders.com
	Web site: http://www.h2oriders.com

Island Rover

The *Island Rover* is a 113-foot topsail schooner of William Peterson design. This steel schooner is currently under construction at Flying Point, Freeport, Maine at the site of the Island Rover Foundation home office; a non-commercial shipyard with much volunteer labor although future paid shipwright labor is anticipated.

The future of the vessel's Certifications is still under consideration. The planned voyage range will be all oceans and the schedules will be consistent with the planned research and educational missions of the foundation. The missions include educational opportunities in multi-age level sail training, informing the vessels visitors at every opportunity as to the origin of the materials constituting the vessels construction, promotion of the industrial concepts of: Reduce, Reuse, Repair, Refurbish, Re-utilize, Re-manufacture and Recycle as a means to conserve natural resources and protect the environment, provide a platform from which professional marine oceanographic research can be conducted, promote environmental consciousness and awareness of the environmental impact of modern societies activities on the marine ecosystems of the world.

The *Island Rover* is anticipated to ship with a crew of six – captain, mate, engineer, cook and two deck hands. Passenger efforts will be welcomed in the routine running of the vessel. Fee schedules for passengers and scientists will be established at a future date as the vessel is nearing completion.

Flag:	USA
Rig:	Topsail schooner
Homeport/waters:	Freeport, Maine: worldwide
Who sails?	Groups and individuals of all ages
Season:	Year-round

Specifications:	Sparred length: 113'	LOD: 89'	LWL: 74'
	Draft: 10'	Beam: 22'	Rig height: 105'
	Sail area: 5,000 sq. ft.	Tons: 96 GRT	Power:diesel/electric
	Hull: steel		

Designer:	William Peterson, Murray Peterson Associates, South Bristol, Maine
Built:	Under construction; Flying Point, Freeport, Maine
Crew:	6.
Contact:	Captain Harold E. Arndt
	Island Rover Foundation
	Flying Point
	93 Maquoit Drive
	Freeport, ME 04032
	Tel: 207-865-6621
	E-mail: capt.harold@islandrover.com
	Web site: http://www.islandrover.com

The *Sunderland* is a tall ship built in Lowestoft, England by Samuel Richards in 1885. Her first name was *Civil Lord* and then changed to *Sunderland* when she worked out of the town of Sunderland, England. The *Sunderland,* designed for fishing and carrying cargo, had its first career sailing the heaviest ocean in the world, the North Sea. This vessel is built of English oak on oak with a typical Englich plum stem which creates a lengthening of the waterline and gives her an advantage in sailing speed. The ships from the 1800s are now mostly replicas. English oak is a wood of longevity and it is next to impossible to find lumber of length and age to build such a ship as this today. *Sunderland* fished in the North Sea for 50 years. Her career went from a fishing and cargo vessel to a yacht when she had her first motor installed in the year of 1935, when the commercial use of sailing turned to power engines. She then sailed to the Americas where she was chosen to film the movie "Captains Courageous" making this her second career. This ship is definitely a hard working and lucky ship. She is now on her third career, sailing out of Cabo San Lucas doing pirate historical tours and robbing and pillaging tourists with the rest of the town!

Flag:	Tonga
Rig:	Square rig topsail schooner
Homeport/waters:	Cabo San Lucas, Mexico
Who sails?	Groups and individuals of all ages
Season:	October through August
Cost:	$40 per person per day
Program type:	Passenger day sails

Specifications:			
Sparred length: 105'	LOD: 80'	LOA: 84'
LWL: 70"	Draft: 10' 6"	Beam:19' 6"
Rig height: 85'	Freeboard: 5'	Sail area: 3,079 sq. ft.
Tons: 187 GRT	Power: 120 HP diesel	

Designer:	Sam Richards, Jr.
Built:	1855; Lowestoft, England
Certification:	Safety Certificate from Tonga
Crew:	6. Passengers: 50 (day sails)
Contact:	Captain Mark Belvedere
	Pirate Ship Cruises of Cabo
	Camino al Hotel Hacienda s/n Apt. 2
	Cabo San Lucas, BCS 23410 Mexico
	Tel: 011-52-624-1432714; Fax: 011-52-624-1432714
	E-mail: pirateshipcabo@prodgidy.net.mx
	Web site: http://www.pirateshipcabo.com.mx

Peter Puget

The *Peter Puget* is named after the trusted lieutenant of Captain Vancouver who led several small boat expeditions in the waters that now bear his name, Puget Sound. Long boats like the *Peter Puget* were the tools for exploring the waters of Puget Sound, the San Juan Islands, and the islands of the inner waters of Vancouver Island.

The *Peter Puget* is a reproduction of the type of ship's boat common in the 1790s when Vancouver and Puget explored the Pacific Northwest looking for the Northwest Passage. He (the boat's name is *Peter* after all) is powered by six oars and a two masted standing lug rig. In the waters of Southern California he will join the program of the Pacific Maritime Institute offering Christian sail training adventures to urban youth. Often there are too few youth to man the tall ships *Swift of Ipswich* and *Bill of Rights* which the Institute charter from the L. A. Maritime Institute.

The *Peter Puget* provides an up close experience with the bays, estuaries, and yacht/working harbors of the Southern California region.

Flag:	USA
Rig:	Standing lug
Homeport/waters:	Los Angeles, California: Los Angeles and Long Beach Harbors, Alamitos Bay, Newport Harbor, Mission Bay and San Diego Bay
Who sails?	Middle school through college groups and individuals, adult groups for team building
Cost:	$55 per person per day, group rate $250. $37 per person per day (5-day minimum). Scholarships available.
Program type:	Character building sail training adventures for volunteer crew and paying trainees, using the adventure of exploring bays and harbors to open trainees to the adventure of Christian living and teamwork, marine science and ecology, seaport economics and maritime history. Day long sails, day camp experiences, dockside interpretation.

Specifications:	Sparred length: 20'	LOD: 19' 3"	LOA: 20'
	LWL: 20'	Draft: 13"	Beam: 6' 8"
	Rig height: 17'	Freeboard: 18"	Sail area: 153 sq. ft.
	Hull: wood		

Coast Guard certification:	Six-passenger, uninspected
Crew:	2. Trainees/passengers: 4 - 6 (day sails)
Contact:	Mark R. Klopfenstein, President
	Pacific Maritime Institute
	PO box 1883
	Garden Grove, CA 92840-1883
	Tel: 714-813-7707; Fax: 714-539-2221
	E-mail: markklop@pacbell.net
	Web site: http://www.pacificmaritime.org

The largest brig to be built in Great Britain for over a century, *Stavros S. Niarchos* completed her maiden voyage in October 2000. Representing a significant commitment by the Sail Training Association, *Stavros S. Niarchos* was built to replace the STA's original schooner, *Sir Winston Churchill,* retired after 35 years of service.

Founded in the 1950s, the STA is a charity dedicated to the personal development of young people aged 16-24 through the medium of tall ships' sailing. Youth voyages vary in length from 7 to 12 days. Adult voyages are also operated for those aged 18-69 and range from tall ship day sails to 25 day trans-Atlantic crossings.

The brig, named for her generous benefactor, the late Stavros Spyros Niarchos of Greece, accommodates a total crew of 67. The permanent crew of six professional seafarers is assisted by a volunteer crew of eleven. A further 48 trainees form the voyage crew. While the majority of crew members are British, an increasing number come from continental Europe and the Americas.

Stavros S. Niarchos operates all year round. In the summer months she frequents European and Mediterranean waters, whilst in the winter heads south for the Canaries, Azores and Caribbean.

For current voyage programs and general information about the STA visit the Web site at: www.sta.org.uk

Flag:	United Kingdom
Rig:	Brig
Homeport/waters:	Portsmouth, England: UK and Europe (summer), Caribbean (winter)
Who sails?	Groups and individuals of all ages
Season:	Year-round
Program type:	Sail training for paying trainees

Specifications:	Sparred length: 195'	LOD: 159'	LOA: 159'
	LWL: 133'	Draft: 15'	Beam: 33'
	Rig height: 148'	Sail area: 12,503 sq. ft.	Tons: 493 GRT
	Power: 2x MTU 330KW		

Designer:	Burness, Corlett & Partners & Captain Mike Willoughby
Built:	2001; North Devon, United Kingdom, Appledore Shipbuilders
Crew:	17. Trainees/passengers: 45 (day sails), 48 (overnight)
Contact:	Sail Training Association
	2A The Hard
	Portsmouth, Hampshire PO1 3PT
	England
	Tel: +44 (0) 23 9283 2055; Fax: +44 (0) 23 9281 5769
	E-mail: tallships@sta.org.uk
	Web site: http://www.sta.org.uk

Prince William

Launched by the Sail Training Association in England in 2001, the brig *Prince William* is virtually identical to her sister ship, *Stavros S. Niarchos* (see separate entry). *Prince William* replaced the STA's second schooner, *Malcolm Miller,* retired after 34 years service.

Founded in 1956, the STA was privileged to be the first organization permitted to use the name *Prince William,* in honour of both the young Prince and the STA's long-serving patron, HRH the Duke of Edinburgh.

Now a familiar sight in European waters, *Prince William* hosts a total crew of 67, comprising six professional permanent crew, eleven volunteer crew and 48 voyage crew trainees. Youth voyages, (16-24 years), and adult voyages, (18-69), afford opportunities for personal development through the excitement and challenge of sailing a tall ship.

During the summer *Prince William* sails between ports in Great Britain, usually visiting continental Europe and Eire en route. In the winter months she is based in Portsmouth and hosts tall ship day sails along the south coast of England.

For current voyage programs and general information about the STA visit the Web site at: www.sta.org.uk

Flag:	United Kingdom		
Rig:	Brig		
Homeport/waters:	Portsmouth, England: UK and Europe		
Who sails?	Groups and individuals of all ages		
Season:	Year-round		
Program type:	Sail training for paying trainees		
Specifications:	Sparred length: 195'	LOD: 159'	LOA: 159'
	LWL: 133'	Draft:15'	Beam:33'
	Rig height: 148'	Sail area: 12,503 sq. ft.	Tons: 493 GRT
	Power: 2x MTU 330KW		
Designer:	Burness, Corlett & Partners & Captain Mike Willoughby		
Built:	2001; North Devon, United Kingdom, Appledore Shipbuilders		
Crew:	17. Trainees/passengers: 45 (day sails), 48 (overnight)		
Contact:	Sail Training Association		
	2A The Hard		
	Portsmouth, Hampshire PO1 3PT		
	England		
	Tel: +44 (0) 23 9283 2055; Fax: +44 (0) 23 9281 5769		
	E-mail: tallships@sta.org.uk		
	Web site: http://www.sta.org.uk		

Svanen is fully surveyed by the Maritime Service Board in conjunction with the Uniform Shipping Laws of Australia, which enables *Svanen* to operate as a charter and sail training vessel in both coastal and inshore waters. She maintains a yearly program to suit corporate sail training, general charter, and harbor commitments.

Sail training aboard *Svanen* provides team spirit, problem solving, coordination, and initiative opportunities, increasing self-confidence, self-worth, personal goals, and creating new horizons. Equally popular are offshore day sails, weekend packages and adventure holidays, and harbor cruises. *Svanen* will tailor programs to the client's voyage requirements.

Flag:	Australia
Rig:	Barquentine, three-masted
Homeport/waters:	Port Jackson, Sydney, New South Wales, Australia: New South Wales and Queensland, Australia coast
Who sails?	Middle school students and individuals of all ages. Affiliated with organizations serving disadvantaged children.
Season:	Year-round
Cost:	$120 per person per day
Program type:	Sail training for professional crew and paying trainees. Sea education in cooperation with accredited institutions and organized groups. Passenger day sails and overnight passages.

Specifications:			
	Sparred length: 130'	Draft: 10' 1"	Sail area: 3,385 sq. ft.
	LOD: 130'	Beam: 22' 4"	Tons: 119 GRT
	LOA: 98' 4"	Rig height: 87' 3"	Power: diesel
	LWL: 120'	Freeboard: 3'	Hull: Danish oak

Built:	1922; Frederikssund, Denmark
Certification:	Waterways Authority, New South Wales, Australia – 1E & 2C Survey
Crew:	5. Trainees: 25 (day sails), 30 (overnight)
Contact:	Laurence Nash Kalnin, Managing Director
	Svanen Charters Pty. Ltd.
	148-152 Regent St.
	Redfern, NSW 2016, AUSTRALIA
	Tel: 61-2-9698-4822; Fax: 61-2-9699-3399
	E-mail: medind@fl.net.au
	Web site: http://www.charterguide.com.au/main/search/boat/default.asp

Marc P. Binard
Water Music Charters
AB 20459
Marsh Harbour
Abaco, Bahamas
Tel: 242-367-2295; Fax: 242-367-3029
E-mail: islandoc2001@yahoo.com

Fleet of 75 Classic Boats
Mr. Julio Blanco
Asociacion Argentina de Veleros Clasicos
Juncal 867, p. 3
C1062ABE
Buenos Aires, Argentina
Tel: 54-11-4373-0321; Fax: 54-11-4393-2468
E-mail: jcblanco@fibertel.com.ar

LOS ANGELES

MARITIME MUSEUM

Tall Ships Are Coming!

ORGANIZATIONS WHICH DO NOT OPERATE
VESSELS BUT DO OFFER SAIL TRAINING
OR SEA EDUCATION PROGRAMS

ActionQuest

ActionQuest summer adventure programs offer teenagers the excitement of yachting while living aboard, developing new friendships through teamwork, and acquiring valuable, lifelong, leadership skills. Shipmates gain certification in sailing and scuba diving with marine science, water skiing, and windsurfing during their three weeks on board. Most shipmates arrive with no previous experience, yet the first time they set sail from the dock, it will be a shipmate who takes the helm under the guidance of licensed sailing masters. Programs operate in the Caribbean, Mediterranean, Galapagos, Australia, and South Pacific. Attracting over 480 teens from 37 states and 18 countries, ActionQuest creates an environment in which teens can discover the extraordinary in their lives and expand both geographical and personal horizons. ActionQuest also offers a high school semester afloat (Argo Academy) and 80-and 40-day college level programs (Sea-mester programs).

Contact: ActionQuest
PO Box 5517
Sarasota, FL 34277
Tel: 941-924-6789 or 800-317-6789; Fax: 941-924-6075
E-mail: info@actionquest.com
Web site: http://www.actionquest.com

America True Tall Ship Semester for Girls

The Tall Ship Semester is the only extended academic sail training program for high school girls. Provided through schools in the San Francisco area, the semester offers young women a chance to learn, to accept new challenges, and to succeed at new accomplishments. The students have an opportunity to develop confidence, life skills, and a sense of teamwork within a tangible community.

The program begins ashore in San Francisco, with students tackling their introductions to Oceanography, Maritime Literature, Coastal History, the Mathematics of Navigation, and Seamanship. The class then embarks on a seven-week voyage aboard a tall ship, where each student stands watch and performs the duties of a deckhand as they explore such regions as the Sea of Cortez, and Mexico's western coastline or the Caribbean. Following the voyage, the students return to their school communities, completing their portfolios and projects while working as an intern in the local maritime community.

Active as both crewmembers and scholars, the students learn to take risks and accept responsibility, discover new cultures, new possibilities, and new personal horizons. These lessons will serve them throughout their lives.

Contact: Nettie Kelly, Program Director
America True Tall Ship Semester for Girls
Pier 17
San Francisco, CA 94111
Tel: 415-433-4287: Fax: 415-433-9910
E-mail: truetssg@americatrue.org
Web site: http://www.americatrue.org

Bluewater Maritime School

Bluewater Maritime School is a US Coast Guard approved training facility. Our approved courses include, Operator of Uninspected Passenger Vessels, Master to 200GRT, Apprentice Steersman of Towing Vessels, Able Seaman, Commercial Assistance Towing and Auxiliary Sail as well as STCW instruction.

We also offer Prep Courses for 500/1600 GRT. We're located in a suburb of Jacksonville, FL and have arrangements with the city to host ASTA vessels in addition to accommodating individual students.

All Courses are taught by professional mariners with substantive commercial experience.

Contact: Captain Bob Russo
Blue Water Maritime School
2292 Mayport Road #31
Atlantic Beach, FL 32233
Tel/Fax: 904-247-3366
E-mail: tugco@aol.com

Boston University Explorations in Learning: Summer Learning For All Ages

In the summer of 2000, Boston University's Maritime Program was the proud recipient of ASTA's Sail Training Program of the Year Award. Participants of the Maritime Program spent two weeks aboard the Tall Ship *Rose* where they explored maritime history and gained hands-on experience as night watch, ship's crew, and deck hands. This summer, Boston University offers three maritime courses aboard the *Alabama* through its new Explorations in Learning program. In *Maritime History in the Atlantic World*, June 15-June 29, you'll learn the art of sailing and discover the role that seafaring played in the development of trade and empires in Europe, Africa, and the Americas. If New England's seafaring history is more appealing, then consider *Maritime History of New England*, running June 29-July 13. For literature buffs, *Classics of Maritime Literature* will focus on the works of 19th and 20th Century authors, August 10-August 24.

Explorations in Learning goes beyond the sea and offers non-traditional, one-of-a-kind learning adventures on the Gulf of Maine, Martha's Vineyard, in New Hampshire, Boston, and as far away as Europe.

Contact: Robyn Friedman
Explorations in Learning
Boston University Metropolitan College
755 Commonwealth Avenue
Boston, MA 02215
Tel: 617-353-2978
E-mail: explore@bu.edu
Web site: http://www.bu.edu/explorations.

Buffalo Maritime Heritage Foundation, Inc.

The Buffalo Maritime Heritage Foundation was founded to promote visits of sail training vessels to the Great Lakes and the City of Buffalo, and to promote sail training in the area. Visiting ships are berthed in the beautiful park setting of the Erie Basin Marina and other close by slips. Tall ships from around the world have visited including *Christian Radich*, *Pride of Baltimore II*, *America*, and *Bounty*. Potable water, electricity, telephone service, showers and waste disposal facilities are readily available on the dock. Stores are located close by in the downtown area. Buffalo is still the western terminus of the Erie Canal, which made the city prosperous and famous. The canal is used today for yachts transiting from Albany on the Hudson River, and for recreational boating and barge traffic. Buffalo is 18 miles (26 km) south of Port Colborne, the Lake Erie (western terminus) of the Welland Canal, and we can help ships with their transit through the canal. Buffalo is only 20 minutes (18 miles) from Niagara Falls by automobile, closer than any other major American or Canadian city.

Contact: RADM Edmund de Castro, Jr. NYNM
Buffalo Maritime Heritage Foundation, Inc.
120 Delaware Avenue, Suite 100
Buffalo, NY 14202-2704
E-mail: jdecastro@jdecastro.com
Web site: http://www.transportationlaw.jdecastro.com

The Coalition for Buzzards Bay

The Coalition for Buzzards Bay is a nonprofit, membership organization dedicated to the restoration, protection and sustainable use and enjoyment of Buzzards Bay and its watershed. Formed in 1987, The Coalition works to improve the health of the Bay for all through education, conservation, research and advocacy. Our programs include: Baywatchers, a bay-wide water quality monitoring program - the largest in Massachusetts - which utilizes volunteers to monitor trends in coastal water quality from Westport to Woods Hole; a Bay Lands Center supporting the conservation of important watershed open space and habitat; environmental education programs for school children and adults, and a Baykeeper advocacy program to support the cleanup and protection of Buzzards Bay. The Coalition for Buzzards Bay is supported by more than 1,500 individuals, families, businesses and organizations and managed by an 18 member volunteer Board of Directors. Based in New Bedford, a staff of eleven and hundreds of volunteers support the Coalition's work on behalf of a clean and healthy bay.

Contact: Mark Rasmussen, Executive Director
                        17 Hamilton Street,
                        New Bedford, MA 02740
                        Tel: 508-999-6363
                        E-mail: cbb@savebuzzardsbay.org
                        Web site: http:// www.savebuzzardsbay.org

Drayton Harbor Maritime

Drayton Harbor Maritime (DHM) is a private, nonprofit, 501(c)(3) organization whose mission is "to preserve, restore, and interpret the past and present maritime, marine, and estuarine heritage of Drayton Harbor, Washington, and its associated waters." Headquartered in Blaine, Washington, DHM owns and operates the historic *Plover* pedestrian ferry. Built in 1944 to transport workers between the Alaska Packers Association (APA) cannery on Tongue Point (end of Semiahmoo Spit) and the City of Blaine, *Plover* travels her original route, providing visitors a voyage back in time and an interpretation of Drayton Harbor.

In co-operation with Whatcom County Parks, DHM also provides docents and staff for the Semiahmoo Park Museum, located on Semiahmoo Spit. The Museum houses a modest collection of displays and artifacts depicting the area's maritime history.

With grant funding and the assistance of Trillium Corporation, which owns Tongue Point, DHM is spear-heading the restoration of a portion of the old cannery wharf complex, against which, in its hey-day, ships of the famous APA "star fleet" (*Star of India*, etc.) moored. Upon completion, the dock will be available for use by visiting tall ships, include interpretive signage, and will be the western terminus for *Plover's* route.

Contact: Richard Sturgill, Executive Director
                        Drayton Harbor Maritime
                        1218 4th Street
                        Blaine, WA 98230
                        Tel: 360-332-5742 or
                        Kenneth Ely, Chairman
                        E-mail: drkenely@juno.com

The Foundation of the Los Angeles Maritime Museum

The Los Angeles Maritime Museum, founded in 1980, is located at Berth 84 in the Port of Los Angeles. The Museum focuses on the maritime history of Southern California, and has a large collection of ship models, carvings, and sailors' knot work on display. The museum also offers changing exhibits, quarterly speakers forums, and a gift shop. Museum members may tour the harbor on the historic tug, *Angels Gate*.

The Museum's educational affiliate is the Los Angeles Maritime Institute, offering character building sail training experiences for at-risk youth. The institute operates the topsail schooners *Bill of Rights* and *Swift of Ipswich*. In April 2002, the twin 90-foot wooden brigantines *Irving Johnson* and *Exy Johnson* were launched. These new additions to the sail training fleet will offer on-board laboratories and classrooms.

Contact: Museum Director: Dr. Pete Lee (310-548-7618)
                        Museum Curator: Marifrances Trivelli (310-548-7618)
                        LA Maritime Institute President: Captain James Gladson
                        (310-833-6055)
                        Los Angeles Maritime Museum
                        Berth 84, Foot of 6th Street
                        San Pedro CA 90731
                        Tel: 310-548-7618; Fax: 310-832-6537
                        E-mail: curator@lamaritimemuseum.org

Friends of Brookline Sailing

Friends of Brookline Sailing is a community group which supports the sailing program at the Brookline (Massachusetts) High School. The school has a sailing team which competes in the Massachusetts Bay League in the Spring and a beginner/novice instructional program in the Fall, which is run through Community Boating, Inc. in Boston.

The programs are located on the Charles River, in Boston. One of the objectives of Friends of Brookline Sailing is to assist the high school in locating coaching candidates for both the Spring and the Fall programs. Persons interested in such positions should contact Thomas Urmy at the address below.

Contact:
Thomas V. Urmy, Jr.
29 Chestnut Place
Brookline, MA 02445
E-mail: turmy@shulaw.com

Girl Scouts of the USA

Girl Scouts sail into the futute, in boats small to tall! Whether learning from sailing around a pond or around the world, girls say the "best part's the fun!" A sailing ship is a superb "camp of the sea," where girls can focus on goals like teamwork and leadership through environmental action, international friendship, maritime heritage, arts, technology, science, careers, etc. Indeed sail training is a great way to "just add water" to Girl Scout handbooks, badges, interest projects and the progression of activities for every age level. Starting with basic safety for the youngest Daisy Girl Scouts through sailing adventures for teenage Senior Girl Scouts, Girl Scouts and volunteer leaders in over 300 local Girl Scout councils are always eager for more local, national and international opportunities for fun and learning under sail!

Still on course with adventures, we're expanding the Connecticut Girl Scouts tall ship "FriendShip Amistad" ambassadors program; involving more girls in port and underway in TALL SHIPS CHALLENGE® Pacific Coast 2002, Great Lakes 2003, and Atlantic Coast 2004; planning a Girl Scout Mariner reunion with the newly launched brigantines *Irving Johnson* and *Exy Johnson* from the Los Angeles Maritime Institute; Girl Scouts Sail into the Future at the GSUSA National Convention in Long Beach, CA in October of 2002; and other exciting "wider opportunities" under sail! *Girl Scouts. Where Girls Grow Strong.*

Contact:
Kathleen Cullinan, Camping Consultant
Girl Scouts of the USA
420 Fifth Avenue - 15th Floor
New York, NY 10018-2798
Tel: 212-852-8553; Fax: 212-852-6515
E-mail: kcullinan@girlscouts.org
Web site: http://www.girlscouts.org

Glacier Society, Inc.

The purpose of the Glacier Society is to restore and operate the USS/USCG *Glacier* as a functioning museum ship honoring all who served in the exploration of the North and South Poles. The USS/USCG *Glacier* made 29 voyages to the Antarctic and 10 voyages to the Arctic under both the U.S. Navy and U.S. Coast Guard command—one of the few vessels to serve under the colors of both the USN and the USCG. Both in port and while underway, the Glacier Society will provide hands-on training to children and adults while teaching the history of exploration of the Poles. She will serve as a learning platform for K-12 students and as a scientific platform for university students including real-time Internet links to active polar research stations.

Picture yourself aboard the *Glacier* as her educational odyssey begins from San Francisco to the East Coast after restoration. We are looking for volunteers to participate in this exciting adventure! Volunteer opportunities include restoration, archival research and fundraising.

Contact:
Ben Koether, Chairman
Glacier Society, Inc.
905 Honeyspot Road
Stratford, CT 06615
Tel: 203-375-6638; Fax: 203-386-0416
E-mail: benkoether@glaciersociety.org
Web site: http://www.glaciersociety.org

SAIL TALL SHIPS!

Golden Gate Tall Ships Society

The Golden Gate Tall Ship Society (GGTSS) is a California nonprofit organization dedicated to educating people in nautical skills and supporting the preservation and operation of traditional sailing vessels, particularly tall ships.
Goals and strategies include:
- Provide opportunities for sail training experiences for young people.
- Provide sailing and shipboard education for members.
- Support shore-side education.
- Support tall ships visiting San Francisco Bay.
Golden Gate Tall Ships Society (formerly Sausalito Tall Ships Society) provides scholarships for young people aboard tall ships, including high school students in San Francisco.

Contact: Gale Brewer, President
                          Golden Gate Tall Ship Society
                          PO Box 926
                          Sausalito, CA 94966
                          Tel: 415-332-6999
                          E-mail: info@ggtss.org
                          Web site: http://www.ggtss.org

HANSA Foundation

The HANSA Foundation's goals are: to provide a sail training-based opportunity for North American and European young people, aged 15-25, principally from the Gulf of Maine community and the Hanseatic cities of the North Sea and the Baltic; to join an intercultural exchange with internationally mixed crews of trainees; to place North American trainees aboard Hanseatic sail training ships, and reciprocally European youth aboard North American ASTA ships; to provide programs on and in association with their partners, all of which are ASTA members; to make sail training opportunities available to all youth through need-blind scholarships, bridging the gap between the ASTA Sail Training Scholarship and STAG (Sail Training Association of Germany), whose trainee scholarships are restricted to German citizens or residents; and to build cultural and economic bridges with our largest European trading partner, Germany.

Contact: David Schurman, Executive Director
                          HANSA Foundation
                          PO Box 69
                          North Reading, MA 01864
                          Tel: 781-944-0304;
                          Fax: 781-944-2469
                          E-mail: info@sailtraining.com
                          Web site: http://www.sailtraining.com

Headwaters to Ocean

The only program of its kind in the Columbia River Basin, H2O is dedicated to fostering community-based stewardship of these awe-inspiring rivers through hands-on experience. Founded in 1995 by veterans of sail training programs world-wide, H2O has inspired over 11,000 people to make small changes in their behavior to create healthier watersheds and stronger communities, carrying out its education-to-action mission.

Contact: Kiirsten Flynn, Program Manager
                          Headwaters to Ocean (H2O), Inc.
                          3945 SE Hawthorne Boulevard
                          Portland, OR 97214
                          Tel: 503-228-9600
                          E-mail: HQ@h2ocean.org
                          Web site: http://www.h2ocean.org

Herreshoff Marine Museum

The Herreshoff Marine Museum bordering Narragansett Bay is arguably Rhode Island's most important maritime historical site. From 1863 to 1945, the Herreshoff Manufacturing Company produced the world's finest yachts, the first United States Navy torpedo boats, and a record eight consecutive successful defenders of the America's Cup. Rhode Island's oldest boat *Sprite* (also the oldest catboat in the US) and *Reliance*, the largest America's Cup boat ever built and featured on the Rhode Island State Quarter, were Herreshoff designs.

The America's Cup Hall of Fame brings alive the history of the America's Cup, tracing advances made in the design, construction and sailing in cup competition, while providing permanent recognition to those who demonstrated outstanding performance and sportsmanship.

Museum activities include presentation of an extensive collection, educational programs for adults and youth, a boat restoration program, research, scholarship, outreach programs and community events.

Contact:
Teri Souto
Herreshoff Marine Museum
One Burnside Street, PO Box 450
Bristol, RI 02809
Tel: 401-253-5000
E-mail: t.souto@herreshoff.org
Web site: www.herreshoff.org

Independence Seaport Museum

The Independence Seaport Museum is located on the Delaware River at Penn's Landing in downtown Philadelphia. The Museum is a private, nonprofit institution dedicated to the collection, preservation, and interpretation of materials relating to maritime history, with a particular emphasis on the Delaware Bay and River.

Located in a newly renovated, multi-million dollar facility, the Museum houses permanent and changing exhibit galleries, classrooms, an active boat building shop, and a specialized maritime library. Museum visitors can tour the 1944 US Navy submarine BECUNA and the cruiser OLYMPIA, launched in 1895. The 1934 Trumpy motor yacht *Enticer* is maintained and operated in the charter trade.

The Museum regularly provides berths for visiting vessels and has jointly offered educational programs with sail training vessels such as *Niagara*, *A.J. Meerwald* and *Pioneer*.

Contact: Karen Cronin, VP Operations
Independence Seaport Museum
211 South Columbus Boulevard
Philadelphia, PA 19106
Tel: 215-925-5439; Fax: 215-925-6713
E-mail: kcronin@indsm.org
Web site: http://www.phillyseaport.org

Lake Champlain Maritime Museum- Burlington Schooner Project

Lake Champlain Maritime Museum's most ambitious undertaking to date, the building of the *Lois McClure*, an 1862-class canal schooner at the King Street Ferry Dock in Burlington Vermont. Modeled after the *General Butler* and *OJ Walker*, two historic shipwrecks located within a mile of the

construction site, the BSP hopes to re-connect present day residents, visitors and school children to the rich commercial history of Burlington and Lake Champlain's archaeological legacy. After a spring 2004 launching, we will re-create a traditional journey down the lake, through the Champlain Canal to the ports of the Hudson River and on to the South Street Seaport Museum. When not traveling, the *Lois McClure* will be a permanent feature of the Burlington waterfront. The ship, with her tall wooden masts, will become a tangible link to the evolution of Burlington. The Burlington Shipyard is located at the King Street Ferry Dock on the Burlington Waterfront. Watch or lend a hand as experienced crafts-men fashion timber, iron, cotton and canvas into a working schooner. Interesting exhibits and hands-on activities for the whole family. Free to the public, open 7 days a week.

Contact: Mike LaVecchia
                         1 King Street
                         Burlington VT. 05401
                         Tel: 802-864-9512
                         E-mail: mail- wmsc@together.net

Landing School of Boatbuilding and Design

Established in 1978 and located in Kennebunkport, Maine, The Landing School of Boatbuilding and Design is a non-profit post-secondary career school dedicated to providing the highest quality vocational education in boatbuilding, yacht design, and marine systems technology available. The School was created to provide a gateway to the marine industry for students seeking career opportu-nities in the marine trades focusing on both recreational and commercial watercraft in both power and sail. The Landing School's ability to reinforce and preserve traditional skills and knowledge while advancing the art and science of boat design, construction, outfitting and repair through the integra-tion of modern techniques and contemporary materials is recognized and valued throughout the marine industry. Our School has earned an international reputation for program quality, and, as an educational institution, is considered by many in the marine industry to be unequaled. The graduates and hundreds of alumni of the School are highly sought after for their craftsmanship, productivity, work ethic, and passion for their chosen careers in, on, and around boats.

Contact: Landing School of Boatbuilding and Design
                         P.O. Box 1490
                         Kennebunkport, Maine 04046
                         Tel: 207-985-7976; Fax: 207-985-7942
                         E-mail: landingschool@cybertours.com
                         Web site: http://www.landingschool.org

National Maritime Historical Society

The National Maritime Historical Society is an educational organization dedicated to promoting greater awareness and appreciation of America's seafaring heritage. The Society advances seafar-ing knowledge through its quarterly magazine Sea History as well as through its other publications and through programs with schools, museums and universities.

We are currently pursuing "Young America Defends the Hudson," a program commemorating the 225th anniversary of the American Revolution and the pivotal role played by the Royal Navy and American forces to take and defend the waterway that could have divided the colonies.

The Society is also active in historic ship preservation, publication and occasional research pro-jects. It is funded by a large and active membership, which all who cherish the seafaring heritage are invited to join.

In 2001, NMHS initiated "Passage Making," a campaign to build a sound financial future for the Society so that its members, trustees and staff can continue to advance the causes we serve: Communication, the Maritime Education Initiative, and Historic Ship Preservation. In pursuit of this goal, our new mission statement is:

"To preserve and perpetuate the maritime history of the United States and to invite all Americans to share in the challenging heritage of seafaring."

Contact: National Maritime Historical Society
                         5 John Walsh Boulevard
                         PO Box 68
                         Peekskill, NY 10566
                         Tel: 914-737-7878: Fax: 914-737-7816
                         E-mail: nmhs@seahistory.org
                         Web site: http://www.seahistory.org

National Outdoor Leadership School

The National Outdoor Leadership School (NOLS) has a 30-year history of excellence in outdoor education and leadership. Today, NOLS runs eight branch schools around the world and courses on five continents. Sail training is available on open boats in Baja California, Mexico, on keel boats in Desolation Sound, British Columbia, and as a cultural experience aboard dhows in Kenya, East Africa. These courses are run as self-reliant sailing expeditions. Training in a multitude of other skill areas is available from sea kayaking to mountaineering, hiking, horse packing, and more. Leadership, safety and judgment, and minimum-impact camping are central themes throughout every NOLS experience. College credit is available on most courses through the University of Utah. NOLS is a private, non-profit educational corporation.

Contact: Hans Trupp, NOLS Mexico Sailing Program Supervisor
            Baja California Sur
            E-mail: hans_trupp@nols.edu

Northwest Schooner Society

Seattle's Northwest Schooner Society (NWSS) provides a unique opportunity for teens and adults to experience a piece of American history aboard fully restored "floating classrooms." The Society is a nonprofit, tax-exempt organization, founded in 1994 to allow more people to experience the excitement and challenge of old-fashioned seamanship, twenty-four hours a day.

The Northwest Schooner Society sponsors voyages of different lengths on historic ships through their own multidisciplinary educational program. Under billowing canvas, schools and youth groups experience real-life application of science, math, history, and geography. Programs are designed to bring out the best in teenagers, introducing youngsters to an inner strength they never knew they had while they haul sail to harness the elements. From their homeports in Bellingham and Seattle, they sail the stunning and protected waters of Washington State and British Columbia. The Society organizes environmental cruises on the 1924 schooner Zodiac, the largest sailing ship on the West Coast. The Society also owns and operates the 87-foot steel power yacht *Rebecca*, built in 1947.

Contact: Bill Vonk
            Northwest Schooner Society
            PO Box 9504
            Seattle, WA 98109
            Tel: 800-551-6977; Fax: 206-633-2784
            E-mail: bvonk@nwschooner.org
            Web site: http://www.nwschooner.org

Ocean Voyages, Inc.

Ocean Voyages was founded 23 years ago to provide participatory educational sailing programs throughout the world. Programs are open to sailing enthusiasts of all ages. Most programs run from one to four weeks in length. Ocean Voyages works with educators and institutions to design customized programs for youth participation for "youth of all ages." Ocean Voyages also has extensive experience in scientific research projects and documentary and feature films.

Ocean Voyages works toward preserving our maritime heritage and sailing arts, and providing opportunities for people to gain sailing education and seafaring experience. Coastal and inter-island programs are available in addition to offshore passage-making and around-the-world voyaging opportunities. Program areas include: Hawaii, California, the Pacific Northwest, Galapagos Islands, Aegean Sea, Caribbean, French Polynesia, and New Zealand, as well as Pacific and Atlantic Ocean crossings. Many of the international vessels that Ocean Voyages works with participated in Tall Ships 2000® and OpSail 2000 as wel as ASTA's TALL SHIPS CHALLENGE® Race Series.

Contact: Ocean Voyages
            1709 Bridgeway
            Sausalito, CA 94965
            Tel: 415-332-4681 or 800-299-4444; Fax: 415-332-7460
            E-mail: sail@oceanvoyages.com
            Web site:http://www.oceanvoyages.com

SAIL TALL SHIPS!

Philadelphia City Sail

Philadelphia City Sail is a nonprofit, maritime educational program working primarily with inner city youth of Philadelphia. The schoolship *Northwind*, a 75-foot topsail schooner, serves as an educational platform to introduce students to sailing, maritime history, and the marine sciences. While on board, students set sail and have an opportunity to explore the world of plankton, study the water quality of the Delaware River, and learn about the past, present, and future of the Philadelphia waterfront.

Philadelphia City Sail's school-year program is a partnership with The Academy of Natural Sciences and is closely aligned with the Philadelphia School District. In combination with a summer program, the schoolship services over 3,000 students each year.

Contact:
Mark Fallon, Education Director
Philadelphia City Sail
PO Box 43235
Philadelphia, PA 19129
Tel: 215-271-3400; Fax: 215-271-0234
E-mail: Phcitysail@aol.com
Web site: http://www.phillyfriend.com/citysail.htm

The Port Alberni Maritime Heritage Society

The Society is a non-profit community based organization incorporated in 1984 with a mandate to aid in the preservation and exhibition of the maritime history and heritage of Port Alberni, and the west coast of Vancouver Island. The Society advises the Alberni Valley Museum on the development of maritime projects and collections. It also has membership in the Vancouver Maritime Museum, and the World Ship Society (Vancouver Chapter).

Two significant Port Alberni harbor front heritage attractions have recently been completed by the society. They are; THE MARITIME DISCOVERY CENTRE, and the restoration of the Canada Coast Guard historic BAMFIELD LIFEBOAT.

The DISCOVERY CENTRE is open daily during the summer months, and features a changing exhibit each year. Children's special events and "hands on" learning experiences are offered from time to time. MEMBERSHIP: $10.00 Canadian Annually.

Contact:
Port Alberni Maritime Heritage Society
PO Box 330
Port Alberni, BC V9Y 7M8 Canada
E-mail: PA_Maritime_Heritage_Society@hotmail.com

Project Link, LTD.

Project Link was founded in 1984 to facilitate the incorporation of special-needs students into regular classroom settings. Project Link recently expanded the scope of its mission to include all students both before and after graduation. The new focus of the organization relates directly to the maritime world, taking special advantage of the coastal opportunities of Boston Harbor and vicinity.

Project Link is working with a number of Boston area schools to develop a program that will allow students to interact with personnel aboard several sailing vessels, providing real-life, real-time elements to issues and problems being discussed in class. Two such Internet links have been established with the *Picton Castle* and the USCG Barque *Eagle*. The study course will culminate with a sail aboard *Firebird*, a 47-foot Alden yawl. In addition to this program, Project Link helps students discover meaningful careers in the maritime field following high school graduation.

Contact:
John V. Henderson, Executive Director
Project Link, Ltd.
PO Box 167
Manchester, MA 01944
Tel: 978-768-7469; Fax: 617-357-5834
E-mail: projlink@ma.ultranet.com

Rose Island Lighthouse Foundation

The Rose Island Lighthouse is located in lower Narragansett Bay, Rhode Island – a mile offshore and a century in the past. Beyond the reach of Newport's utility lines and services, the recently restored lighthouse is managed by the non-profit Rose Island Lighthouse Foundation as an independent, energy efficient, environmental education center that is directly dependent on forces of nature like rainwater and wind-powered electricity. The light in the tower was joyously relit on August 7, 1993 and is listed again on the charts. The Lighthouse is also listed on the National Register of Historic Places.

Home to historic keepers and their families for over a hundred years, the Lighthouse today abuts a 17- acre protected wildlife refuge that is owned by the Foundation. Both properties are maintained by modern keepers who sign on for a week at a time as part of our environmental education program, which also includes overnights in the museum, as well as school field trips and special group tours.

We welcome you to become part of our effort to keep the light shining in the hearts and minds of the next generation of the Earth's keepers. See how the past can provide answers for the future at Rose Island – a historic, living museum and environmental education center.

Contact: Charlotte Johnson, Executive Director
Rose Island Lighthouse Foundation
PO Box 1419
Newport, RI 02840
Phone: 401-847-4242; Fax. 401-847-7462
E-mail: Charlotte@RoseIsland.org
Web site: http://www.RoseIslandLighthouse.org

Sail America

Sail America was founded in 1990 by members of the US sailing industry who wanted to play a very active role in growing sailing as a sport, an industry, and a way of life. Its over 600 members represent every segment of the industry from manufacturers to sailing schools, charter companies to publications. It is the only nonprofit industry association exclusively working to promote the growth of the sailing industry.

Sail America's mission statement is: "To promote the growth of the sailing industry." To achieve this they have developed programs and events which will significantly increase participation in sailing. Sail Expo® St. Petersburg, Atlantic Sail Expo®, Pacific Sail Expo®, Strictly Sail® Chicago, and Strictly Sail® Miami not only boost sales for the businesses involved, but serve to educate sailors and non-sailors. Special events and over 300 seminars – a compilation of the best technical. safety, and entertainment presentations offered to the sailing public – take place during the Sail Expo® and Strictly Sail® events.

Contact: Scot West, Executive Director
850 Aquidneck Avenue, Unit B-4
Middletown, RI 02842-7201
Tel: 401-841-0900; Fax: 401-847-2044
E-mail: scotw@sailamerica.com
Web site: http://www.sailamerica.com

Sail Newport

Sail Newport is a non-profit organization dedicated to offering public access to the sport of sailing. To accomplish its mission, we offer educational programs and foster one-design racing in Narragansett Bay. As Rhode Island's Public Sailing Center, the organization endeavors to make it easy and affordable to learn and enjoy the sport of sailing at any age, with its youngest students starting at age seven. Sail Newport also offers a rental fleet of J/22s and Rhodes 19s for use seven days a week during the sailing season.

The broad array of educational programs for youth and adults include novice, intermediate, and advanced levels of instruction. In addition, Sail Newport custom designs sailing programs for schools, colleges, community groups, municipal organizations, youth groups, and disabled organizations. The organization is especially proud of its Scholarship Program which provides financial aid to eligible community families.

Sail Newport has also earned a reputation for excellence in regatta management and is recognized as the leader in hosting world-class sailing competitions and premiere racing events in New England. Each year, we host a number of renowned national and international events with ample shoreside facilities serving regularly as race headquarters. Some of these events have included Sail

Newport's own annual Newport Regatta™, now in its eighteenth year, the Rolex International Women's Keelboat Championship, the Laser World Championship, Etchells North Americans, Junior Olympic Festivals, the 1998 Hartford World Disabled Championship, the 1998 J/24 North Americans, and the 2000 J/24 World Championship.

Contact: Kim Hapgood, Program Director
Sail Newport, Inc.
60 Fort Adams Drive
Newport, RI 02840
Tel: 401-846-1983
E-mail: kimh@sailnewport.org
Web site: http://www.sailnewport.org

Sail Martha's Vineyard, Inc.

Sail Martha's Vineyard is a 501(c)(3) nonprofit organization dedicated to celebrating and perpetuating Martha's Vineyard's maritime heritage and culture. Its activities encourage island children to be comfortable on the water by offering boat handling and sailing instruction free of charge, adult sailing classes, and support for the high school sailing team for competitive sailors.

Sail Martha's Vineyard supports educational programs in the public elementary schools that familiarize island children with the maritime traditions of Martha's Vineyard, such as their wooden boat project. It attracts interesting and historic vessels to the island, supports such local vessels, and serves as a clearinghouse for other maritime-related organizations and initiatives on the island.

Sail Martha's Vineyard depends entirely on its volunteers and is funded through individual and community contributions and grant support.

Contact: John Christensen, President
or Hope Callen, Administrator
Sail Martha's Vineyard
PO Box 1998
Vineyard Haven, MA 02568
Tel: 508-696-7644; Fax: 508-696-8819
E-mail: sailmv@vineyard.net
Web site: http://www.sailmv.com

Salish Sea Expeditions

Salish Sea Expeditions is a non-profit organization offering diverse science education and sail training programs on Puget Sound onboard the 61' yawl *Carlyn*. Salish provides students, educators, and citizens of all ages with the unique opportunity to directly experience and scientifically explore the Puget Sound marine ecosystem. With guidance from marine educators, Salish students develop a scientific hypothesis and detailed oceanographic sampling and navigation plans for a 2-5 day sailing/research expedition.

During their voyage, students work together to collect and analyze oceanographic samples, sail and navigate the ship, and help with cooking and shipboard chores.

Conducting such a group project fosters cooperation, team building, and positive community problem-solving. It teaches students how to think critically and apply the scientific method. Furthermore, the unique and challenging shipboard environment allows students to master new skills, gain confidence, and see the world from a new vantage point.

Carlyn is designed and rigged to support maximum student participation. It is U.S. Coast Guard certified to carry 38 people and has the capacity to sleep 16. Please see our Web site or call for more information on our diverse array of program offerings. We can even custom-design programs to meet your group's special needs.

Contact: Lori Mitchell, Program Director or
Ellie Linen Low, Executive Director
Salish Sea Expeditions
647 Horizon View Place
Bainbridge Island, WA 98110
Tel/Fax: 206-780-7848
E-mail: info@salish.org
Web site: http://www.salish.org

Save The Bay - People For Narragansett Bay

Save The Bay is a non-profit organization working to protect, restore and explore Narragansett Bay and its watershed. Founded in 1970, the organization was founded on the community's desire to protect our most precious resource.

Save The Bay believes the Bay's future depends on tomorrow's leaders understanding how important the Bay is to our economy, environment and quality of life. The organization delivers education programs to schools, community groups and the general public. It also offers educational experiences in the classroom, along the Bay's shoreline and aboard our education vessel, the *Alletta Morris.*

Save The Bay protects Narragansett Bay by advocating for Bay-friendly legislation, reviewing permits and raising public awareness. It restores the Bay to full health by improving salt marshes, building fish ladders and transplanting eelgrass to the Bay.

Contact: Save The Bay
434 Smith Street
Providence, RI 02908
Tel: 1-800-NARRBAY
E-mail: savebay@savebay.org
Web site: http://www.savebay.org

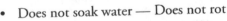
SAIL TALL SHIPS!

Seattle Area Sea Scouts

Yankee Clipper, Sea Scout Ship 97, has trained youth between the ages of fourteen and twenty-one nautical skills such as sailing, seamanship, navigation, aquatics, communications, leadership, as well as izenship and character building. *Yankee Clipper* also uses a 14' C-Lark and Lido, and 10' Sea Scouter s ing dinghies.

Affiliated with the Boy Scouts of America and the West Seattle Lions Club, *Yankee Clipper* was buil 1943 by the US Navy, and lengthened and coverted to a sail training vessel in 1950. She sails the wat of Puget Sound and British Columbia. *Yankee Clipper* has participated in numerous events featuring cl sic vessels and is the recipient of awards and accolades including being named "historic tall ship" of Southwest Seattle Historical Society.

Meetings are held weeky, overnight cruises monthly and longer cruises in the summer. In the fall, crew conducts Ecology Tours on the Duwamish River.

Contact:

Captain John Kelly
5271 45th Avenue SW
Seattle, WA 98136
Tel: 206-932-0971

US Merchant Marine Academy

The United States Merchant Marine Academy is located on Long Island Sound at Kings Point, N York. The USMMA, founded in 1943, is the fourth of the five federal service academies. Its mission is to tr young men and women for civilian and military careers in the nation's maritime and intermodal transpor tion system. During a four-year course of study, midshipmen spend one year at sea as cadets aboard co mercial merchant ships, where they gain valuable practical experience. The remaining three years are sp at the Academy. Upon graduation, individuals receive a Bachelor of Science degree, a US Coast Gua license as deck or engineer officer, and a commission as an Ensign in the US Naval Reserve. Tuition, roo and board are provided by the federal government, in exchange for a 5-8 year service obligation in the ci ian transportation industry, active duty military, or Naval Reserve.

The Academy has long recognized the leadership and seamanship skills gained through sail traini and supports an extensive waterfront program. This includes a five-boat offshore sailing team, an inter-c legiate sailing team, and an extensive instructional and recreational fleet. All midshipmen are required learn to sail, and nearly 20% participate in the extracurricular programs. Midshipmen operate and maint all small craft and serve in all billets, from skippers watch captains and navigators.

Contact:

CDR Eric Wallischeck,USMS, Sailing Mast
Yocum Sailing Center
US Merchant Marine Academy
Kings Point, NY 11024-1699
Tel: 516-773-5396
E-mail: wallischecke@usmma.edu
Web site: http://www.usmma.edu

Ventura County Maritime Museum

Located on Fisherman's Wharf at the corner Channel Islands Boulevard and Victoria Avenue Oxnard, California, the Ventura County Maritime Museu is the focal point of Channel Islands Harbor's enterta ment center, and where maritime history comes alive.

The Museum is dedicated to the interpretation world maritime history, and is acknowledged as housi the finest collection of marine art and ship models on t Pacific Coast. The art collection spans four centuries marine painters, beginning with the 17th century Dut and Flemish masters and ending with the work of conte porary artists such as John Stobart and David Thimga An international parade of models of historic ships ma up a "Genealogy Of Sail" presentation representing ne ly 5,000 years of sailing history. Temporary exhibits feat ing both local and internationally recognized artists, well as timely subjects of maritime interest, assure th there is always something new to appeal to and attract repeat as well as first-time visitors. The Museum also has an active elementary education program targeted to grades 4 through 7, featuring California, American, and ancient maritime history. The Museum combines its programs with the Channel Islands Marine Floating Lab, which offers an oceanography program, to provide students with a rich, rewarding field trip to Channel Islands Harbor. These programs touch about 4500 students each year.

The Museum is open seven days a week; hours are 11 to 5. Suggested donation is $3.00 for adults, $1.00 for children under 12. Group tours, special activities for school groups, and social events can be arranged.

Contact: David Leach, Operations Manager
             Ventura County Maritime Museum
             2731 S. Victoria Avenue
             Oxnard, CA 93035
             Tel: 805-984-6260; Fax: 805-984-5970
             E-mail: VCMM@aol.com

Williams College - Mystic Seaport – Maritime Studies Program

The Maritime Studies program of Williams College and Mystic Seaport offers undergraduates the opportunity to focus a semester on the study of the sea. Students take four Williams College courses at Mystic Seaport: maritime history, literature of the sea, marine science (either oceanography or marine ecology), and marine policy. Academics are enhanced by hands-on maritime skills classes in sailing, shipsmithing, celestial navigation, or sea music. There are opportunities to climb aloft on square-riggers.

Four field seminars are incorporated into the curriculum each semester. Aboard a 130-foot stay-sail schooner, students voyage offshore for nearly two weeks in the North Atlantic each fall and in the Caribbean each spring semester. These expeditions involve intensive student participation. Students also travel to Nantucket and the Port of New York for the Atlantic Coast Field Seminar, and out west to California and Oregon to compare and contrast the flora, fauna, history, and environmental issues of the Pacific Coast.

Students return to Mystic and apply knowledge gained in their field experiences toward research projects in history, marine science, and marine policy. A full semester of credit is granted through Williams College (equivalent to 18 transfer credits). Financial aid is available.

Contact: Kelly Smit, Assistant Director of Admissions
             Williams-Mystic Maritime Studies Program
             Mystic Seaport
             75 Greenmanville Avenue, PO Box 6000
             Mystic, CT 06355-0990
             Tel: 860-572-5359; Fax: 860-572-5329
             E-mail: admissions@williamsmystic.org
             Web site: http://www.williamsmystic.org

Wooden Boat Foundation

The Wooden Boat Foundation is an organization as unique as the seaport town that is its home. The Wooden Boat Foundation is a non-profit organization operating on the waterfront of the Victorian seaport of Port Townsend Washington, a community that is world famous for its maritime culture and its wooden boats.

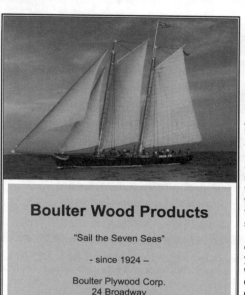

The Wooden Boat Foundation celebrates and preserves traditional maritime skills, culture and heritage through education and community participation. Made famous by hosting the premier wooden boat festival of the United States, beginning its tradition of education and celebration in 1977. The Foundation provides a broad variety of programs from our *Living Waterfront program*, guiding groups of young students through experiences in the famous trade shops and boatyards of our community to, our *Summer Youth Sea Camp* and *Adventure at Sea* programs aboard traditional training vessels and the tall ship *Adventuress*. The foundation has over 400 volunteers, 40 small craft, and is Port Townsend's waterfront community center, where people come to sail, row, be Sea Scouts, mentors, or armchair sailors in our maritime library.

The Foundation's traditional vessel chandlery also provides the one stop source for all of your traditional vessel hardware, bo'sonry, and wood working needs. Proceeds from the chandlery and the Wooden Boat Festival help to fund our educational programs.

Contact: Chris Kluck
380 Jefferson Street
Port Townsend, WA 98358
E-mail: info@woodenboat.org
Web site: http://www.woodenboat.org

WoodenBoat School

The WoodenBoat School is located on a 64-acre waterfront campus in Brooklin, Maine. Founded in 1981, the school's twin focus is on wooden boat building and seamanship taught by experienced professionals in the marine industry. Sailing courses are taught by experienced, licensed instructors on cutters, Friendship sloops, ketches, and more than 20 assorted small craft ranging from sailing prams to Herreshoff 12-1/2's. Instruction in related crafts such as lofting, marine mechanics, marine survey, painting and varnishing, marine photography, navigation, and marine art is also offered. Accommodations are available at the school. Courses are also offered at various off-site locations around the country

Contact: Rich Hilsinger, Director
                            WoodenBoat School
                            PO Box 78
                            Brooklin, ME 04616
                            Tel: 207-359-4651; Fax: 207-359-8920
                            Web site: http://www.woodenboat.com

The Yorktown Foundation

The Yorktown Foundation, located in Yorktown, Virginia at the mouth of the York River as it enters the Chesapeake Bay, is a nonprofit organization dedicated to preserve and perpetuate the special historic character of Yorktown (site of Revolutionary War victory in 1781).

One goal is to revitalize the waterfront and give visitors a sense of this colonial port. This $12M effort includes a dock designed specially for tall ships and cruise ships that want to experience the historic village of Yorktown or take a short trip (14 Miles) to Williamsburg. The project is on schedule for completion the summer of 2003. Visiting ships will add to the total educational experience at Yorktown.

Contact: Gary Freeman
                            Yorktown Foundation
                            P.O. Box 43
                            Yorktown, VA 23690
                            Tel: 757-890-1335; Fax: 757-898-3806
                            E-mail: gintail@earthlink.net

Youth Adventures, Inc.

Youth Adventure, Inc. is the oldest nonprofit sailing organization in the Pacific Northwest. Founded in 1959, Youth Adventures purchased the 1913 schooner *Adventuress* and began to offer a sail training program for "youth of all ages." This limited program became more active in the 60s when stewardship of the historic schooner was assumed by Ernestine "Erni" Bennett. For the next 25 years, Erni and a dedicated group of volunteers operated sail training programs aboard the venerable ship for thousands of youth, adults, and seniors - in Girl and Boy Scout, school, environmental education, elderhostel and other groups.

In 1991, Youth Adventures passed ownership and stewardship of the *Adventuress* to Sound Experience, a nonprofit environmental education and sail training organization. Since then, Youth Adventure has continued to help fund regional sail training and sea education programs, youth scholarships, and related activities.

In recognition of her commitment to sail training, Erni Bennett was presented the ASTA Lifetime Achievement Award in 1998. Know to many as "Mrs. B," Erni passed away at the age of 83 in August 2001. However, her sail training legacy will continue on through the newly established Ernestine Bennett/American Sail Training Association Scholarship program as will her enduring example of supporting sailing-based, lifelong learning opportunities for "youth of all ages."

Contact: Chuck Fowler
2518 Walnut Road NW
Olympia, WA 98502-4110
Tel: 360-943-2858; Fax: 360-943-5411
E-mail: nwnx@olywa.net
Ken Greff
906 3rd Street
Mukiltea, WA 98275
Tel: 425-353-0945

Photo by Wojtec Wakowski

SOUTH STREET SEAPORT MUSEUM

Sail Training / Marine Education Opportunities

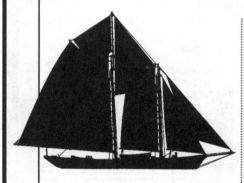

PIONEER
**1885 Iron Hulled
Cargo Schooner**

• School Trips
• Boy Scouts / Girl Scouts
• Charters
• Volunteer Opportunities

LETTIE G. HOWARD
**1893 Gloucester
Fishing Schooner**

• Elderhostel
• Seafaring Camp (with Harvey Gamage)
• Urban Waters
• Team Building

**Recipient, ASTA's 1997
Sea Education Program Award**

Come join us!
For information call (212) 748-8600
or write to us at
207 Front Street
New York, NY 10038

www.southstseaport.org

Ports, businesses,and
associates of tall ships.

Corporate Supporters

Acheson Ventures, LLC

Acheson Ventures, LLC, owner of the vintage gaff topsail schooner Highlander Sea, is committed to showcasing the marine lore of the Port Huron, Michigan area, in addition to providing educational experiences to the public.

One of Michigan's oldest settlements, Port Huron is located where Lake Huron becomes the St. Clair River and is affectionately referred to as the Blue Water Area. Port Huron is home to the historic Port Gratiot Lighthouse (the oldest lighthouse in Michigan), the Huron Lightship Museum, Historic Downtown District, as well as host to a number of annual events including the Feast of the St. Clair, a fascinating reenactment of the fur trading rendezvous, and the Thomas Edison Festival celebrating the great inventor and his youthful years in Port Huron, and Native American celebrations. Every fall the Classic Boat Show features some of the great pleasure boats from area boat builders.

We are very interested in attracting tall ships and tall ship enthusiasts to help celebrate the maritime history of the Blue Water Area.

Contact: Robert Lafean
Acheson Ventures, LLC
600 Fort Street, Suite 101
Port Huron, MI 48060
Tel: 810-966-0900; Fax: 810-966-0990
E-mail: boblafean@advnet.net

City of Richmond, British Columbia, Canada

The City of Richmond is located on Canada's Pacific Coast. Richmond is a unique island city of 165,000 residents. It is favourably located within the Greater Vancouver region in close proximity to downtown Vancouver, the U.S border and is the home of the Vancouver International Airport. Richmond is comprised of a series of islands in the mouth of the Fraser River at Latitude 49° 10' 59.1" N and Longitude 123° 8' 0.7" W.

Richmond welcomes tall ships to our cosy fishing port of Steveston, a fully serviced port with customs, fuel, accommodation and provisions. In the late 1800s, Steveston Village was the busiest fishing port in the world with fourteen fish canneries. Every summer, the harvest of salmon would see the community's population grow by the thousands as Natives, Chinese and Japanese labourers arrived seeking seasonal work. This hard working, hard living community had a rough and tumble lifestyle of gambling, opium-smoking and busy bordellos.

Now over 100 years later, Steveston has evolved into a picturesque working fishing village that comes to life with plenty to see and do. Home to almost 1,000 commercial fishing vessels, Steveston is the largest commercial fishing Harbour in Canada. Along the waterfront fishing boats and freighters ply the waters of the Strait of Georgia. At Fishermen's Wharf, fish boat operators sell fresh salmon, crab, halibut, and shrimp directly from dockside.

For more information about how we can accommodate your vessel contact Steveston Harbour Authority at (604) 272-5539. For more information on the City of Richmond contact (604) 276-4000 or visit our website at www.city.richmond.bc.ca.

Prime Media

At Prime Media Inc, (PMI) we love tall ships, and small ones,too! We're a full service advertising,marketing, public relations, and event management firm with offices in Bloomfieldand New London, Connecticut. With a staff of creative designers, we'veproduced web sites, brochures, logos, videos and more for events, businessesand professionals. After handling thepublic relations and marketing for New London'ssuccessful OpSail 2000 CT, PMI became event managers for the annual Boats Books& Brushes literary, arts and maritime festival in Connecticut. Currently in the planning stages is anothertall ship event with an environmental theme in conjunction with the International Children's Conference on the Environment in July 2003. For information, please contact Richard J.Shenkman at 800 634-1919, extension 700.

Business Partners

Alliance Marine Risk Managers, Inc.

Alliance Marine Risk Managers, Inc. specializes in the consultation and placemenrt of marine insurance for yacht owners and seamen worldwide. Founded and operated by lifelong sailors, Alliance Marine provides the product knowledge and insurance professionals. Equally important to the owner of traditional and historic vessels, Alliance honors and shares the values these vessels represent to the past, present, and future of America's maritime heritage.

Contact: Fredric A. Silberman, President
Alliance Marine Risk Managers, Inc.
1400 Old Country Road, Suite 307
Westbury, NY 11590
Tel: 516-333-7000, 800-976-2676;
Fax: 516-333-9529
Email: AMRM-NY@worldnet.att.net

Charleston Maritime Center, Charleston, South Carolina

Located on the peninsula's edge of the historic district, The Charleston Maritime Center makes a perfect stop for all types of visiting vessels. It is nestled in the center of Charleston's protected harbor and is approximately 3.5 miles from the open sea. Access is direct and immediate from the sea to the dock. No bridges are located from the mouth of the harbor to the docks. While on land, you are in close proximity to the new public library, historic tours and attractions, food and equipment provisioning.

The Charleston Maritime Center has hosted several tall ships to date, including the *Spirit of Massachusetts*, *Liberty Clipper*, *Windy*, *Voyager*, *Bill of Rights*, *Bounty* and the *HM Bark Endeavour*. The Center also hosted Tall Ships 2000® Charleston and welcomed 13 vessels for a week of activities.

The Center is Charleston's premier and only waterfront facility created for the community's use and enjoyment through many varieties of maritime related activities. The good currents and swift winds are especially conducive to races. With plenty of room to dock your boats, you can cruise to the finish line and literally step off your vessel to accept the winning trophy. Showers and free parking are also on-site, so make the most of a good day on the water. Should you prefer a little sightseeing or nightlife, the Charleston Maritime Center is just a few short blocks from the historic district.

Contact: Charleston Maritime Center
10 Wharfside Street
Charleston, SC 29401
Tel: 843-853-3625; Fax: 843-577-6675
E-mail: smithvi@ci.charleston.sc.us

City of New Bedford, Massachusetts

A city built by the sea, New Bedford was once the whaling capital of the world. Herman Melville shipped out of this port in 1841; it inspired him to write *Moby-Dick*. Today, New Bedford is an active seaport with a large fishing fleet & working waterfront. The Seamen's Bethel where Melville worshipped still stands on cobblestoned Johnny Cake Hill. Across the street is the Whaling Museum, the world's largest. New Bedford is homeport to Massachusetts' official vessel, Schooner *Ernestina*. Other attractions: New Bedford Whaling National Historical Park, Rotch-Jones-Duff House/Garden Museum, Buttonwood Park Zoo, Art and Fire Museums, Zeiterion Theatre & several art galleries, as well as many summer festivals. Located approximately 6 nautical miles north of the Intercoastal Waterway west of the Cape Cod Canal, New Bedford harbor features a 3-mi. hurricane barrier, making it the safest haven on the eastern seaboard.

Berthing contact: New Bedford Harbor Development Commission
                                   Tel: 508-961-3000.
Info: New Bedford Tourism/Marketing
                                   Tel: 800-508-5353
                                   Web site: http://www.ci.new-bedford.ma.us

City of New London, Connecticut

New London's new, $20 million waterfront park offers a half mile promenade and five piers to visiting vessels and tourists from around the world. This deep water port welcomes tall ships and luxury cruise lines as a destination port for travel up and down the Eastern Seaboard. Floating docks for transient boaters are available to the public, and kayakers and canoers can launch from a car-top boat ramp. The City Pier Plaza has a fiber-optic lighted stage area to entertain thousands for events year round. SeaPony Express offers cruises and charters in the river and Long Island Sound. Customs House Pier can accommodate large and small vessels and nearby mooring fields welcome visiting sailors. A dinghy dock allows access to the water frontpark and downtown New London. New London and Southeastern Connecticut have everything visitors look for when planning travel experiences. Visit the best in the arts, family attractions, quiet beaches, the world's largest casinos and Yankee heritage, all in a bustling New England port.

Contact: City of New London, Connecticut
                                   Richard M. Brown, City Manager
                                   181 State Street
                                   New London, CT 06320
                                   Tel: 860-447-5201; Fax: 860-447-7971

City of Sarnia, Ontario, Canada

Sarnia hugs the St.Clair River, and shores of the one of the world's largest freshwater lakes, Lake Huron. It is one of the busiest recreational boating and shipping regions of the Great Lakes. Here, the landmark twin Blue Water Bridges join Ontario with Port Huron, Michigan, just an hour north of Detroit.

For thousands of years, natives have inhabited the area. The first European settlers arrived early in the 19th century. They named their community "The Rapids" for the fast-flowing St. Clair River. In 1836, The Rapids was renamed Port Sarnia, but in 1856 it was given a final new name, which was Sarnia.

Sarnia marks the northern starting point of the St. Clair Parkway, one of three parkway systems in the province. The city boasts approximately 20 kilometers (12 miles) of waterfront and is home to over 73,000 residents. One of the features of the Sarnia Bay district is Centennial Park, home to the annual Christmas-themed Celebration of Lights and a variety of summer festivals. The Sarnia Highland Games have been held in Centennial Park for two decades. Dow People Place, located within the park, is an outdoor entertainment stage featuring regular summer concerts. Beside Sarnia Bay Marina is a 100 foot wide model of the Great Lakes. The ample outdoor park settings create an ideal environment for waterfront picnics and location to view the busy river activity. Annually more than 5,000 freighters pass by Sarnia, traveling up and down the St. Clair River. Two cruise boats run regular excursions from Sarnia and Point Edward out onto Lake Huron.

The area enjoys a moderate climate, rarely receiving significant snowfalls, but often just enough to put glimmer on the ground for the lights festival. Summers are hot but a cool breeze off the lake or a dip in its refreshing waters makes Sarnia a perfect vacation spot.

Contact: City of Sarnia, Ontario
                                   Henk Vanden Ende
                                   946 Toro Street
                                   Sarnia, Ont, N7V 3N9 Canada
                                   Tel: 519-333-6344
                                   E-mail: henkv@ebtech.net

City of Wilmington, North Carolina

Located in Southeastern North Carolina, Wilmington is an area rich in history and culture. The city, bounded to the west by the Cape Fear River and to the east by the Intracoastal Waterway, is the leading port of North Carolina and a very popular tourist destination.

The city provides public dock space in historic downtown Wilmington, along a scenic riverfront overlooking the USS NORTH CAROLINA Battleship Memorial. Visitors can enjoy one of the largest and finest National Historic Registry districts in the nation. Numerous galleries, gardens, shopping/dining establishments, recreational activities, a vibrant night life and our newly expanded riverwalk are all within walking distance of the docks.

The community has a strong commercial and recreational maritime history. The city is host to several annual festivals/events that draw thousands of people to downtown Wilmington's riverfront. The city of Wilmington enthusiastically welcomes the opportunity to host tall ships and sail training vessels.

Contact: R.T. Jones, Dockmaster
City of Wilmington
Public Services and Facilities
P.O. Box 1810, 302 Willard Street
Wilmington, N.C. 28402
Tel: 910-520-6875 (Dockmaster)
Tel: 910-341-7855 (Public Services & Facilities)
Web site: http://www.ci.wilmington.nc.us

Conventures, Inc.

Conventures, Inc. is New England's largest event marketing and management firm. Conventures specializes in maritime events and strategic marketing communications services to assist your special event or your vessel marketing initiatives. Conventures is New England's largest special events company with a department specializing in tall ship and maritime festivals. Our expertise include sponsorship development and fulfillment, merchandising programs, ship recruitment, and ship representation.

In the last decade, Conventures has produced over ten successful maritime festivals including Sail Boston 1992®, The Boston Seaport Festival™, 1998 Bicentennial Salute of the USS CONSTITUTION™, Sail Boston 2000®, and Sail Detroit™ 2001.

Contact: David H. Choate, Conventures, Inc.
One Design Center Place, Suite 718
Boston, MA 02210
Tel: 617-439-7700; Fax: 617-439-7701
E-mail: dchoate@conventures.com
Web site: http://www.conventures.com

Coos Bay/North Bend PC

Oregon's Bay Area—Coos Bay, North Bend, and Charleston—invites you to visit our beautiful bay area on the southern Oregon Coast. The Port of Coos Bay is a deepwater port and well equipped to handle tall ships. The Coos Bay Pilots Association and the U.S. Coast Guard have the expertise needed to bring vessels into Coos Bay and guide them safely to dockside. Should you offer tours to the public, we also have funds to advertise on major television networks, newspapers and magazines to help promote your visit. We will consider financial assistance to visiting tall ships to help offset costs. Coos Bay City Dock is located across the street from city center, and we welcome the opportunity to host tall ships and sail training vessels. Should you consider our port, we would be happy to make special arrangements to welcome your tall ship!

Contact:

Beverly Saukko, Executive Director
Coos Bay/North Bend Promotion & Convention Bureau
500 Central – Room 10
Coos Bay, OR 97420
Tel: 541-269-8921; Fax: 541-267-5615
E-mail: tourism@harborside.com
Web site: http://www.oregonbayarea.com

Dirigo Cruises, Ltd.

Since 1973, Dirigo Cruises has offered educational voyages with emphasis on celestial navigation, nature expeditions, sail training, and midshipman programs. Operating in New England, the Caribbean, the Indian Ocean, and the South Pacific, Dirigo Cruises has programs for people of all ages.

Contact:

Captain Eben M. Whitcomb, Jr.
39 Waterside Lane
Clinton, CT 06413
Tel: 860-669-7068;
Fax: 860-669-2297

Fall River Area Chamber of Commerce

The 16th Annual Fall River Celebrates America Waterfront Festival, August 8-11, 2002, will be a family-oriented, alchohol-free, series of events and exhibits at Battleship Cove and Heritage State Park on the historic Fall River, Massachusetts waterfront. Tall ships, Portuguese Night, multi-cultural events, three entertainment stages, fireworks, children's entertainment, sailing regatta's, International Food and Dessert Fair, arts and crafts, and six-division parade are a few of the many events that will take place. In addition, there are year-round attractions such as the Battleship MASSACHUSETTS, the Marine Museum at Fall River, the Old Colony and the Fall River Railroad Museum, and the Fall River Carousel. The festival is produced by the Chamber of Commerce in cooperation with the City of Fall river, the Fall River Cultural Council, The FIRSTFED Charitable Foundation, and other businesses. Tall ships interested in participating and for further information:

Contact:

Jim Haskins
Fall River Chamber of Commerce
Director of Membership Services
Tel: 508-676-8226; Fax: 508- 675-5932
E-mail: jhaskins@fallriverchamber.com
Web site: http://www.fallriverchamber.com

Hallett Traditional Sails, LLC

Hallett Traditional Sails is dedicated to building authentic and historic sails with truly traditional materials and techniques. We also offer the very best modern traditional sail that also has the authentic look but uses more modern materials, creating a sail that will last longer. Hallett Traditional Sails is a partnership with Hallett Canvas and Sails, fusing modern techniques such as computer design and sail cutting with traditional hand finishing.

Our sail makers have over 50 years of traditional sail making experience. They have worked on projects from small dinghies sails to ships sails for boats such as the HMS *Rose*, the *Eagle*, *Radiant*, *Bounty*, and many more. Our expertise under the guidance of Heidi Sawyer sets apart our sails and service from all the rest. We are committed to forming the relationship needed to provide you with a product that fits your needs.

Contact: Heidi Sawyer, Sailmaker
P.O. Box 247
34 Atlantic Avenue
Rockland ME 04841
Tel: 207-594-9810; Fax: 207-594-9815
E-mail: hallettsails@hotmail.com
Web site: http://www.hallettcanvasandsails.com

Historic Promotions, Inc.

Historic Promotions is a full service company representing tall ships worldwide. We provide diverse services to client ships, ports, corporate and non-profit sponsors, educational programs, and festival operators. Some of the services provided for tall ship events include historic reenactments, youth education programs, corporate entertainment, charter, and securing long-term sponsorships.

After nearly three decades of financing, international trade, and corporate development, founder and President, Ron Prichep, turned his sights to the sea. "Bringing ships together with ports produces meaningful experiences for so many and maintains ships on the seas to continue our maritime heritage." Using business development and marketing expertise, Historic Promotions, generates income for tall ships so they may fulfill their mission as living museums and educational venues. Historic Promotions organizes annual voyage schedules to optimize income opportunities, and matches ships with events, to increase the public's appreciation of nautical heritage, history, technology, craftsmanship and life. Historic Promotions can assist with most business needs of the maritime community and many of its services are paid for based upon actual performance or by the sponsors.

Contact: Ronald Prichep, President
8361 Robert Place
Manassas, VA 20112-3111
Tel: 703-530-0626; Fax: 703-530-8669
E-mail: ronprichep@aol.com

Ocean Navigator School of Seamanship

The Ocean Navigator School of Seamanship offers the following seminars for offshore sailors in approximately ten locations around the country:

- Introduction to Celestial Navigation
- Understanding Meteorology and Marine Weather
- Offshore Seamanship and Heavy Weather Seamanship Under Sail
- Introduction to Offshore Emergency Medicine
- Navigation – Basic to State of the Art
- Marine Diesel Engine Operation and Maintenance
- Marine Electrical Systems Operation and Maintenance
- The On Board Computer
- High Tech Systems for the Average Cruising Yacht

The seminars are fast-paced and fairly intense, designed for experienced sailors. A knowledge of basic skills is assumed although most seminars begin with a review of those skills. In many cases the subject is too broad to produce experts overnight, but in every case you will go away with a full appreciation for the subject and the ability to go on learning from that day forward. The school's mission is to teach present and future offshore sailors important knowledge and techniques that will make them better voyagers and navigators.

Contact:

Ocean Navigator School of Seamanship
PO Box 760
Rockport, ME 04856
Tel/Fax: 207-236-7014
E-mail: education@oceannavigator.com
Web site:http://www.oceannavigator.com

Sail Baltimore

Sail Baltimore is a nonprofit, community organization dedicated to offering maritime educational experiences to the general public, visitors, local citizens, children, and disadvantaged youth. Other goals are to stimulate the economy of the City of Baltimore and surrounding communities, to increase regional tourism, provide a forum and network for encouraging business development opportunities, and to foster international cultural exchange.

This mission is accomplished through recruiting, planning, and hosting visits of various types of ships whose presence in the harbor offers an educational but non-commercial experience. Sail Baltimore also produces special events designed to attract people to the city's waterfront, including several successful tall ship events and water parades over the past 27 years.

Contact:

Sail Baltimore
1809 Thames Street
Baltimore, MD 21231
Tel: 410-752-7300;
Fax:410-522-3405
E-mail: info@sailbaltimore.org
Website:http://www.sailbaltimore.org

Sail New London

Bring your appetite when you set sail for *Boats Books & Brushes* with a *Taste of Connecticut*, two popular festivals partnered to form one unique literary, arts, food and maritime event, September 6-8, 2002, on New London, CT's historic waterfront. Visit authors for readings and book signings and watch artists painting on the piers. Sample gourmet food and fine wine and beer served by 40 of Connecticut's finest chefs and restaurants. Enjoy art exhibits, maritime history, live music, and story-tellers. Children can take part in hands-on arts and crafts adventures, visit Museum Village, and hear "Spooky Stories by the Sea." Sailing and boating enthusiasts can tour the USCG E*agle* at City Pier and watch the Class C tall ships race in the 3rd Annual New London Schooner Challenge. For more information call the Chamber of Commerce of Eastern Connecticut at 860-443-8332 or visit www.sail-newlondon.com.

Sail San Francisco

Sail San Francisco is a nonprofit organization founded to foster international friendships and good will in the San Francisco Bay Area. The organization hosts events such as international tall ship gatherings and supports local youth focused tall ship sailing programs which are designed to enhance leadership skills, self-esteem and experience with intercultural exchanges. Special emphasis is placed on community outreach during international tall ships visits. Sail San Francisco strives to offer a variety of free events and ensure that these events are accessible to disabled individuals. Exchanges between local and foreign tall ship crews and under-served residents and students of the Bay Area who share the same language are also a priority.

Sail San Francisco successfully brought the 'Gold Rush Sail' visit of international tall ships, their crew and many educational and cultural events to more than two million Bay Area visitors and residents in July, 1999. Work is underway to host the next international tall ship visit to San Francisco in 2002.

Contact:

Alison Healy, Executive Director
Sail San Francisco
2801 Leavenworth Street, 2nd floor
San Francisco, CA 94137
Tel: 415-447-9822; Fax: 401-447-7320
E-mail: info@sailsanfrancisco.org
Web site: http://www.sailsanfrancisco.org

SAILFEST

SAILFEST was created in 1976 as a celebration of New London, Connecticut's sailing history. It is a community volunteer effort produced by The Downtown New London Association (DNLA), a non-profit group of approximately 50 merchants in the Downtown area. Southeastern Connecticut's premier summertime event takes place the second weekend in July.

SAILFEST is a street and harbor festival which attracts approximately 300,000 over the weekend. During the event tall ships dock at the City's new 20-million dollar waterfront park. SAILFEST also features a parade, amusement rides, free entertainment, food and craft vendors lining downtown streets and a WORLD CLASS fireworks display described as always one of the largest in the Northeast. Proceeds from the SAILFEST are returned to the community and used to fund other DNLA projects and activities designed to promote the waterfront and business district. The DNLA is committed to promote the Downtown New London area through quality special events and activities that showcase the culture and heritage of the region. Tall ships interested in participating in SAILFEST please contact Barbara Neff.

Contact: Barbara J. Neff
PO Box 1096
New London, CT 06320
Tel: 860-444-1879
E-mail: sailfest@snet.net
Web site: http://www.sailfest.org

Savannah Waterfront Association

In the 1970s, the city of Savannah, Georgia implemented a major urban renewal program to revitalize the waterfront. Old cotton warehouses have been transformed, and the Savannah Waterfront Association hosts many exciting festivals to bring people to the river. Today, Savannah's historic waterfront is lined with more than 100 unique shops and galleries, fabulous restaurants, seductive nightspots, and elegant inns and hotels. The docking facilities were updated in the last six years, and Savannah has hosted several tall ships and has plans for an annual tall ship festival. The Savannah Waterfront Association is a nonprofit organization whose purpose is the promotion and preservation of the historic waterfront.

Contact: Gordon Varnedoe, Executive Director
Savannah Waterfront Association
PO Box 572
Savannah, GA 31402
Tel: 912-234-0295; Fax: 912-234-4904
E-mail: waterfests@aol.com
Web site: http://www.savriverstreet.com

Société du Vieux-Port de Montréal (Old Port Montreal Corporation, Inc.)

Since May 1992, the Old Port of Montréal has been offering Montréalers, yachting tourists, and tall ships a quality marina The Port d'Escale. Located in the Jacques Cartier Basin, the Port d'Escale is equipped with a full range of up-to-date facilities to accommodate sailboats over 200 feet, docking on floating docks. Tucked into the heart of the Old Port, a few steps away from downtown Montréal, this secure facility provides a quiet haven for the ships mooring there. Because of its varied activities and its unique atmosphere, the Old Port is an important site for recreation and tourism in Montréal. Set a heading for the Port d'Escale, and discover Montréal in style.

Contact: Sylvain A. Deschamps, Harbourmaster
333 de la Commune Street West
Montréal, QUE H2Y 2E2 Canada
Tel: 514-283-5414; Fax: 514-283-8423

Tall Ships® Cruise Club

The Tall Ships® Cruise Club (TSCC) is a division of the Landings Travel Agency of Sarasota, Florida in business since 1983. Dedicated to bringing luxury level cruises to the tall ships experience, the TSCC delivers on three levels of travel experience.

Since 1997 the TSCC has planned Tall Ships® Rendezvous Cruises in Europe featuring a major maritime port festival and the start of a leg of the annual Tall Ships® races. In 1997, *Crystal Harmony* was in Stavanger, Norway; in 1999, Lerwick, Scotland; in 2000 it was Stockholm, Sweden; and in 2001 the Tall Ships® Rendezvous was in Bergen, Norway. In 2002, the TSCC has arranged with Silversea Cruises to be on the *Silver Cloud* to rendezvous with the fleet of tall ships in La Coruna, Spain. In 2003 aboard the *Crystal Symphony* again the TSCC will be in St. Petersburg, Russia for the 300th anniversary of the founding of this magnificent port city by Peter the Great and then cruise on to the 2003 Tall Ships® Rendezvous in Gdynia, Poland.

The TSCC also arranges group cruises that give an actual tall ship cruising experience on tall ships such as *Star Clipper* and *Royal Clipper*.

Finally, the Tall Ships® Cruise Club is designing maritime heritage land-tours to the grand European maritime museums and other historical nautical venues of the UK, Ireland and France.

Contact: Dewey Kennell
             Tall Ships® Cruise Club
             Landings Travel Agency
             4986 S. Tamiami Trail
             Sarasota, FL 34231
             Tel: 800-299-1125
             E-mail: deweykennell@earthlink.net

Village of Greenport, Long Island, New York

Located in the beautiful, deep and superbly protected waters of the Gardiners/Peconic Bay system of eastern Long Island, Greenport Harbor has been a uniquely appealing destination for mariners since the dawn of American history. Modern-day Greenport remains true to this heritage. A seaborn visitor arriving today steps off the boat, and back in time, to enjoy an authentic working seaport where a car is unnecessary.

Deep water dockage for large and small vessels is available at a municipally owned marina in the heart of a downtown waterfront listed on the National Register of Historic Places. Stores, galleries, and services including those catering to mariners, such as welding, hauling, carpentry and marine hardware, even a hospital, are but steps away. A waterfront park has been developed upland of the marina which boasts a vintage carousel, an outdoor amphitheater and boardwalk. Additional boardwalk will soon connect the marina to a transportation center where bus, rail, and ferry connections are available to Shelter Island, New York City, and destinations throughout Long Island.

Greenport is keenly interested in visits by tall ships and sail training vessels and will make special arrangements to host traditional sailing vessels, their crews and trainees.

Contact: Mayor David E. Kapell
Village of Greenport
236 Third Street
Greenport, New York 11944
Tel: 631-477-3000
Fax: 631-477-1877

GreenportHarbormaster:
516-702-4381

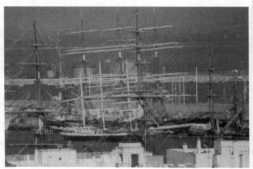

356

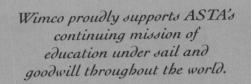

Photo by Phil Holys

SAIL TALL SHIPS!

Associate Members

Life Members
Mr. Henry H. Anderson, Jr.
Mr. and Mrs. John Benson
Captain Joseph M. Davis
Mr. Murray Davis
Captain Robert S. Douglas
Mr. Ronald V. Gallo
Mr. John M. Hopkins
Mr. Jonathan T. Isham
RADM Michael A. Martin
Mr. Thor H. Ramsing
Mr. Frederic S. Sater
Captain Cornelius Vanderstar
Dr. A. R. G. "Robin" Wallace
Mr. Edward B. Watson, Jr.
Mr. Robert W. Rathall
Mr. Arthur W. Young

Patrons
Mr. Peter Manigault

Supporting Members
Mr. and Mrs. Steven H. Baker and Family
Mr. Hal G. Barstow
Mr. Arthur Birney
Mr. and Mrs. Peter Boudreau
Mr. and Mrs. Thomas J. Gochberg
Mr. and Mrs. Frederick E. "Ted" Hood, Sr.
Mr. George Lewis, Jr.
Mr. Per H. M. Lofving
Mr. Jeffrey N. Parker
Mr. Joseph A. Ribaudo
Captain and Mrs. Christopher Rowsom
Captain and Mrs. Walter Rybka
Mr. David A. Steen
Mr. and Mrs. David Evan Thomas
Ms Alix T. Thorne
Mr. F. C. "Bunky" Wichmann, Jr.
Captain Eric J. Williams III, USCG (Ret.)

Family Members
Mr. Alexander M. Agnew
Mr. and Mrs. Paul Barker
Mr. and Mrs. Robert Bechtel
Captain Peg Brandon and Mr. Tony Cave
Mr. and Mrs. James T. Chadwick
Mr. and Mrs. Ted Cochran
Mr. and Mrs. Jim Cole
Ms Deborah Cooper and Family
Dr. and Mrs. Marshall Cushman
Mr. Leverett Davis and Family
Mr. and Mrs. Tim Driskel
Dr. and Mrs. Daniel Eardley
Mr. and Mrs. James C. Greenway III
Mr. Frederick W. Guardabassi
Ms Patricia E. Hartle and Captain Laurence Gellerman
Captains Deborah Hayes and John Beebe-Center
Mr. Jerry Hilgendorff
Dr. and Mrs. Cameron Hinman
Ms and Mr. Krista and Derek Klett
Mr. Stanley Martin and Family
Captain Henry E. Marx and Family
Mr. and Mrs. John McNaughton
Mr. and Mrs. Daniel A. Mello
Ms Jacqueline Moore and Mr. Blau
Mr. and Mrs. Colin Mudie
Mr. and Mrs. Clarke Murphy
LCDR and Mrs. Eugene A. Peterman
Mr. John Rae
Ms Deborah Raven-Lindley
Captain and Mrs. Andrew Reay-Ellers
Mr. Don Reed and Family
Mr. and Mrs. R. Norton Richards
Ms Stephanie K. Strong-Irwing
Mr. Wojtec Wacowski
VADM and Mrs. Thomas R. Weschler, USN (Ret.)
Mr. Thomas Wing
Captain and Mrs. David V. V. Wood, USCG (Ret.)
Mr. and Mrs. Dudley L. Wright
CAPT Peter C. Wylie

Individual Members
Mr. Richard A. Adams
CAPT Raymond W. Allen, USN (Ret.)
Mr. Michael Allen
Mr. Nicholas Alley
Mr. Michael J. Anderson
Ms Clara Anderson
Mr. Roger W. Archibald

Ms Cindy Arnold
Mr. Michael Auten
Ms Mary Baker
Ms Susan Baker
Captain Thomas Baker II
Mr. B. J. Barden
Mr. Aaron S. Barker
Ms Emily Barker
Ms Mavis Barkley
Mr. J. Burr Bartram, Jr.
Mr. Elmar Baxter
Ms Debra Beaman
Ms Secundra Beasley
Captain Austin Becker
Mr. Scott Beglinger
Mr. Robert Bein
Mr. Mark Belvedere
Mr. Jack Bennett
Captain Sean Sexton Bercaw
Mr. Erik Berliner
Mr. David Bierig
Mr. Brian W. Billings
Mr. James A. Bising
Mr. Andrew Bisset
Mr. Jim Bjork
Mr. Thomas D. Blanchard, Jr.
Mr. David H. Blomberg
Ms Irene Bodnaruk
Ms Constance L. Boehm
Mr. Lucio Bolognani
Ms Beth Bonds
Mr. Eric Bradish
Mr. Michael E. Brannigan
Mr. Mark K. Branse
Captain Jesse A. Briggs
Mr. Geoff Briggs
Mr. Harvey Brillat
Dr. Jeffrey Brodsky
Ms Margaret Brookhouse
Mr. James Brooks
Mr. Richard M. Brown
Mr. S. D. Brown
Ms Gay Lorraine Burgiel
Mr. Craig K. Burton
Mr. Richard Canfield
Ms Diane L. Carey
Mr. Bob Carlisle
Dr. Michael S. Carlson
Dr. R. Bruce Carruthers
Ms Jeanne Cassidy
Mr. Wilmot V. Castle, Jr.
Ms Marion Oates Charles
Captain G. Andy Chase
Mr. Gerin B. Choiniere
Mr. Randall Christian
Mr. Mike Christie
Mr. Richard J. Clark
Captain Martyn J. Clark
Ms Christine Cleary
Mr. Ward Cleaveland
Captain Timothy C. Clifford
Mr. Rick Clolek
Mr. Richard G. Cobler
Ms Susanna Cointot
Mr. William Colby
Mr. Timothy Collyer
Mr. Lawrence Conlin
Captain Stephen Connett
Mr. Michael J. Convery
Mr. Tim Cordes
Dr. Stanton G. Cort
Mr. Rich Cosgrove
Mr. Harold Joseph Coughlin, Jr.
Mr. Alan Creaser
Captain George W. Crowninshield
Dr. David R. Damon
Ms Laurie Dann, President
Mr. Thomas E. Dasson
Mr. Mike Dawson
Mr. Mickey DeBoef
Ms Nancy Dessenberger
Mr. Kevin DeVries
Mr. John Dignan
Mr. Edward M. Dolan
Mr. John C. Dommerman
Mr. Ryan Downing

Ms Elizabeth B. Doxsee
Mr. Michael F. Dugan
Mr. Bart Dunbar
Ms Connie Dusckas
Mr. Kevin Dykema
Mr. Richard Dykstra
Ms Patricia Dzintarnieks
Mr. David Eddy
Mr. Richard J. Edwards
Mr. Tom Ehbrecht
Mr. Gordon J. Eisenbart
Mr. Randy Ellerman
Mr. G. Elliott
Ms Luann Elvey
Mr. Peter Equi
Ms Pam Erickson
Ms Barbara J. Ettner
Ms Emily Evans
Mr. Joe Ewing
Mr. Christopher Ferszt
Captain Ted Finley
Mr. John Fischer
Mr. Doug Fischer
Mr. Harland Fish
Mr. David E. Fleenor
Ms Edie Flynn
Mr. Patrick Flynn
Mr. David J. Foley
Mr. Robert Foulke
Mr. Chuck Fowler
Mr. Iver C. Franzen
Mr. Walter Freisewinkel
Mr. Tim Frush
CAPT Jack Fuechsel, USCG (Ret.)
Mr. Yoshitatsu Fukawa
Mr. Stephen K. Galpin
Ms Lori Ganton
Mr. Richard J. Gay
Mr. Thomas A. Gemmell
Ms Cindy Giles
Mr. Andrew Gledhill
Mr. Thomas A. Goodall
Mr. Javier Gorords
Mr. John Graefe
Ms Meg Graustein
Captain Ken Greff
Mr. Dan Grehrice
Mr. John B. Griffith
Ms Janet Grimm
Mr. Konrad Groeschell
CAPT Donald F. Grosse, USCG (Ret.)
Captain Chad H. Grubb
Mr. William M. Gruber
Mr. John Guldi
Mr. Jack Hagedorn
Mr. Richard Haggblad
Mr. Ed Hale
Captain Paul C. Haley
Mr. Scott Hamann
Mr. Al Hamilton
Mr. Gary Hamman
Mr. Herbert T. Hand
Ms Lynne P. Hanhilammi
Mr. Eric M. Hansen
Mr. John Harrow
Mr. David F. Hart
Mr. Mike Haslam
Ms Joanne Hatch
Mr. and Mrs. Brian Healey
Ms Alison Healy
Mr. Hanns-Georg Karle Heil
Mr. Carl Heise
Ms Kitty McKoon Hennick
Mr. Carl Herzog
Mr. Money Hickman
Ms Barb Hicks
Mr. Richard Hill
Mr. James E. Hilyard
Captain David W. Hiott IV
Ms Sharon Hirsch
Mr. Michael G. Hoag
Mr. Russell Holterman
Mr. Phillip Holysh
Ms Mary Honti
Mr. Stephen D. Hopkins
Mr. Nicholas C. Horvath
Mr. Evans Hoyt
Captain Alan Ross Hugenot
Mr. Chuck Hukari
Ms Jody Hulsebosch

Mr. Richard L. Jacoby
Ms Jennifer Jeffries
RADM Tim Jenkins, USNR (Ret.)
Mr. Robert P. Johnson
CDR Robert A. Johnson, USN (Ret.)
Ms Anne Johnson
Mr. Patrick Johnson
Mr. Ellsworth O. Jones
Mr. Thomas Hadley Josten
Mr. Ken Kaelin
Mr. Tom Kastle
Mr. Donald Keel
Ms Nettie Kelly
Captain and Mrs. Arthur Kimberly
Mr. Richard King
Ms Barbara Kirby
Mr. Brian Kliesen
Mrs. Mitzi Koch
Mr. Edward Kothe
Mr. Kurt Krimphove
Mr. Roy H. Kruse
Mr. Wil Langdon
Mr. Anthony Lanza
Mr. Kurt Larson
Ms Melanie Laur
Mr. David Leanza
Mr. Timothy Lee
Ms Linda Leggitt
Mr. Ron Leggitt
Mr. Thomas E. Leonard
Ms Katherine Leonard
Mr. Francis A. Lewis III
Mr. James Lida
Ms Nancy Linden
Ms Patricia H. Lock
Mr. Richard C. "Chad" Loebs, Jr.
Ms Patricia R. Longan, Ph. D.
Mr. James Longstreet
Ms Sally H. Lunt
Mr. John H. Lynch
Ms Lauren Elizabeth Marchand
Mr. John C. Marcum
Mr. David B. Markell
Ms Robyn Marquez
Ms Holly K. Martin
Mr. Paul H. Martinez, Esq.
Mr. Ralph L. Mason
Mr. David T. Matthews
Ms Chris Maurer
Mr. Ross L. Mayberry
Mr. George McCarror
Mr. Leander McCormick-Goodhart
Miss Dorothy H. McGee
Mr. Neil McLaren
Ms Agnes McLean
Captain Brian S. McNamara
Mr. Greg McPhee
Captain Donald McQuiston
Mr. John D. McShane
Mr. Johann Meister
Mr. Jerry Menzies
Mr. Jerry Mergler
Ms Trina Meyer
Mr. Paul Meyer
Mr. Randy Michaels
Mr. Greg Michales
Mr. Roger Michalski
Captain Jan Miles
Mr. Tim Miller
Mr. Wayne Miller
Mr. Robert Miorelli
Mr. Mark E. Mitsock
Mr. David Moreno
Mr. Eric Morrison
Mr. Henry E. Moseley
Ms Deanna Moseley
Dr. M.S. Moyer
Mr. Jay Mullen
Mr. Dale Murphy
Ms Melissa Murphy
Mr. Ryan Mynsberge
Mr. Takamasa Nakagawa
Mr. Kazuko Nakagawa
Mr. Hisakazu Nakayama
Ms Jesse Leah Nankin
Mr. and Mrs. Ken and Julie Neal-Boyd
Mr. James Nelson
Mr. Charles Nelson
Mr. Tod Neuenschwander
Mr. Frank A. Newton

SAIL TALL SHIPS!

Mr. Ralph J. "Buzz" Nichols
Mr. Paul C. Nicholson, Jr.
Ms Gretchen Nielsen
Mr. Donald L. Nock
CAPT John T. O'Brien, USN (Ret.)
Ms Kathy Odiorne
Mr. Brian Olson
Mr. Patrick O'Malley
Ms Cathy Onsted
Mr. David Onsted
Ms Lynn Ann Oschmann
Mr. John Osgaad
Mr. Gordon John Owen
Mr. Lincoln Paine
Ms Kimberly Paltridge
Mr. Tim Paul
Mr. Eric S. Peden
Captain Randall S. Peffer
Ms Kristina Isabella Pentek
Mr. Thomas M. Pepin
Mr. Stephen Perloff
Mr. Charles E. Perry
Ms Annie Perry
Ms Eve Perry
Mr. Albert Petatan
Mr. David Peterson
Mr. Kevin S. Petrone
Ms Annmarie Petrosky
Ms Carmen Petrosky
Mr. Thomas J. Pfister
Mr. Lindsey Philpott
Mr. Edward V. Pietka
Mr. Joseph D. Pignato
Ms Louisa Pittman
Ms Erna Place
Mr. Eric Pratt
Mr. Rich Predku
Mr. Kenneth Prest
Mrs. Donna Prieur
Mr. Justin Pritchard
Captain Ulrich Pruesse
Captain Gunther K. Reher
Ms Melissa Reichert
Mr. James E. Reiff
Ms Sandra Rellinger
Ms Sandra Reno
Mr. Alan Rice
Ms Nancy H. Richardson
Ms Ellen Rieton
Miss Stephanie Robb
Ms J. Catherine Roberts
Ms Candice A. Rogie
Mr. William Roland
Ms Elizabeth Romano
Ms Elizabeth E. Roosevelt
Mr. Mark Rosenstein
Mr. Greg R. Rossi
Mr. Jeff H. Rothman
Mr. Jack Rovics
Ms Laura Rowan
Mr. Ken Ruppel
Captain Robert D. Rustchak
Ms Erica Sachs
Mr. H. Alexander Salm
Mr. David E. Sargent
Mr. Roy Savage
Mr. Jesse Schaffer
Ms Deborah Schellenberg
Mr. David Schenk
Mr. Donald S. Scheu
Mr. Ken Schmitt
Mr. Michael Schoettle
Mr. Arent H. Schuyler, Jr.
Mr. Gary Schwarzman
Mr. W. E. Seaman
Mr. H. J. Sefcovic
Mr. Horton R. Shaw
Ms Jamilyn Shaw
Mr. Kelly Shawl
Mr. Karen Shawl
Mr. Paul H. Sheehan
Mr. Douglas Sheets
Captain Christopher B. Sheldon
Captain Randall M. Sherman
Mr. Rudolph C. Shokal
Ms Sarah Skacelas
Mr. Daniel Skira
Ms Karla M. Smith
Ms Caroline J. Smith
Mr. Travis Smith

Mr. Steve Sohus
Ms Sally Somsel
Mr. James E. Spurr
Mr. Ray Stache
Mr. Wallace C. Stark
Senator John Stauffer
Captain M. Jeremy Steele-Perkins
Ms Susan C. Steiner
Mr. Mike Stevens
Mr. Les Stevenson
Ms Kaari Sullivan
Mr. Clyde Sundberg
Mr. Robert J. Surprenant
CAPT Harold J. Sutphen, USN (Ret.)
RADM Rothesay C. Swan, AO CBE
Ms Judy SwansonUSCG, Ret.
Ms Barb Swierzbin
Captain William Taylor, USCGR (Ret.)
Mr. James Taylor
Mr. Donald F. Teal
Ms Arnota Tejchma
Mr. Robert Thorsten
Mr. Steve Tompkins
Ms Shari Torka
Mr. Mark Treat
Mr. Thompson Tully
Mr. Wilfred van Breukelen
Mr. Jason Van Every
Mr. Jason Van Every
Mr. David B. Vietor
Mr. Sebastian Pablo Viora
Ms Sue Wagener
Ms Donna Walker
Ms Gayle Wallace
Ms Angela Walter
Mr. Shel Wappler
Mr. John Wargo
Mr. Paul Warner
Ms. Erika Washburn
Mr. James A. Washburn
Mr. David G. Watson
Mr. Collin Webb
Mr. Robert L. Webb
Captain Jim Wehan
Mr. Earl Weintraub
Mr. Fred Were
Mr. Tim Whiting
Mr. Michael Wick
Mr. Jerome Widenhouse
Captain John C. Wigglesworth
Commodore John A. Willett
Mr. Joseph A. Willhelm
Mr. Jonathan S. Wisch
Mr. Matt Wise
CAPT Christopher Withers, USN (Ret.)
CAPT Elizabeth G. Wylie, USN (Ret.)
Mr. Charles Zechel
Mr. Jim Zielake

Junior Members

Ms Lynda D. Burris
Ms Rachel J. Cortez
Ensign Daniel Doyle, USN
Mr. Ian Glass
Mr. Bryan Ross Hammond
Mr. Caitlin Harwood
Mr. James W. Hiney
Ms Laura Hockensmith
Ms Kelly Iacono
Mr. Kent J. Ingalls
Mr. Matt Johnson
Ms Arielle Knuttel
Mr. Nicholas Landholt, Jr.
Ms Sara Levine
Mr. Kenneth J. Martin
Ms Jennifer L. McDermott
Ms Vera Miller
Ms Lily Morris
Mr. Marc Muldoon
Ms Lucie Patching
Ms Rebecca "Becca" Priddy
Mr. Gregory Rubelmann
Mr. Dustin Schaefer
Mr. Andrew Scime
Mr. Mark W. Smith
Ms Maroya Spalding
Ms Liz Tabor
Ms Laura A. Trulson
Mr. Bradford S. Woodworth

2001 Annual Appeal Donors

Thank you!!! The American Sail Training Association thanks the following generous contributors to our Float the Boat! 2001-2002 Annual Appeal Campaign. Working together with members, vessels, educators, ports and others, the American Sail Training Association is helping to change young people's lives through sail training experiences and celebrating the histories and traditions that made the United States of America and Canada great maritime nations.

Mr. Alexander M. Agnew
Mr. Henry H. Anderson, Jr.
Mr. Jeffrey E. Anthony
Mr. Roger W. Archibald
Mr. Peter A. Aron
Captain Richard P. Bailey
Mr. and Mrs. Benjamin B. Baker
Mr. Mike Bancroft and Ms Julia Bancroft
Mr. Hal G. Barstow
Mr. J. Burr Bartram, Jr.
Mr. Elmar Baxter
Mr. and Mrs. Samuel Bell, Jr.
Captain Sean Sexton Bercaw
Mr. Alvin A. Bicker
Mr. Timothy Blanchard
Ms Constance L. Boehm
Mr. Michael Blau and Ms. Moore
Mr. and Mrs. Peter Boudreau
Mr. James "Carl" Breed
Mr. Harvey Brillat
Mr. Nicholas Brown
Mr. Richard M. Brown
Mr. and Mrs. Thomas K. Burgess
Ms. Gay Burgiel
Judge and Mrs. Levin H. Campbell
Mr. Levin H. Campbell, Jr.
Mr. Richard Canfield
Dr. Michael S. Carlson
Mr. John K. Castle
Captain G. Andy Chase
Ms Linda Christenson
Mr. Stephen H. Clark
Dr. Matthew Claybaugh, Ph.D
Mr. Ward Cleaveland
Ms Alice Collier Cochran

Mr. and Mrs. Steve Colgate
Mr. Harold Joseph Coughlin, Jr.
Mr. Robert Craig
Mr. Thomas D. Cullen
Dr. and Mrs. Marshall Cushman
Dr. David R. Damon
RADM J. Edmund de Castro, Jr., NYNM
Mr. Nicholas B. Dill, Jr.
Mr. Dexter Donham
Mr. and Mrs. Duncan Doolittle
Mr. Edward du Moulin
Mr. Bart Dunbar
Mr. and Mrs. Robert W. Engle
Mr. Peter Equi
Mr. Hal Fessenden
Mr. Toby Field
Mr. Michael Ford
Mr. Chuck Fowler
Mr. Robert L. Freeman
Mr. A. George Gebauer
Mr. and Mrs. Morton Gibbons-Neff, Jr.
Captain James L. Gladson
Captain Robert C. Glover III
Mr. and Mrs. Thomas J. Gochberg
Mr. and Mrs. Robert Goddard
Mr. Michael Gomez
Mrs. L. K. Gosling
Mr. Bob Gray
Dr. and Mrs. Donald S. Gromisch
Mr. Frederick W. Guardabassi
Mr. and Mrs. J. Robert Gunther
Ms Ellen Gutekunst
Mr. Richard Haggblad
Captain Paul C. Haley
Mr. George H. Hartmann
Dr. and Mrs. David Hayes

Captains Deborah Hayes and John Beebe-Center
Mr. and Mrs. J. Garry Hoyt
Mr. and Mrs. Sven Hubner
Mr. & Mrs. Victor Illonardo
Mr. Ole W. Johannessen
Mr. John Johnson
CDR Robert A. Johnson, USN (Ret.)
Mr. Steve Johnson
Mr. Thomas Hadley Josten
Captain John E. Kelly
Captain Thomas K. Kelly
Mr. James Kerr, Esq.
Ms Day Ketcham
Dr. and Mrs. Charles Langston
Mr. George Lewis
Ms Patricia H. Lock
Mr. Per H. M. Lofving
Mr. Bruce Long
Ms. Ginny Long
Mr. and Mrs. Ron Lowenstein
Mr. John K. McColloch
Mr. and Mrs. Ian McColough
RADM Dennis McCoy, USN (Ret.)
Ms Jennifer L. McDermott
Mr. Thomas M. McKenna
RADM James F. McNulty, USMS (Ret.)
Mr. and Mrs. Daniel McSweeney
Mr. and Mrs. Peter A. Mello
Mr. John F. Millar
Captain and Mrs. Stuart K. Mills
Captain George H. Moffett, Jr.
Captain Marshall A. Monsell
Mr. Robert S. Montgomerie-Charrington
Mr. and Mrs. Clarke Murphy
Mr. James Murphy
Mr. Hisakazu Nakayama
Commander Randall A. Neal, USN
Mr. and Mrs. Ken and Julie Neal-Boyd
Mr. Tony O'Connor, Sr.
Mr. Martin J. O'Meara, Jr.
Mr. and Mrs. Richard S. Palmer
Mr. Jonathan H. Pardee
Mr. Jeffrey N. Parker
Mr. Rafe Parker
Mr. A. Lauriston Parks, Esq.
Mr. Jed Pearsall
Mr. Edward V. Pietka

Mr. and Mrs. R. Daniel Prentiss
Ms Lisette Prince de Ramel
Captain Doug Prothero
Mr. Joseph A. Ribaudo
Ms Nancy H. Richardson
Mr. Lloyd M. Rives
Mr. George I. Rockwood, Jr.
Rodgers Family Foundation
Ms Elizabeth E. Roosevelt
Captain and Mrs. Christopher Rowsom
Mr. and Mrs. Edmund S. Rumowicz
Captain and Mrs. Walter Rybka
Mr. H. Alexander Salm
Mr. and Mrs. William L. Saltonstall
Mr. Frederic S. Sater
Mr. Rick Scarano
Mr. Michael Schoettle
Mr. W. E. Seaman
Dr. and Mrs. Charles Shoemaker, Jr.
Mr. Fredric A. Silberman
Ms Robin M. Skuncik
Mr. & Mrs. Graeme Smith
Mr. Scott Smithwick
Mr. and Mrs. Stephen W. Spencer
Mr. Ray Stache
Mr. Wallace C. Stark
Captain M. Jeremy Steele-Perkins
Ms Jennifer Stewart
Mr. and Mrs. E. MacGregor Strauss
CAPT Harold J. Sutphen, USN (Ret.)
Dr. and Mrs. Edward Tarlov
CAPT and Mrs. Kenneth W. Thompson, USCG (Ret.)
Ms Alix T. Thorne
Captains Jeff and Ellen Troeltzsch
True North of Clinton, LLC
Vice Admiral Sir George Vallings, KCB
Captain Cornelius Vanderstar
Mr. John Wargo
Captain Jim Wehan
Mr. Mark Weinheimer
V Adm and Mrs. Thomas R. Weschler, USN (Ret.)
Mr. F. C. "Bunky" Wichmann, Jr.
Captain John C. Wigglesworth
Commodore John A. Willett
CAPT David V.V. Wood, USCG (Ret.)
CAPT Elizabeth G. Wylie, USN (Ret.)

Thank You!

Other Sail Training Associations

The following organizations have functions corresponding to those of the American Sail Training Association. Please contact them for information about sail training opportunities in their respective countries.

AUSTRALIA
Australian Sail Training Association (AUSTA)
PO Box 196
Crows Nest, NSW 2065
AUSTRALIA
Tel: +61 2 9906 1277
Fax: +61 2 9906 1030
E-mail: avboz@ozemail.com.au

BELGIUM
Sail Training Association Belgium (STAB)
Grote Singel 6
B-2900 Schoten
BELGIUM
Tel: + 32 3 6580 006

CANADA
Canadian Sail Training Association
Canadian Sailing Expeditions
PO Box 2613
Halifax, NS B3J 3N5
CANADA
Tel: +1 902 429 1474
Fax: +1 902 429 1475
doug@canadiansailingexpeditions.com
Web site:
www.canadiansailingexpeditions.com

DENMARK
Danish Sail Training Association (DSTA)
Attn: Mr Steen Bjerre
Soendergade 12
DK 9000 Aalborg
DENMARK
Tel: + 45 98 10 29 15
Fax: + 45 98 10 00 15
E-mail: info@steen-bjerre.dk

FINLAND
Sail Training Association Finland (STAF)
Risto Villikari
Hietasaarenkuja 6
FIN-00180 Helsinki

FINLAND
Tel: +358 9 685 2616
Fax:+358 9 685 2615
E-mail: purjelaivasaatio@kolumbus.fi
Web site: www.kolumbus.fi/nuorpurj/

FRANCE
Sail Training Association France (STA France)
France - Voiles - Equipages
8 rue Jean Delalande
F-35 400 Saint-Malo
FRANCE
Tel: + 33 2 99 82 35 33
Fax: + 33 2 99 82 27 47

GERMANY
Sail Training Association Germany (STAG)
Hafenhaus, Columbusbahnhof
D-27568 Bremerhaven
GERMANY
Tel: + 49 471 945 5880
Fax: + 49 471 945 8845
Web site: www.sta-g.de

INDONESIA
Sail Training Association of Indonesia (STA Ina)
APLI - Mabes TNI Al Cilangkap
Jakarta 13780
INDONESIA
Tel: +62 21 872 3162
Fax: +62 21 871 1358
E-mail: dispot@centrin_med.ld

ITALY
Sail Training Association Italia (STAI)
Yacht Club Italiano
Porticciolo Duca degli Abruzzi
I-16128 Genova
ITALY
Tel: + 39 010 254 3652

SAIL TALL SHIPS!

Fax: + 39 010 246 1193
Fax: + 39 010 251 6168
E-mail: staitaly@tin.it

JAPAN
Sail Training Association of Japan (STAJ)
Memorial Park Tower A
2-1-1 Minato-Mirai
Nishi-ku, Yokohama
Kanagawa 220-00 12
JAPAN
Tel: + 81 45 680 5222
Fax: + 81 45 680 5225
E-mail: LDD00622@nifty.ne.jp

THE NETHERLANDS
Sail Training Association Netherlands
(STAN)
Postbus 55
NL-2340 AB Oegstgeest
THE NETHERLANDS
Tel and Fax: + 31 71 515 3013

NORWAY
Norwegian Sail Training Association (NSTA)
c/o Jostein Haukali
Stokkahagen 54
N-4022 Stavanger
NORWAY
Tel: +47 5156 0621
Fax: +47 5156 0621
info@nsta.no
www.nsta.no

POLAND
Sail Training Association Poland (STAP)
PO Box 113
ul.Zjednoczenia 3
PL-81-963 Gdynia
POLAND
Tel: + 48 58 20 6580
Fax: + 48 58 20 6225

PORTUGAL
Portuguese Sail Training Association
(APORVELA)
Centro de Operacoes
Doca do Terreiro do Trigo

1100 Lisboa
PORTUGAL
Tel: +351 21 887 6854
Fax: +351 21 887 3885
E-mail: Aporvela@telepac.pt
Web site: www.Aporvela.pt

RUSSIA
Sail Training Association Russia
(STAR)
Admiral Makarov State Maritime
Academy
Kosaya Linia 15a, RU-199026
St. Petersburg
RUSSIA
Tel: + 7 812 217 1934
Fax: + 7 812 217 0682

SOUTH AFRICA
Sail Training Association of South
Africa (STASA)
P O Box 479
5 Vesperdene Road
Green Point
8051 Capetown
SOUTH AFRICA
Fax: +27 21 797 3671

SWEDEN
Sail Training Association of Sweden
(STAS)
Christer Samuelsson
C/O MAN B&W Diesel Sverige AB
Box 2331
403 15 Göteborg
SWEDEN
Tel: + 46 31 17 62 95
Fax: + 46 31 13 15 64

UNITED KINGDOM
Sail Training Association (STA)
2A The Hard
Portsmouth PO1 3PT
UNITED KINGDOM
Tel: + 44 23 92 832055
Fax: + 44 23 92 815769

Membership Opportunities

In 2003, the American Sail Training Association will celebrate the 30th anniversary of its founding. A lot has happened over that period, including growing the organization from a handful of vessels that sailed in the Northeastern United States to now nearly 250 tall ships and sail training vessels that navigate the world's lakes, bays, seas and oceans providing character building experiences and lifelong memories for thousands of youth of all ages each year.

A very important factor in ASTA's development over the years has been the strength of our membership. Without the support of our members, many of the education and scholarship programs that we offer such as the Henry H. Anderson,Jr. Sail Training Scholarship, the ASTA Professional Crew Development Grants and the ASTA Vessel Assistance Grants would not be possible.

We offer several levels of membership:

Associate Membership

Individual - $50 per year
Benefits:
- Complimentary copy of *Sail Tall Ships!* A Directory of Sail Training and Adventure at Sea.
- Subscription to Running Free, our semi-annual newletter covering tall ships news and events.
- Subscription to e-RUNNING FREE our new monthly email newsletter.
- 15% discount on all ASTA merchandise sold through the ASTA Ship Store
- Discounts to attend ASTA Annual Conference
- Invitations to attend ASTA's Regional Meetings, Education and Safety Forums and other Special Events

Junior - $25 per year
Open to sailors 22 years of age or younger
Benefits:
- All of the benefits of Individual Membership above

Family - $75 per year
Open to two members at the same address
Benefits:
- All of the benefits of Individual Membership above
- Two ASTA or TALL SHIP CHALLENGE® lapel pins

Supporting - $250 per year
Benefits:
All of the benefits of Family Membership above
- Two ASTA or TALL SHIPS CHALLENGE® Coffee Mugs (New members only)
- An autographed copy of *Tall Ships – The Fleet for the 21st Century* by Thad Koza, a beautiful coffee table book featuring color photographs of 150 sail train-

ing vessels in the international fleet. (New members only)
- Listing in Sail Tall Ships! A Directory of Sail Training and Adventure at Sea

Patron - $1,000 per year
For individuals wishing to express a greater commitment to ASTA's mission
Benefits:
- All of the benefits of Supporting Membership above

Organizational Memberships
(Dues are based on a calendar year January 1 – December 31)

Business Partners - $350 per year
For ports, businesses, and associates of sail training and tall ships.

Corporate - $1000 per year
For ports, businesses and associates of sail training and tall ships wishing to express a greater commitment to ASTA's mission.

Affiliate Membership - $200 per year
Open to non-profit organizations which do not operate their own sail training vessel, but do offer sail training, sea education or maritime history programs (Scouts, schools, colleges, etc.)

Benefits:
- A 150-word listing in the ASTA directory *Sail Tall Ships!* A directory of Sail Training and Adventure at Sea.
- A listing of your Organization on the ASTA website. We provide a hot link to your website and appreciate reciprocity.
- The opportunity to post help wanted ads in the very popular Billet Bank on the ASTA website. The Billet Bank is the most visited section of the ASTA website all year long and is the most effective service for matching professional sail trainers and open positions.
- 10 complimentary copies of Sail Tall Ships for your staff and volunteers;
- A subscription to Running Free, ASTA's newsletter to be published in June and October;
- Discounts for staff to attend ASTA's Annual Conference on Sail Training and Tall Ships.
- Invitations to attend ASTA Regional Meetings, educational and safety forums and other special events.
- A subscription to our new monthly email newsletter, e-RUNNING FREE, which covers a wide range of useful and news breaking topics. Additionally, your membership makes you eligible for the Highlighted Program section.
- 15% discount on all ASTA merchandise and apparel in stock in the ASTA Ship's Store.

Sail Training Organization 1, 2, or 3
Open to those organizations operating vessels. Membership dues is based on the organization's annual budget. STO1: Less than $250,000 / $300 per year,

STO2: $250,000-$500,000 / $400 per year, STO3: Over $500,000 / $500 per year.

Benefits:
- A full page listing, including a photo of your vessel, in the ASTA directory *Sail Tall Ships!* (additional vessel listings available for additional charges.)
- Eligibility for the Henry H. Anderson, Jr. Sail Training Scholarship Program for trainees that sail aboard your vessel(s).
- Eligibility for the ASTA Professional Crew Development Grant Program.
- Eligibility for the ASTA Vessel Assistance Grant Program
- The opportunity to post help wanted ads in the very popular Billet Bank on the ASTA website.
- A listing of your Organization on the ASTA website. We provide a hot link to your website and appreciate reciprocity.
- Access to the ASTA Insurance Program, which provides first class security at affordable rates.
- 10 complimentary copies of Sail Tall Ships for your staff and volunteers;
- A subscription to Running Free, ASTA's newsletter to be published in June and October;
- A subscription to our new monthly email newsletter, e-RUNNING FREE, which covers a wide range of useful and news breaking topics. Additionally, your membership makes you eligible for the Highlighted Program section. We just heard from the Highlighted Program in our first edition of e-RUNNING FREE that they received interest as a direct result of their profile.
- Discounts for staff to attend ASTA's Annual Conference on Sail Training and Tall Ships.
- Invitations to attend ASTA Regional Meetings, educational and safety forums and other special events.
- 15% discount on display advertising in Sail Tall Ships!
- 15% discount on all ASTA merchandise and apparel in stock in the ASTA Ship's Store.
- Additional copies of *Sail Tall Ships!* at production cost (plus shipping) for resale.

In addition to the above direct benefits, ASTA works on a regular basis with the Coast Guard, Customs and Immigration and other government agencies on behalf of the sail training industry.

We are also working on several additional projects that will bring added benefits in the upcoming year to you as an ASTA member. We are exploring an ASTA member discount program for STCW training courses and we are working on providing a member's section to our website which will allow you to communicate with other ASTA members on topics that you face as professional sail trainers.

We look forward to having you come aboard and join the ASTA Crew with the above membership that best suits your interest and budget! Not only will you become a member of the largest sail training association in the world, but you will be supporting the youth education and leadership development programs that can help shape young people's lives!

Membership Application

s! I/We want to join the American Sail Training Association!

me: _____

ganization: _____

ssel(s): _____

iling Address: _____

y: _____ State/Province: _____ Postal/Zip: _____

untry: _____ *

one: _____ Fax: _____

Mail: _____

ase enroll me/us in the following membership category:

sociate Memberships

sociate memberships are renewable on date of anniversary.

_____ Individual $50   _____ Supporting $250

_____ Junior $25   _____ Patron $1,000

_____ Family $75

ganizational Memberships

ganizational Memberships are for calendar year (January 1 through December 31).

_____ Corporate $1000   _____ Business Partner $350

_____ Affiliate $200

Sail Training Organizations

_____ Budget less than $250,000 $300

_____ Budget between $250,000 and $500,000 $400

_____ Budget greater than $500,000 $500

or all addresses in Canada or Mexico, please add US $16 to cover the additional postage and handling sts. For addresses outside of North America, please add US $24.

yment of dues:

_____ Check or money order enclosed (US dollars please)

_____ Visa or MasterCard

rd number: _____ Expires: _____

me on card: _____ Signature: _____

il or fax this form to:

ASTA
PO Box 1459
Newport, RI 02840 USA
Fax: +1 401.849.5400
or join via ASTA's Web site at: http://www.tallships.sailtraining.org

29th Annual Conference on

Sail Training and Tall Ships

ASTA's Annual Conference on Sail Training and Tall Ships

ASTA's Annual Conference on Sail Training and Tall Ships gathers ships' masters, port representatives, public officials, marine suppliers, naval architects, program administrators, festival managers, preservationists, environmentalists, crewmembers, and educators. Topics concerning vessel operations, regulatory issues, management, educational programming, and safety at sea are addressed each year, as are sessions on media relations, marketing, funding, communications, and port event organization.

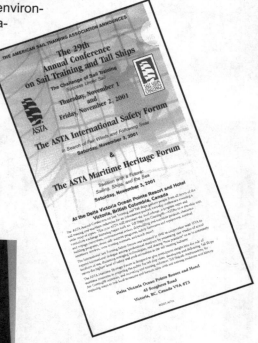

Held annually during the first week in November, the ASTA Conference on Sail Training and Tall Ships is both fun and informative and offers oceans of networking opportunities.

Plan to join us November 7, 8, 9, 2002 in Toronto, Ontario, Canada for the 30th Annual Conference.

The International Sail Training Safety Forum

The International Sail Training Safety Forum, initiated in 1992 in cooperation with the ISTA, expands the international dialogue among professional mariners by presenting case studies of actual incidents at sea, discussing emerging technologies, and sharing "best practices" so as to constantly insure a high level of safety and professionalism in the sail training industry. Professionals engaged in sail training, sea education, vessel operations, and tall ship events from throughout the world participate in this annual symposium. Topics covered have included preparing for heavy weather, hypothermia, technology and forecasting, survival gear and much more. The American Sail Training Association hosts the Safety Forum during odd-numbered years, in conjunction with the Annual Conference on Sail Training and Ships.

The 8th Annual ASTA/ISTA International Sail Training
Safety Forum held in Boston, MA in November, 1999.

ASTA Biennial Education Under Sail Forum

ASTA's new Education Under Sail Forum made it's grand premiere in Chicago in 2000! This was the first of what is planned to be a program-focused complement to the International Safety Forums biennial series. Inspired by a night watch suggestion from Captain Jesse Briggs and led by Captain Jim Gladson from LA Maritime Institute, the theme for 2000 was "How Do You Know if You're Making a Difference? Outcomes Measurement and Sail Training."

Designed to inform and inspire excellence in the development and delivery of educational experiences under sail, the forum overflows with creative exchanges among captains, crew, administrators, teachers, program developers, curriculum designers, and others.

In 2002, the Education Under Sail Forum will be held on Saturday, November 9, in conjunction with the 30th Annual Conference on Sail Training and Tall Ships, in Toronto, Ontario, Canada.

Above, Nancy Richardson and Captain Jim Gladson, Co-organizers of the first Biennial Education Under Sail Forum held in Chicago in November of 2000. Left, Dr. Sidney Thompson, keynote speaker.

ASTA Maritme Heritage Forum

The ASTA Maritime Heritage Forum is designed to give participants insight into the role of maritime museums in preparing the public for tall ship visits, developing and delivering Tall Ships Are Coming!® activities, and recruiting and training volunteer Tall Ships® Ambassadors by exploring ways to link local museums and historic sites with sail training traditions and history.

Introduced in 2001 in conjunction with the 29th Annual Conference on Sail Training and Tall Ships, the forum - "Tradition with a Future: Sailing, Ships and the Sea"- included a tour of the Maritime Museum of British Columbia and offered a series of seminars covering topics such as *Tall Ships as Magnets:* Attracting New People and Programs, *Ship Tours:* More Than Just a Walk Across the Deck, and *Sea Chests and Sea Bags:* Traditions Go to School.

The ASTA Sail Training Rally

Bucket Brigade

Rowing

Knot-Tying

In the 1980s, ASTA developed the concept of the Sail Training Rally; a competition among crews, both at sea and ashore. These rallies provide trainees with an opportunity to demonstrate their seamanship skills in a friendly but competitive format. Shoreside events such as knot tying, tug-of war, bucket brigade, rowing, walk the plank, and heaving line toss/hawser pull, allow the general public to observe the sort of teamwork and maritime skills that are learned on board sail training vessels at sea.

Heaving Line Toss and Hawser Pull

Tug-of-War

ASTA Regional Meetings.

Regional—Atlantic, Pacific and Great Lakes—meetings are held late winter/early spring. These meetings are less formal than our annual Conference, but like the Conference, we encourage our professional members to submit ideas for locations and topics.

The regional meetings offer an opportunity for the host to showcase their facility and programs while providing an intimate setting for attendees to network. A typical regional meeting may include a tour, special presentation, safety demonstration, day sail, luncheon and reception.

In 2001, the Pacific Regional Meeting was held in Richmond, British Columbia, Canada – the opening port in ASTA's TALL SHIPS CHALLENGE® Pacific Coast 2002 Summer race series. It was hosted by the City of Richmond and sponsored by the Radisson President Hotel and Tourism Richmond.

The Great Lakes Regional Meeting, often held in conjunction with the Canadian Sail Training Association's annual meeting and safety forum, was hosted by the Erie Maritime Museum in Erie, Pennsylvania, and sponsored by the Erie Port Authority and the Flagship Niagara League.

The 2001 Atlantic Regional Meeting was held in Baltimore, Maryland, and hosted by the Living Classrooms Foundation and the USS Constellation Foundation.

Planning usually starts in November with meetings held in February, March or April. If your organization would like to host a regional meeting, please send a letter of interest along with a proposed agenda to ASTA.

Henry H. Anderson, Jr. Sail Training Scholarship

ASTA Sailing Vessel Assistance Grant

ASTA Crew Development Grant

The Henry H. Anderson, Jr. Sail Training Scholarship, ASTA Sailing Vessel Assistance Grant, and ASTA Crew Development Grant programs were established in 1999. The first is designed to assist young people between 14 and 19 to achieve a sail training experience aboard USCG or national equivalent-inspected ASTA member vessels. Scholarships are available to both individuals and groups. The second is designed to assist ASTA member vessels which may not be USCG-inspected in maintenance and improvement projects that will better enable them to further ASTA's missions. The Crew Development Grant program is designed to help keep motivated crewmembers in the ASTA fleet by assisting them in upgrading their professional qualifications through training.

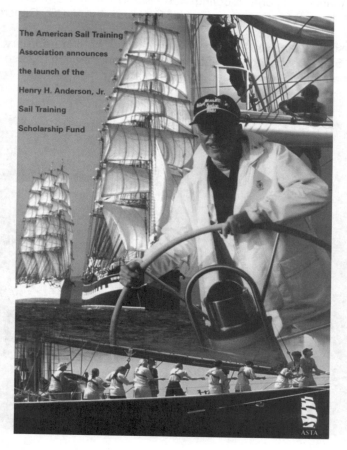

The American Sail Training Association announces the launch of the Henry H. Anderson, Jr. Sail Training Scholarship Fund

ASTA Publications

Sail Tall Ships! **A Directory of Sail Training and Adventure at Sea** first appeared in 1980, and is now in its fourteenth edition. The directory provides program and contact information for member vessels and sail training associations throughout the world. To help fulfill ASTA's mission, the directory is also distributed through maritime museums and their affiliated shops, marinas, maritime events, and sail training programs, as well as bookstores, libraries, high school guidance counselors, university career resource centers, and education conferences throughout the United States and Canada.

Guidelines for Educational Programs Under Sail defines ASTA standards for sail training and sea education within the framework of the Sailing School Vessels Act. This manual defines criteria and indicators of effectiveness for the design, delivery, and evaluation of curricula, instruction, and program administration. In addition to the core of safe seamanship education, the guidelines apply to all aspects of sail training: adventure, education, environmental science, maritime heritage, and leadership development.

The **ASTA Training Logbook** enables trainees to keep a personal log of their sea time and to document their progress in sail training, and records a progression of skill-building activities in nautical science, safety, seamanship, and navigation. Completion of course work and sea time must be certified by either the instructor or the ship's master.

The **International Safety Forum Proceedings**, an annual publication of the International Safety Forum, is a record of the papers submitted and discussions held on various aspects of sail training safety and operations, emergency procedures, professional training and qualifications, vessel design and construction, etc. The Forum has been held each year since 1992, and copies of each year's proceedings are available through ASTA's Ship's Store.

A Quick Guide to the Regulations Pertaining to Sail Training Vessels Visiting US Waters gives non-US vessels a sense of the regulations governing all ships visiting ports in the United States and provides contact information for each of the federal authorities enforcing those regulations.

Tall Ships by Thad Koza, published by TideMark Press with a foreword by ASTA's Executive Director, Peter A. Mello, is available through the ASTA Ship's Store. This beautiful book features four-color photographs of 150 sail training vessels in the international fleet.

ASTA Website

www.tallships.sailtraining.org is your portal to the world of sail training and tall ships. Links to ASTA member vessels and affiliates make it easy to learn more about opportunities under sail, the ships that can take you to sea, and shore-based programs. The ASTA Web site also provides links to tall ship events such as the TALL SHIPS CHALLENGE® series (during the series in the Great Lakes last August, the ASTA website received over 635,000 hits) and to international sail training associations and resources around the world.   Information on upcoming ASTA events such as the Annual June Fundraiser, the Annual Conference on Sail Training and Tall Ships, regional meetings, and the Annual Appeal can also be found on the Web site.

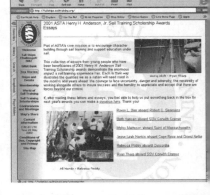

ASTA Scholarship and Grant criteria as well as printable application forms are available on the Web site - where you can also read first-hand accounts of the life-changing effects of sail training experiences in the form of essays and stories written by past scholarship recipients.

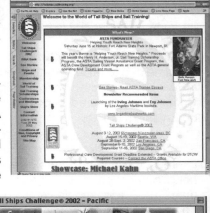

An on-line Billet Bank provides notice of positions available aboard ASTA member vessels. The Billet Bank is the most visited section of the ASTA website all year long and is the most effective service for matching professional sail trainers and open positions. ASTA Oraganizational Members are invited to post available positions using the standarized form found on the ASTA Web site. New information is added on a daily basis and billets remain posted for 90 days unless ASTA is otherwise advised. (ASTA does not endorse any specific program or individual, but simply shares information as it becomes available.)

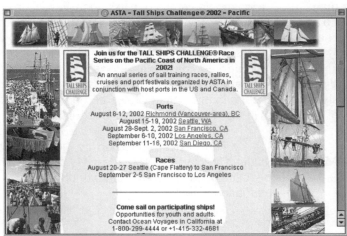

To learn more about the American Sail Training Association and how you can get involved. Visit the ASTA Web site today!

ASTA Newsletter

RUNNING FREE is the American Sail Training Association's semi-annual newsletter providing in depth coverage of ASTA events including the TALL SHIPS CHALLENGE® Series, the ASTA Annual Conference on Sail Training and Tall Ships, the International Safety Forum, the ASTA Education under Sail Forum and the ASTA Maritime Heritage Forum.

e-RUNNING FREE was launched in January 2002 and is a monthly email newsletter guiding you to what's new at ASTA, with our professional member organizations and in the sail training world in general. In addition to current topics in e-RUNNING FREE, check out the regular features like the Highlighted Program, TALL SHIPS CHALLENGE® News, the ASTA Treasure Hunt and the ASTA Book of the Month. To subscribe or to offer feedback, send email to newsletter@sailtraining.org.

Book of the Month Club

The American Sail Training Association is proud to announce that Baker Books of North Dartmouth, Massachusetts is the sponsor of the ASTA Book for the Month and the ASTA Book Buying Program. For every book that is purchased from them via the ASTA website, Baker Books will donate a share of the purchase price to ASTA (15% with the exception of rare and out of print books). There are millions of titles available to you just a click away. So next time you go to buy a book online go to **www.tallships.sailtraining.org** and place your order to support ASTA!

Baker Books
Purveyors of Information & Imagination

ASTA Gallery

Check out the new gallery section on the ASTA
website. Here you will find extraordinary maritime artwork,
photographs and ship models. It's a great place to look for that
special birthday or holiday gift and by shopping here you'll be supporting the programs of the American Sail Training Association.
Check in on a regular basis to see what's new
and exciting.

Ships Store

Located on the ASTA Web site (www.tallships.sailtraining.org) the Ship's Store is the place to go for ASTA Gear, Event Merchandise and ASTA Publications. Hats, polo's, t-shirts, belts, calendars, ASTA flags, coffee mugs and lapel pins are just some of the items you can purchase through the ASTA Ship's Store.
Looking for a unique gift for someone special?
Visit the ASTA Ship's Store today!

SAIL TALL SHIPS!

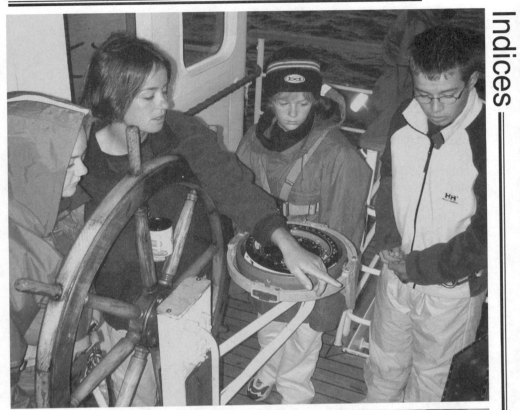

Photos by Wojtek Wacowski

SAIL TALL SHIPS!

Advertisers' Index

Geographical Index

SAIL TALL SHIPS!

SAIL TALL SHIPS!

Alphabetical Index

SAIL TALL SHIPS!

*The mission of the American
Sail Training Association is to
encourage character building
through sail training, promote
sail training to the North
American public, and support
education under sail.*